HTML, XHTML, and CSS

Your visual blueprint™ for designing effective Web pages

by Rob Huddleston

WILEY

Wiley Publishing, Inc.

HTML, XHTML, and CSS: Your visual blueprint™ for designing effective Web pages

Published by
Wiley Publishing, Inc.
10475 Crosspoint Boulevard
Indianapolis, IN 46256

www.wiley.com

Published simultaneously in Canada

Library of Congress Control Number: 2008926447

ISBN: 978-0-470-27436-1

Manufactured in the United States of America

10 9 8 7 6 5 4 3 2 1

Trademark Acknowledgments

Contact Us

For general information on our other products and services please contact our Customer Care Department within the U.S. at 800-762-2974, outside the U.S. at 317-572-3993, or fax 317-572-4002.

For technical support please visit www.wiley.com/techsupport.

The Windmills of La Mancha

Fabled in song and legend, the windmills of La Mancha dot a fertile but arid plateau in central Spain. Although Miguel de Cervantes brought them fame in his classic novel *Don Quixote de La Mancha*, the windmills are in fact important to the region's agricultural industry. Wheat, barley, oats, wine grapes, and saffron are produced there, but perhaps La Mancha's most famous product is the unique cheese made exclusively from the milk of the Manchego sheep. Explore La Mancha and the rest of Spain with *Frommer's Spain*, available wherever books are sold and at www.Frommers.com.

WILEY

Sales

Contact Wiley
at (800) 762-2974
or (317) 572-4002.

PRAISE FOR VISUAL BOOKS...

"This is absolutely the best computer-related book I have ever bought. Thank you so much for this fantastic text. Simply the best computer book series I have ever seen. I will look for, recommend, and purchase more of the same."

—David E. Prince (NeoNome.com)

"I have several of your Visual books and they are the best I have ever used."

—Stanley Clark (Crawfordville, FL)

"I just want to let you know that I really enjoy all your books. I'm a strong visual learner. You really know how to get people addicted to learning! I'm a very satisfied Visual customer. Keep up the excellent work!"

—Helen Lee (Calgary, Alberta, Canada)

"I have several books from the Visual series and have always found them to be valuable resources."

—Stephen P. Miller (Ballston Spa, NY)

"This book is PERFECT for me — it's highly visual and gets right to the point. What I like most about it is that each page presents a new task that you can try verbatim or, alternatively, take the ideas and build your own examples. Also, this book isn't bogged down with trying to 'tell all' — it gets right to the point. This is an EXCELLENT, EXCELLENT, EXCELLENT book and I look forward to purchasing other books in the series."

—Tom Dierickx (Malta, IL)

"I have quite a few of your Visual books and have been very pleased with all of them. I love the way the lessons are presented!"

—Mary Jane Newman (Yorba Linda, CA)

"I am an avid fan of your Visual books. If I need to learn anything, I just buy one of your books and learn the topic in no time. Wonders! I have even trained my friends to give me Visual books as gifts."

—Illona Bergstrom (Aventura, FL)

"I just had to let you and your company know how great I think your books are. I just purchased my third Visual book (my first two are dog-eared now!) and, once again, your product has surpassed my expectations. The expertise, thought, and effort that go into each book are obvious, and I sincerely appreciate your efforts."

—Tracey Moore (Memphis, TN)

"Compliments to the chef!! Your books are extraordinary! Or, simply put, extra-ordinary, meaning way above the rest! THANK YOU THANK YOU THANK YOU! I buy them for friends, family, and colleagues."

—Christine J. Manfrin (Castle Rock, CO)

"I write to extend my thanks and appreciation for your books. They are clear, easy to follow, and straight to the point. Keep up the good work! I bought several of your books and they are just right! No regrets! I will always buy your books because they are the best."

—Seward Kollie (Dakar, Senegal)

"I am an avid purchaser and reader of the Visual series, and they are the greatest computer books I've seen. Thank you very much for the hard work, effort, and dedication that you put into this series."

—Alex Diaz (Las Vegas, NV)

Credits

Project Editors
Timothy J. Borek
Sarah Hellert

Senior Acquisitions Editor
Jody Lefevere

Copy Editor
Lauren Kennedy

Technical Editor
Grey Hodge

Editorial Manager
Robyn Siesky

Business Manager
Amy Knies

Senior Marketing Manager
Sandy Smith

Manufacturing
Allan Conley
Linda Cook
Paul Gilchrist
Jennifer Guynn

Book Design
Kathryn Rickard

Production Coordinator
Erin Smith

Layout
Andrea Hornberger
Jennifer Mayberry

Screen Artist
Jill A. Proll

Cover Illustration
Steven Amory

Proofreader
Broccoli Information Management

Quality Control
Caitie Kelly

Indexer
Sherry Massey

Vice President and Executive Group Publisher
Richard Swadley

Vice President Publisher
Barry Pruett

Composition Director
Debbie Stailey

About the Author

Rob Huddleston has been developing Web pages and applications since 1994, and has been an instructor since 1999, teaching Web and graphic design to thousands of students. His clients have included the United States Bureau of Land Management; the United States Patent and Trademark Office; the State of California and many other federal, city and county agencies; the United States Army and Air Force; Fortune 500 companies such as AT&T, Wells Fargo, Safeway, and Coca-Cola; software companies including Oracle, Intuit, and Autodesk; the University of California, San Francisco State University, the University of Southern California; and hundreds of small businesses and non-profit agencies. Rob is an Adobe Certified Instructor, Certified Expert, and Certified Developer, is an Adobe User Group Manager, and was named as an Adobe Community Expert for his volunteer work answering user questions in online forums. Rob lives in northern California with his wife and two children.

Rob is the author of *XML: Your visual blueprint to creating expert websites using XML, CSS, XHTML, and XSLT,* published by Wiley Publishing in 2007. You can visit Rob's blog at www.robhuddleston.com.

Author's Acknowledgments

This book is dedicated to my wife Kelley and my children, Jessica and Xander. Without your love and support, I couldn't possibly do this. It's impossible for me to express my love enough.

I also would like to thank Jody Lefevere and the entire team at Wiley for their hard work in making this book. They are a fantastic group of people to work with.

As always, I need to thank my parents for their support and for being the "proud parents" who keep the rest of the family informed of my goings-on when I get too involved writing to do so.

Lots of people have said that the secret to being happy is to do what you love. Almost nine years ago, Terry Twomey took a chance and hired me as an instructor. I'm not sure what I would be doing today if he hadn't taken that chance, but I know I wouldn't be doing what I love. So thank you Terry, and thank you as well to Mel, Pete, Charles, Tyler, Tesfa, Tony, Matt, and Jane. Your patience and guidance when I was getting started allowed me to get here today, and I will be forever grateful.

TABLE OF CONTENTS

TABLE OF CONTENTS

TABLE OF CONTENTS

HOW TO USE THIS BOOK

HTML, XHTML, and CSS: Your visual blueprint for designing effective Web pages uses clear, descriptive examples to show you how to use HTML, XHMTL, and CSS to create flexible, standards-based Web pages. If you are already familiar with HTML and XHTML, you can use this book as a quick reference for many HTML and XHML tasks.

It is suggested that you read this book in order, from beginning to end, as each chapter builds on the concepts from those that preceed it. However, the book is structured so that you can also skip sections that cover topics with which you are already familiar.

Who Needs This Book

This book is for the experienced computer user who wants to find out more about HTML and XHTML. It is also for more experienced Web designers who want to expand their knowledge of the different features that the languages have to offer.

Book Organization

HTML, XHTML, and CSS: Your visual blueprint for designing effective Web pages has 19 chapters and 3 appendixes.

Chapter 1, "Introducing HTML and XHTML," introduces the basic concepts and syntaxes of the languages, along with companion languages such as CSS and JavaScript. It also offers an overview and comparison on some of the tools available to create Web pages, and explains fundamental concepts about Web browsers and servers. Finally, it offers ideas as to how to plan a Web site.

Chapter 2, "Introducing HTML Basics," gets you started with coding your first HTML document. It shows how to add the required structure tags and save and preview your page. It then discusses adding headings, paragraphs, line breaks, horizontal rules, and comments to your page. It also discusses the importance of using logical formatting in your pages.

Chapter 3, "Creating Hyperlinks," shows you how to link documents together. It discusses strategies for planning the navigation of your site, structuring your files, and understanding file paths. Then, it shows how to create links to other documents, other Web sites, other places on pages, and e-mail addresses. It also shows how to control the tab order for links, display tooltips, and test your links.

Chapter 4, "Working with Images," covers the topics around adding images to your pages. It discusses

acceptable file formats, shows how to add images to pages, how to set alternate text, and specify the size of images. It also shows how to use images as links and how to add an icon to display in the browser's address bar.

Chapter 5, "Using Tables," shows how to work with data tables in Web pages. It covers adding tables, and modifying those tables with headers, column and row span, borders, widths, white space, and table sections and columns.

Chapter 6, "Using Lists," discusses how to add lists to your page. It shows how to add bulleted, numbered, and definition lists, and how to nest lists within other lists.

Chapter 7, "Formatting the Text on Your Page," introduces text formatting with CSS. It covers the basic units of measurement that can be used, and shows how to set the size of text and the font to be used. It then discusses how to use colors, and shows how to apply those colors to various aspects of your page. It then shows how to control other aspects relating to typography, including the space between lines, making text bold or italic, and aligning text.

Chapter 8, "Apply More Formatting to Your Page," introduces background colors and images and shows how to control them. It also covers padding, borders, and margins on elements, and shows how to set their width and height. It shows how to style links, tables and lists, and how to customize cursors.

Chapter 9, "Working with Other CSS Selectors," discusses how to apply styles to more than one element at a time, and use the span and div elements, classes, and IDs to further control the appearance of your page. It also details more specialized CSS controls such as contextual selectors, pseudo-classes and pseudo-elements, and how to set rules as important. Finally, it shows how to move your styles to external documents that can control all of the pages in your site.

Chapter 10, "Laying Out Your Page," covers topics showing how to create layouts using CSS. It shows how to use floats and positioning to achieve layouts, work with overflow text, and use minimum and maximum height and width settings. It then shows several practical examples, such as replacing a heading with an image and creating tabbed navigation. It then covers the creation of style sheets for print and common CSS hacks.

Chapter 11, "Adding Forms," shows how to create forms to capture user information from your site. It covers the various form controls provided in XHTML, how to group form controls for improved usability, and discusses strategies for processing the form data.

Chapter 12, "Working with JavaScript," teaches you how to implement the powerful scripting language into your sites. It shows how to add JavaScript to your pages, and use it to validate forms, open new windows, hide and display page contents, and swap images. It also shows how to debug JavaScript errors.

Chapter 13, "Making Your Site Accessible," discusses how to ensure that all users, including those with disabilities, can access the information on your site. After introducing the concepts behind Web accessibility, it shows how to make tables, images, forms, and site navigation accessible, and how to test for accessibility.

Chapter 14, "Adding Specialized Markup," shows how to add special characters to your pages, how to add addresses, and use quoted text, abbreviations and acronyms, and code samples on your page.

Chapter 15, "Creating an RSS Feed," includes an introduction to XML and RSS, and shows how to create a feed so that other sites can subscribe to yours and display selected information on their pages.

Chapter 16, "Using Content from Other Sources," shows how to create a blog and use it on your site, display RSS from other sites, show pictures from Flickr, maps and calendars from Google, advertising, social bookmarks, and search boxes.

Chapter 17, "Getting Your Site Listed on Search Engines," covers topics that show how to best ensure that your page will appear in popular search engine results, including using meta elements data and the Google Web master tools. It also shows how to prevent search engines from cataloging pages.

Chapter 18, "Testing and Validating Web Pages," teaches how to look for and avoid common HTML, XHTML, and CSS mistakes, and introduces tools you can use to check your pages for these errors.

Chapter 19, "Publishing Your Site," shows how to sign up with a Web host, buy a domain name, and upload your site to a Web server.

Appendix A is a complete XHTML reference.

Appendix B is a CSS reference.

Appendix C is a Web accessibility reference.

What You Need to Use This Book

To perform the tasks in this book, you will need a computer with a Web browser such as Microsoft Internet Explorer or Mozilla Firefox and a text editor. All of the code examples are written using Notepad, but they can be successfully completed in any code editor. Several examples require an active Internet connection to complete.

The Conventions in This Book

A number of styles have been used throughout *HTML, XHTML, and CSS: Your visual blueprint for designing effective Web pages* to designate different types of information.

`Courier Font`

Indicates the use of code such as tags or attributes, scripting language code such as statements, operators, or functions, and code such as objects, methods, or properties.

Bold

Indicates information that you must type.

Italics

Indicates a new term.

An Apply It section takes the code from the preceding task one step further. Apply It sections allow you to take full advantage of HTML, XHMTL, and CSS.

Extra

An Extra section provides additional information about the preceding task. Extra sections contain the inside information to make working with HTML, XHMTL, and CSS easier and more efficient.

What's on the Web Site

The accompanying Web site, www.html2008vb, contains the sample files for *HTML, XHTML, and CSS: Your visual blueprint for designing effective Web pages*.

Introducing HTML

Less than twenty years after its invention, the World Wide Web has become ubiquitous. Today, there are tens of billions of Web sites worldwide, and the number continues to grow at an almost exponential rate. There are many factors that have contributed to the growth of the Web, but one of the most important is that Hypertext Markup Language (HTML), the language in which Web pages are written, is easy to learn, and best of all, free.

History of HTML

The World Wide Web was invented in 1990 by Tim Berners-Lee. Berners-Lee worked at the European Particle Physics Laboratory (CERN) in Geneva, and at the time, no one operating system had come to dominate the market. Therefore, the visiting scientists at CERN were bringing in their own computer systems, and despite the fact that they were working together on cutting-edge technologies, they had no real way to share their data with one another except on paper.

In the 1960s, scientists at IBM developed the Standard Generalized Markup Language (SGML), which is a language for creating other languages. Also in the 1960s, researchers at Brown and Stanford Universities developed hypertext, a method of relating similar information.

Berners-Lee developed HTML by combining these two concepts: He took the idea of hypertext and applied it via SGML. He also developed the Hypertext Transfer Protocol (HTTP), which allows networked computers to exchange HTML documents, and the first browser/editor, which he called WorldWideWeb, a name later adopted for the entire system.

The first time Berners-Lee used these new technologies was on Christmas Day, 1990. It took several years to really catch on, but by 1995, new companies such as Yahoo! and Amazon.com were founded, and along with the Netscape browser, the Web quickly took off from there.

Versions of HTML

HTML went through several iterations in the early days when only a few people, mostly at universities, were using it. Berners-Lee first publically promoted the concept of HTML online in 1991, but it was not until 1993 that the Internet Engineering Task Force formally adopted an HTML specification as a "working draft." Two years later, they published the HTML 2.0 specification (note that, technically, there was never an HTML version 1.0).

HTML 3.0 was proposed in 1995, but was deemed too complex for implementation by browsers. It was fairly quickly supplanted by HTML 3.2, the first truly popular version of the language. Unfortunately, version 3.2 introduced a host of browser-specific elements and attributes that had been adopted by browser manufacturers such as Netscape and Microsoft, creating challenges for Web designers who wanted to create pages that would correctly display across multiple browsers.

Realizing that what had begun as a fairly simple text markup language was fast becoming too complex to manage, the World Wide Web Consortium (W3C), the body that had been established to manage the development of future versions of HTML and other Web-related technologies, released HTML 4 in 1997. This marked an attempt to find a common ground between the needs of future developers to have an easy-to-use and easy-to-learn yet robust language while preventing the then-millions of existing pages from breaking in newer browsers. The goal of this new version was to encourage Web designers to move away from the bloated, browser-specific code they had been forced to write and instead return their HTML documents to the original ideas of the language; they would then focus solely on the underlying structure of the document instead of visual formatting, which would now be handled by Cascading Style Sheets (CSS), the newly-developed formatting language of the Web.

The "Flavors" of HTML 4.01

HTML 4 (and the update version 4.01) has three versions. HTML 4.01 Transitional encourages, but does not require, designers to move from the presentation-heavy code of earlier HTML and begin using CSS for formatting. HTML 4.01 Strict requires that only structure-based code be used, with all formatting handled by CSS. The third, less commonly-used HTML 4.01 Frameset allows developers to create pages that utilize frames for page layout.

HTML Elements and Tags

HTML is made up of *elements*, which describe to the browser how a particular piece of text should be treated. Elements are expressed in HTML as tags, which consist of the element surrounded by angle brackets, or the greater than and less than symbols. An example of a tag that uses the `html` element is `<html>`.

Attributes

There are times when you need to expand on the information you are providing in a tag. For example, it is not enough to simply tell the browser that you want to display an image on the page; you need to tell it which image to display. This additional information for tags is given through *attributes*. Attributes appear after the element but before the final angle bracket in an opening tag. Attributes consist of the attribute name, an equal sign, and a value, which will be enclosed in quotation marks.

```
<img src="images/logo.gif">
```

Note that attributes are never repeated in the closing tag, and whenever you use more than one attribute in a single tag, they can be presented in any order.

Container and Empty Tags

Most HTML tags will surround a block of text, thus marking it up. These tags use elements that describe both when the markup needs to begin, and when it ends. For example, if you want to make some text bold, you need to tell the browser both when to begin making the text bold and when it should stop doing so. These *container tags* use an opening tag, which has the element and the angle brackets, and a corresponding closing tag, which includes a forward slash after the opening bracket and before the element.

```
<strong>Some text to be made bold-
faced</strong>
```

While the majority of tags are containers, there are a set of tags that essentially represent instructions to the browser, and thus have no matching closing tag. For example, while it makes sense that you need to tell the browser where to begin and end bold text, it likewise makes sense that you only need to tell the browser where to place an image — it has no logical end point, and therefore no closing tag. These are called *empty tags*, as they do not contain content.

HTML Syntax Rules

While I have already noted that HTML uses a very loose syntax, there are still a few things about which you need to be aware.

- **HTML is case-insensitive**. You can use any case you want for elements, attributes, and attribute values. You can also freely mix and match cases, but being consistent will make your code easier to read.

- **HTML is whitespace-insensitive**. Within tags, the element must immediately follow the opening angle bracket. After that, however, you can put as much space as you wish, including carriage returns, between the element and any attributes, between attributes, and before the closing bracket. Outside of tags, you can use any whitespace characters, again including carriage returns, within your content without affecting the final display in your browser. Browsers always ignore more than one consecutive whitespace character, and always ignore tabs and carriage returns.

- **When using attributes, you can enclose the value of the attribute in single or double quotation marks**. Some attribute values need not have quotation marks at all, but it is easier to simply always use them rather than try to figure out which cases require them and which do not.

Introducing XHTML 1.0

While development of HTML continued, the W3C was also hard at work on another markup language. The Extensible Markup Language (XML) was designed to allow developers to create documents that focused solely on the actual data of their page, without regard to how such data might eventually be displayed. XML relies on a much stricter syntax than HTML. While beginners may find the loose syntax of HTML easy to learn, languages with stronger syntaxes are ultimately easier to debug and manage.

To provide Web designers with the tools they needed to be better able to troubleshoot pages, the W3C released Extensible HTML (XHTML) 1.0, ultimately intending that it replace HTML 4.01. XHTML uses the same set of elements and tags as HTML, and even includes the same three "flavors" — Transitional, Strict, and Frameset. However, it requires that pages be written in the much stricter XML syntax.

XHTML Syntax Rules

Although HTML and XHTML share a set of elements, there are several important differences between the syntaxes of each:

- **XHTML is case-sensitive**. All elements and attributes must be lowercase.

- **XHTML requires that attribute values be quoted**. You can use single or double quotation marks, but you must always use them.

- **XHTML requires that all attributes have values**. While rare, there are a few scattered examples of HTML attributes that have no value, and instead use a single word. In XHTML, these must have a value, which is always the name of the attribute repeated as the value. An example is the input element, used for forms (see Chapter 11 for details). When the input element is used to create a radio button, and you wish to have the button selected by default, HTML uses the checked attribute. In XHTML, it is written `checked="checked"`.

- **XHTML requires that tags be properly nested**. It is almost always possible to nest tags within other tags. For example, much of the content on your page will be in paragraphs, which use the `p` element. Within a paragraph, you may have text that you want to be both bold (using the `strong` element) and italic (using `em`). The code in this case would be `<p>Some <strong><em>bold, italic</em></strong> text.</p>`. Here, the `em` tag is nested within the `strong`, which is in turn nested within the `p`. This is the proper XHTML syntax, where the tags close in the opposite order from which they were opened, and each element is completely nested within the other. HTML would allow for `<p>Some <strong><em>bold, italic</strong></em> text.</p>`, where the order of the closing tags is reversed.

- **XHTML requires closing tags**. As was discussed previously, HTML has container tags that surround marked-up text and empty tags that merely give an instruction to the browser. In XHTML, even empty tags must be closed. You can either add the closing tag immediately after the opening, as in `<img src="images/picture.gif"></img>`, or simply add the forward slash before the closing angle bracket: `<img src="images/picture.gif" />`. Either is allowed, but the latter is preferred if for no other reason than it takes less code.

The one syntax rule that is the same between HTML and XHTML is that both are whitespace-insensitive.

Declaring the "Flavor" of XHTML

For your XHMTL document to be considered valid, you must begin the document with a *document type declaration.* This statement informs the browser which "flavor" of XHTML you are using to write your code. Although the declarations, also called *DOCTYPES*, look complex at first, they will always be exactly the same on every document that uses that type, so you can simply copy and paste them from one document to the next.

The XHTML Transitional DOCTYPE:

```
<!DOCTYPE html PUBLIC "-//W3C//DTD XHTML 1.0
Transitional//EN"
"http://www.w3.org/TR/xhtml1/DTD/xhtml1-
transitional.dtd">
```

The XHTML Strict DOCTYPE:

```
<!DOCTYPE html PUBLIC "-//W3C//DTD XHTML 1.0
Strict //EN"
"http://www.w3.org/TR/xhtml1/DTD/xhtml1-
strict.dtd">
```

The XHTML Frameset DOCTYPE:

```
<!DOCTYPE html PUBLIC "-//W3C//DTD XHTML 1.0
Frameset//EN"
"http://www.w3.org/TR/xhtml1/DTD/xhtml1-
frameset.dtd">
```

Declaring the XHTML Namespace

Because XHTML documents are technically written in XML, it is necessary to also define the XHTML namespace for your document. This is a fairly technical XML detail, and fully understanding its purpose is not necessary, especially considering that, like the DOCTYPE, it will always be the same on every one of your documents (regardless of which DOCTYPE you are using). It is added as an attribute to the first tag in your page, which uses the `html` element:

```
<html xmlns=" http://www.w3.org/
1999/xhtml>.
```

Advantages of XHTML

Writing XHTML only requires a small amount of additional effort beyond writing HTML, and yet it provides several advantages. First, you can validate XHTML documents using one of several free online resources. Browsers will not throw errors or attempt to inform you in any way when they encounter mistakes in your Web page coding. Instead, they will simply ignore any elements or attributes they do not understand and continue trying to render the page as best they can. Unfortunately, this can make troubleshooting problem pages difficult. XHTML documents with a proper DOCTYPE declaration can be checked against a *validator*, which lets you know if there are problems and allows you to fix them.

Second, XHTML requires that you write better, cleaner code, which will prove much easier to edit and maintain later. Third, XHTML is "future-proof," meaning that because you declare the version of the language you are using right from the beginning, browsers into the distant future should be able to correctly render your pages.

Writing XHTML Strict documents also allows you to separate the content of your page, the XHTML, from the presentation of your page, the CSS, giving you much more flexibility in your designs. This topic is explored in greater detail throughout this book.

Introducing Cascading Style Sheets

The W3C developed CSS in an effort to provide a more robust formatting language for the Web. CSS can be used with any Web page, regardless of whether you are using HTML or XHTML, and regardless of the DOCTYPE you choose.

Versions of CSS

The original specification of CSS, version 1.0, was released at the end of 1996. It introduced text formatting, including bold and italic typefaces, indents, and spacing; the ability to add foreground and background colors to elements; alignment for most elements; and margins, padding, and borders on elements.

Version 2.0 was adopted about eighteen months later. Its most useful additions were most of the positioning properties used for page layout and media types that allow designers to target style sheets to specific uses.

Version 3.0 is still under development by the W3C, with no specific timeframe for adoption.

Browser Support for CSS

Perhaps the most commonly cited reason for not adopting CSS is concerns over browser support. While these concerns were at one time well justified, today few browsers lack significant support for CSS.

Of the major browsers on the market today, all fully support CSS 1.0, and all support most if not all of the properties in CSS 2.0. In fact, some browsers such as Mozilla Firefox even support some features in CSS 3.0, although they do so sporadically.

However, not all browsers implement CSS exactly according to standards, so there are still significant differences in the ways in which pages may render. It is absolutely imperative that, as a Web designer, you test each of your pages on a variety of browsers to ensure that it functions properly.

Basic CSS Syntax

CSS relies on a completely different syntax from XHTML. Instead of elements and tags, CSS uses *rules*, which are made up of a selector and declarations.

The *selector* is a reference to the portion of the XHTML document that should be formatted. The selector can be an XHTML element, or a special CSS selector such as an ID or class. ID and class selectors will be discussed in Chapter 9.

Declarations are made up of property-value pairs. Each property is separated from its value by a colon, and each declaration is separated from the next by a semicolon. The whole set of declarations is enclosed in curly braces:

```
p { color: #ff0000; font-weight:bold; }
```

CSS selectors are case-sensitive, while the declarations are case-insensitive. CSS is whitespace insensitive.

Properties that contain more than one word, such as font-weight, separate the words with hyphens. If a property value needs more than one word, such as in the name of a font like Times New Roman, that value needs to be in quotation marks.

Inheritance

XHTML documents are made up of nested sets of elements, creating parent-child relationships. Many, but not all, CSS properties inherit from parent-to-child elements. For example, if you have a paragraph that contains a span, the span will inherit most of the parent's properties, especially those regarding text and font styles.

Advantages of CSS

While it is more difficult to learn CSS formatting than HTML formatting, there are many advantages to using it:

- **CSS provides many formatting options not available in HTML**. Some examples include the ability to add borders and background colors to any element, control the spacing between lines, override default formatting options, and implement layout controls.

- **Pages that use CSS load and render more quickly**. Because your XHTML documents are smaller when you use CSS, the browser can download the pages more quickly; and because it contains only the code needed for the content, it renders more quickly as well. Subsequent pages in your site see an even bigger speed increase, because the CSS document has already been downloaded and cached by the browser.

- **You can reformat an entire site**. By separating your content and your presentation, you can change the formatting on your entire site from a central location — your CSS file. Therefore, it is possible to reformat your site without having to dig into individual content pages. You can find an example of this capability at www.csszengarden.com, which is a site that presents a single page with many different formats, all using CSS.

- **You can repurpose your site without rewriting it**. These days, more and more users are viewing pages on alternate devices such as cell phones. This creates both a unique challenge and a unique opportunity to designers. The challenge is in designing pages that can look good on a 19-inch widescreen computer display and a 3-inch cell phone screen. By having all of your presentational code in CSS, you can switch layouts dynamically as your users move from one device to the next, again without having to rewrite any of your underlying XHTML.

The Cascade

As you build your style sheets, you will encounter many instances where you have more than one style rule applying to the same element on your page. In these cases, the *cascade* specifies how conflicts are resolved. Style rules that are closer to the element in question take precedence over those farther away. Also, more specific rules override less specific rules, so an ID selector that targets one specific element will take precedence over a general element. Only declarations directly in conflict will be overridden, so a declaration from a less-specific selector will apply if the more-specific selector is silent on that property.

For example, take the following two rules:

```
p {color:#999999; font-weight:bold; }
p#heading {color:#000099; }
```

A paragraph with an ID of `heading` would be dark blue, using the `color:#000099` from the more-specific `p#heading` rule but would also be bold, as the more-specific rule does not state a `font-weight` property, so the less-specific rule using the element selector applies.

Linking and Importing

Keep your style sheet information in a separate document. This separates content from presentation, a key consideration behind the development of CSS. It also enables you to apply the same style sheet to multiple pages, so you can create one design for your entire Web site.

CSS provides for two ways to attach a CSS style sheet to an XHTML page. The more common is to use the XHTML `link` element:

```
<link rel="stylesheet" type="text/css"
href="path_to_css_document" />
```

All three attributes are required. The value of the `rel` attribute is almost always `stylesheet`, and the value of `type` is always `text/css`.

The second method is to import your style sheet through the special CSS `@import` rule, which appears within an XHTML style tag:

```
<style type="text/css">
@import ("path_to_css_document");
</style>
```

The two methods are not mutually exclusive. If you use both, rules in the imported style sheet will take precedence over rules in the linked style sheet, which enables you to force certain properties to be overridden.

Introducing JavaScript

n the early days of the Web, a need arose to allow designers to provide some sort of interactivity for their users. Netscape, at the time the developer of the most popular browser, developed a scripting language for that purpose.

A Brief History of JavaScript

JavaScript was first introduced in Netscape version 2 in 1996. It was originally called LiveScript, but as Netscape was also adding support for Java to the browser, they decided to change the name. Several months later, Microsoft introduced their version of the language, called JScript, along with Internet Explorer (IE) version 3.0. JScript was intended to be compatible with JavaScript, with a different name simply to avoid trademark issues, although it did introduce several new features.

Later, Microsoft submitted JScript to Ecma International, an organization that develops and maintains standards for computer systems. Today, both JavaScript and JScript try to maintain compatibility with the standardized version, which is called ECMAScript, although both still retain certain variations from the standard.

Running JavaScript

In order to run, your JavaScript code must be interpreted by an application. In most cases, the application being used to run it will be a Web browser. However, many other applications support JavaScript in some form today, including Adobe Reader, which can interpret scripting contained in Portable Document Format (PDF) documents. Some commercial applications rely on the language to implement many aspects of the program itself. For example, many of the dialog boxes in Adobe Dreamweaver CS3 are written in HTML, with their functionality provided by JavaScript.

Writing JavaScript

JavaScript is text-based, and can be written in any text editor. Any editor designed to assist in writing Web pages is likely to provide help in the form of code hints and syntax highlighting for JavaScript.

Browser Support

Every major modern browser offers full support of JavaScript. Microsoft's IE officially supports ECMAScript, but this in effect means it supports JavaScript. Non-Microsoft browsers tend to claim to not support JScript, although that language's close relationship to ECMAScript means that other browsers effectively do support it.

JavaScript Is Not Java

Java is a very powerful object-oriented programming language from Sun Microsystems. JavaScript is a scripting language. Java is designed to allow developers to create full desktop applications, and in fact many of the applications that you run on your computer are likely written in Java. JavaScript is designed to enhance the capabilities of Web browsers. Except for the name, the two languages in fact have absolutely nothing in common. While it is common for beginning Web designers to confuse the two, care should be taken not to as there is no help available for Java that would be useful for JavaScript programming, and vice versa.

Advantages of JavaScript

As a scripting language, JavaScript is fairly easy to learn and implement. Unlike compiled languages such as Java or C#, JavaScript developers do not need any additional software to run their applications; they can use any modern browser instead.

JavaScript allows developers to achieve many effects not offered by HTML. For example, HTML form controls are extremely limited, and offer little in the way of validation controls to ensure that the data being entered is what is expected. JavaScript allows developers to write as complicated a validation scheme as they need on top of the form.

JavaScript can also work in conjunction with CSS to achieve advanced visual effects such as drop-down menus, accordian effects, and much more.

The Rise and Fall of Dynamic HTML

In the late 1990s, many Web sites began to want to expand the capabilities of the browser beyond merely presenting HTML, and saw JavaScript as a way of doing this. Dynamic HTML (DHTML) was an attempt at combining HTML, JavaScript, and CSS to produce many exciting visual effects. However, wide adoption of DHTML was hindered by important differences in browser implementation, at times requiring two completely different scripts to render in Netscape and Microsoft browsers. Many DHTML effects sacrificed usability and accessibility in the name of "cool" effects, and the language has been abandoned for the most part today.

Disadvantages of JavaScript

The biggest problem with using JavaScript is that all browsers allow users to disable it. Although few users actually take this step, there are enough people out there who sometimes or always surf the Internet with JavaScript disabled to cause problems for sites that rely on it for mission-critical site content.

Disabled users often encounter problems with JavaScript as well. Given much of the implementation of the language revolves around creating visual effects, assistive technologies such as screen readers for the blind often lack the capability to correctly interpret JavaScript effects.

For these reasons, you should always be sure to provide an alternative to JavaScript effects, and avoid using the language for anything that would cause the site to break entirely in non-script environments. For example, you should never use JavaScript to completely render your navigation.

Ajax: DHTML, Take Two

Ajax, or Asynchronous JavaScript and XML, was developed as a way to allow developers to extend on the concepts of DHTML while fixing many of its problems. Most Ajax development is done through pre-built JavaScript libraries, saving developers time in having to rewrite code. The better, more widely adopted libraries focus on good usability and accessibility, and also provide many features previously unavailable, such as the ability for JavaScript to refresh only a portion of a Web page. The extremely popular Google Maps application (http://maps.google.com) is an example of Ajax.

JavaScript Libraries

Today, many libraries of JavaScript functions exist that enable developers to implement complex scripting effects while requiring that they write little or no script themselves. These libraries free developers from having to spend time coding and debugging applications, and allow them instead to focus on the end-user experience.

Understanding Creation Tools

B ecause XHTML, JavaScript, and CSS are all written in plain text, you do not necessarily need a specialized tool to create even the most complicated Web pages. Notepad on Microsoft Windows and SimpleText on Apple Macintosh computers are both basic text editors that you can use for Web pages. However, an editor specifically designed for the purpose of creating Web pages will help in many ways.

Code Editors

Code editors are applications that allow you to type your code directly. Unlike simple text editors, code editors will provide many tools to make design easier.

Most code editors share common features:

- **Line numbers**. Debuggers for JavaScript and other programming languages and validators for XHTML and CSS will all return error messages that reference line numbers, so having an editor that shows those numbers makes finding the errors easier.

- **Code hints**. Many editors will display a list of available elements or attributes as you type. Obviously, this saves you from having to have the exact names memorized, but it also helps in reducing your typing time as you can generally only type a few letters of the name before having the editor finish it for you; it also reduces spelling errors.

- **Tag completion**. Editors specifically designed for Web pages will add closing tags where needed, again saving you the time of having to type them.

- **Integrated reference or help functions**. Most editors will include in their help system a complete list of elements, attributes, and a description of each.

- **Color coding and syntax highlighting**. Almost every editor will color code elements and attributes in XHTML, properties and rules in CSS, and language constructs in JavaScript, making the code easier to read and errors easier to spot.

Eclipse

Eclipse is very widely used open source editor. It was originally built for Java developers, but has many plug-ins that extend its capabilities to include other languages, including XHTML, CSS, and JavaScript. It can be downloaded free of charge from www.eclipse.org. Eclipse is available for both Windows and Macintosh.

Macromedia HomeSite

HomeSite is a very feature-rich code editor. Given Macromedia's acquisition by Adobe, there has been little new development of the product, and Adobe has given no indication as to whether they will continue developing it in the future. A free 30-day trial of HomeSite is available at www.adobe.com/products/homesite. HomeSite is only available for Windows.

TopStyle

This editor was developed by the original creator of HomeSite, Nick Bradbury. It currently exists in both a commercial version and a free version with a smaller feature set. TopStyle's main focus is on CSS, and though it can be used to create XHTML, many developers use it solely for editing their style sheets. TopStyle is available only for Windows. Information about TopStyle can be found at www.newsgator.com/Individuals/TopStyle/Default.aspx.

BBEdit

A popular editor amongst Macintosh developers is BBEdit from Bare Bones Software. It features many of the standard features of text editors, along with powerful search tools that can search across documents and utilize regular expressions, as well as a built-in File Transfer Protocol (FTP) client. You can purchase BBEdit at www.barebones.com.

TextMate

TextMate was developed as an alternative to BBEdit for Macintosh users. It is an extremely configurable editor, allowing users to create their syntax highlighting schemes, create macros to extend the program's functionality, and save snippets to reuse code later. A free trial and purchase information for TextMate can be found at www.macromates.com.

While code editors tend to give designers more direct control over their code, visual design editors tend to allow for faster workflows as they save time: The developer has to type little if any code. More importantly, they present the designer with a visual representation of the final page, allowing for a more natural design process. Visual editors are often referred to as WYSIWYG (What You See Is What You Get) editors, although none of them present an absolutely perfect rendering of how the page will appear in a browser.

Features that you will find in most visual editors include:

- A visual design view with a representation of a browser's display

- Toolbars or panels for inserting common elements and modifying their properties

- A visual CSS editor for simplified style sheet creation and modification

- An integrated FTP or other publishing tool for uploading completed pages

- Powerful site management features that allow for integrated file management

- A code view for manually entering or modifying code if needed

Adobe Dreamweaver CS3

Dreamweaver is a feature-rich, powerful design tool. Considered by many to be the industry standard amongst Web designers, Dreamweaver not only supports the features mentioned previously, but it also has tools for creating dynamic, database-driven Web sites with a minimal amount of code. Its focus is on designing standards-based XHTML pages. Dreamweaver CS3 is the first version of the program released by Adobe, and includes support for Adobe's Ajax library, called Spry. Dreamweaver also has tight integration with other Adobe products, including easy insertion of Flash movies and round-trip graphic editing from Fireworks and Photoshop. You can download a 30-day trial of Dreamweaver from www.adobe.com/products/dreamweaver. Dreamweaver is available for both Macintosh and Windows.

Microsoft Expression Web

Expression is Microsoft's latest entry in the visual design tool market, replacing the now-discontinued FrontPage. Unlike its predecessor, Expression is geared towards professional designers and is being placed as a direct competitor to Dreamweaver. It supports CSS and standards-based design, and also features tools that allow developers to create pages that use Microsoft's ASP.NET server-side technology. You can download a trial of Expression from www.microsoft.com/expression/products/overview.aspx. It is only available for Windows.

Adobe GoLive

Before their acquisition of Macromedia, Adobe's Web development tool was GoLive. Its best features focus on its integration with other Adobe products, in particular Photoshop, from which it supports round-trip editing of graphics, and InDesign, which allows designers to take complex print layouts and convert them to Web-friendly layouts. While GoLive is no longer a part of the Creative Suite product line, having been replaced by Dreamweaver, it is still in active development, with a new version, GoLive 9, that was released in 2007. Visit www.adobe.com/products/golive to download a trial version. Like other Adobe products, GoLive is available in both Macintosh and Windows versions.

Microsoft FrontPage

Even though it has been officially discontinued by Microsoft, FrontPage remains a popular editor. FrontPage was originally designed to make creating Web pages as easy as creating documents in a word processor such as Microsoft Word. Even though it had a very simple interface and required little or no learning, it tended to lack many features professionals desired, and its reliance on creating code that would only render correctly in IE made creating cross-browser and cross-platform pages difficult. Still, its ease of use more than compensated for that in many people's eyes.

Understanding Web Browsers

Regardless of which tool you use to design your pages, you should keep in mind that, ultimately, you are designing for the browser. That is the tool on which your users will view your page. Unfortunately, from the early days of Web development, browsers have posed numerous problems for designers.

The Browser Wars

In 1994, Marc Andreessen and Jim Clark, both of whom had been working for several years on the Web in its earliest implementations, founded the Netscape Corporation and published Netscape Navigator, the first widely adopted Web browser. Netscape Navigator quickly became the most popular browser in the world, but in 1995 Microsoft released IE 1.0 as an add-on feature to Windows 95.

The two companies would fiercely compete for the browser market for the next several years in what became known as the "browser wars." Unfortunately, both for designers and HTML, the competition mostly revolved around each browser releasing a new version with new features — proprietary HTML elements or attributes. This was ultimately the reason behind the development of HTML 4.01, XHTML 1.0, and CSS, so in the end, the Web community benefited more from the browser wars than they were hurt by them.

The browser wars eventually ended as IE benefited from its tight integration with Windows while the operating system gained dominance. In 1999, Netscape was purchased by AOL, which uses the brand to this day but officially disbanded the company in 2003.

Internet Explorer

By far the most dominant browser on the market today is Microsoft Internet Explorer, or IE. The fact that it is installed by default on every copy of Windows ensures that it will continue to dominate the market for the foreseeable future.

From a Web designer's perspective, this is both good and bad. The good is that if your page displays correctly on IE, you can be sure that in most situations the vast majority of your users will see your page as you do. The bad is that IE has long been the least standards-compliant browser on the market, so getting your page to display correctly on it, while still maintaining the appearance of the page on other browsers, can be challenging.

In 2006, Microsoft released IE 7. They introduced several new features in this version, but for designers, the most important aspect was the news that IE 7 would adhere much closer to standards than past versions, and correctly implement several CSS rules that before had been either ignored by IE or incorrectly rendered.

All users of Windows Vista have IE 7 by default. At this time, it is the only version of IE that will work on Vista. Most Windows XP users have by now also upgraded to IE 7, although significant numbers still use IE 6.

For many years, Microsoft developed a version of IE for Macintosh computers. Oddly, this version of IE often displayed pages differently from the Windows versions, at times being more standards-compliant, and at times less. In 2006, Microsoft announced the end of development of the Mac version of IE.

Mozilla Firefox

In 1998, Netscape created the Mozilla Organization, which would continue the development of their browser as an open source project. Mozilla is the name of the underlying rendering engine used by many browsers today, and is a combination of Mosaic, the name of the browser Andreessen and Clark built before founding Netscape, and Godzilla.

Today, Mozilla supports several open source projects, the most relevant being the Firefox browser. Firefox is designed as a standards-compliant browser, which means that if you create your page following the rules of XHTML and CSS set forth by the W3C, your page should display correctly in Firefox. Due mostly to this, Firefox is often the primary browser on computers used by Web developers.

Firefox is currently in version 2.0, and is available for Windows, Macintosh, and most Unix machines. You can download the browser for free from www.getfirefox.com.

Apple Safari

Apple announced in 2003 that they had developed their own browser, to replace Internet Explorer for Macintosh as the default browser on Mac OS X. Beginning with the release of OS X version 10.3, Safari was bundled with the operating system; as of the release of version 10.4, it is the only browser included.

Because Safari is based on the WebKit rendering engine, rather than Mozilla, early versions had some rendering oddities that made designing pages for it more challenging. Today, however, it is mostly standards compliant, so pages that render correctly on Firefox will almost certainly render correctly on Safari.

For many years, the biggest challenge for the majority of designers in dealing with Safari was the fact that it was only available for the Mac. This changed in 2008 when Apple released Safari 3 for both Mac and Windows. Safari is available as a free download from www.apple.com/safari/download.

Opera

The Opera browser, from Opera Software in Norway, was for a very long time the only browser for which you had to pay. Therefore, it did not develop as strong a following as its feature set should have allowed. When Opera 8 was released and it was announced that it would be free, more people decided to take a look.

Opera has long been standards-based, but its most recent version, 9.2, features tools that allow designers to see what their pages may look like on very small screens, so those designers who wish to develop pages for mobile devices will often use Opera for this purpose.

Opera is available for Windows and Macintosh from www.opera.com/download.

Which Browser Should You Use?

Which browser you use for general Web use is a completely personal decision. However, for Web design, you need to have as many of the browsers listed previously as you can. In general, you will want to design initially with the more standards-based browsers, such as Firefox, in mind, and then modify your page as needed to fix problems in the less standards-based browsers, such as Internet Explorer.

Worrying About Old Browsers

A lot of clients and bosses may have read or heard something saying that their pages should be built to support older versions of browsers, particularly older versions of Internet Explorer such as 5 or 5.5, or Netscape 4.7. These browsers offer varying levels of support for modern design principals, especially CSS, and can pose a significant challenge to designers. The obvious answer to the question about whether or not to support them is to determine if anyone is actually still using them. Unfortunately, accurate browser usage statistics for the Web as a whole are hard to come by and will vary greatly. The good news, though, is that you do not need statistics for the Web as a whole — you only need to care about which browsers *your* users have, and that is a statistic that is easy to come by, because your Web server will have logs of that. So before you start rebuilding your page for Netscape 4.7, check your server logs. Odds are good that it will show that you have little or no users still on old browsers, and you are free to stop worrying about them.

Understanding Web Servers

While the browser is the palette for which you design your pages, Web servers play an important role as well. As a Web designer, you do not need to understand servers to the point that you would feel comfortable administering a server — hopefully, that will be someone else's job. However, a basic understanding of servers and how they work will enable you to better appreciate their role in getting your pages to your users.

The Client-Server Model

The Internet and all of its associated applications, including the Web, use a client-server networking approach. Early client-server networking relied on so-called "dumb terminals" on the client side, which were little more than monitors connected to the network that relied on the server to do all of their processing. Today, of course, your users will be using full-fledged computers that are much more powerful than the servers of old. However, these clients must still connect to a server in order to receive Web documents.

HTTP

Berners-Lee, in creating the Web, established a new protocol that would allow for the transmission of hypertext documents over a TCP/IP connection. He dubbed this the Hypertext Transmission Protocol, or HTTP. While few users of the Internet have any knowledge of what it is or why it exists, one cannot escape being aware of HTTP as it, of course, begins most Web addresses.

TCP/IP

Networking relies on established protocols to ensure that the computers on both sides of the connection are able to communicate and exchange their data as needed. The most important protocols for the Internet are the Transmission Control Protocol (TCP) and the Internet Protocol (IP). TCP allows for the delivery of that data, while IP establishes a consistent addresses format that allows machines anywhere in the world to find one another. TCP/IP dates back to the 1960s, and in fact the co-developers of the protocols are often referred to as the "fathers of the Internet." Every computer that wishes to directly connect to the Internet needs to have a unique IP address. Currently, the most widely adopted form of IP is version 4, in which addresses are expressed as four numbers between 0 and 255, separated by periods or dots. IP version 4 yields just over 4 billion unique addresses. However, the ever-increasing popularity of the Web has created a shortage of addresses, so a new version of IP, version 6, is beginning to gain use. IP version 6 uses a new address scheme that will yield a seemingly endless supply of address (3.4×10^{38} total).

Web Servers

A *Web server* is merely a piece of software that runs on a computer that is connected to the Internet and allows its files to be shared. While many people use the term to refer to the physical machine on which the Web server software is running, it is important to remember that a Web server is actually software. While many Web servers exist, by far the two most popular and widely used are Internet Information Services by Microsoft and the Apache Web Server from the Apache Software Foundation.

Regardless of the manufacturer, Web servers all do essentially the same thing. They listen for requests to be made via HTTP, and respond to those requests, usually by finding the document the user has asked for and sending it to them. For basic HTML documents, the server will not open or read the document, but will instead merely send it off to the browser.

Internet Information Services

Microsoft's entry in the Web server market, Internet Information Services (IIS), was introduced in 1995 on the Windows NT Server operating system. Since then, the company has released a new version of IIS with each new iteration of its server-based operating system, so today versions exist to run on Windows 2000, Windows XP, Windows 2003, and Windows Vista. While each new version has sought to improve security, the basic feature set of the server has remained mostly unchanged. One of the nicest features of IIS is its graphic user interface, which makes configuring the server much easier than its competitors.

IIS unfortunately only runs on Windows, and only on the version of Windows for which is was designed. It is free, and is included along with any of the versions of Windows mentioned previously with the exception of Windows XP Home Edition, which does not include or support IIS.

Apache Web Server

The main competitor for IIS is the open source Apache Web Server. Maintained by the non-profit Apache Software Foundation, this lightweight server will run on practically any operating system, including Macintosh, various Unix installations, and Windows. Macintosh OS X ships with Apache preinstalled.

When it was originally developed, software engineers took a series of existing software components and pieced them together to create the server. Thus, it was literally "a patchy" server, and when it was released, Apache decided to keep the Apache variation of that name for the server itself as well as the foundation.

Officially, Apache lacks any user interface for configuration. Instead, users must modify a text file, http.config, in which all of the server's settings are kept. This file can be daunting to the uninitiated, but with some explanation and a little practice, it becomes fairly simple to maintain the server. There are several third-party implementations that provide some sort of graphical interface for configuration as well.

Default Documents

Often, users will make a request to a Web server without asking for a specific document. This always occurs when a user merely enters the domain name of a site, as typing in **www.wiley.com**. In these cases, the browser is essentially coming to the server and merely asking to connect instead of requesting a document. The server, however, still needs to send a document back to the user, so every server has a setting that allows the administrator to determine a set of special filenames that will be served by default. Apache has long set the list to index.html and index.htm, while Microsoft has always insisted on preconfiguring IIS to look for Default.htm. Most of the time, the server administrator will add index.htm and index.html to the IIS settings, as these have become well established as default filenames for Web site's home pages.

Root Folders

Installing a Web server on your computer opens an obvious security hole in your machine — you are running software that invites others to connect to you and retrieve files. To counteract this issue, servers are configured to retrieve documents from one specific folder on the machine's hard drive. It can see and send files from subfolders of the root, but it cannot go above the root to any other directory. The root is the directory in which all of your Web pages, and any supporting files such as CSS documents, images, Flash movies, and anything else must be located. The server will be unable to locate any files stored outside of the root directory. When setting up your computer on which you plan to develop Web pages, you should mimic this functionality of the server and make sure that your pages will continue to work after you transfer them to the server.

Plan Your Web Site

When you begin work on your Web site, there will be an urge to simply sit down at the computer, open up your editor, and start creating. However, you will soon find that you start running into roadblocks, as you continually need to tweak your navigation, find new content, or even reach a point where you are simply unsure of what to do next.

Instead of this haphazard approach, you should force yourself to sit down and carefully plan your site before you ever begin typing anything. You can do this planning on the computer or on paper — whichever is easier for you.

Why Do You Want a Web Site?

The first thing to determine is exactly why you are creating a Web site. What exactly do you hope your users will get out of it? With billions of sites on the Web, the odds are extremely good that there are already sites out there that provide the same or similar information or goods or services that your site will. So ask yourself, why would someone want to use your site instead of someone else's? Occasionally, you may even talk yourself out of building the Web site at all if you cannot satisfactorily answer this question.

Who Are Your Users?

No traditional brick-and-mortar company would consider opening a new location without performing thorough market research, and yet few Web sites do the same. You need to know who your users are, at least in a general sense, before you begin any development. Are they more likely to be young or old? How much education are they likely to have? How much income? Are they likely to be computer and Web savvy or not? All of these questions should influence your approach to your pages. Computer professionals expect a much different experience when they visit a site than computer neophytes. The former group is more likely to be using higher-end hardware and software and high-speed connections, so you can feel more comfortable using multimedia on your site if that is your target. If, on the other hand, you expect a lot of users from rural areas where high-speed connections are less common and you expect your users to be much less technically inclined, then you need to adjust your site contents accordingly.

Where Will You Get Your Content?

Content is king on the Web. People surf the Web for a lot of different reasons, but in the end they are all looking for one thing: content. The content of your site will primarily be the text and images on your pages. If you are building a personal site, then obviously the content will come from you. Corporate sites may have a team of developers to help create the content. Content may already exist, either in printed form, which will require that it be input into a computer, or it may already exist electronically and can possibly be copied and pasted from some other application.

If you plan to offer multimedia on your site, you will possibly have an even bigger hurdle to overcome, as the creation of music and video requires much more time and energy and will certainly involve other, likely expensive equipment and software. Either way, you will want to have a good idea of what your content will be and where you will get it before you start work on the site, and especially before you attempt to give an employer or client a proposed deadline for completion of work on the site.

What Will the Visual Design Look Like?

While you should focus on content first and foremost, the Web is without a doubt a primarily visual medium, and what your site looks like is important. Most professional designers will sketch out many different designs before they settle on the one they want. Some use computer graphics programs such as Adobe Photoshop or Adobe Fireworks for this purpose, while others simply draw rough sketches on paper. Once you settle on a design, you can begin to figure out how the content will fit and make changes to the design as needed. Note that good Web sites modify the design to fit the desired content, not the other way around, as content is by far the more important of the two. Ask yourself this: Would you be more likely to return to an ugly site that gave you the information you need, or a gorgeous site that had little to offer beyond the looks? Hopefully, of course, you will not have to make this choice on your site, and will instead have something that is both functional and pretty; just remember that functional should take precedence.

Organize Your Files

As was already mentioned in the section on Web servers, all of your Web site's assets — the HTML documents, images, style sheets, multimedia, and so on — need to be placed within a single directory on your computer as you develop your site, as this is how they will work once on the server. However, it is not considered a best practice to place all of these files loose in one directory. It is not uncommon for even small sites to have many hundreds of files, and larger sites can reach into the tens of thousands. From the very beginning of the design process, you should have a plan for the organization of the files on your site. You can change this organization later, but unless you are using a tool with site management features such as Adobe Dreamweaver, moving a file from one directory to another late in the development process can mean having to edit hundreds of your Web pages to fix now-broken links.

The only file that absolutely must reside directly in the root folder is the home page. Some designers choose to put all of the top-level documents — the documents that represent the main sections of the site — in the root as well. At the very least, you will want a folder to store your images, and if you are using multimedia, you probably want a folder for that as well. If any of the main sections of the site will have multiple files, placing them in a subdirectory of the root will help keep you organized.

The most important thing to keep in mind is that there is not one "correct" way to organize the files. If you are working alone on the site, then you should use whatever organizational scheme makes the most sense to you. If you are working in a team, then you all need to sit down and discuss how you will stay organized.

Create a Basic Web Page

While every Web page will be slightly different, each will contain the same set of basic structure tags. Properly formed Extensible Hypertext Markup Language (XHTML) documents will begin with the appropriate document type declaration. Following that, they will have an `<html>` tag, which needs to contain the `xmlns` attribute. This tag will contain all of the rest of the content of the page, so its opening tag will immediately follow the DOCTYPE and its closing tag will be the last one the page, as the DOCTYPE does not have a closing tag.

Your document will then be divided into two sections. The top section is the `head`, into which you will eventually place information used by the browser and search engines. Within the `head`, you need to put your `title`.

The page `title` is used by search engines to help catalog the page, so you want to be sure that it contains your company or organization name and a descriptive name for the page. Perhaps more importantly, the page `title` appears on the browser's title bar at the top of the screen, and helps identify the page to your user. If a user likes your page and adds it to her favorites or bookmarks, the `title` will be the default name of the page.

The second section is the body. All of the content of the page — everything that the user actually sees in the browser windows — will go in the `body`. In most documents, the `body` will contain the overwhelming majority of the code.

These four elements — `html`, `head`, `title`, and `body` — are required on every page.

Create a Basic Web Page

① Open your desired editor to a new document.

Note: *You can open Notepad in Windows by clicking Start → Programs → Accessories → Notepad.*

② Type the document type declaration.

The example shown uses XHTML Transitional.

Note: *See Chapter 1 to learn more about document type definitions.*

③ Type the `html` element's opening tag.

④ Add the `xmlns` attribute.

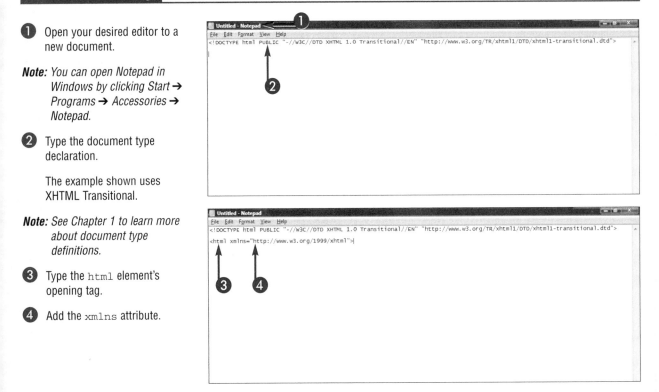

5 Type the head element's opening tag.

6 Type the title element's opening tag.

7 Type a descriptive title for the page.

8 Add the closing title tag.

9 Add the closing head tag.

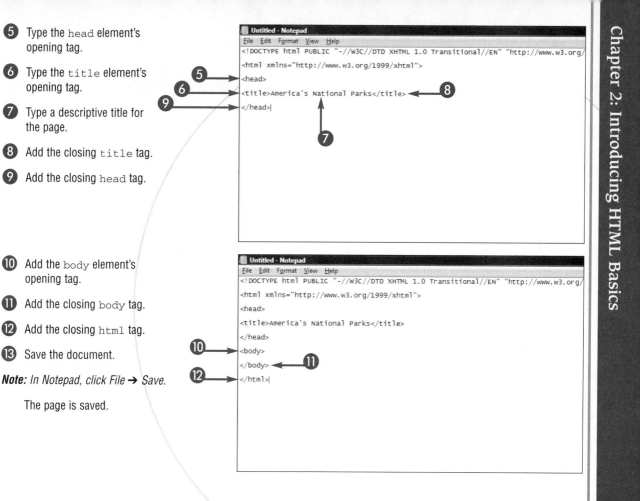

10 Add the body element's opening tag.

11 Add the closing body tag.

12 Add the closing html tag.

13 Save the document.

Note: *In Notepad, click File → Save.*

The page is saved.

Extra

Web browsers are designed to be very forgiving when they interpret pages, so your document will most likely display correctly if you omit one or more of these tags. However, just because the browser will display the page anyway, does not mean you should not always include them. Leaving them out will cause your page to fail to validate properly, which will in turn make troubleshooting other potential problems more difficult. Screen readers and other assistive technologies for persons with disabilities may have difficulty reading the page correctly or may fail altogether.

You cannot format the text in the title in any way, and you cannot include any other html tags within it. If you do, those tags will appear directly on the title bar instead of being interpreted and rendered correctly. The appearance of the text on the title bar is determined by the browser itself and by the users when they choose themes for their pages; it is something over which you simply have no control.

Save and Preview a Web Page

You will want to periodically save the changes to your page and preview it in one or more Web browsers. You should get in the habit of saving the page every few minutes, so that if there is a power failure or some other issue with your computer, you will not lose — and have to redo — too much work.

When you save your page, be sure that you save it into the folder that you set up to hold all of your Web documents. Web page filenames should be long enough to be descriptive of their content, while being short enough that they are not inconvenient to type. They can contain only letters, numbers, dashes, and underscores. Filenames on the Web *cannot contain spaces*. Be very careful to watch for this and correct any files where you accidently used spaces. Many browsers will simply fail to

display a page otherwise. Your filename may end up being case-sensitive, so it is considered a best practice to use all lowercase letters in the filename.

Your document will need either an .htm or .html extension. There is no practical difference between them, and which you choose to use is ultimately personal preference. Editors specifically designed for Web pages should add the extension for you.

Your home page will need to have the filename required by your server for default documents, most likely index.htm or index.html.

Once the document is saved, you will want to open it in a Web browser to be sure that it is displaying correctly. All browsers have an "open file" functionality that allows you to open a Web page from your local file system.

Save and Preview a Web Page

① Open a Web page in your editor.

Note: In Notepad, click File → Open.

② Save the page.

Note: In Notepad, click File → Save As.

The Save As dialog box appears.

③ Navigate to the folder that will contain your Web pages.

④ Type an appropriate filename.

⑤ If necessary, type the file extension, using either .htm or .html.

Note: In Notepad, you have to set Files of Type to All Files to prevent the program from adding its own .txt extension.

⑥ Open Internet Explorer.

⑦ Click File ➔ Open.

The Open dialog box appears.

Note: *If you are using Internet Explorer 7, you will need to right-click in the toolbar area and select Menu Bar to see the menus.*

⑧ Click Browse to navigate to the folder in which you saved your file.

⑨ Open the file.

The page opens in the browser.

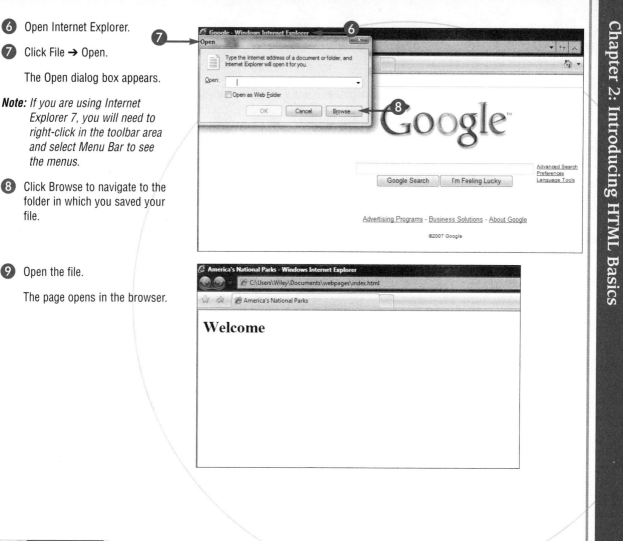

Extra

All browsers render basic XHTML the same, so it will not yet be obvious why you need to test your pages in more than one browser. The differences between the browsers become apparent once you start implementing Cascading Style Sheets (CSS) and JavaScript, at which time it becomes necessary to view each page in every browser you think your users may have. Most likely, this will include Internet Explorer 6 and 7, Firefox, and Opera on Windows, and Safari on Macintosh.

If you use a visual design tool such as Adobe Dreamweaver or Microsoft Expression Web, do not rely on the visual design view in those programs in lieu of actual testing in the browsers. The visual design views are there to give you an idea as to what your page will look like. They cannot represent the differences in browsers, and so will rely either on a single browser's rendering engine, or some other engine that might try to approximate a middle ground amongst the most popular browsers. Either way, this view cannot substitute for viewing your page in the real thing. Additionally, these tools may not activate certain key features of your page, such as JavaScript, and they may display certain elements for design purposes, such as hidden table borders, that would be otherwise invisible in the browser.

Create Headings

Many studies have confirmed that most people do not read Web pages. Rather, they tend to skim them, picking out the bits of information that they need and then closely reading only that portion of the page. You should design your pages with this reading habit in mind. The best way to allow your user to quickly skim the page for relevant information is to use XHTML headings.

XHTML provides for six levels of headings, represented by the h1, h2, h3, h4, h5 and h6 elements. You should use the h1 element to denote the most important topic on the page. Subtopics of that heading should be marked up with h2 elements, while subtopics of those second level headings should use h3, and so forth. For example:

```
<h1>Mount Lassen Volcanic National
Park</h1>

<h2>Getting There</h2>
```

All of the headings will display by default in a bold typeface. Each also has a default size, with the first level of heading being the largest, and each other level progressively smaller. All of the headings are block-level elements, meaning that they will have space above and below them on the page. And all of these default display properties can be overridden by CSS, so you should make sure to use the correct heading level for the text in question.

Create Headings

① Open an XHTML document in your editor.

Note: In Notepad, click File → Open.

② Beneath the opening body tag, type the h1 element's opening tag.

③ Type the text for the heading.

④ Type the closing h1 tag.

⑤ Type the h2 element's opening tag.

⑥ Type the text for the heading.

⑦ Type the closing h2 tag.

⑧ Save the page.

Note: *In Notepad, click File → Save.*

The file is saved.

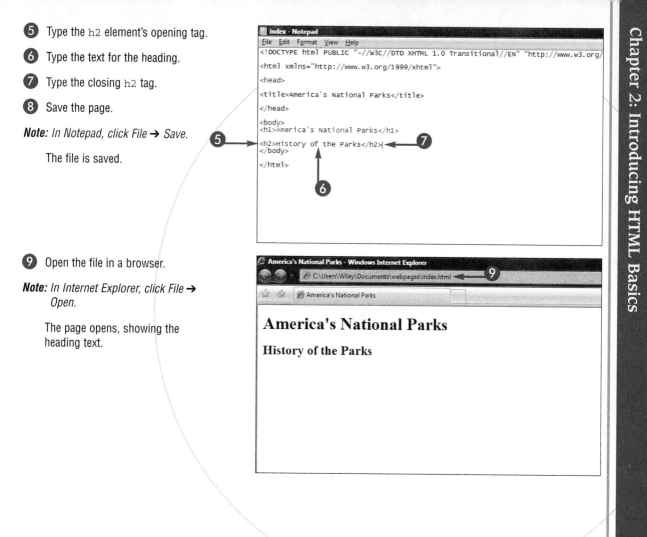

⑨ Open the file in a browser.

Note: *In Internet Explorer, click File → Open.*

The page opens, showing the heading text.

Create Paragraphs

The main portion of your content will be made up of paragraphs of text. In traditional publishing, paragraphs were denoted by indenting the first line of text. Many modern forms of publishing have abandoned the first-line indent and instead place space above and below the text of the paragraph, just as this book does. The Web uses this same practice.

You must remember, however, that XHTML is whitespace insensitive, so actually adding space above and below blocks of text in your code has no effect on their final display. In fact, if you put text in your code without any XHTML elements around it, it will appear in the browser as a solid block, regardless of what spacing you may have used.

Therefore, XHTML provides for a paragraph element, p. Any text that you wrap with <p> tags will appear as a paragraph, with space above and below. You must be sure to add a closing tag at the end of the paragraph.

Many beginners become concerned about the apparent double spacing that seems to occur with paragraphs on Web pages. In the early days, there was no real way to achieve fractional line heights, so by default the browsers will place a whole line both above and below the paragraph. Many designers think that this looks like too much space, but here again, CSS can help as it does allow you to precisely control the height of the line. As with other aspects of your Web page, you should focus at this point only on getting your content entered using the proper tags and worry about the visual design later.

Create Paragraphs

1. Open a Web page in your editor.

2. In the body of the document, add a p element's opening tag.

3. Add text to the paragraph.

4. Add the closing p tag.

⑤ Add a second opening p tag.

⑥ Add text for the second paragraph.

⑦ Add a closing paragraph tag for the second paragraph.

⑧ Save the page.

⑨ Open the page in a Web browser.

The page opens, showing the paragraphs.

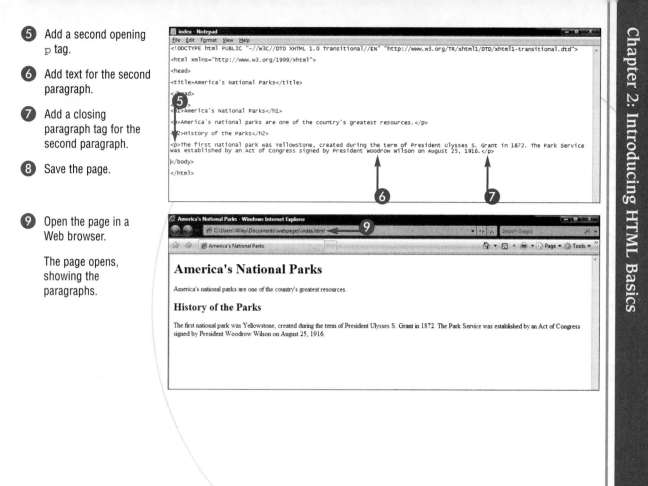

Extra

HTML made certain closing tags optional, including the one for the paragraph. The browser would know to begin a new paragraph when it encountered another opening p tag, and would thus know to end the prior paragraph. Some designers went so far as to use the opening p tag to mark the end of each paragraph, rather than the beginning.

While you may encounter this practice in legacy Web pages you edit, you should avoid it. XHTML solves this inconsistency by simply requiring that every tag be closed. More important, using the proper combination of an opening tag at the beginning of the paragraph and a closing tag at the end maintains the logic behind the language. The p is supposed to be a container element, so the paragraph in question should be enclosed within the tag. Strict XHTML, in fact, does not allow any text to appear directly in the body of the document, but rather requires that it be enclosed in some block-level element.

Add Line Breaks

By default, lines of a paragraph wrap with the size of the browser window. However, there are times where you will want to force lines of a paragraph or other block of text onto new lines. In XHTML, you accomplish this via the use of the break element, br. One of the simplest elements in the language, br simply instructs the browser to insert a line break.

Remember that in XHTML, all elements must be closed. The br element is one of the empty elements in the language, meaning that it does not contain or wrap around text. It is essentially an instruction to the browser to start the following text on a new line. In HTML, it would simply be written <br>, but in XHTML, it must contain the trailing slash to close it: <br />.

A common example of the element would be in formatting an address on several lines:

```
<p>1600 Pennsylvania Ave. NW<br />

Washington, D.C. <br />

20006</p>
```

Keep in mind that simply placing code on separate lines will not achieve the desired effect. The code above could as easily be written in one line without changing the display in the browser; hence the need for the br element.

Add Line Breaks

① Open a Web page in your editor.

This example shows index.html.

```
index - Notepad
File Edit Format View Help
<!DOCTYPE html PUBLIC "-//W3C//DTD XHTML 1.0 Transitional//EN" "http://www.w3.org/
<html xmlns="http://www.w3.org/1999/xhtml">
<head>
<title>America's National Parks</title>
</head>
<body>
<h1>America's National Parks</h1>
<p>America's national parks are one of the country's greatest resources.</p>
<h2>History of the Parks</h2>
<p>The first national park was Yellowstone, created during the term of President U
was established by an Act of Congress signed by President Woodrow Wilson on August
</body>
</html>
```

② Add a paragraph element's opening tag.

③ Add the first line of text.

```
index - Notepad
File Edit Format View Help
<!DOCTYPE html PUBLIC "-//W3C//DTD XHTML 1.0 Transitional//EN" "http://www.w3.org/
<html xmlns="http://www.w3.org/1999/xhtml">
<head>
<title>America's National Parks</title>
</head>
<body>
<h1>America's National Parks</h1>
<p>America's national parks are one of the country's greatest resources.</p>
<h2>History of the Parks</h2>
<p>The first national park was Yellowstone, created during the term of President U
was established by an Act of Congress signed by President Woodrow Wilson on August
<p>The national headquarters of the US National Park Service is located at:|
</body>
</html>
```

④ Add a break tag.

⑤ Add another line of text.

⑥ Add the paragraph's closing tag.

⑦ Save the file.

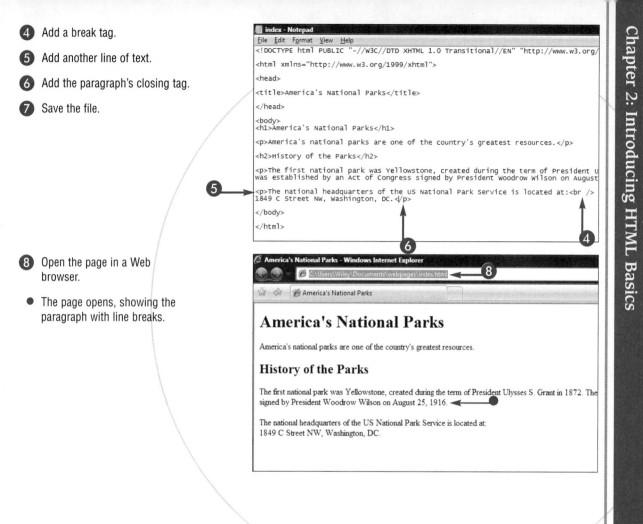

⑧ Open the page in a Web browser.

● The page opens, showing the paragraph with line breaks.

Extra

The br element will not normally take attributes, but in HTML Transitional and XHTML Transitional documents, you will commonly see it used with a clear attribute, whose values will be set to either right, left, or both. This attribute allows the designer to use the break tag to prevent the content that follows from continuing a *float*, a common technique used for CSS-based layouts that I cover later in this book.

HTML Strict and XHTML Strict do not allow the clear attribute, as it is solely presentational. You can achieve the same effect via the use of style sheet rules, in which case the br tag will contain either an id or, more often, a class attribute.

You should always take care that you are using the proper tag in the proper context. Reserve the use of br for those instances where you have several lines of text that are logically part of the same paragraph or other block and merely wish to display on separate lines, instead of using it in place of paragraphs simply to avoid the extra space between lines; you can control this through style sheets.

Add Horizontal Rules

At times, you may wish to divide your page visually into sections. On particularly long pages, a rule can be used to let your user know that they are starting a new section or topic. While not required, logic would dictate that most rules would be followed by a new heading, likely an `h1`. You can insert horizontal rules into your page with the `hr` element. It is an empty element, and so must contain the trailing slash to close the tag in XHTML.

```
<hr />

<h1>Start of a new section ... </h1>
```

Older versions of HTML included a series of presentational attributes that allowed you to set the width (length), height (thickness), and color of the rule. Today, all of those attributes have been deprecated in favor of CSS.

The default appearance of the rule is fairly plain and even using style sheets to alter the color or width of the rule still leaves much to be desired visually. Therefore, some designers omit the tag altogether and divide their page by inserting a custom image in its place. This can create a much more visually interesting design, as long as care is taken to ensure that non-visual users can still understand that the content that follows is a new logical section of the page.

Add Horizontal Rules

1 Open a Web page in your editor.

2 Add content.

3 Add an `hr` tag.

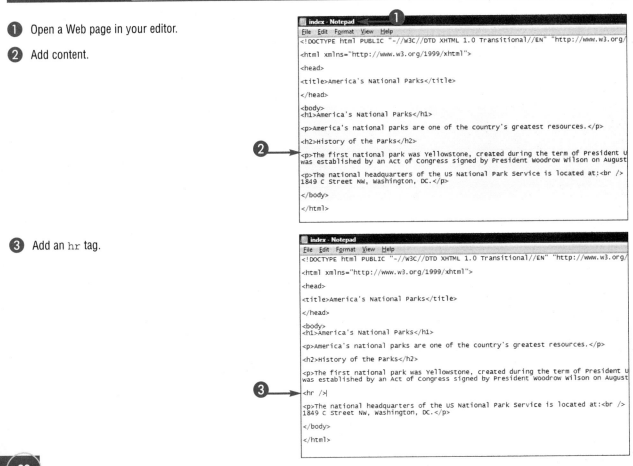

④ Add an h2 element's opening tag.

⑤ Add new heading text.

⑥ Add the closing h2 tag.

⑦ Add a paragraph of text below the heading.

⑧ Save the page.

⑨ Open the page in a Web browser.

● The page opens, showing the horizontal rule.

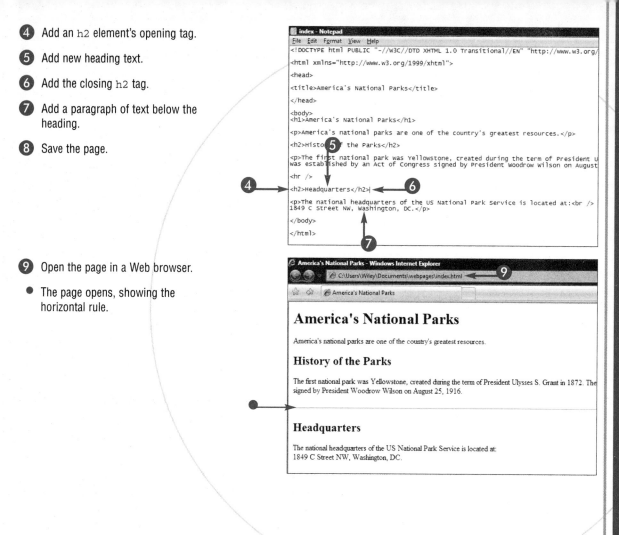

Horizontal lines on a page have been called *rules* for centuries. In fact, you are probably familiar with the term, because you have most likely purchased college-ruled notebook paper before. According to the Oxford English Dictionary, the term is derived from Old French *reule*, which in turn came from the Latin *regula*, meaning "straight stick," and has the same word origin as a ruler that you use for measurement. Traditional letterpress printing used a straight piece of some rigid material, often steel but possibly copper, brass, or zinc, that was the same thickness as the text to create rules.

Horizontal rules should be used sparingly on your pages. If you have a section of the document that is a completely different topic from the one above, you might consider whether that content would be better suited existing on a completely separate document. Early Web designers would at times have a series of rules together, often with different widths, to create visual designs, but this practice has been largely discontinued in favor of images or CSS borders.

Add Comments to the Code

E ven though you will primarily focus on your end user's experience while developing pages, you should also consider making your page as easy as possible to edit later, either for you or for other Web developers you may work with. Writing to existing Web standards and making sure you write good code is the main way in which you help yourself later, but adding comments is an important aspect of this as well.

Comments are notes you can put in your source code. Their contents are not displayed in the browser window, but they remain in the source code for you or other developers to view later. A common practice is to put a comment near the top of the page to make note of when the page was created, who created it, and any

modifications made since its creation. You can also use comments to denote the beginning or end of sections of the page, or note where future additions might be added.

Comments in XHTML begin with an angle bracket followed by an exclamation mark and two dashes. They end with two dashes and the closing angle bracket. All content between the opening and closing marker for the comment will not be displayed in the browser.

```
<!-- This is a comment. -->
```

Comments can span as many lines of code as needed. Comments can appear anywhere within your document after the DOCTYPE. Be aware that you should not place anything before the DOCTYPE, as doing so may cause some browsers to render your page incorrectly.

Add Comments to the Code

1 Open a Web page in your editor.

2 Near the top of the code, after the DOCTYPE declaration, type `<!--` to begin a comment.

3 Add text with the title of the page, your name as author, and the date.

④ Close the comment by typing `-->`.

⑤ Save the page.

```
index - Notepad
File Edit Format View Help
<!DOCTYPE html PUBLIC "-//W3C//DTD XHTML 1.0 Transitional//EN" "http://www.w3.org/

<!--
Title: America's National Parks
Author: Rob Huddleston, rob@robhuddleston.com
Date: 11/4/07|
-->|

<html xmlns="http://www.w3.org/1999/xhtml">

<head>

<title>America's National Parks</title>

</head>

<body>

<h1>America's National Parks</h1>

<p>America's national parks are one of the country's greatest resources.</p>

<h2>History of the Parks</h2>

<p>The first national park was Yellowstone, created during the term of President U
was established by an Act of Congress signed by President Woodrow Wilson on August

<hr />

<h2>Headquarters</h2>

<p>The national headquarters of the US National Park Service is located at:<br />
1849 C Street NW, Washington, DC.</p>

</body>

</html>
```

⑥ Open the page in the browser.

● The page opens. The comment does not appear in the browser window.

```
America's National Parks - Windows Internet Explorer
C:\Users\Wiley\Documents\webpages\index.html       ⑥

America's National Parks

America's National Parks

America's national parks are one of the country's greatest resources.

History of the Parks

The first national park was Yellowstone, created during the term of President Ulysses S. Grant in 1872. The
signed by President Woodrow Wilson on August 25, 1916.

Headquarters

The national headquarters of the US National Park Service is located at:
1849 C Street NW, Washington, DC.
```

Extra

It is important to remember that although the comment does not appear in the browser window, it still exists in the code. Since their inception, browsers have allowed users to view the source code of Web pages. Therefore, you should be careful to never have anything confidential in your comments.

While comments certainly help future editing of pages, they also add file size to the page, so you must strike a balance between having sufficient comments in your code to improve readability while not overly bloating it. Make sure all of your comments are succinct and on topic.

Comments can also be useful to temporarily hide or disable features of your page. If, for example, you have a link on your navigation bar to a page that is not yet completed or available online, you can comment out the link. This effectively hides it until such a time as the page becomes available, at which point you can simply remove the comment to bring back the link.

Apply Logical Formatting

Most of the visual presentation of your page should be handled through CSS. CSS is much more powerful, and provides many more formatting options, than HTML; and separating your presentation from your content makes your pages more versatile.

However, there are times when formatting is not used for purely presentational effects; instead, it enhances the underlying logic of the page. The default styling of headings is an example of this: You apply heading tags around text not just to make them bigger and bold, but also to logically specify that this text is more important than others, and that it describes the topic that follows.

Within a paragraph or other block of text, there will be times when you wish to make the text either bold or italic

or both. If you are doing this for purely presentational purposes, such as making the name of the company stand out, then you should use CSS. However, if you are applying bold or italic to text so that you can emphasize the content, then you are applying logical formatting — the difference in visual appearance has some meaning to the code.

You can denote that text should be displayed in a bold typeface by using the strong element, and italic by using the em element, which is short for emphasis. It should be obvious that these will be container tags — you need to tell the browser both when to start applying the bold or italic, and when to stop. You can nest either of these within the other to get bold and italic text.

Apply Logical Formatting

① Open a Web page in your editor.

② Add a paragraph element's opening tag.

③ Add text to the paragraph.

④ Add a strong element's opening tag.

⑤ Type the text to be bold.

6 Close the `strong` tag.

7 Finish the text in the paragraph.

8 Save the page.

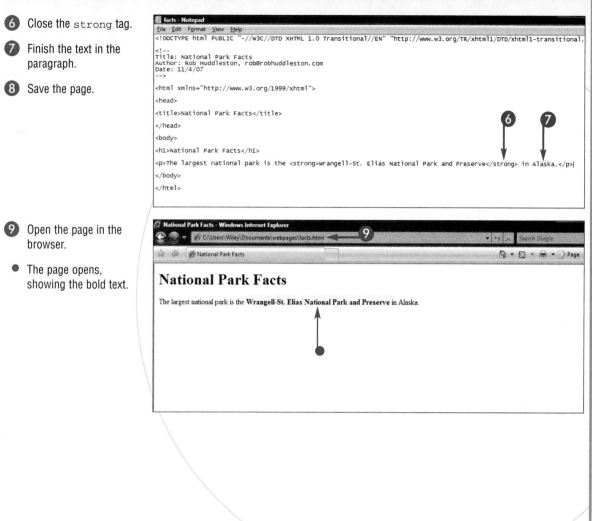

9 Open the page in the browser.

● The page opens, showing the bold text.

Extra

There are several other tags that will result in italicized text, but they have different logical meanings. For example, both the `address` element and the `cite` element will cause text to be rendered as italic. Those elements will be discussed in later chapters.

Many designers use the `b` and `i` elements to designate bold or italic text, respectively, instead of `strong` and `em`. While the display in the browser is identical, the underlying meaning is less clear. When you use `strong`, you are telling the browser that the text should be bold because it is being strongly emphasized. When you use `b`, you are telling the browser to make the text bold, but not providing any reason *why* it should be bold. Both `b` and `i` have been deprecated from XHTML, so they are not valid in XHTML Strict.

Logical formatting is preferred primarily because screen readers for the blind and other accessible devices are helped if the page maintains its own internal logic.

Plan Your Navigation

A key, often-overlooked ingredient in having a successful Web site is creating good navigation. Ideally, your site's navigation should be second nature to your users. They should not have to think too hard — or at all — about how to get from one section or page in your site to the next. Some examples of sites with fantastic navigation are Amazon.com, Yahoo, and eBay. All three have very intuitive links and buttons that just about anyone can understand instantly.

Good navigation does not happen by accident. It must be carefully planned from the beginning to succeed.

The best way to learn good navigation is to study these examples and other sites and figure out what they are doing right so that you can emulate it on your own pages.

Levels of Navigation

Most sites rely on several levels of navigation. Level 1 navigation provides links to the main pages of the various sections of the site and the home page. Most likely, the level 1 links will appear in some form on every page. Within each section, level 2 navigation takes users to the pages of that section. Level 2 links will probably appear on each page within the section, but not on pages outside the section. Larger sites may break down links even further, with third- or even fourth-level links in some sections.

User-Centric versus Designer-Centric

Perhaps the most common mistake made by designers when working on navigation is that they plan their site's structure and navigation based on what they want or are used to. However, the Web is a user-centric environment. Your users will have very little time and most likely no money invested in your site when they visit, so if it does not provide them with exactly what they need, they will quickly go elsewhere. In general, users have a very low threshold for frustration when using Web sites.

Many organizations, however, still approach the layout of the site and navigation from an internal perspective. Your company has department A, department B, and so forth, so you may be tempted to organize your site so you have department A's pages together, and then department B's, and so on. The problem here is that your users are unlikely to know or care how your company is organized internally.

Take, for example, a rural county government's site. If a citizen finds a dead animal in front of his house and needs to call someone to have it removed, he will likely go to the county's Web site and get the number for the department. But who does he call? The local police? Animal control? The fire department? The forest service? In a traditional Web site layout, where each of these agencies would have separate sections of the Web site, the citizen would have to dig through each section before finding the answer. Instead, the county could organize its site based on the needs of the user, so there could be a section devoted to people who live in the county and need services, a section for those who work there, and for those who visit. The site then becomes about the user, instead of the agencies.

Navigation Structure Does Not Have to Equal Page Structure

It is as important that you plan how you will organize the documents that make up the site as it is that you plan your navigation. The difference between the two is that the former is for your needs, while the latter is for your users'. In the previous county government example, it might make sense for the county Web master to have a folder in the site devoted to the police pages, and another folder for the fire department. But that does not necessarily mean that the site's navigation must follow the same pattern. Simply remember that the site's navigation needs to fulfill the needs of the user, not the needs of the developer.

The Design Should Serve the Navigation, Not Vice Versa

The site's visual design is an important aspect to the success of the site, and should not be overlooked. However, it is far less important than the design of the navigation and the content. Many professional designers have made the mistake of sacrificing links because they would not fit into a preconceived visual design. This is a huge mistake. If the necessary navigation does not fit the design, then the design needs to change. Your users do not really care what the page looks like, as long as it is reasonably attractive.

Consistent Look and Feel

Your navigation should look and feel consistent throughout the site. Avoid having a dramatically different appearance or placement for the level 1 links on various pages. Level 2 links should appear in the same place in every section. It is okay, and at times even desirable, to have the links appear with a different color scheme across sections to let the user know that they are, in fact, in a different section of the site, but the overall appearance should remain the same. Amazon.com implements this strategy very well.

Links Must Be Obvious

Your users should never have to hunt for a link. The size, appearance, and placement of links should make it instantly clear to users that this is something they can click. The actual text of the link should make it clear what users can expect to see when they click the link. Once again, study the top successful sites on the Web, including Amazon.com and eBay, to see excellent examples of this. Many blogs, on the other hand, fail miserably in this regard with links that are difficult to find.

Test, Test, Test

The only way to be sure that your navigation is succeeding is to have actual users test the pages. You can do Web site testing in a formal, proctored environment if budget allows, or informally by simply asking users to visit and use the page, and then respond back to you with their thoughts. There are two important factors to keep in mind with successful testing. First, your testers must represent actual users, so do not have highly technically inclined people test a site aimed at computer novices. In a company, having the secretaries test the site is as important, if not more so, than having the CEO test it. Second, your test should mimic real-world situations. Do not give specific instructions, but instead simply ask the users to go to the site and act as they would normally. If they get stuck somewhere or lost, the fault is in the design of the site, not in the user. Real-world users will not take the time to ask for help, but will instead simply leave the site, so these are critical issues that must be solved.

Structure Web Site Files

Keeping your files organized is another important factor in maintaining a successful Web site. Most file structure organization will be invisible to your user, but it will help you to be as efficient as possible in your work.

The Root Directory

Because your Web server will store all of your files under one directory on its drive, you must do the same on your development computer. The exact location of the directory in which you store your files is unimportant, but you need to establish this Web root folder before you do any other work. Every page in your site, and all of the site's assets, including style sheets, images, audio and video files, and everything else that will appear on the Web must be in this directory and a subfolder of it.

Assets

Other site assets should be organized as you see fit. If you will be using more than one external style sheet, you should consider creating a "styles" directory. If your site will serve video, audio files, or Adobe Flash movies, they may need separate folders as well.

Some advocate for the creation of an "assets" folder off the Web root, which will contain separate folders for the site's images, style sheets, audio, video, Flash, and any other non-HTML files.

Subfolders Under the Root

Except for the very smallest of sites, you will almost certainly want to place subfolders under the root directory to organize your files. Some designers keep a single level of subfolders, while others, particularly those dealing with very large sites, nest folders several levels deep. The only important factor is that the site's organization be logical and work for you.

Images

Just about every designer agrees that images should always be stored in a folder dedicated to that purpose. Most designers actually call this folder "images," although it can be named just about anything. Very large, graphics-heavy sites may find the need to organize the images within the folder into subfolders.

Most sites can work with a single images directory located off the root, but some larger sites prefer each section to have its own images directory within the section's folder. The thing to keep in mind again is that there is no one correct approach and you must find for yourself what works best.

Directory Naming Rules

Each directory in your site needs to be named according to the same rules that govern the naming of files. The names, therefore, can only consist of letters, numbers, dashes, and underscores, and cannot contain spaces or other special characters.

The directory name will appear as part of the address to the page. Therefore, it should be long enough to be descriptive while staying short enough to not be difficult to type. Users can derive some idea as to the meaning of the page or section that they are looking at from the directory name, and some search engines will catalog pages in part based on the directory name, so you should make sure that you avoid meaningless abbreviations. While sometimes necessary for organization, too many levels of subfolders can hinder this process and should be used with care.

Understanding
File Paths

To link to pages within your site, you must understand file paths and URLs.

The Uniform Resource Locator

Web pages are found based on their Uniform Resource Locator, or URL. A URL represents a path to a page on the Web.

```
http://www.wiley.com/WileyCDA/WileyTitle/
productCd-0470274360.html
```

The URL for this book's companion Web site begins with the protocol used to communicate with the server; in this case, as in most Web pages, it is http://. Following that is the name of the server, www, and the server's domain name, wiley.com. After the domain name, you can follow

the path to the file, so in this case the file, productCd-0470274360.html, is in a directory called WileyTitle, which is, in turn, called WileyCDA. The WileyCDA directory would most likely be located under the Web root.

It is worth noting that the previous assumptions may not be completely correct. Many advanced Web sites that are using databases to populate their content, as in the case of Wiley Publishing, will use programmatic techniques to generate URLs that do not necessarily represent the physical file path, but for our purposes in illustrating the structure of a URL, that is unimportant.

Getting from Page A to Page B

When you want to create a link to a page in your site from another page in the same site, you need to provide a path from the page that will contain the link to the page that is the link's target. There are essentially three methods of providing this path.

Relative Paths

The most common method for providing link paths is to use a relative path. In this scenario, you provide the path to the page to which you are linking, starting at your current location. It is similar to providing directions to tourists you encounter on the street: You tell them how to get where they need to go, starting at your current location.

BACKING UP

If you need to set a path that moves up in the directory tree, for example going from a subfolder to its parent, then you can use two dots.

Site-Root Relative Paths

The next method is a site-root relative path, where you always give the location of the page relative to the root folder, regardless of the location of the page on which the link exists. Site-root relative paths can at times be easier to calculate, and are particularly helpful if you want to use the exact same navigation code across pages. Because the paths to each page will be the same regardless of the location of the calling page, you can safely copy and paste the code from one page to the next and be sure that your links will continue to work.

Absolute Paths

The final method of addressing paths is the absolute path. Using absolute paths is similar to how you address envelopes in the mail: You give the complete address, regardless of your current location. In an absolute path, you provide the complete URL to each page in every one of your links.

Path Examples

Let us say that the site at www.mycompany.com has a home page, an index.html in the root folder of the site, and a products1.html page in a products folder, which is located in the root. To get from index.html to products1.html:

● The relative path would be products/products1.html.

● The site-root relative path would be the same, products/products1.html.

● The absolute path would be http://www.mycompany.com/products/products1.html.

The path from products1.html to index.html:

● Relative: ../index.html

● Site-root relative: index.html

● Absolute: http://www.mycompany.com/index.html

Create a Link to a Page in Your Site

Hyperlinks are the key concept behind the Web. Giving developers the ability to link from one resource to another related resource was one of the driving forces behind their development. In XHTML, you use the a element, which is short for "anchor." The purposes of most other elements in the language are clear from their names, but this one is not always and will sometimes confuse beginners. The logic behind the anchor is that you are essentially anchoring one document to the other when you create the link.

The anchor element has one required attribute, href. The value of href will be the path to the target resource. You can use a relative, site-root relative, or absolute path when creating links to pages within your site. Generally, relative paths will be the easiest to manage and maintain. In some cases, you might choose to use site-root relative paths, but you will almost never use absolute paths for local links.

The default appearance of a link varies as the user interacts with the page. Initially, it will be blue. Once the link's target page has been visited by the user, the link turns purple. When it is activated, it will be red. Links are always underlined by default, but this behavior, along with the colors of the links, can be changed with style sheets.

Create a Link to a Page in Your Site

1 Open a Web page in your editor.

2 Below the body element's opening tag, add a paragraph tag.

3 Add the anchor element's opening tag.

4 Within the opening tag, add an href attribute.

5 Set the value of the attribute to a relative path to another page in your site.

6 Add descriptive text to describe the target resource.

7 Add the anchor's closing tag.

8 Add the paragraph's closing tag.

9 Save the page.

⑩ Open the page in a browser.

⑪ Click the link.

● The target page opens in the browser.

The text you use to describe your link — the text that you place between the opening and closing anchor tags that your user will click — should somehow describe the page to which your user will be taken. Perhaps the most common mistake many designers make, including many long-time professionals who should know better, is to use non-descriptive text in a link. The worst is perhaps "click here," which has become so overused as to become something of a cliché. "Click here" is not descriptive in the least; it is also insulting the user's intelligence, because it can be assumed that she *knows* she is supposed to click the link.

Less obvious but all too common is to have a good, descriptive sentence, but then not link the descriptive words. For example, you may see a sentence such as "Buy this book here." In this case, either the entire sentence should be the link, or at least the words "Buy this book," as those are what actually describe what will happen — the user will be taken to a page to buy something. Unfortunately, many designers will simply link "here," thus losing the descriptive value.

Create a Link to a Page on the Web

You can link to other sites on the Web as well as pages within your own site. External links use the exact same syntax as internal ones, so you will still use the anchor element with an `href` attribute. The only difference is that you must use an absolute path to describe the location of the other resource.

You must remember that absolute paths always contain the *complete* URL. A very common mistake made by beginners is to forget the protocol at the beginning of the path. You must begin with http://, https://, or whatever the site to which you are linking requires in order for the link to work.

If the page to which you are linking is being hosted on a server that is running some version of Unix or Linux, the path to the page will be case-sensitive. If it is on a Windows server, then it will not be. As there is no simple way to tell which operating system the site might be using, you should err on the side of caution and assume that the path you type into your code needs to match exactly, including case.

An easy way to ensure that you get the correct and complete path to an external page is to use your Web browser to go to the page to which you want to link and then copy the address from the browser. You can then paste the link into your code. This solves any issues with capitalization, spelling, or missing parts of the path.

Create a Link to a Page on the Web

① Open your Web browser.

② Navigate to a page to which you wish to create a hyperlink.

③ Right-click the browser's address bar.

④ From the context menu, click Copy.

The address to the page is copied to the clipboard.

⑤ Open a Web page in your editor.

⑥ Add a paragraph element's opening tag.

⑦ Add an anchor element's opening tag.

⑧ Within the opening tag, add an `href` attribute.

⑨ Paste the Web address you copied from the browser as the value of the attribute.

⑩ Type a description of the target.

⑪ Add the anchor's closing tag.

⑫ Add the paragraph's closing tag.

⑬ Save the file.

⑭ Open the page in a Web browser.

⑮ Click the link.

The target page opens in the browser.

```
 facts - Notepad
File Edit Format View Help
<!DOCTYPE html PUBLIC "-//W3C//DTD XHTML 1.0 Transitional//EN" "http://www.w3.org/

<!--
Title: National Park Facts
Author: Rob Huddleston, rob@robhuddleston.com
Date: 11/4/07
-->

<html xmlns="http://www.w3.org/1999/xhtml">

<head>

<title>National Park Facts</title>

</head>

<body>

<p><a href="http://www.nps.gov">National Park Service Home Page</a></p>

<h1>National Park Facts<h1>

<p>The largest national park is the <strong>Wrangell-St. Elias National Park and P

</body>

</html>
```

```
 National Park Facts - Windows Internet Explorer
  C:\Users\Wiley\Documents\webpages\facts.html
   National Park Facts

National Park Service Home Page

National Park Facts

The largest national park is the Wrangell-St. Elias National Park and Preserve in Alaska.
```

Extra

Due to well-publicized lawsuits, copyright infringement is a big topic, and often leads designers to question what kinds of resources to which they are allowed to create links. The important concept to remember with copyrights is that you violate them when you try to claim that someone else's work is your own, or when you do something that causes the legal owner to potentially lose revenue from her work, as is the case with sharing music files. Linking to a Web page does not violate either of these principals. When you provide a user with a link to someone else's page, you are not claiming that their work is your own, and if this person makes money off of the page, you are merely driving more people to her and are, in fact, helping her make money. The Web was designed to encourage this kind of cross-promotion.

The one limitation here is that you will be unable to provide a link to a page that requires the user to log in before it can be accessed. In this case, your user will be required to provide his username and password to access the page.

Create a Link Within a Page

I f you have a very long page, one that will require the user to scroll through many screens worth of information, it can be helpful to provide navigation near the top to the important headings. That way, your user will not have to scroll to get the data they want, but can instead simply click a link and be taken right to the correct spot on the page.

When linking to another page within your site or to an external site, the implied first step is that the page or site to which you are linking needs to exist. When creating links within a page, you need to create the spot on the page to which you will link as well as the link itself.

The older method of creating the target for the link is to use the name attribute of the anchor tag, which is

provided in place of the href. The name's value must follow the rules of a Web filename, using letters, numbers, dashes, and underscores but no spaces. In addition, it must be unique on the page.

The newer method, supported by every major modern browser, is to add an id attribute to an existing element at the spot to which you are linking. Like the name, id must not contain spaces and must be unique.

The link itself will use the anchor tag with an href attribute. In this case, the value of href will contain a pound or hash sign (#), followed by the name or id to which you are linking.

Create a Link Within a Page

1 Open a Web page in your editor.

2 At the spot at which you wish to link, add an anchor element's opening tag.

3 Add the name attribute.

4 Set the value of the name to a one-word, unique description of this spot on the page.

5 Add the closing anchor tag.

6 At another spot on the page, add an id attribute to an existing element.

7 Set the value of the id to a one-word, unique description of this spot on the page.

8. Near the top of the page, add an anchor element's opening tag.

9. Add an `href` attribute to the tag.

10. Set the value of the `href` to a pound or hash, followed by the `name` attribute you added in Steps 3 and 4.

11. Add a description of the target of the link.

12. Add a closing anchor tag.

13. Add an anchor element's opening tag.

14. Add an `href` attribute to the tag.

15. Set the value of the `href` to a pound or hash, followed by the `id` attribute you added in Steps 6 and 7.

16. Add a description of the target of the link.

17. Add a closing anchor tag.

18. Save the page.

19. Open the page in a browser.

20. Click each of the links to test them.

The browser scrolls to the target of the link.

Note: *You will need to use either the browser's back button or the scroll bar to move back to the top of the page to click the second link.*

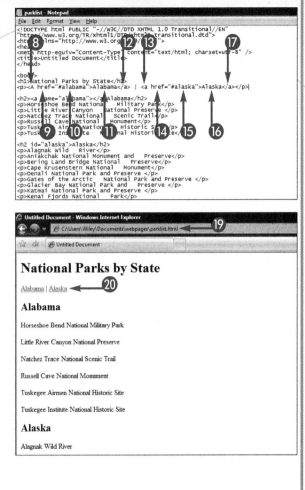

Extra

You can use either the `name` or the `id` for links within a page as every browser your users are likely to be on today will support both. However, you should be aware that the `name` attribute has been deprecated, so you cannot use it on XHTML Strict documents and should not use it in XHTML Transitional.

In addition to the fact that `name` is deprecated, using `id` as the target of the link has other advantages. First, it requires one less tag in your document. Whereas when using `name` you need to add another anchor tag, when using `id` you are simply leveraging existing elements. Second, the `id` attribute is used for many other purposes in your Web page, and, in fact, may already exist in your code. Two of these additional uses that will be discussed in later chapters are that it allows you to apply styles to a specific element and it allows you to manipulate the element in JavaScript.

Create a Link to an E-mail Address

The simplest way to provide the ability for users to contact you from your site is to provide a link to your e-mail address. The syntax for this is similar to the other links: You have an a element with an href attribute. In this case, the value of the href will be the word mailto, a colon, and the address to which you are linking.

Be aware that while this is a simple technique, there are disadvantages. First, your user must be on his own computer, because the link works by having the browser activate the user's e-mail program and address a new message to the e-mail specified in the link. While it is possible to configure some browsers to use a Web-based

e-mail service for these links, you can safely assume that few users will know how to do this, and fewer still will take the time to do so on a public machine. Therefore, a certainly not insignificant portion of your users will simply be unable to use the link to contact you. Second, spammers will very quickly find this link and begin sending mail to it. They can use the same technology that search engines rely on, but in the case of the spammers, they are looking specifically for these links on the valid assumption that this is an e-mail address that is being closely monitored, and is thus an ideal target for them.

The alternative to an e-mail link is a form, which will be covered in detail in Chapter 11.

Create a Link to an E-mail Address

① Open a Web page in your editor.

② Add a paragraph of text enclosed in paragraph tags.

③ Within the paragraph, add the anchor element's opening tag.

④ Within the opening tag, add an href attribute.

⑤ Set the value of the attribute to mailto: and your e-mail address.

⑥ Add descriptive text to describe the target resource.

Note: You should be sure that this text informs the user that clicking the link will send an e-mail.

⑦ Add the anchor's closing tag.

⑧ Save the page.

⑨ Open the page in a browser.

⑩ Click the link.

Your e-mail client will open with a new message addressed to the e-mail you added in Step 6.

Apply It

You can add additional headers to the e-mail such as a from address, cc, bcc, subject, or body. In the `href` value, add a question mark after the e-mail address, then the name of the field, an equal sign, and the value. If you are adding more than one, separate each field and value pair with an ampersand.

```
<a href="mailto:someone@mycompany.com?cc=ceo@mycompany.com&subject=Contact+from+website">Send
us an email</a>
```

Note that the values for each field cannot contain special characters. If you need to add spaces, as in the previous example, substitute the plus sign. Any other character needs to be represented by its URL entity. See Appendix A for a reference of these codes.

Set Tooltips for Links

When clicking a link, your user should have an understanding of what she will encounter when she views the link's target. Users can become frustrated when they click a link that merely says "Contact Us" and end up with their e-mail program in front of them, or when they follow a link to a PDF and were not expecting Adobe Reader to open.

The best way to make sure that users will know what to expect is to make sure you use descriptive text for the link. However, you can further describe the link in a tooltip that will appear when the user mouses over the link.

Adding tooltips to links requires that you add the `title` attribute to the anchor tag. The text you add as the value of `title` will appear as a tooltip on every modern browser.

Some designers attempt to fool search engines by adding additional search engine-friendly text to the `title` attribute in the hopes that it will enhance their rankings. Unfortunately, this does little to your search engine ranking, will most likely confuse your user, and should be avoided. Use only text that will enhance your user's experience by giving them additional information about the link in the title.

Note that some browsers, particularly older versions, may not show the `title`'s tooltip. Also, some users may move their mouses over the link and click it before the tooltip appears. Therefore, the `title` should not be the primary method of providing useful information. Instead, it should merely add to the information given in the link's text.

Set Tooltips for Links

① Open a Web page in your editor.

② Below the body element's opening tag, add a paragraph tag.

③ Add the anchor element's opening tag.

④ Within the opening tag, add an `href` attribute.

⑤ Set the value of the attribute to a relative path to another page in your site.

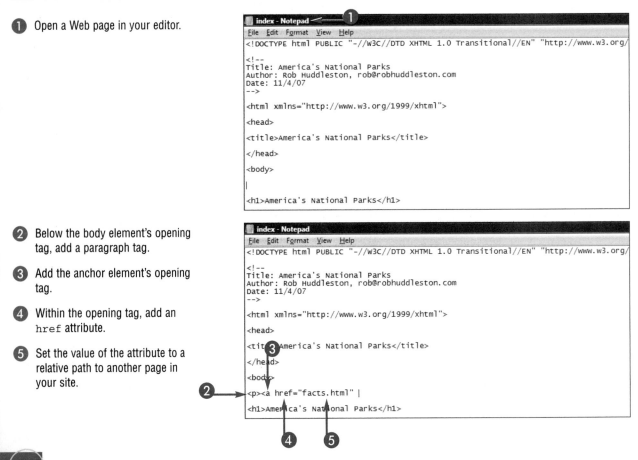

6 Add a `title` attribute to the anchor.

7 Set the `title`'s value to an additional description of the link's target page.

8 Add descriptive text to describe the target resource.

9 Add the anchor's closing tag.

10 Add the paragraph's closing tag.

11 Save the page.

12 Open the page in a browser.

13 Mouse over the link.

● The title displays as a tooltip in the browser.

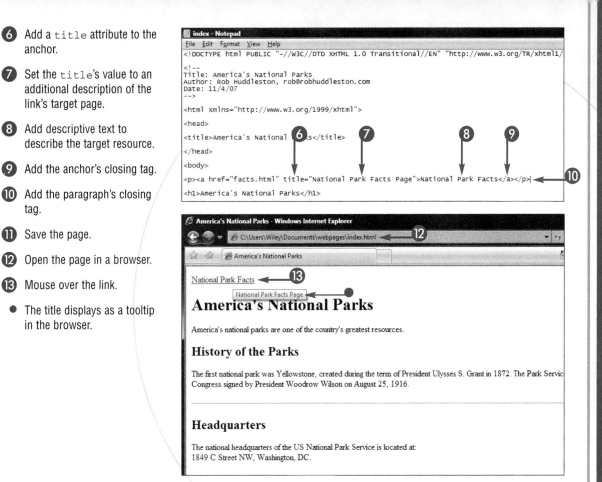

Test Your Links

Y ou must be certain to test each link on each page to ensure that it works correctly. Broken links not only frustrate users, but they also present an unprofessional or unfinished appearance for your site.

Most Web editing tools have some sort of link checker in them, but you should never rely on these tools. Computer software is only capable of verifying that the link is targeting a page that exists, but it cannot tell if the page in question is the one you intended as the target. It is very easy, for example, to select the wrong file if you are using a tool that allows you to browse for a file and builds the link for you rather than you typing the code directly.

For external sites, it is too easy to mistype the address, resulting in either a broken link or possibly worse, a link

to a site other than the one you intended. There are unfortunately unscrupulous Web developers who buy domain names that are close matches to some of the most popular sites on the Web but represent common misspellings of those domains.

Just as important as testing your links when you first design your page is testing them again periodically through the life of the site. This is particularly important for external links, especially those that link to pages other than the home page of a site. The owner of the external site may move pages, significantly change their content, or take them down altogether. Just because a link worked when you created it does not mean it will continue to work later.

Test Your Links

① Open your page in a browser.

② Click a link on the page.

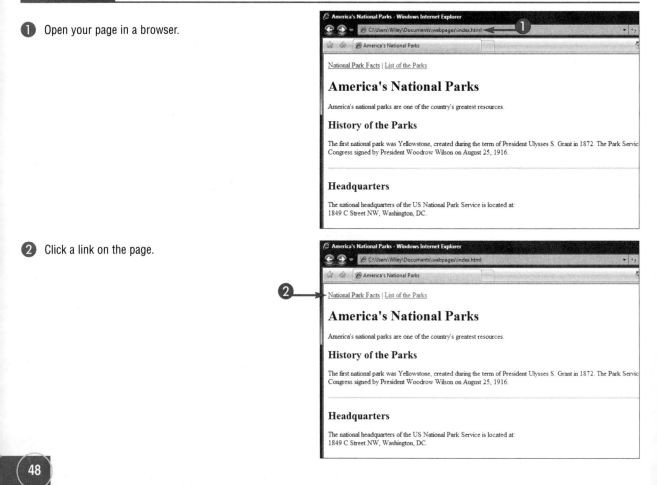

- The new page appears, as in this example, or an error occurs.

③ If the link worked, click the Back button and try the next link.

③

National Park Service Home Page

National Park Facts

The largest national park is the **Wrangell-St. Elias National Park and Preserve** in Alaska.

④ If the link did not work, fix its target in your code and try again.

```
<!DOCTYPE html PUBLIC "-//W3C//DTD XHTML 1.0 Transitional//EN" "http://www.w3.org/TR/xhtml1/DTD/xhtml1-transitional.dtd">
<!--
Title: America's National Parks
Author: Rob Huddleston, rob@robhuddleston.com
Date: 11/4/07
-->
<html xmlns="http://www.w3.org/1999/xhtml">
<head>
<title>America's National Parks</title>
</head>
<body>
<p><a href="facts.html" title="National Park Facts Page">National Park Facts</a> | <a href="parklist.html" title="List of the National Parks">List of the Parks</a></p>
<h1>America's National Parks</h1>
<p>America's national parks are one of the country's greatest resources.</p>
<h2>History of the Parks</h2>
<p>The first national park was Yellowstone, created during the term of President Ulysses S. Grant in 1872. The Park Service was established by an Act of Congress signed by President Woodrow Wilson on August 25, 1916.</p>
<hr />
```

④

Extra

Testing your links is a good chance to have someone else take a look at your site. By asking a third party to test the links, you can check not only that they actually work, but also make sure that the link text is relevant. If you user reports to you that he got to a page other than the one he was expecting, but you verify that the link is pointing to the correct page, then most likely the link text is leading the user to expect something else and should be modified.

Further, this kind of testing can ensure that your users do not have to click too many links to get where they want to go. Carefully observing your tester — without directly guiding him — and getting honest feedback after the test will reveal if the user became frustrated or felt that he was lost, both of which are signs of navigation that needs to be rethought.

Understanding Image File Formats

When creating images, you have many formats from which to choose, from common open formats supported by most image-editing tools to proprietary ones supported by only a few. When creating Web pages, the choices are much simpler, as only three formats are available.

Graphics Interchange Format

The Graphics Interchange Format, or GIF, is perhaps the most common image format on the Web. The format, which was invented by CompuServe in 1987, actually predates the Web.

Color Palette

The biggest limitation of a GIF is its color palette. GIFs are 8-bit images, meaning that they can contain a maximum of 256 colors. When the format was originally developed, 8-bit monitors were the norm, so the limitation did not seem like something likely to impede support for the format. Due to this, GIFs are best suited for line art and images with large blocks of solid color.

Compression and Optimization

GIFs use a lossless compression technique to reduce their size. This compression results in considerably smaller files without loss of quality. Designers can optimize an image by selecting precisely which colors they wish to preserve. Each color removed from the image will reduce the overall file size.

Legal Issues

The format uses the LZW (for Lempel-Ziv-Welch, the names of its creators) compression technique, which was patented by Unisys at the time CompuServe invented GIFs. As the Web became more popular, the popularity and usage of the GIF increased along with it, and in the mid-1990s, Unisys attempted to enforce its patent on the compression technique by requiring commercial Web sites to pay a fee for the use of the format. This resulted in widespread condemnation of both Unisys and CompuServe, and Unisys was never able to adequately enforce the patent.

Between 2003 and 2004, the patent expired in the various countries in which it had been filed, and the format is now available for free open use worldwide.

Animation, Interlacing, and Transparency

Three of the biggest advantages of the format are its support for animation, interlacing, and transparency.

A GIF can be saved with a series of individual images within the same file. This, along with embedded control data, allows the image to display simple animation. The popularity of animated GIFs has declined sharply with the increasing popularity of Adobe Flash and the need for more complex animation and interaction.

GIFs also allow for individual scan lines of the image to be stored out of order, allowing the browser to display the image through progressive passes. On the very slow connections that were the norm in the early days of the Web, this allowed users to cancel the download of an image if they were able to see that it was not what they wanted before the entire image displayed.

One color on the image can be designated as transparent. This allows designers to display a nonrectangular image on a colored background, and is a popular technique. In fact, transparency support is perhaps the most important feature in maintaining support for GIFs.

Joint Photographic Experts Group

In the early 1990s, the Joint Photographic Experts Group published a new graphics standard, which was named after the group: JPEG. Technically, the format is the JPEG Interchange Format, although common convention simply refers to it as JPEG. The early Windows operating system limitation of a three-character file extension resulted in the JPG abbreviation, which is commonly used when referring to the format.

Color Palette

Unlike GIF, the JPEG format uses a 24-bit file, giving designers approximately 16.7 millions colors in which to work. Thus, JPEG is ideal for continuous-tone images. JPEGs do not tend to have as sharply defined edges as do GIFs, and images with only a few colors or large blocks of the same color will tend to be larger as a JPEG than as a GIF.

Optimization

JPEGs rely on a lossy compression technique that essentially deletes data from the image using a series of complex algorithms. Thus, as the file size of a JPEG is reduced, so is its quality. Experience and practice with the format will allow you to discover the point at which the image is as small as it can be while maintaining acceptable quality.

Portable Network Graphics

Portable Network Graphics, or PNG, is a file format developed in response to the Unisys GIF patent battle.

Features

PNG was intended as a replacement for GIF, and features many improvements on the older standard. In particular, by the time PNG was developed, the 256-color limitation of GIFs was becoming a problem: PNG is 24-bit, and supports 16.7 million colors like JPEG. However, unlike JPEG, PNGs support transparency and interlacing. The former supports designating a single color in the palette as transparent, as with GIF, or creating an alpha channel, which allows for partial transparency. The latter uses a technique superior to that used in GIF, resulting in a clearer initial preview of the image, although most high-speed connections used today render the issue of interlacing moot.

PNGs rely on a lossless compression technique known as *deflate* that is not protected by any patent and is highly efficient at compressing the image without reducing its quality.

PNGs do not directly support animation, leaving this to the realm of the GIF, although several extensions to the format do. To date, support for these extensions varies widely.

Browser Support

The most significant issue in the use of PNG has been very slow browser support. While the format has been fully implemented in most browsers, including Mozilla Firefox, Apple Safari, and Opera, Microsoft's Internet Explorer was slow to support the format and its features. Internet Explorer did not support the format at all until version 3, and versions 3 through 6 did not support the format's alpha transparency feature. This feature was added for Internet Explorer 7. Because Internet Explorer is by far the most widely used Web browser, its lack of full support of the PNG image format has hindered the format's widespread use.

Choose the Appropriate Format

Which format you choose mostly depends on your intended use for the image. GIFs, with their limited palette but support for transparency, are commonly used for line art, logos, and buttons. JPEG is the best format for photographs, as those images need the deeper color palette and are expected to be nontransparent and rectangular.

A PNG can be used anytime a nonanimated GIF is used, although its 24-bit color depth also makes it a suitable replacement for JPEG. PNGs are particularly useful when a richer color palette is needed along with transparency, such as in cases where there are images with gradients or shadow effects.

Add an Image to Your Page

The Web is primarily a visual medium, so few pages will not be enhanced by adding images. Whether they are corporate logos, buttons, photographs of products, or merely visual elements added for flair, the images on your page can make the difference in the overall appearance of your page.

Most modern graphics programs give you the ability to either create images from scratch or modify existing digital images to a suitable format for the Web. Once the image is created or saved, you can easily display it on your page. A Web page can in theory have as many images as you wish.

You can add images to your Web page using the XHTML img element. The img element takes a required src attribute, in which you specify the path to the image that is to be displayed. Just as with hyperlinks, you can use a relative, site-root relative, or absolute path to specify the source.

```
<img src="images/yosemitevalley.jpg" />
```

The img is an empty element, which makes sense as it is an instruction to the browser to place the image at that point, and is not marking up any text. As such, it needs to end with a closing slash in XHTML documents.

Note that you are not directly embedding your image into your page; rather, you are including code that tells the browser to request the image from the server, download it, and then display it in the appropriate spot on the page. Therefore, it is necessary to remember to upload all of your images to your Web server along with your Web page files.

Add an Image to Your Page

1 Open a Web page in your editor.

2 In the place in which you wish to add the image, type an img element's opening tag.

3 Add the src attribute.

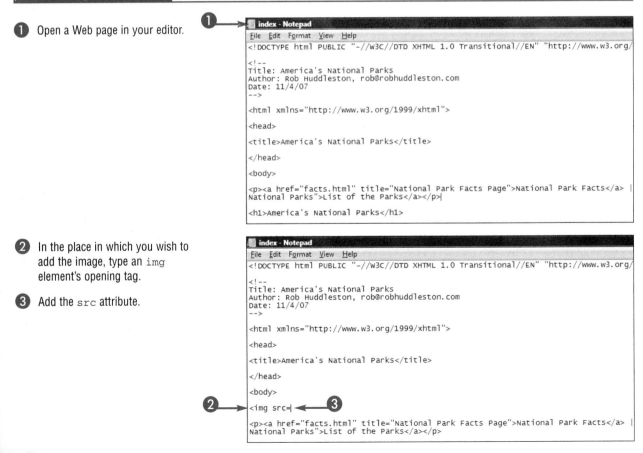

④ Set the attribute's value to the path to the image you wish to include.

⑤ Add the closing slash to the tag.

⑥ Save the page.

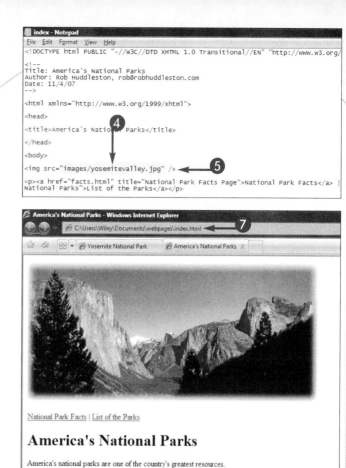

⑦ Open the page in your browser.

The page opens, showing the image.

Because an absolute path is legal in the `img` tag's `src` attribute, some designers rely on a process called *hotlinking*, whereby they link directly to another site's images. This is a practice that should be avoided. If the owners of a site feel that they might have images that are being hotlinked, they may implement scripts to block it, causing the image on your page to either appear broken or possibly appear as an another image altogether (one the other site uses to replace the one to which you linked). Even if the other site does not block hotlinking, you still have the possibility that they will move, rename, or remove the image from their server, thus breaking the link on your page.

As with any other resource you place on your page, you need to be sure that any images you use are those to which you have a legal right. You must assume that any image you see on another Web site is protected by copyright, and unless that site specifically grants you permission to use the image, you will be in violation if you use it, either by directly hotlinking to it or by saving it and using a copy local to your server.

Specify Alternate Text for an Image

Even though the Web is indisputably a primarily visual medium, you should not ignore your visually impaired users. Chapter 14 contains a full discussion of the issues around making your Web site friendly and usable to disabled persons; however, one aspect of making your site accessible to the visually impaired is actually required by XHTML: adding alternate text to your images.

To be valid, every `img` tag must contain both a `src` attribute and an `alt` attribute. The `alt` attribute allows you to describe the image in text. This text will then be read by screen readers, the software the visually impaired use to surf the Web and, in fact, use on their computers in general.

This so-called "alt text" needs to be an accurate description of the image in question. You do not need to describe every detail of the image; instead, your aim is for users who cannot see the image to nonetheless get an idea of what it represents. A picture of a snow-capped mountain, for example, might have alt text of "snow-capped mountain" or, if it is a specific peak, perhaps "snow on top of Mount Lassen." Do not include the words "picture of" or "image of" in the alt text. Images that contain text should have their alt text set to the words on the image.

Images that are merely visually "flair" on the page, such as those used in place of horizontal rules, still need an `alt` attribute, but it needs to be set to an empty string, as in `alt=""`. Screen readers will ignore these images.

Specify Alternate Text for an Image

① Open a Web page in your editor.

② In the place in which you wish to add the image, type an `img` element's opening tag.

③ Add the `src` attribute.

④ Set the attribute's value to the path to the image you wish to include.

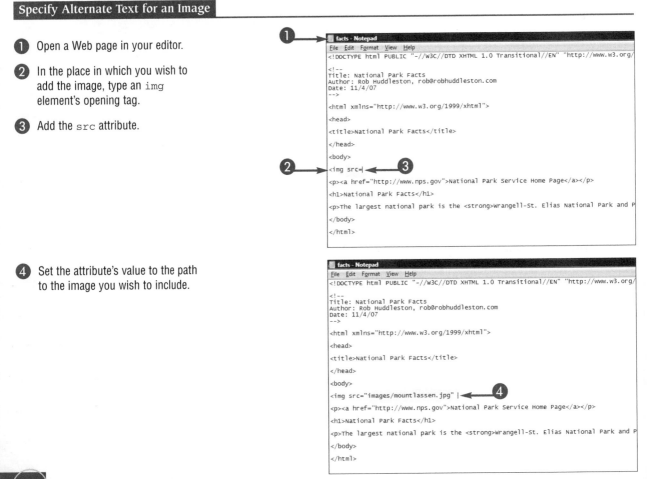

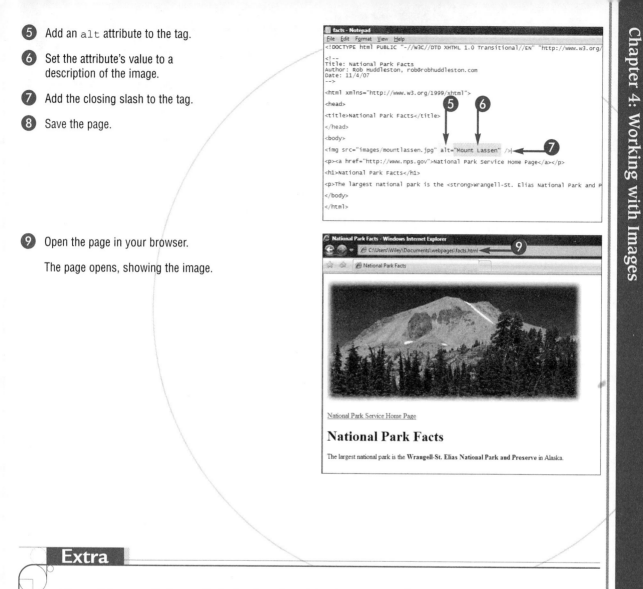

⑤ Add an `alt` attribute to the tag.

⑥ Set the attribute's value to a description of the image.

⑦ Add the closing slash to the tag.

⑧ Save the page.

⑨ Open the page in your browser.

The page opens, showing the image.

Extra

Microsoft Internet Explorer will display the value of the alternate text when your user mouses over the image as a tooltip. This behavior, while useful for testing alternate text, is not standard and not supported by any other browser. If you wish to have a tooltip display on mouse over, use the `img` tag's `title` attribute instead, as this is supported by every browser. Most designers set the `title` and the `alt` attributes to the same value, but if they are different, Internet Explorer correctly displays the `title` text instead of the alternate text.

The alternate text is also displayed when the image cannot be viewed, either due to network or connection problems or, more often, an incorrect `src` attribute being set in the code. Anytime you see alternate text on your page instead of your image, check to be sure that the `src` attribute's value is correct and that the image has been uploaded.

Specify the Size of an Image

When the browser downloads an image, it will determine the dimensions of the image and display it accordingly. However, keep in mind that the image is, in fact, merely linked to the page, not embedded in it. This means that the browser actually makes several passes at the page: First, it reads through and renders the XHTML, laying out elements as needed. Then, it begins again from the top of the code and requests, downloads, and displays each image.

When it makes its first pass through the document, it will leave only enough space for the images as is required for its broken image icon. Later, when it downloads the image, it will have to adjust the layout to fit the actual size of the image, which can cause the whole page to seem to shift around. If your user has already begun reading the text, this shifting can be extremely annoying

as she is likely to lose her place on the page. Forcing the browser to continue adjusting the layout also slows down its rendering of the page.

You can avoid all of this by specifying the size of each image in your code. By adding width and height attributes to the img tag, with values set to the pixel dimensions of the image, you tell the browser how much space it should leave in its initial pass through the page, thus ensuring that it will not have to adjust anything, and speeding up the entire process. You can also be sure that your layout will still look as planned if any of the images fail to load correctly, as there will still be the planned-for space on the page in their place.

Use your image editing software to determine the size of each image.

Specify the Size of an Image

① Open a Web page in your editor.

② In the place in which you wish to add the image, type an img element's opening tag.

③ Add the src attribute.

④ Set the attribute's value to the path to the image you wish to include.

⑤ Add an alt attribute and an appropriate value.

⑥ Add a width attribute and a value equal to the width of the image.

7 Add a height attribute with a value equal to the height of the image.

8 Add the closing slash to the tag.

9 Save the page.

10 Open the page in your browser.

The page opens, showing the image.

Extra

The width and height attributes are not required, but for the reasons outlined previously, it is strongly recommended that you always provide them. In addition, you want to make sure that you always provide the *correct* width and height of the image. It is technically legal to use other values, causing the browser to display the image either larger or smaller than it actually is, and even distorting it by providing values for the width or height that are not proportional. The problem with doing this is that it does not, in fact, resize the image; instead it merely has the browser change its display.

The main issue with this is that the browser is simply not very good at resizing images, and is likely to cause distortion, noise, or pixelization when it resizes the image. Resizing the image in a real image editor can avoid these problems. If the image is not the size you want it, use an image editing tool to resize and resample it, and then set the width and height attributes to the new values from the editor.

Using Images as Links

While most of the links on your page will be text, you can use images instead. Images are frequently used for a page's primary navigation. E-commerce sites frequently display an image of a shopping cart as a link to that area of the site, and use images of their products to link to product details.

Using an image as a link simply involves combining what you know about creating hyperlinks with what you know about inserting images. The hyperlink will use the anchor tag with the `href` attribute. However, instead of providing descriptive text between the opening and closing tags, you will insert an image. The `img` tag will be constructed exactly as in previous sections, with appropriate `src`, `alt`, `width`, and `height` attributes.

Likewise, the anchor tag is constructed in the same way as shown in Chapter 3.

An unfortunate side effect of using an image as a link is that the browser will display the image with a border around it, set to the same color as the page links. Initially, it was thought that there needed to be some sort of visual clue to the user indicating that the image was a link. The image itself will hopefully be all the clue the user needs, so most designers hide the image border. You can do this through HTML, by adding a border attribute to the `img` tag with a value set to `0`, but this attribute is not valid in XHMTL, and you should use CSS instead.

Using Images as Links

① Open a Web page in your editor.

② Add an anchor element's opening tag.

③ Add the `href` attribute, set to the appropriate value, and the closing bracket.

④ Type an `img` element's tag.

⑤ Add the `src` attribute.

⑥ Set the attribute's value to the path to the image you wish to include.

⑦ Add an `alt` attribute with an appropriate value.

8. Add a `width` attribute and a value equal to the width of the image.

9. Add a `height` attribute with a value equal to the height of the image.

10. Add the closing slash to the tag.

11. Add the closing anchor tag.

12. Save the page.

13. Open the page in your browser.

The page opens, showing the image.

14. Click the image to test the link.

● Mouse over the image to display the link URL in the status bar.

National Parks by State

Alabama | Alaska

Alabama

Horseshoe Bend National Military Park

Little River Canyon National Preserve

Natchez Trace National Scenic Trail

Russell Cave National Monument

Tuskegee Airmen National Historic Site

Extra

While images for links can be much more visually interesting than plain text, they have several big disadvantages. First, they add to the overall file size for the page. Second, they are much more difficult to edit — instead of simply changing the text in a Web page file, you must open your graphics editor, find the original image, change it, and then re-optimize and re-export it. If you lose the original image, you may find that you have to re-create the image from scratch in order to edit it. Third, they can be more difficult for disabled users, although this can be mitigated by ensuring that you use proper alternate text. Keep in mind that the alternate text needs to describe the image itself, not the target of the link.

Perhaps the biggest advantage of using images for links, other than their obviously more attractive overall appearance, is that if your image contains text, you can use any font you wish, instead of being limited to the few fonts available for the Web. The issue of fonts on the Web will be explored in detail in Chapter 7.

Add a Favorites Icon

Many large sites employ a favorites icon on their pages. This is a small graphic, usually the logo of the site, which appears on the browser's address bar next to the Web site's address, and on the Favorites or Bookmarks menu if the user adds the page to their favorites.

The most challenging process of adding a favorites icon to your site is creating the icon in the first place. Older browsers required that the image be an actual icon — a file with an .ico extension — and many designers did not have the necessary software on their machines to create such an image, as most graphics editors did not support the format. Ironically, today most leading editors do in fact support the format, while at the same time browsers have stopped requiring it and now support GIF and PNG images.

Once the image has been created, you can add it to your site by adding a `link` element to your page. The `link`

element must be in the `head` of the document. It takes three required attributes:

- The `rel` attribute is set to a value of `shortcut icon`.

- The `href` attribute has as its value the path to the icon itself.

- The `type` attribute is set to the appropriate MIME type for the image.

If the file is an ICO, the type will be `image/vnd.microsoft.icon`; if a GIF or PNG, it will be `image/gif` or `image/png`, respectively.

Many browsers will detect an image called favicon.ico in the root of the Web site and use it automatically, even if no link tag is included in the document. This saves you from having to add the tag to each document, but you must create an ICO file instead of using a GIF or PNG.

Add a Favorites Icon

① Open a Web page in your editor.

② In the `head` of the document, add a `link` element's tag.

③ Set the `rel` attribute to `shortcut icon`.

④ Set the `href` to the path to the favorites icon.

⑤ Set the type to the appropriate type for the image.

⑥ Type the closing slash for the `link` tag.

⑦ Save the page.

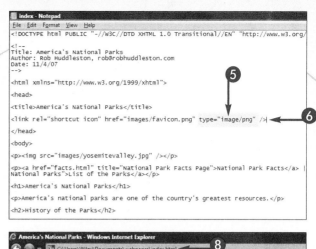

⑧ Open the page in your browser.

● The page opens, showing the favorites icon on the browser's address bar.

Add a Table to Your Page

Tables allow you to present large blocks of data to your users in an organized fashion. Phone lists, product specification grids, and calendars are just a few of the possible uses for tables on a Web page.

Tables are arranged in rows and columns, similar to the layout in a spreadsheet application like Microsoft Excel. In XHTML, you use a minimum of three elements to create a table and its parts. The `table` element defines the table itself. Then, each row of the table is defined by the table row element, `tr`, which is short for table row. Finally, each individual cell is created by use of the `td` element, which is short for table data. Each of these elements' tags wraps around the other, so a `td` can only appear between the opening and closing `tr`, which must in turn appear within a table's opening and closing tags.

Note that in XHTML, you do not directly define the columns of a table; columns are instead calculated by the browser based on the maximum number of cells in any given row.

There is no limit as to the number of rows that may appear in a table on a page. Likewise, you can, in theory, have as many columns as you wish, although you will want to try to avoid having so many columns as to force the user to scroll horizontally on the page.

Any content is allowed within a table cell. You can have images, text formatted in any way, hyperlinks, or anything else. In fact, you can place any XHTML elements that you can legally place within the body of a document within a `td`.

Add a Table to Your Page

1. Open a Web page in your editor.

2. Add a table element's opening tag.

3. Add a `tr` element's opening tag.

4. Add a `td` element's opening tag.

5. Add content to the cell.

6. Add a closing `td` tag.

7. Repeat Steps 4 to 6 to add additional cells to the row.

8. Add a closing `tr` tag.

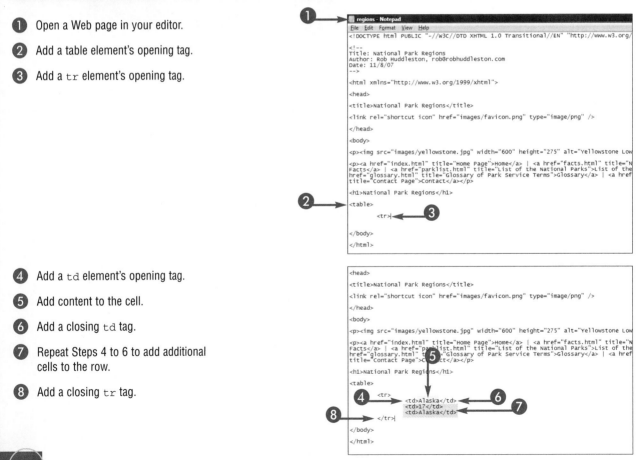

9 Repeat Steps 3 to 8 to add additional rows to the table.

10 Add a closing `table` tag.

11 Save the page.

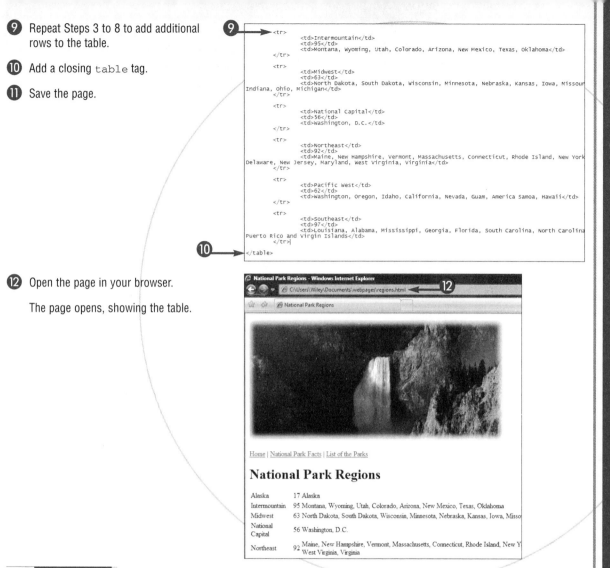

```
    <tr>
            <td>Intermountain</td>
            <td>95</td>
            <td>Montana, Wyoming, Utah, Colorado, Arizona, New Mexico, Texas, Oklahoma</td>
    </tr>
    <tr>
            <td>Midwest</td>
            <td>63</td>
            <td>North Dakota, South Dakota, Wisconsin, Minnesota, Nebraska, Kansas, Iowa, Missour
Indiana, Ohio, Michigan</td>
    </tr>
    <tr>
            <td>National Capital</td>
            <td>56</td>
            <td>Washington, D.C.</td>
    </tr>
    <tr>
            <td>Northeast</td>
            <td>92</td>
            <td>Maine, New Hampshire, Vermont, Massachusetts, Connecticut, Rhode Island, New York
Delaware, New Jersey, Maryland, West Virginia, Virginia</td>
    </tr>
    <tr>
            <td>Pacific West</td>
            <td>62</td>
            <td>Washington, Oregon, Idaho, California, Nevada, Guam, America Samoa, Hawaii</td>
    </tr>
    <tr>
            <td>Southeast</td>
            <td>97</td>
            <td>Louisiana, Alabama, Mississippi, Georgia, Florida, South Carolina, North Carolina
Puerto Rico and Virgin Islands</td>
    </tr>
</table>
```

12 Open the page in your browser.

The page opens, showing the table.

Extra

Few elements in XHTML generate more debate in the Web community than tables. The language itself provides no tools or methods for laying out pages. Early users of the Web were primarily scientists who were uninterested in creating multicolumn layouts. However, as the Web gained wider acceptance, the need for some sort of layout control became necessary, and the only elements in the language that came close to providing it were the table elements. For years, most if not all Web sites used tables to define not tabular data, but the layout of the page as a whole.

This approach has many problems. It requires large amounts of code to implement, tends to create major problems for disabled users and search engines, and is difficult to maintain. About its only advantage is that, compared to the alternative, it is very easy to learn.

That alternative, and the approach used in this book, is to use the properties provided by Cascading Style Sheets (CSS) to position elements on the page. To learn more about laying out Web pages using CSS, see Chapter 10.

Add Headers to Your Table

Most tables will require a row or column of headers to define for the user the data that row or column represents. Often, the data in the table will be meaningless without headers.

Table headers are represented in XHTML by the `th` element, which will be used in place of the `td` for the header cells. Thus, you are not defining an entire row or column as a header, but rather individual cells. This way, it is possible to have headers in both a row and a column. An example of a table that might use both is a product comparison chart, where the left column might contain product names, which are logically headers, while the top row contains features, which should likewise be marked as headers. While there is no requirement that

the header cells be in the top row or left column of the table, there will rarely be a time when they make sense anywhere else.

By default, the contents of a header cell will be displayed in the browser using a bold typeface and will be horizontally centered in the cell. You can modify both of these display properties through CSS. While other text in the table can be made bold and centered, this should be avoided so as to prevent confusion with the headers. If it is required, be sure to use CSS to achieve this result, and not `th` tags, which should *only* be used to markup the actual header cells. Conversely, a lot of inexperienced Web designers manually center and bold the text in `td` cells along the top row instead of simply using the `th` element.

Add Headers to Your Table

1 Open a Web page in your editor that contains a table.

2 Add a `tr` element's opening tag just below the opening table tag.

```
regions - Notepad
File  Edit  Format  View  Help
Facts</a> | <a href="parklist.html" title="List of the National Parks">List of the
href="glossary.html" title="Glossary of Park Service Terms">Glossary</a> | <a href
title="Contact Page">Contact</a></p>

<h1>National Park Regions</h1>

<table>
        <tr>|          2

        <tr>
                <td>Alaska</td>
                <td>17</td>
                <td>Alaska</td>
        </tr>

        <tr>
                <td>Intermountain</td>
                <td>95</td>
                <td>Montana, Wyoming, Utah, Colorado, Arizona, New Mexico, Texas,
        </tr>
```

3 Add a `th` element's opening tag.

4 Add header text.

5 Close the `th`.

```
regions - Notepad
File  Edit  Format  View  Help
Facts</a> | <a href="parklist.html" title="List of the National Parks">List of the
href="glossary.html" title="Glossary of Park Service Terms">Glossary</a> | <a href
title="Contact Page">Contact</a></p>
                                          4
<h1>National Park Regio   </h1>

<table>
       3 tr>          <th>Region</th>|   ←   5

        <tr>
                <td>Alaska</td>
                <td>17</td>
                <td>Alaska</td>
        </tr>

        <tr>
                <td>Intermountain</td>
                <td>95</td>
                <td>Montana, Wyoming, Utah, Colorado, Arizona, New Mexico, Texas,
        </tr>
```

6 Repeat Steps 3 to 6 for each additional header.

7 Add the closing `tr` tag.

8 Save the page.

9 Open the page in your browser.

The page opens, showing the table and its headers.

Extra

You can specify longer or shorter names for the contents of your header row by adding an abbreviation using the `abbr` attribute to the `th`. Its value will be the longer or shorter version of the cell's content. Some browsers may display this instead of the content if space allows. Note that while it is called "abbreviation," it can actually represent a longer version of the text.

```
<table>
    <tr>
        <th abbr="Sunday">Sun</th>
        <th abbr="Sunday">Sun</th>
        <th abbr="Sunday">Sun</th>
        <th abbr="Sunday">Sun</th>
        <th abbr="Sunday">Sun</th>
        <th abbr="Sunday">Sun</th>
        <th abbr="Sunday">Sun</th>
    </tr>
</table>
```

Create Cells That Span Rows or Columns

ometimes it may be necessary to break up the strict grid of a table and represent data that spans more than one cell. This technique was used frequently by designers using tables for layout, but it has its place in properly coded data tables as well.

A classic example is a calendar. There have been attempts to contrive CSS to properly display calendars on the Web, but a calendar is an example of tabular data, and would be properly marked up as such. In a traditional seven-day grid for a calendar, only the rare nonleap year February that happens to begin on a Sunday is going to fit the grid perfectly. Every other month will have days at the beginning or end of the grid, or both, that are not part of the current month. Some

designers may choose to represent these days as individual empty cells, but others may wish to show them as a single cell, possibly filled with some sort of miscellaneous information, or perhaps left empty.

Spanning rows can be achieved via the rowspan attribute of either the td or th element. Columns can be spanned using the similar colspan attribute. Both take as their value an integer representing the number of cells to be spanned. Care needs to be taken to ensure that you still end up with the correct number of cells overall. A row that contains a colspan in one of its cells will have a correspondingly lower number of overall cells, while a rowspan will require missing cells from an equal number of rows. You cannot span fractional cells.

Create Cells That Span Rows or Columns

① Open a Web page that contains a table in your editor.

② Within the table, add a tr element's opening tag.

③ Add a td element's opening tag.

④ Add a colspan attribute to the td.

⑤ Set the value to the number of cells to be spanned.

⑥ Add content to the td.

⑦ Close the td.

⑧ Close the tr.

⑨ Repeat Steps 2 to 8 to add additional spanned rows to the table.

⑩ Save the page.

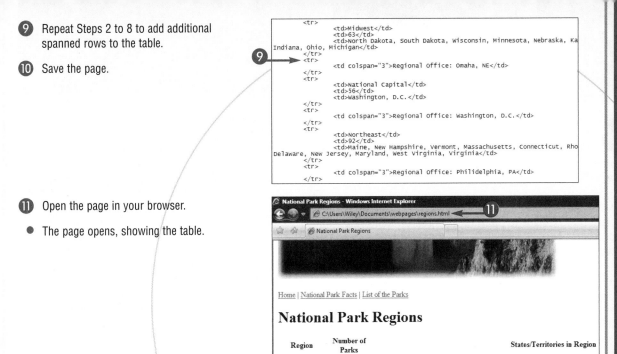

```
        <tr>
                <td>Midwest</td>
                <td>63</td>
                <td>North Dakota, South Dakota, Wisconsin, Minnesota, Nebraska, Ka
Indiana, Ohio, Michigan</td>
        </tr>
        <tr>
                <td colspan="3">Regional Office: Omaha, NE</td>
        </tr>
        <tr>
                <td>National Capital</td>
                <td>56</td>
                <td>washington, D.C.</td>
        </tr>
        <tr>
                <td colspan="3">Regional Office: washington, D.C.</td>
        </tr>
        <tr>
                <td>Northeast</td>
                <td>92</td>
                <td>Maine, New Hampshire, Vermont, Massachusetts, Connecticut, Rho
Delaware, New Jersey, Maryland, West Virginia, Virginia</td>
        </tr>
        <tr>
                <td colspan="3">Regional Office: Philidelphia, PA</td>
        </tr>
```

⑪ Open the page in your browser.

● The page opens, showing the table.

National Park Regions - Windows Internet Explorer

C:\Users\Wiley\Documents\webpages\regions.html

National Park Regions

Home | National Park Facts | List of the Parks

National Park Regions

Region	Number of Parks	States/Territories in Region
Alaska	17	Alaska
Regional Office: Anchorage, AK		
Intermountain	95	Montana, Wyoming, Utah, Colorado, Arizona, New Mexico, Texas, Oklahoma
Regional Office: Denver, CO		
Midwest	63	North Dakota, South Dakota, Wisconsin, Minnesota, Nebraska, Kansas, Iowa, Michigan
Regional Office: Omaha, NE		
National Capital	56	Washington, D.C.
Regional Office: Washington, D.C.		

Extra

Creating particularly complex table layouts using `rowspan` and `colspan` is possible. You can, for example, use both `rowspan` and `colspan` together in a single cell to create a large cell that spans both horizontally and vertically. It may be necessary and helpful to sketch out these complex tables before you attempt to build them to make sure that you get the right number of overall cells. Unfortunately, browsers will not return an error if you have too many cells in a row or column, but will instead simply attempt to render the table as you coded it. This often results in cells "hanging" off the side of the table or below it.

It is possible to leave cells of a table empty. A truly empty cell, where you simply have the opening and closing `td` tags adjacent — `<td></td>` — will not display consistently across all browsers; some will draw the cell and others will leave a blank space where it should be. To achieve consistency, you should make sure that you have some content in the cell, even a blank space. See Chapter 15 for details on how to enter empty spaces that will still be rendered by the browser.

Set the Border of the Table

By default, browsers will not display borders on a table. You can display the border of a table using the `border` attribute of the `table` tag. The value of the border will be an integer representing the width of the border in pixels; rarely will a value other than 1 be used.

Additional attributes existed prior to HTML 4.01 and XHTML 1.0 to set the color of the border; Microsoft even had attributes, specific to Internet Explorer, that allowed for controlling the shading of the border by setting alternate colors for the "dark" and "light" sides of the table. All of these attributes have been deprecated and should not be used.

The biggest disadvantage to setting table borders via the attribute is that it is an all-or-nothing approach. It is not possible to have a border around the outside of the table, but not the cells, or around only some of the cells. You

cannot have a border around some cells that differs from that around others.

You can solve all of those issues by using CSS for the border instead. Given borders are ultimately presentational, it is better to use CSS regardless. CSS gives you much more control over the appearance of the border, and aspects such as border color are more widely supported. Using CSS to set the table borders will be discussed in Chapter 8.

While using CSS for borders is the preferred method for final sites, setting the border using the attribute is helpful while building and debugging the page, especially when using a complex table with row and column spans. You can add the `border` attribute to the table while you build the page, and then delete it in favor of CSS once the table is properly built.

Set the Border of the Table

① Open a Web page that contains a table in your editor.

② In the `table` element's opening tag, add a `border` attribute.

③ Set the value of the attribute to `1`.

④ Save the page.

⑤ Open the page in the browser.

The page opens, showing the visible table border.

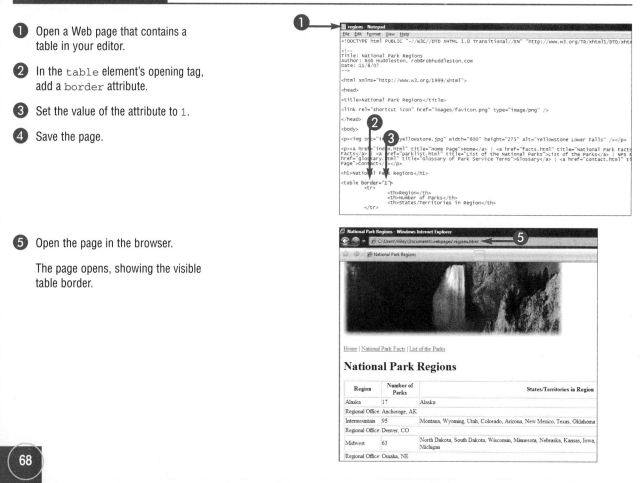

Set the Width of a Table

By default, a table will be as wide as it needs to be to display its contents. If the contents are too wide to fit the browser window, the table will only be as wide as the window. The only exception is if the table contains images or some other content that cannot be wrapped, in which case the table will expand to the width of the content, possibly forcing the user to scroll horizontally.

You can control this behavior through the `width` attribute to the `table` element, and can set the width in either pixels or a percent. If the former, the table will be a set width regardless of the size of the user's monitor; if the latter, it will expand and collapse to a point if the width of the browser window should change.

You can also apply the `width` attribute to table cells, either regular or headings. While never officially supported in any version of HTML, browsers have long allowed designers to set the width on the `tr` element as well to set an overall width of a row.

You should remember that the browser will ignore any widths that it cannot render if they are smaller than the content. Also, if you set a width of a table, and then set widths on rows or cells that exceed or do not add up to the table's width, the smaller number will be ignored in favor of the larger.

As with borders, you can achieve far better control of your table by setting the width using CSS instead of this attribute, which has been deprecated.

Set the Width of a Table

1 Open a Web page that contains a table in your editor.

2 In the `table` element's opening tag, add a `width` attribute.

3 Set the value of the attribute to an appropriate value.

4 Save the page.

5 Open the page in the browser.

The page opens, showing the table set the desired width.

Add Space Within a Table

Whitespace is an important element in any design, and data tables are no different. Insufficient space between data points can be difficult to read, particularly if the table is set to not display borders.

XHTML provides two attributes to control the whitespace in tables. The first, `cellpadding`, sets the amount of space in pixels between the contents of the cell — the actual data — and the edge of the cell. The second, `cellspacing`, controls the space between individual cells. Both are attributes of the `table` element. You cannot set differing amounts of space around individual cells.

The defaults for each of these attributes vary from one browser to the next. In general, both `cellspacing` and `cellpadding` will default to two or three pixels each. Most designers prefer to set them manually to ensure consistency across browsers.

You can also use CSS to control these values. CSS contains a `padding` property to replace `cellpadding` for tables, and a `margin` property in place of `cellspacing`. With CSS, it is possible to have individual cells with different amounts of either. However, not all browsers support the use of `padding` and `margin` on table cells consistently. Therefore, neither the `cellpadding` nor `cellspacing` properties have been deprecated; both are valid even in XHTML Strict. Until consistent browser support becomes the norm, you should continue to rely on the attributes.

A value of 0 is legal for both attributes. Setting `cellpadding` and `cellspacing` to 0 was a common technique of designers who used tables for layout to "stitch" together a large image over a series of table cells. In data tables, you will most likely always want a positive value for `cellpadding`, although setting `cellspacing` to 0 may make sense in some designs.

Add Space Within a Table

① Open a Web page that contains a table in your editor.

② In the `table` element's opening tag, add a `cellpadding` attribute.

③ Set the value of the attribute to a positive integer.

④ Add a `cellspacing` attribute.

⑤ Set the value of the attribute to a positive integer.

⑥ Save the page.

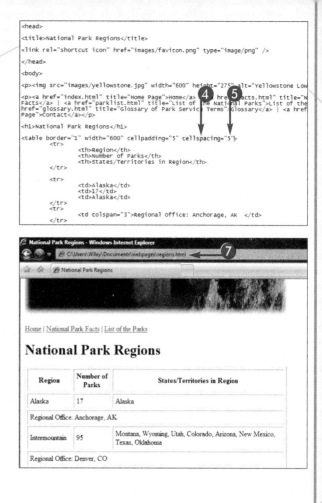

```
<head>
<title>National Park Regions</title>
<link rel="shortcut icon" href="images/favicon.png" type="image/png" />
</head>
<body>
<p><img src="images/yellowstone.jpg" width="600" height="275" alt="Yellowstone Low
<p><a href="index.html" title="Home Page">Home</a> |  href=    acts.html" title="N
Facts</a> | <a href="parklist.html" title="List of the National Parks">List of the
href="glossary.html" title="Glossary of Park Service Terms">Glossary</a> | <a href
Page">Contact</a></p>

<h1>National Park Regions</h1>

<table border="1" width="600" cellpadding="5" cellspacing="5">
        <tr>
                <th>Region</th>
                <th>Number of Parks</th>
                <th>States/Territories in Region</th>
        </tr>

        <tr>
                <td>Alaska</td>
                <td>17</td>
                <td>Alaska</td>
        </tr>
        <tr>
                <td colspan="3">Regional office: Anchorage, AK  </td>
        </tr>
```

⑦ Open the page in the browser.

The page opens, showing the added space.

National Park Regions

Home | National Park Facts | List of the Parks

National Park Regions

Region	Number of Parks	States/Territories in Region
Alaska	17	Alaska
Regional Office: Anchorage, AK		
Intermountain	95	Montana, Wyoming, Utah, Colorado, Arizona, New Mexico, Texas, Oklahoma
Regional Office: Denver, CO		

Apply It

You can specify `cellpadding` and `cellspacing` in percent values if you wish. When using percents, you must include the % symbol. Without it, the browser will assume pixels.

```
<table cellpadding="10%" cellspacing="5%">
    <tr>
            <th>Name</th>
            <th>Phone</th>
    </tr>
</table>
```

Define Sections
of a Table

Most data tables are likely to be made up of two or three sections. At the top, you will have one or more rows that contain the headers. At the bottom, one or more rows may make up a footer. In between, you have the main body of the table, the data.

XHTML provides a set of elements to denote these three sections: thead, tbody, and tfoot. These tags wrap around the rows that make up each section of the table. Each section can contain one or more rows, although the header and footer will each rarely contain more than one.

Unlike other XHTML elements, the three table section elements do not alter the default display of the table in the browser. Looking at a page with a table in a normal visual browser, it is impossible to tell if the designer used these tags or not.

When defining the sections in your code, you need to create them out of order. The first section will be the thead, but the tfoot needs to immediately follow it, *before* the tbody. This is because the browser needs to know what the footer information is before is can properly lay out the table.

Defining these sections out of order can be a bit confusing, and it may help to initially create the table in the more logical order, with the footer at the bottom, and then cut and paste those rows into the correct place when you are finished creating the table.

Define Sections of a Table

1 Open a Web page that contains a table in your editor.

2 Below the table element's opening tag, add a thead element's opening tag.

3 Immediately following the closing tr tag, close the thead.

4 On the line below the closing thead, add a tfoot element's opening tag.

5 Add an opening tr tag.

6 Add a td element's opening tag.

7 Add a colspan attribute with a value equal to the number of columns in the table.

8 Add data for the cell.

⑨ Type `</td>` to close the `td` tag.

⑩ Type `</tr>` to close the `tr` tag.

⑪ Type `</tfoot>` to close the `tfoot` tag.

⑫ On the next line, add a `tbody` element's opening tag by typing `<tbody>`.

⑬ After the final closing `tr` of the table, close the `tbody` tag by typing `</tbody>`.

⑭ Save the page.

⑮ Open the page in the browser.

The page opens. The changes have not affected the table's appearance.

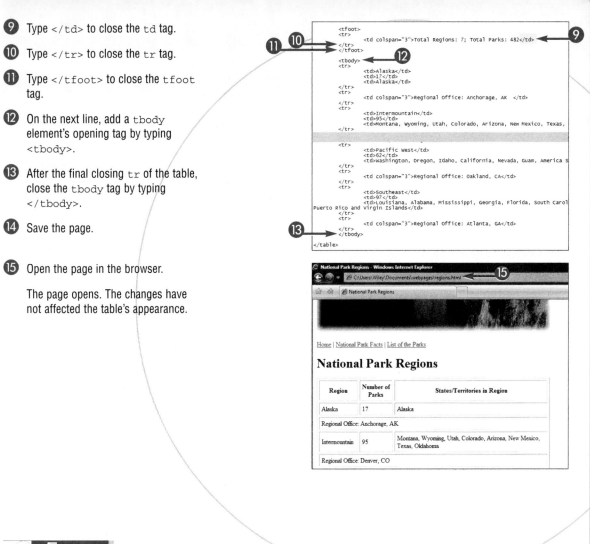

Extra

The table section elements serve three main purposes. First, they assist in making your table more accessible by adding additional underlying logic to the page that helps screen readers and other assistive devices make sense of the table. Second, they provide wrappers for similar rows of the table that can be used by style sheets for formatting.

And third, least apparent but perhaps most useful, is if you have a very long table with hundreds of rows and your user attempts to print it, the table will span many pages. However, under normal circumstances she will loose the header information after the first page. If you use these elements, most modern browsers will automatically repeat the information from the `head` section at the top of each page in a printout, and repeat the `tfoot` information at the bottom of each page.

Define
Columns

Tables on Web pages are created in terms of rows and cells. When you are coding your table, you create the columns by default as you add cells — the highest number of cells in any row of the table will be the number of columns of the table.

There are times, however, that you may wish to explicitly define columns in the table. For example, if you want to define a width for a particular column, either through the use of the `width` attribute or through CSS, you technically need to set that width on each cell in the affected column. Browsers will actually let you define the width on a single cell, and then will use that value for the entire column, but if you should later delete the cell that contains the width, you will lose it — hence the need to define it on every cell.

However, this creates bloated code that is hard to maintain. Imagine that you have hundreds of rows, and need to alter the width that is set in every cell. Instead, you can explicitly define columns in your code and apply the width to the column in one place using the `col` element.

The `col` element will appear at the top of your table code, after the `table` element's opening tag but before any actual data. It does not establish a column or add data, but instead merely allows you to apply attributes or styles, which will then be carried through to the cells of that column.

You can add an optional `span` attribute to the column to have its properties apply to multiple adjacent columns. You want to be sure that you have one `col` element for each column in your table. The `col` is an empty element, and needs to contain a trailing slash to be properly closed.

Define Columns

① Open a Web page that contains a table in your editor.

② After the `table` element's opening tag, add a `col` element's opening tag.

③ Add a `width` attribute.

④ Set the value of the width.

⑤ Add a slash to the end of the tag to close it.

⑥ Repeat Steps 2 to 5 for each additional column.

⑦ Save the page.

```
</head>
<body>
<p><img src="images/yellowstone.jpg" width="600" height="275" alt="Yellowstone Low
<p><a href="index.html" title="Home Page">Home</a> | <a href="facts.html" title="N
Facts</a> | <a href="parklist.html" title="List of the National Parks">List of the
href="glossary.html" title="Glossary of Park Service Terms">Glossary</a> | <a href
Page">Contact</a></p>
<h1>National Park Regions</h1>
<table border="1" width="600" cellpadding="5" cellspacing="5">

        <col width="150" />
        <col width="50" />          ←——⑥
        <col width="400" />

        <thead>
```

⑧ Open the page in the browser.

The page displays in the browser.

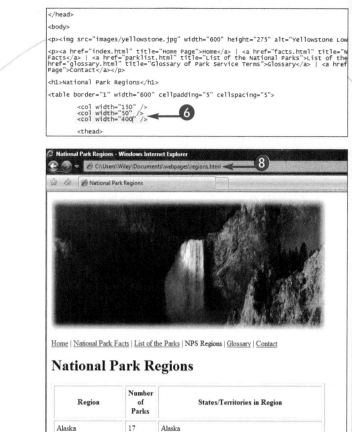

You can use the `colgroup` element to group columns together and apply widths or styles to multiple columns at once.

```
<table>
    <colgroup width="50%">
        <col width="50%">
        <col width="50%">
    </colgroup>
    <col width="50%>
```

Note that in this case, the `col` elements within the group are given widths relative to the group, not to the page itself.

Add a Bulleted List to Your Page

Most Web sites contain lists. Whether you are an e-commerce site displaying your products, or a non-profit site showing your members, you need lists. All navigation on the Web can be argued to be a list; after all, navigation is really nothing more than a list of links to the other pages on the site.

Perhaps the most common type of list on Web sites is an *unordered*, or bulleted, list. Any list that contains items that do not need to appear in a particular order will be an unordered list. The list is defined via the `<ul>` tag. Within the `<ul>` tag block, each item is denoted by a list item element: `<li>`. Here is the basic setup of an unordered list:

```
<ul>

    <li>List Item</li>

    <li>List Item</li>

</ul>
```

Lists can contain any number of items, and the actual contents of a list item can be just about any other markup.

Add a Bulleted List to Your Page

① Open a Web page in your editor.

② Within the body, add an opening `ul` tag.

```
parklist - Notepad
File  Edit  Format  View  Help
<!DOCTYPE html PUBLIC "-//W3C//DTD XHTML 1.0 Transitional//EN" "http:/
<html xmlns="http://www.w3.org/1999/xhtml">
<head>
<meta http-equiv="Content-Type" content="text/html; charset=utf-8" />
<title>Untitled Document</title>
</head>

<body>

<a href="/index.html"><img src="images/muirwoods.jpg" alt="Muir Woods

<h1>National Parks by State</h1>
<p><A href="#alabama">Alabama</a> | <a href="#alaska">Alaska</a></p>

<h2><a name="alabama"></a>Alabama</h2>

<ul>

</body>
</html>
```

③ Add an opening `li` tag.

④ Add an item for the list.

⑤ Add the closing `li` tag.

```
parklist - Notepad
File  Edit  Format  View  Help
<!DOCTYPE html PUBLIC "-//W3C//DTD XHTML 1.0 Transitional//EN" "http:/
<html xmlns="http://www.w3.org/1999/xhtml">
<head>
<meta http-equiv="Content-Type" content="text/html; charset=utf-8" />
<title>Untitled Document</title>
</head>

<body>

<a href="/index.html"><img src="images/muirwoods.jpg" alt="Muir Woods

<h1>National Parks by State</h1>
<p><A href="#alabama">Alabama</a> | <a href="#alaska">Alaska</a></p>

<h2><a name="alabama"></a>Alabama</h2>

<ul>
    <li>Horseshoe Bend National Military Park</li>

</body>
</html>
```

6 Repeat Steps 3 to 5 for any additional items you wish to add to the list.

7 Add the closing `ul` tag.

8 Save the page.

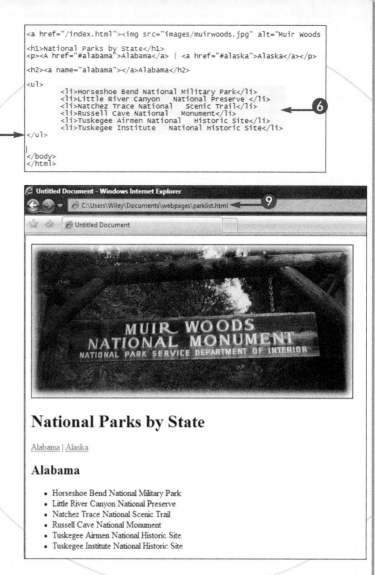

9 Open the page in a Web browser.

The page opens, showing the bulleted list.

Extra

In addition to displaying the list items with a bullet, browsers indent the contents of the list. In the early days of the Web, some designers would misuse the `ul` element for indentation, presenting it without `li` elements, but as style sheets give the ability to precisely indent any element when used in its proper context, this practice has been mostly abandoned.

Style sheets also give the ability to change the bullet itself. While a presentational attribute, `type`, existed for both `ul` and `li`, it has been deprecated and is not allowed in XHTML Strict documents. The attribute only provided three options for unordered lists: an empty circle, a filled circle, and a square. With style sheets, you can still use any of those options, but the bullet may also be replaced entirely with a custom image. See Chapter 8 for more information on this technique.

Add a Numbered List to Your Page

The second most common type of list on Web pages are *numbered*, or ordered, lists. Browsers will automatically control the numbering of items of the list, so you can freely add, remove, and rearrange the items without needing to worry about the numbers themselves.

The main element for ordered lists is ol. Like the ul element, the `<ol>` tag wraps around the entire list. Each item of the list is marked with an li element, just as with unordered lists. An example of an ordered list might be:

```
<ol>

    <li>Chop onions</li>

    <li>Heat onions and olive oil in the
pan</li>

    <li>Pour sauce over meat</li>

</ol>
```

While they are used much less frequently than unordered lists, you will nonetheless encounter plenty of opportunities to make use of ordered lists on your pages.

Add a Numbered List to Your Page

1 Open a Web page in your editor.

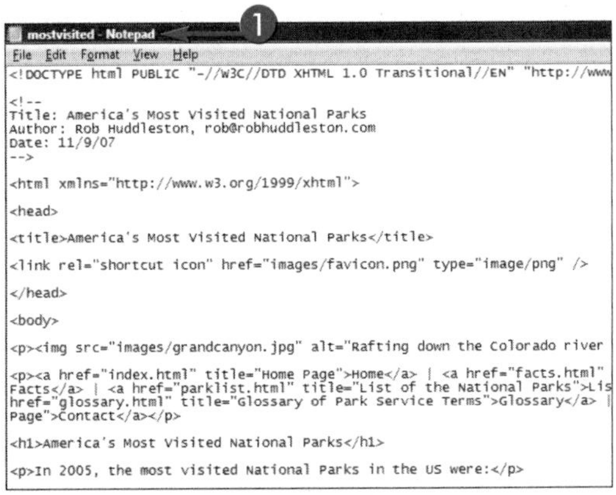

2 Within the body, add an opening ol tag.

3 Add an opening li tag.

4 Add an item for the list.

5 Add the closing li tag.

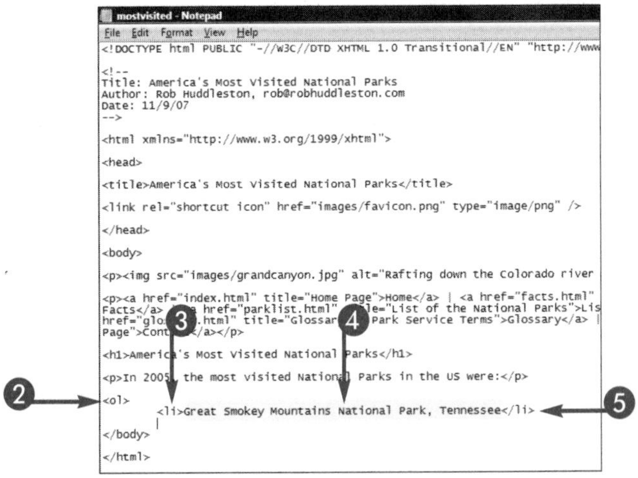

6 Repeat Steps 3 to 5 for any additional items you wish to add to the list.

7 Add the closing `ol` tag.

8 Save the page.

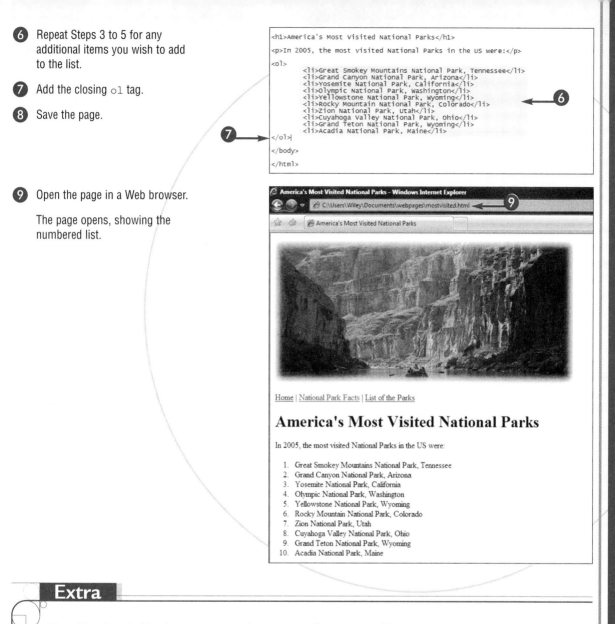

```
<h1>America's Most Visited National Parks</h1>

<p>In 2005, the most visited National Parks in the US were:</p>

<ol>
        <li>Great Smokey Mountains National Park, Tennessee</li>
        <li>Grand Canyon National Park, Arizona</li>
        <li>Yosemite National Park, California</li>
        <li>Olympic National Park, Washington</li>
        <li>Yellowstone National Park, Wyoming</li>
        <li>Rocky Mountain National Park, Colorado</li>
        <li>Zion National Park, Utah</li>
        <li>Cuyahoga Valley National Park, Ohio</li>
        <li>Grand Teton National Park, Wyoming</li>
        <li>Acadia National Park, Maine</li>
</ol>

</body>

</html>
```

9 Open the page in a Web browser.

The page opens, showing the numbered list.

America's Most Visited National Parks — Windows Internet Explorer

C:\Users\Wiley\Documents\webpages\mostvisited.html

America's Most Visited National Parks

Home | National Park Facts | List of the Parks

America's Most Visited National Parks

In 2005, the most visited National Parks in the US were:

1. Great Smokey Mountains National Park, Tennessee
2. Grand Canyon National Park, Arizona
3. Yosemite National Park, California
4. Olympic National Park, Washington
5. Yellowstone National Park, Wyoming
6. Rocky Mountain National Park, Colorado
7. Zion National Park, Utah
8. Cuyahoga Valley National Park, Ohio
9. Grand Teton National Park, Wyoming
10. Acadia National Park, Maine

Extra

Transitional and older documents can rely on two attributes to modify the list. The `type` attribute allows you to override the character used for the numbering. By default, browsers will use an Arabic numeral for each item. Setting type to a value of `a` results in lowercase alphabetic characters being used, while a type of `A` sets the list to use uppercase alphabetic characters. A type of `i` uses lowercase Roman numerals, and type `I` uses uppercase Roman numerals.

The `start` attribute can be used to set the list to begin at something other than 1. Even if you are using a non-alphabetic type, `start` will always be represented by a number. Therefore, if you have a list set with a type of `a` (for lowercase alphabetic characters) and you wish the list to begin at c, you would set `start` to 3.

Both the `start` and `type` attributes have been deprecated in favor of style sheets, but you may encounter them in legacy documents.

Add a Definition List to Your Page

E arly versions of HTML supported many different list types. Today, only three remain. By far the most common is the unordered list (ul). Second is the ordered list (ol). A fairly distant third is the *definition* list. While unordered and ordered lists have a variety of possible uses, the definition list's formatting is such that it is really only useful for its original intended purpose: providing a set of terms and their definitions.

The list itself is defined with the dl element. Each term in the list is marked with a definition term element, dt. Each term's definition is then marked with a dd element.

By default, browsers will display the term on its own line. The definition will appear below it on a new line, indented.

An example of a definition list might be:

```
<dl>

    <dt>W3C</dt>

    <dd>World Wide Web Consortium – the
body that determines standards for web
technologies.</dd>

</dl>
```

Add a Definition List to Your Page

1. Open a Web page in your editor.

2. Within the body, add an opening dl tag.

3. Add an opening dt tag.

4. Add the term you are defining.

5. Add the closing dt tag.

6. Add an opening dd tag.

7. Add the definition for the term.

8. Add the closing dd tag.

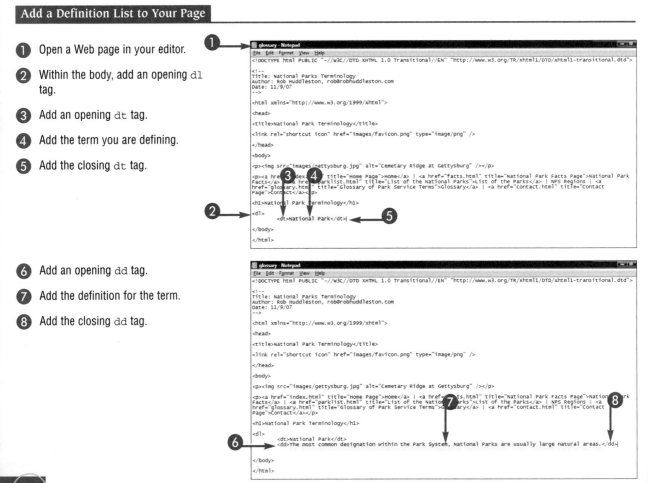

9 Repeat Steps 3 to 8 for any additional items you wish to add to the list.

10 Add the closing dl tag.

11 Save the page.

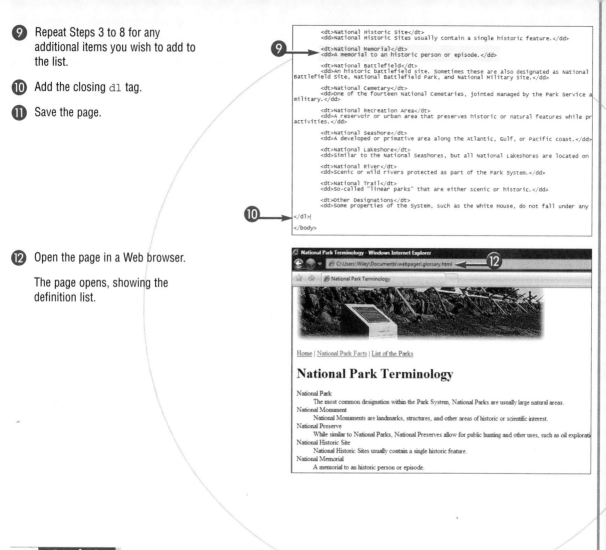

```
                  <dt>National Historic Site</dt>
                  <dd>National Historic Sites usually contain a single historic feature.</dd>

                  <dt>National Memorial</dt>
                  <dd>A memorial to an historic person or episode.</dd>

                  <dt>National Battlefield</dt>
                  <dd>An historic battlefield site. Sometimes these are also designated as National
Battlefield Site, National Battlefield Park, and National Military Site.</dd>

                  <dt>National Cemetary</dt>
                  <dd>One of the fourteen National Cemeteries, jointed managed by the Park Service a
military.</dd>

                  <dt>National Recreation Area</dt>
                  <dd>A reservoir or urban area that preserves historic or natural features while pr
activities.</dd>

                  <dt>National Seashore</dt>
                  <dd>A developed or primative area along the Atlantic, Gulf, or Pacific coast.</dd>

                  <dt>National Lakeshore</dt>
                  <dd>Similar to the National Seashores, but all National Lakeshores are located on

                  <dt>National River</dt>
                  <dd>Scenic or wild rivers protected as part of the Park System.</dd>

                  <dt>National Trail</dt>
                  <dd>So-called "linear parks" that are either scenic or historic.</dd>

                  <dt>Other Designations</dt>
                  <dd>Some properties of the System, such as the White House, do not fall under any
</dl>|
</body>
```

12 Open the page in a Web browser.

The page opens, showing the definition list.

Apply It

You can have more than one term associate with more than one definition if you wish.

```
<dl>
      <dt>Theater</dt>
      <dt>Theatre</dt>
      <dd>A building, room or stage for the presentation of plays or movies.</dd>
      <dd>A large geographic area of military activities.</dd>
</dl>
```

Nest a List Within a List

E ach list type supports the possibility of nesting another list within it, so an unordered list may be nested within another unordered list, or within an ordered list, or in the definition of a definition list. Likewise, ordered lists may be nested within the other list types, and so forth.

While nested lists are fairly common on the Web, they are rarely properly coded. For unordered and ordered lists, the common practice is to nest the list outside of any li tags. However, according to the HTML and XHTML specifications, the only element allowed directly within an ol or ul tag is the li. Therefore, it is necessary to include the entire nested list, including the ol or ul tags, within an li block, not outside it.

All three list elements — ul, ol, and dl — are block-level elements. The dt element only allows for inline elements, so a nested list of any type could only appear within the dd tag of a definition list.

Browsers will increase the level of indentation with each nested list. They will also alter the bullet for unordered lists. Assuming that the bullet is not being altered via a style sheet, the outermost list will use a closed circle, while the first level of a nested list will use an open circle. Should lists be nested further, the remaining levels will use a square bullet. This same structure will apply to unordered lists nested within other list types, so an unordered list within an ordered list will use the open circle as its bullet. Nested ordered lists do not change their type.

Nest a List Within a List

1. Open a Web page in your editor.

2. Within the body, add an opening ul tag.

3. Add an opening li tag.

4. Add an item for the list.

5. Add an opening ul tag within the list item.

6. Add an opening li tag.

7. Add an item for the nested list.

8. Add the closing li tag.

9. Repeat Steps 6 to 8 for each additional item on the nested list.

10. Add the closing ul tag.

11. Add the closing li tag.

12. Add another opening li tag.

13. Add another item for the outer list.

14. Add the closing li tag.

Note: *To create hyperlinks, see Chapter 3.*

15. Add the closing ul tag.

16. Save the page.

17. Open the page in a Web browser.

The page opens, showing the nested lists.

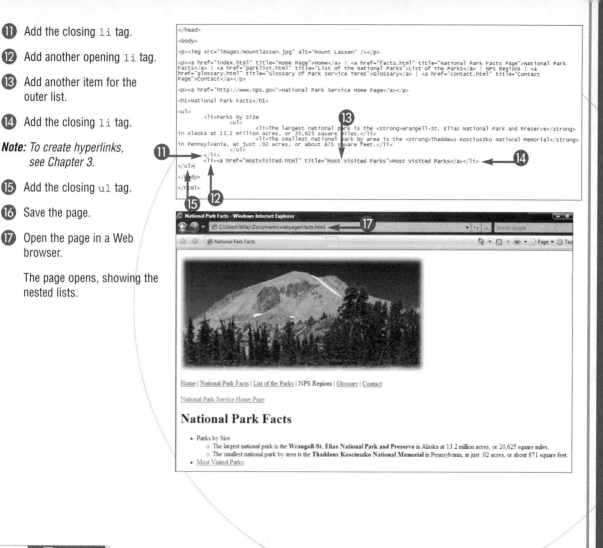

Extra

When coding complicated sets of nested tags, especially when the nesting will use many of the same elements as in the example here, where you have sets of li tags that exist in different parent elements, it becomes very important to properly structure your code.

Because HTML and XHTML are whitespace insensitive, you are free to add as much whitespace to your code as you wish. A standard practice is to place each element on its own line. For elements with a lot of content, as is the case with the items that contain the nested lists, it is recommended that the opening tag be placed on its own line, with the nested items each on their own lines, and the closing tag on a line by itself.

Just as important is the indentation of the code. By using tabs or multiple spaces, you can clearly delineate the parent-child relationships in the code. For example, you want to make sure that the nested list items are indented further than the non-nested items.

Get Started with Cascading Style Sheets

Cascading Style Sheets (CSS) give you much greater control over the presentation and formatting of your page. Style rules can be placed in embedded styles directly within a Web page, or in external style sheets, which is discussed in Chapter 9. To create an embedded style sheet, you need to add a `style` tag block to the head of the document. The tag will take one required attribute, `type`, which must be set to a value of `text/css`.

Within the tag block, you will create your style rules. Each rule will consist of a *selector*. There are many types of selectors that you can use; this chapter looks at the most basic of those: the element selector. An element selector is merely an XHTML element that is being used somewhere on the page and contains the content you wish to format.

After the selector, you will have one or more declarations, which are in turn made up of *property* and *value* pairs. The properties and values are separated by a colon, and each pair is separated from each other pair by a semicolon. The entire block of declarations is wrapped by a pair of curly braces to offset it from the selector.

A simple example of an embedded style sheet might look like this, which creates a style named *p* with text colored #ff0000:

```
<style type="text/css">

p        {color:#ff0000;}

</style>
```

Get Started with Cascading Style Sheets

① Open a Web page in your editor.

② In the head section of the document, add a `style` element's opening tag.

③ Add the `type` attribute.

④ Set the attribute's value to
text/css.

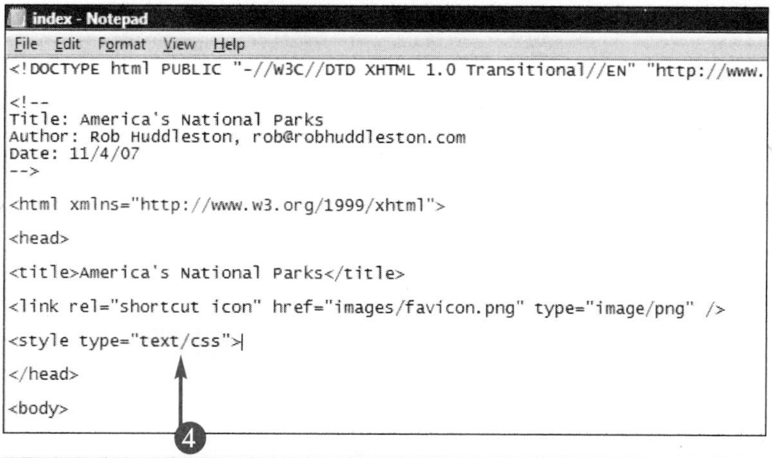

```
index - Notepad
File  Edit  Format  View  Help
<!DOCTYPE html PUBLIC "-//W3C//DTD XHTML 1.0 Transitional//EN" "http://www.
<!--
Title: America's National Parks
Author: Rob Huddleston, rob@robhuddleston.com
Date: 11/4/07
-->
<html xmlns="http://www.w3.org/1999/xhtml">
<head>
<title>America's National Parks</title>
<link rel="shortcut icon" href="images/favicon.png" type="image/png" />
<style type="text/css">|
</head>
<body>
```

④

⑤ Add a closing style tag.

⑥ Save the document.

The document is saved.

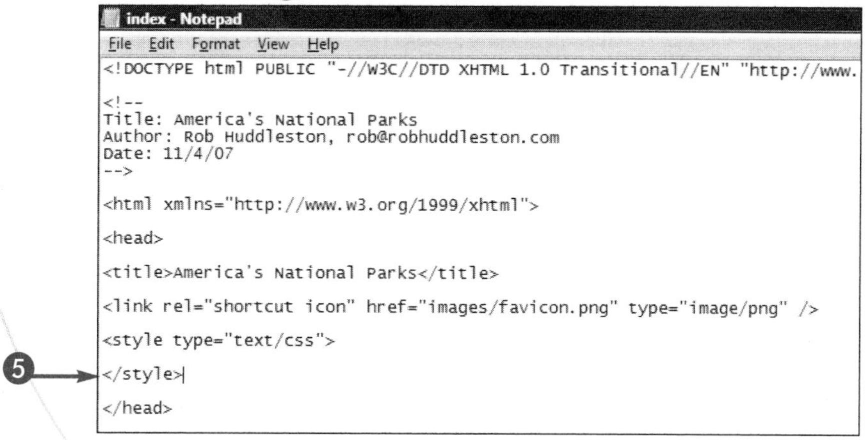

```
index - Notepad
File  Edit  Format  View  Help
<!DOCTYPE html PUBLIC "-//W3C//DTD XHTML 1.0 Transitional//EN" "http://www.
<!--
Title: America's National Parks
Author: Rob Huddleston, rob@robhuddleston.com
Date: 11/4/07
-->
<html xmlns="http://www.w3.org/1999/xhtml">
<head>
<title>America's National Parks</title>
<link rel="shortcut icon" href="images/favicon.png" type="image/png" />
<style type="text/css">
</style>|
</head>
```

⑤

Extra

Just as in XHTML, CSS is whitespace insensitive, so you should add plenty of whitespace to your code to enhance readability. One common technique is to place each selector and the opening curly brace on a single line, then each declaration on its own line, and then the closing curly brace. Indenting the declarations can make the code even easier to read.

```
p {
    color:#ff0000;
    font-weight:bold;
}
```

You should also note that the semicolon on the final declaration is technically optional. However, it is a good idea to always use it. That way, if you add additional declarations to the rule, you will not need to remember to add the semicolon to the existing code.

Understanding Units of Measurement

Many of the properties you use in your style sheets will require that you specify a unit of measurement, whether it be the size of text or the length of a line. CSS supports a wide array of units, and understanding how each works will potentially save you hours of debugging time.

The "Real World" Units

Most CSS properties allow you to use inches, centimeters, and millimeters as valid units. While all of these are units with which you are already familiar, they are usually avoided by designers. The inch is simply too big of a unit to be effective, especially if the designer is concerned with the appearance of the page on very small screens such as mobile devices.

Centimeters and millimeters are small enough to be generally usable, but all three units have another liability: A computer

monitor does not always render an inch, centimeter, or millimeter at its real size. Depending on the resolution settings of your monitor, one inch on the screen may not equal one inch on a ruler held up to the screen. It is, therefore, difficult to predict exactly how a page will look on different screens if using these units.

In CSS, inches are specified with in, centimeters with cm, and millimeters with mm.

Points and Picas

CSS supports units of measurement that are totally unfamiliar to most Web designers, although they have existed for centuries. The pica was developed in the eighteenth century and represents ⅙ of an inch. It has been used by typographers and graphic artists since then, but is rarely known outside of those industries.

A foot is divided into inches, and likewise a pica can be divided into points. Each point is 1/12 of a pica, so therefore, there are 72 points in one inch. Anyone who has used a computer word

processor knows that fonts are measured in points, but few understand that it is an actual unit of measurement. Standard 12-point text is therefore ⅙ of an inch tall.

Points and picas are favored by graphic designers migrating to the Web because they are units with which they are familiar. In fact, many non-designers will naturally lean towards using points for font measurement. However, given both are based on the inch, both suffer from the same problem as using inches.

CSS uses pt to set points and pc for picas.

Pixels

Your computer screen displays images by filling in small squares with information that, when viewed together, make up an image. These squares are technically called *picture elements*, which has been shortened to pixels.

You can set measurements in CSS to pixels. As it is truly the only unit of measurement that you computer natively understands, it would stand to reason that pixels might be the ideal unit to use in your design. While many of the properties

that take length will, in fact, best be set in pixels, others will not work, due to the fact that the precise size of a pixel cannot be predicted. Different monitors will have different pixels sizes, but more important, changing the resolution of the screen can cause the same monitor to use a different size for the pixel.

The pixel is represented in CSS by px.

Ems and Exes

If you find points and picas confusing, then ems and exes may seem even odder. Like the former, these are units that have been used by designers for centuries, but unlike points and picas, neither is based on any specific unit. Instead, an em is simply the height of an uppercase "M" in the current font. For purposes of CSS design, an em can, therefore, be seen as the equivalent to the font size, so if the font had been set to 12 points, 1 em would also be 12 points. Ems are useful for setting fractional sizes, so in the previous example, you might set the height of a line of text to 1.5 ems, or 18 points.

An ex is theoretically equal to the size of a lower-case letter "x" in the font, referred to as the *x-height*. While fonts will vary the actual height of an x for artistic reasons, few font definition files include an exact measurement for the x-height, so browsers will almost always simply treat it as .5 em. Due to the potential for inconsistencies, most designers avoid using ex as a measurement.

The big advantage to using ems or exes is that, because both are proportional to the font size, both will scale nicely. The previous example noted setting the line height using ems. If you do this, and then later increase the size of the font, the line height will remain 1½ times the font size.

Percents

The unit that is perhaps the easiest to comprehend is the percentage. Almost every property that supports units of measurement allows you to set that unit as a percent. The only potential point of confusion is in understanding exactly what the unit is a percentage of.

All XHTML documents are made up of a series of nested elements — a paragraph, for example, may be nested within the body, which is, in turn, nested within the `html` element. When using percentages, the unit is a percent of the parent element's unit. Therefore, if a paragraph's font size is 95%, it means that it is 95% of the body's size, whatever that may be.

As with using ems, the biggest advantage of using percentages is scalability. If you set all of your font sizes in points, and then wish to increase the size of all of the text on the page, you must change every font size reference. Instead, if you set everything to percents, then you would only need to change the size of the text on the body element and everything else would scale accordingly, as all of the content on the page is ultimately a descendent of the body.

Relative versus Absolute Measurements

While the argument could be made that every unit of measurement is relative on a computer screen, browsers define inches, centimeters, millimeters, points, picas, and pixels as absolute units, and percents, ems, and exes as relative ones.

The real meaning here is that once an element is set in one of the absolute units, its size will not be affected by the size of any other element, while the relative units allow elements to scale.

Practice and experience will teach you when it is best to use an absolute unit, and when a relative unit will work better.

No Default Unit

In CSS, there is no default unit of measurement, so one must always be provided. Browsers are inconsistent in how they handle measurements where no unit is provided; some will arbitrarily assign a unit, while others will ignore the property altogether as being invalid. Therefore, you should take care to always specify the unit.

Set the Size of Text on a Page

Before CSS, designers were forced to use the HTML font element and its size attribute to control the size of text on the page. In addition to adding a lot of extra code to the page, this approach limited designers to seven arbitrary font sizes, represented simply by the numbers 1 through 7. Size 7 was the largest, displayed in most browsers as approximately equal to 36 point text, while size 1 was smallest, mapping to roughly 8 points.

Today, this system has been abandoned in favor of the CSS font-size property. You can use just about any unit you wish in specifying font sizes, except the strange 1–7 system of old. In addition to setting the sizes exactly by specifying a value and its unit, you can use one of nine keywords. The absolute keywords xx-small, x-small, small, medium, large, x-large, and xx-large are

intended as direct replacements to the old 7-size system, although not all browsers map the CSS keywords to the old HTML sizes. Two relative keywords, smaller and larger, can be used to decrease or increase the size of the text based on the selected element's parent element's size. Few designers use these keywords, as most prefer the more precise control offered by setting sizes with a specific unit.

Any element in XHTML that renders text can take font-size. Some elements that serve as containers to text-based elements but do not take text themselves, such as table, tr, ul, and ol, can take font-size and correctly pass the size down to the children that contain text, while others do not. This behavior can be inconsistent across browsers, and must be carefully tested before implementation.

Set the Size of Text on a Page

① Open a Web page in your editor.

② In the head, type `<style type="text/css">`.

③ Type the closing style tag, `</style>`, on a new line.

```
index - Notepad
File  Edit  Format  View  Help
<!DOCTYPE html PUBLIC "-//W3C//DTD XHTML 1.0 Transitional//EN" "http://www.

<!--
Title: America's National Parks
Author: Rob Huddleston, rob@robhuddleston.com
Date: 11/4/07
-->

<html xmlns="http://www.w3.org/1999/xhtml">

<head>

<title>America's National Parks</title>

<link rel="shortcut icon" href="images/favicon.png" type="image/png" />

<style type="text/css">

</style>

</head>
```

④ Add an element selector and the opening curly brace.

⑤ Add the font-size property.

```
index - Notepad
File  Edit  Format  View  Help
<!DOCTYPE html PUBLIC "-//W3C//DTD XHTML 1.0 Transitional//EN" "http://www.

<!--
Title: America's National Parks
Author: Rob Huddleston, rob@robhuddleston.com
Date: 11/4/07
-->

<html xmlns="http://www.w3.org/1999/xhtml">

<head>

<title>America's National Parks</title>

<link rel="shortcut icon" href="images/favicon.png" type="image/png" />

<style type="text/css">

p {
          font-size:
</style>
```

⑥ Set the value.

Note: *Be sure to include a unit unless you are using one of the keywords.*

⑦ Add the closing curly brace.

⑧ Save the page.

⑨ Open the page in a browser.

● The page opens, showing the text in the specified size.

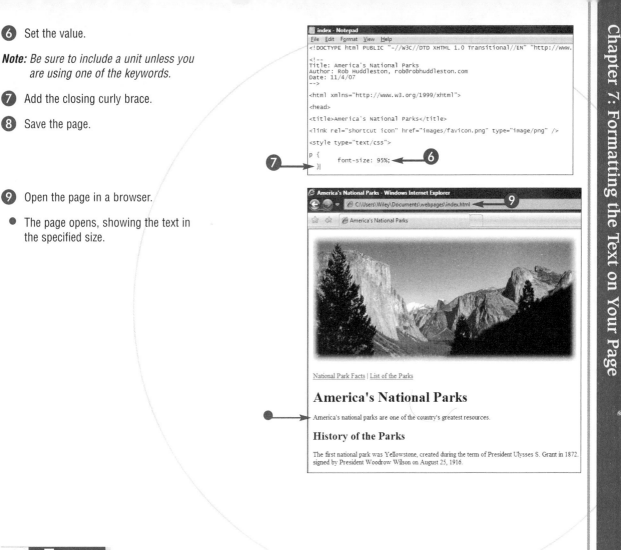

Extra

In addition to the added flexibility gained when setting font sizes using percents, you also gain an important accessibility advantage. Browsers have the capability to allow users to resize text on the page so that users with poor eyesight can make the text larger and easier to read. Most browsers will allow users to resize the text under any condition, but unfortunately, Microsoft Internet Explorer will only allow for this resizing if you, the designer, set the font size using a relative unit of measurement. If you use any of the absolute units — inches, centimeters, millimeters, picas, points, or pixels — your users will not be able to resize if they use Internet Explorer. Microsoft partially solved this issue in version 7 of the browser by adding a Page Zoom feature that scales every element on the page, not just the text, but the text sizing functionality remains unchanged.

If you set a font-size for the body of the document, you will, in essence, set a default size for all elements on the page, as they are all descendents of the body element.

Set the Font on a Page

Most browsers use Times New Roman, or some variant of it, as the default for text on the page. Many designers, however, would prefer to have better control over the font, which is achieved through the `font-family` property.

When you specify the font for the page, you are not embedding any actual font information; rather, you are merely instructing the browser as to which font you wish it to use. In order for that instruction to succeed, you need to specify a font that already exists on the user's machine. This use of what are called *device fonts* represents a significant limitation in the range of available fonts. While you can in theory specify any font you want, in practice only four fonts can be all but guaranteed to exist on your user's machine: Arial, Courier, Times New Roman, and Verdana.

Should you specify a font that your user does not have installed, the browser will revert to its default. To reduce the possibility of not finding a match, designers will often give a list of possible fonts, including a generic font family, such as `Arial, Helvetica, sans-serif`. The list is evaluated in order from left to right, so in this case, the browser would use Arial, but if it could not be found, then it would use Helvetica; if neither are present, the browser would use its default sans serif font.

The font names are not case-sensitive, but they do need to match the name of the actual font file, which is not necessarily the common name for the font. For example, Microsoft Word shows a common Office font as Comic Sans, but the actual name that must be used is MS Comic Sans.

Set the Font on a Page

① Open a Web page that contains an embedded style sheet in your editor.

● This embedded style sheet specifies the size of body text (enclosed in `p` tags).

② Add an element selector and the opening curly brace.

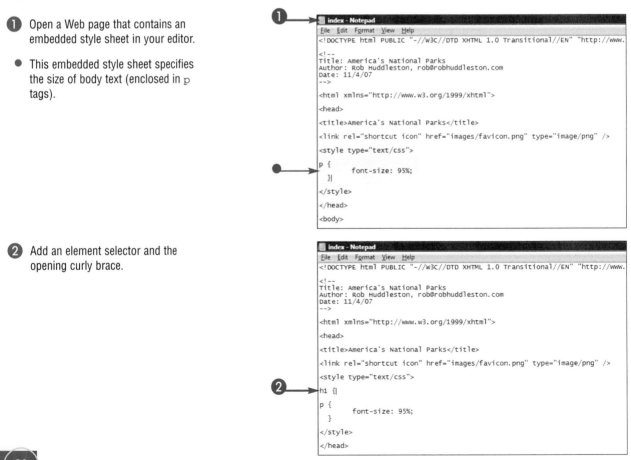

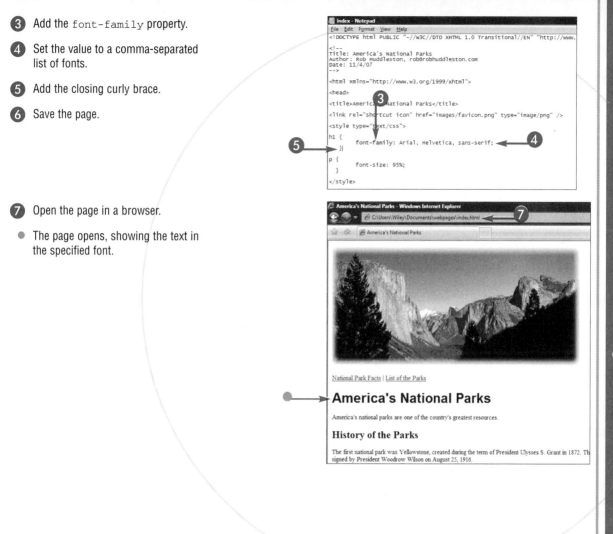

③ Add the `font-family` property.

④ Set the value to a comma-separated list of fonts.

⑤ Add the closing curly brace.

⑥ Save the page.

⑦ Open the page in a browser.

● The page opens, showing the text in the specified font.

Extra

Font names that contain more than one word, such as Times New Roman or MS Comic Sans, must be in quotation marks. You can use either double or single quotation marks. One-word font names do not need quotes.

The most commonly supported generic font families are serif, sans-serif, and monospace. *Serifs* are the "feet" found on the ends of letters in fonts such as Times New Roman. While not universally accepted, a common belief is that serifs originated in ancient Rome by the necessities of carving letters into stone. The precise origin of the word serif is not known, but *sans* is French for without, so a sans serif font is one without serifs, such as Arial. Monospace fonts are those where every letter takes the same horizontal space, so an *I* and an *M* will be the same width. Monospace fonts were widely used by typewriters; today, they are mostly used to represent code in technical manuals (such as this one).

Using Color on the Web

Computer monitors today are capable of displaying millions of colors. A basic understanding of how they produce this color will make it easier to create pages that use the colors you want.

RGB

Computer monitors are referred to as *RGB devices* as the colors on them are generated by varying degrees of red, green, and blue light. Early monitors combined the three primaries to produce a total of 256 colors, but today, most monitors are capable of using at least 256 degrees of each color, for a total of 16,777,216 colors.

Television screens are also RGB devices, and, in fact, most modern televisions use very similar, and in some cases identical, technologies as computer screens. Color film was produced by mixing red, green, and blue, and the very earliest color photography involved taking the same image three times, first with a red filter, then a green one, and then a blue one, and combining the plates.

The human eye likewise sees in red, green, and blue. The retina at the back of the eye contains rods and cones that detect varying amounts of these colors and combine them to see the visual spectrum. The human eye can see a much wider range of colors than a monitor is capable of producing.

Graphics Editors and RGB

The other primary color system is CMYK, an abbreviation for Cyan, Yellow, Magenta, and Black. "K" is used for black so that it is not confused with blue. CMYK is the main color space for printing, and your color printer almost certainly contains four inks, one for each of these colors.

Most professional graphics design tools today, such as Adobe Illustrator and Photoshop and Corel Draw, are created to work well with both print and onscreen outputs, and so will support both RGB and CMYK. However, when creating graphics for the Web, you should always work exclusively in RGB, given any device your audience will use to view your pages will be RGB. Any decent graphics tool will allow you to convert an image from CMYK to RGB if necessary. All three of the graphics formats supported by Web browsers — GIF, JPG, and PNG — are RGB-based.

Some graphics applications that were created to primarily target Web graphics, such as Adobe Flash, do not support CMYK at all.

CSS supports three methods of specifying colors to be used on your pages: named colors, RGB, and hexadecimal.

Named Colors

The HTML specification defines sixteen colors that can be referenced by name: `aqua`, `black`, `blue`, `fuchsia`, `green`, `gray`, `lime`, `maroon`, `navy`, `olive`, `purple`, `red`, `silver`, `teal`, `white`, and `yellow`. As the Web evolved, many more named colors were developed, finally including about 140 colors. While most modern browsers support the entire set of named colors, there is no guarantee that they will support any but the standard sixteen, and a few slight variances exist between browsers when they are confronted with the same color.

RGB

A second, rarely used technique is to specify the color via its RGB properties. Each color is expressed as a value between 0 and 255, with the former representing none of the color, and the latter the maximum amount of the color. The three numbers are given in a comma-separated list, which is in turn enclosed in parentheses and preceded by `rgb`:

```
color: rgb(0,216,181);
```

Using this system gives you access to all 16.7 million colors in the RGB space.

Hexadecimal

Hexadecimal is by far the most commonly used method of referencing color on the Web. Originally developed by IBM in the 1960s, hexadecimal is merely a method of counting using a base-16 system, instead of the more familiar decimal system. The additional six digits required are represented by the letters A, B, C, D, E, and F. Hexadecimal enables you to count from 0 to 255 using only two digits, instead of the three required by decimal.

It is possible to mathematically calculate a hexadecimal value from a decimal by dividing the decimal value by sixteen, where the number of times the value divides evenly by sixteen gives you the first digit, and the remainder the second. So 216 divided by 16 is 13 with a remainder of 8. The 13 can be converted to D, and thus the hexadecimal equivalent of 216 is D8.

Most graphics programs and Web editors will provide some method of selecting a color that will simply provide the hexadecimal value.

In CSS, hexadecimal is designated by using a pound or hash symbol, followed by a six-digit hexadecimal value, with the first two digits representing the red, the second two the green, and the third two the blue. The color noted in the previous RGB section would be given as this in hexadecimal:

```
color: #00D8B5;
```

Because hexadecimal is merely a different method of indicating RGB colors, it also enables you to set any color from that color space.

The Web Safe Palette

In the early days of the Web, when monitors were only capable of displaying 256 colors, a set of colors needed to exist that would in theory correctly display. Therefore, a palette of 216 colors was developed, partly to avoid colors reserved by operating systems but also because of their hexadecimal values.

These colors are made up of six possible shades of the three primaries. These shades are represented by the hexadecimal values `00`, `33`, `66`, `99`, `CC`, and `FF`. Thus, any color whose hexadecimal was a combination of those values was "Web safe," while any other color was not. So, `#33CC99` is in this palette, while `#33CC98` would not be.

Unfortunately, the reality of the Web safe palette was that monitors and operating systems vary so greatly that it never truly worked as planned. In fact, a study in the late 1990s found that only 22 of the 216 colors could be counted on to actually display consistently across all 256-color displays.

Because very few users today still rely on 256-color monitors, there is little or no technological reason to continue to restrict your designs to it. However, many programs still rely on it for their default color pickers, Adobe Dreamweaver and Adobe Flash amongst them, and some designers continue to use it as nothing more than a convenient palette from which to choose colors.

Change the Color of Text on a Page

U sing style sheets, you can set the color of the text on your page. Prior to the advent of CSS, this required laboriously wrapping each piece of text that you wanted to change with a `font` tag. Now, you can simply apply a style to whichever tag already exists around the text in question.

The CSS property to set your font color is simply `color`. Technically, `color` applies to the foreground color of the element, but in practical terms, this means the text color, as the horizontal rule is the only element in XHTML that has a foreground that is not text.

When setting the color, you can use a named color, RGB value, or hexadecimal value. When using hexadecimal as most developers do, always remember to precede the value with a pound or hash symbol. Browsers did not enforce

this with the `font` tag, so many developers got lazy and stopped using it. With CSS, most browsers rigidly enforce the rule and will not render colors without the symbol. CSS properties and values are case-insensitive, so while the letters in the hexadecimal value are most often written in uppercase, they do not have to be.

You should develop a complimentary color scheme for your Web site, and be consistent in your use of text colors. First-level headings should always use the same, or at least a similar, color across all of your pages to avoid confusing your users. You should also keep in mind that black text on a white background is by far the color combination that is easiest to read, so if you have large blocks of text on your page, you should consider leaving them black-on-white.

Change the Color of Text on a Page

① Open a Web page that contains an embedded style sheet in your editor.

② Add an element selector and the opening curly brace.

This example creates a formatting rule for the second-level headings (h2).

③ Add the `color` property.

④ Set the value to the hexadecimal code for the color you wish to use.

⑤ Add the closing curly brace.

⑥ Save the page.

⑦ Open the page in a browser.

● The page opens, showing the text in the specified color.

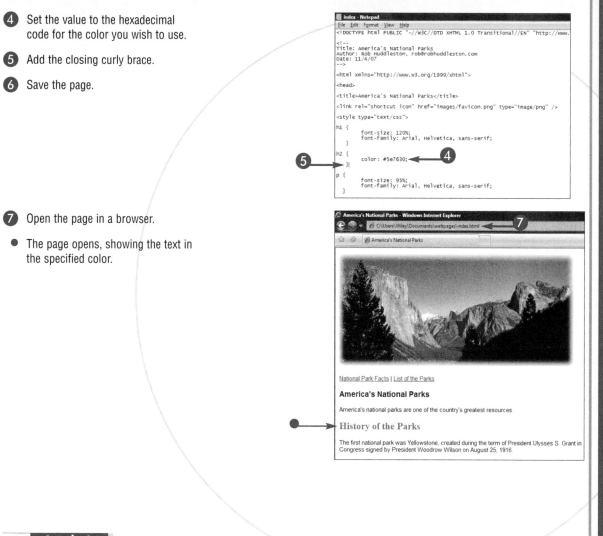

Apply It

You can add single-line comments to your CSS code using two slashes. A multiline comment begins with a slash and an asterisk, and ends with an asterisk and a slash:

```
/*
Define colors
*/
h1 { color: #000066; //dark blue }
p { color: #990000; //maroon }
```

You can use shorthand for the Web safe colors, or any color where the hexadecimal is made up of three pairs of values by using a three digit hexadecimal code instead of six. To do this, simply drop the duplicate values in each pair:

```
h1 { color: #006; /* same as #000066 */}
p { color: #900; /* same as #990000 */}
```

Adjust the Height of Lines

Proper spacing between lines of text is an important factor in readability. Too little space will cause the lines to run together and become difficult to read. Too much space, on the other hand, creates problems where readers' eyes will have difficulty finding the next line as they scan down.

In traditional printing, the space between lines is managed by adjusting *leading*, a term that refers to the strips of lead that were originally used to create spacing. In style sheets, you can use the line-height property instead:

```
p { line-height: 125%; }
```

Except in very rare cases, you should use either a percentage or ems to set the line height. That way, if you later adjust your font size, the line height automatically adjusts proportionally.

There is no absolute right or wrong in determining the proper line height. Most often, you will want a value of between 125% and 150%. When you test your Web site, feedback about text being difficult to read could indicate a problem with your line-height. Personal taste can also come into play here, but should testing indicate a problem, you need to be willing to go with your user's opinions, not your own.

Line-height is used only to adjust the space between lines within a block of text, such as a paragraph. CSS includes another set of properties to adjust the space between blocks, which will be discussed in Chapter 8.

Adjust the Height of Lines

① Open a Web page that contains an embedded style sheet in your editor.

● The style sheet begins here.

② Add an element selector and the opening curly brace.

③ Add the line-height property.

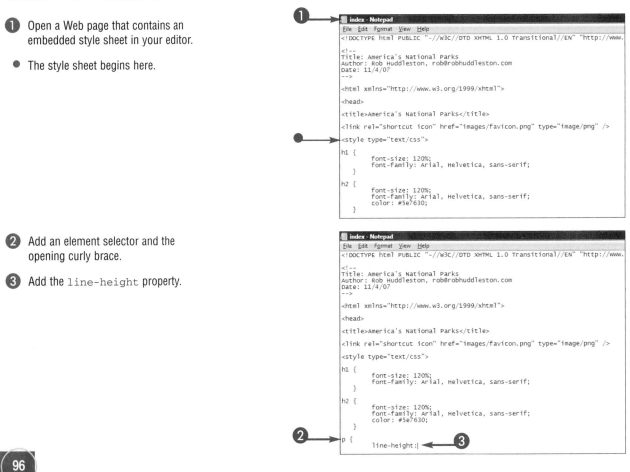

4 Set the value to a percent of the font size.

5 Add the closing curly brace.

6 Save the page.

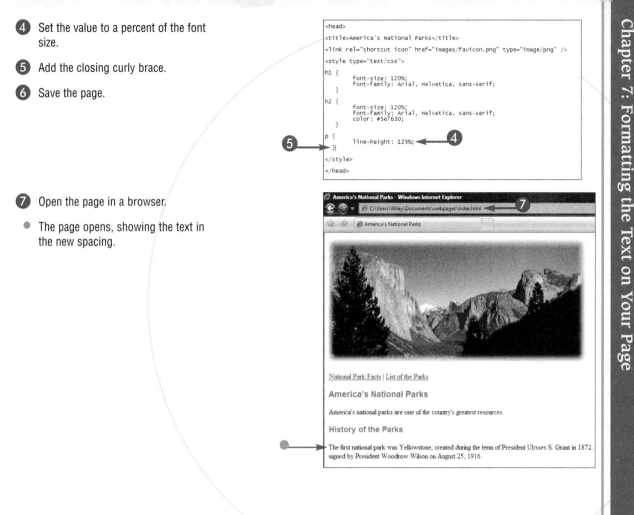

7 Open the page in a browser.

● The page opens, showing the text in the new spacing.

Because both percentages and ems are relative to the font size, they are functionally equivalent, where 1 em is equal to 100%. Thus, 1.4 em equals 140%, and 1.25 em equals 125%. Which unit you choose to use is entirely personal preference. If you have a graphic design background and are familiar with using ems, and in particular with using them to set leading, then that unit will make sense to you and you will most likely prefer it. On the other hand, if you come from another background and are only just learning about ems, you will probably stick with percents.

It is possible to have lines of text actually overlap each other by setting the line-height to a value of less than 100% or less than 1 em. This may be desirable in certain artistic designs, but should obviously be avoided for the main content text on the page.

Older browsers may not support line-height or may support it incorrectly, so if you need to account for version 3 or earlier browsers, be sure to carefully test this property.

Make Text Bold or Italic

You can quickly draw users' eyes to certain words or phrases on your page by making the text bold or italic or both. Bold text in CSS is achieved via the `font-weight` property, while the `font-style` property renders text in italic.

The `font-weight` has many more possible values than might be expected. A value of `bold` renders the text as expected. However, the specification also provides for values of `bolder`, to make the text darker than a normal bold, `lighter` to render the text lighter than normal, and numeric values of `100`, `200`, `300`, `400`, `500`, `600`, `700`, `800`, and `900`. Each of these results in a different degree of boldness, where `500` is the normal weight, the four lower values are degrees lighter, and the others are progressively darker. Unfortunately, no current browser

has support for these additional properties, so in practice `lighter` and `100` through `500` will all render the text as normal, and all other values will render the text as bold.

The `font-style` property supports values of `italic` and `oblique`. Just as with `font-weight`, no browsers support the difference between the two, so as of now they are functionally equivalent.

Both properties also support a value of `normal`, which can be used in nested elements to override an inherited value or to override the default display from the browser. For example, text within any of the headings is by default bold, but applying `font-weight:normal` renders the text without bold; likewise, `font-style:normal` applied to an element such as `cite` or `address` will override the default italicization of those elements.

Make Text Bold or Italic

① Open a Web page that contains an embedded style sheet in your editor.

● The style sheet begins here.

② Add an element selector and the opening curly brace.

③ Add a `font-weight` property.

④ Set the value to `bold`.

⑤ Add the closing curly brace.

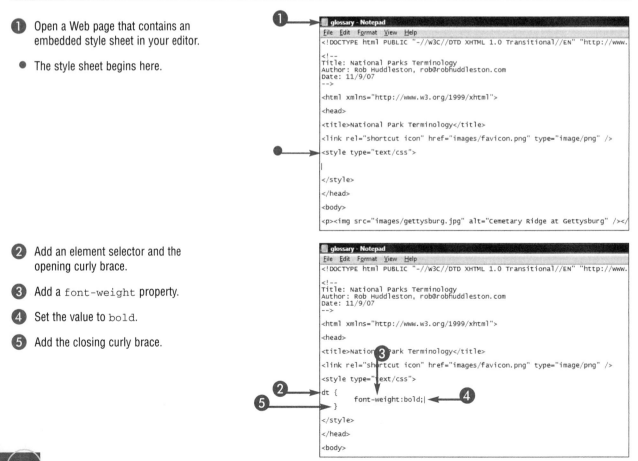

6 Add another element selector and opening curly brace.

7 Add a `font-style` property.

8 Set the value to `italic`.

9 Add the closing curly brace.

10 Save the page.

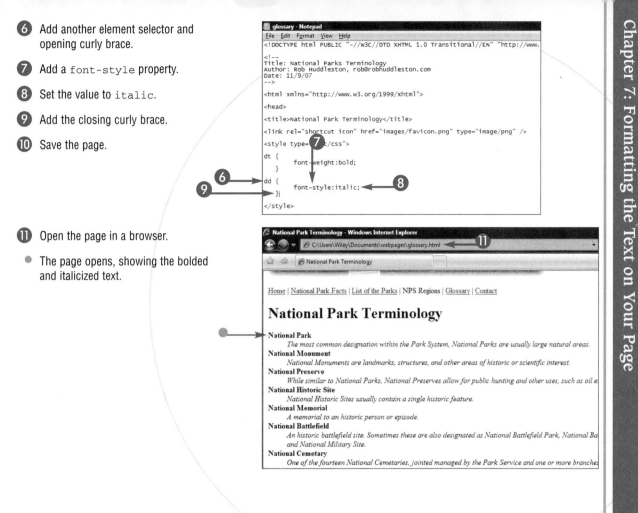

11 Open the page in a browser.

● The page opens, showing the bolded and italicized text.

One aspect of the push to standardization on the Web, and in particular the push to using semantic markup, is a natural confusion as to when it is appropriate to use the XHTML `strong` and `em` elements, and when CSS should be used.

Both `strong` and `font-weight:bold` result in the same visual appearance, as do `font-style:italic` and `em`. The important factor is what the text means non-visually. Using the elements gives some indication as to why the text is bold or italic — it is being emphasized (in the case of `em`) or strongly emphasized (`strong`). Screen readers will often use a different inflection when reading this text to your visually impaired users. The CSS properties, on the other hand, do not indicate any reason, and merely change the appearance. Therefore, you should use the elements when the text is to be bolded or italicized for emphasis, and CSS when you are merely trying to achieve a visual effect, such as making the name of a company stand out in a block of text.

Indent and Align Text

HTML lacked two very common properties for controlling text layout: the ability to indent the first line of text and the ability to align it. Indentation was often faked using non-semantic elements or even images, and while early versions of the language included a center element, simple left or right alignment required the user to bloat the code with the repetitive use of the align attribute. Fully justifying text was simply not supported.

CSS solves both of those issues with the `text-indent` and `text-align` properties. The `text-indent` property allows designers to specify a precise amount by which the first line of a block of text may be indented. As with other measurement-based properties, any valid unit is allowed, but pixels and percents are the most commonly

used units. This property allows designers to achieve the traditional first line indentation common in certain printed media.

The `text-align` property has possible values of `left`, `center`, `right`, and `justify`. The most interesting of these is justify, which provides the effect of fully justified text; that is, text that is aligned with both the left and right margins. Browsers are usually intelligent enough when applying `text-align` set to `justify` to not apply it to the final line of a paragraph. However, justified text, while common in print with its precise layout controls, can be much more difficult to read on a computer screen, particularly if the width of the element if too wide. Therefore, this setting should be carefully tested with users.

Indent and Align Text

① Open a Web page that contains an embedded style sheet in your editor.

● The style sheet begins here.

② Add a `text-indent` property to an existing rule in the style sheet.

③ Set the value to the desired amount of indentation.

4 Add a `text-align` property to an existing rule.

5 Set the value to `center`.

6 Save the page.

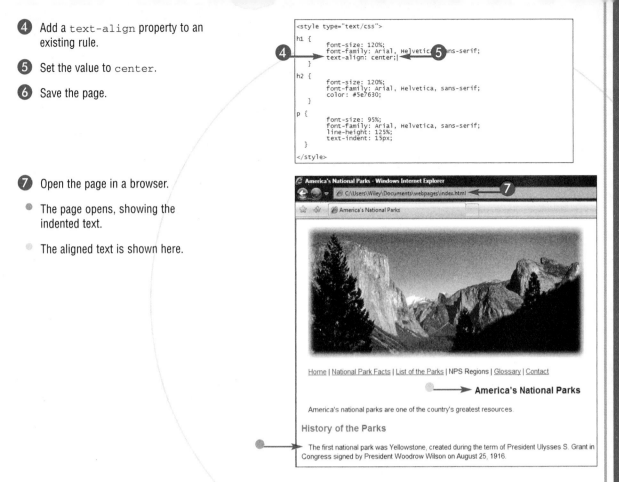

```
<style type="text/css">
h1 {
        font-size: 120%;
        font-family: Arial, Helvetica, sans-serif;
        text-align: center;|
    }
h2 {
        font-size: 120%;
        font-family: Arial, Helvetica, sans-serif;
        color: #5e7630;
    }
p {
        font-size: 95%;
        font-family: Arial, Helvetica, sans-serif;
        line-height: 125%;
        text-indent: 15px;
    }
</style>
```

7 Open the page in a browser.

● The page opens, showing the indented text.

● The aligned text is shown here.

America's National Parks - Windows Internet Explorer

C:\Users\Wiley\Documents\webpages\index.html ← 7

America's National Parks

Home | National Park Facts | List of the Parks | NPS Regions | Glossary | Contact

America's National Parks

America's national parks are one of the country's greatest resources.

History of the Parks

The first national park was Yellowstone, created during the term of President Ulysses S. Grant in Congress signed by President Woodrow Wilson on August 25, 1916.

Extra

Both of these properties have issues with proper inheritance. In theory, one should be able to wrap a series of elements within another element and apply the styles to the parent, thus having them apply to the children. This approach works with many CSS text properties, but has its limits. For simple pages, the most obvious parent element on which to set the styles is the body, as it is already the container for the rest of the content of the page. However, testing will reveal that the `text-indent` property set on the body will affect most block-level elements that are children of the body, such as headings and paragraphs, but content within table cells will not inherit the indentation, so the property must be expressly set for them. This shows that you must always be sure to test your pages in a variety of browsers before deployment.

Using Additional Font Properties

The font-variant property in CSS allows you to use small caps in your text; that is, have the browser render lowercase letters as smaller uppercase letters. Possible values of the property are small-caps and normal, the latter being the default and useful to override inheritance.

```
h1 { font-variant: small-caps; }
```

You should note that some browsers may not support the use of small caps in the currently selected font. In these situations, most will simply render the lowercase letters as uppercase and then size those letters accordingly, but you as a designer have no way to control precisely how much smaller they may be. Certain older browsers may render the text in all uppercase letters of the same size.

Future versions of CSS may support additional values for font-variant.

If you wish to convert text to all uppercase or all lowercase letters, regardless of how they are actually typed, you can apply the text-transform property. Possible values are uppercase, lowercase, and capitalize. The default value for this property is not normal as per usual, but instead none.

```
h2 { text-transform: uppercase; }
```

This property is of particular use in situations where non-designers may be adding content directly to the web page and may not be reliably consistent in their use of capitalization. Forcing headings to all uppercase or to initial capitals can maintain this consistency even if content providers do not.

Using Additional Font Properties

① Open a web page that contains an embedded style sheet in your editor.

● The style sheet begins here.

② Add a font-variant property to an existing rule.

③ Set the value to small-caps;.

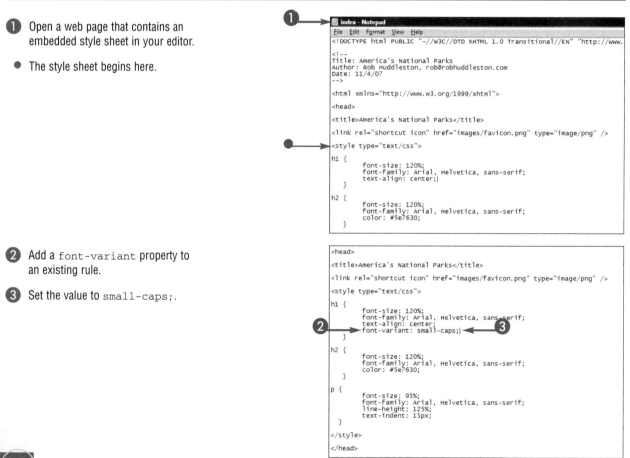

④ Add a `text-transform` property to an existing rule.

⑤ Set the value to `capitalize;`.

⑥ Save the page.

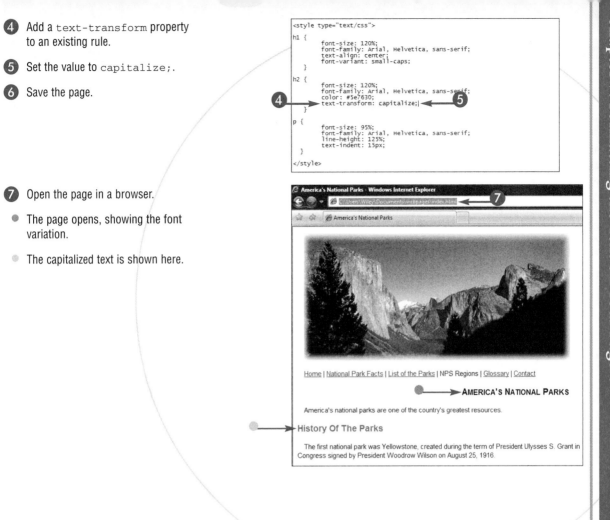

```
<style type="text/css">

h1 {
        font-size: 120%;
        font-family: Arial, Helvetica, sans-serif;
        text-align: center;
        font-variant: small-caps;
    }

h2 {
        font-size: 120%;
        font-family: Arial, Helvetica, sans-serif;
        color: #5e7630;
        text-transform: capitalize;|
    }

p {
        font-size: 95%;
        font-family: Arial, Helvetica, sans-serif;
        line-height: 125%;
        text-indent: 15px;
    }

</style>
```

⑦ Open the page in a browser.

● The page opens, showing the font variation.

● The capitalized text is shown here.

AMERICA'S NATIONAL PARKS

America's national parks are one of the country's greatest resources.

History Of The Parks

The first national park was Yellowstone, created during the term of President Ulysses S. Grant in Congress signed by President Woodrow Wilson on August 25, 1916.

Extra

Font matching in the browser is actually a quite complex process. As much as possible, browsers will attempt to find the precise font required to display each character. For example, if the style sheet sets the font properties to bold, small caps Arial, then the browser will see if the user's machine has a font definition for Arial bold small caps. If such a font exists, it will be used; if not, as is often the case for small caps, then the browser will use what it can — perhaps the Arial bold font — and then attempt to generate an acceptable small caps variant by scaling the uppercase letters accordingly. Given that these calculations actually occur for each character within the text, it is somewhat surprising that font generation is not extraordinarily slow.

When using the `text-transform` property, you should note that a value of `capitalize` will convert the first character of every word to uppercase. While this is often the desired effect, it will not always be perfect. CSS is simply not intelligent enough to determine which words should or should not be capitalized.

Using the Font Shorthand Property

Rather than setting separate properties for the font size, family, line height, bold, and italic, CSS provides a single shorthand property, `font`, that allows you to set all of those properties in a single line.

When using the `font` shorthand, you can set these values in a single space-separated list. However, unlike other shorthand properties in CSS, the order in which you list the values when using `font` is important, as several of the properties being set can take similar values. The generic syntax for the font property is shown below.

```
font: font-style || font-variant || font-
weight || font-size / line-height || font-
family }
```

Note that not all of the values above must be declared, but `font-size` and `font-family` are always required at a minimum. An oddity in this declaration is that the `font-size` and `line-height` properties are separated by a forward slash, instead of the space used to separate all of the others.

A full example of the `font` shorthand is shown here:

```
p { font: italic bold 95%/1.25em Arial,
Helvetica, sans-serif; }
```

While using the shorthand certainly saves coding, many designers avoid it due to the difficulty in remembering the order in which values must be presented and the reduced clarity of the style for other designers.

Using the Font Shorthand Property

① Open a web page that contains an embedded style sheet.

● The style sheet begins here.

② Add an element selector and the opening curly brace.

③ Add a `font` property.

④ Set the desired values for font-style, font-variant, or font-weight.

⑤ Add the desired font-size, a forward slash, and the line-height.

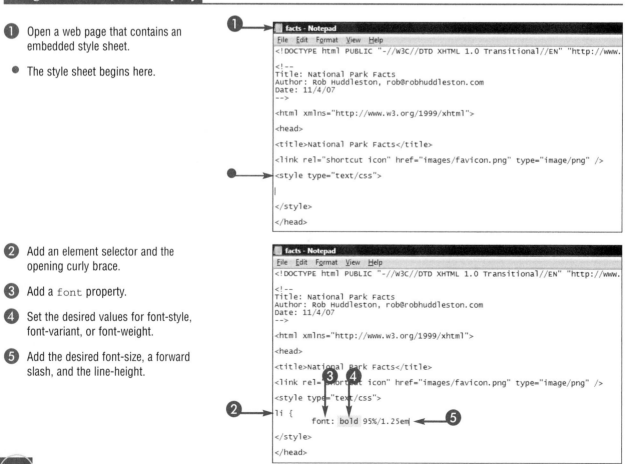

6 Add the desired font-family and a semi-colon.

7 Add the closing curly brace.

8 Save the page.

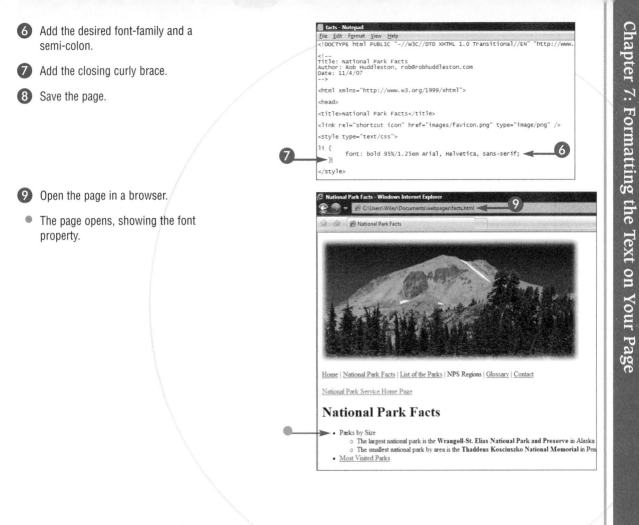

9 Open the page in a browser.

● The page opens, showing the font property.

Extra

Any values not expressly set in the font property will be reset to their defaults, which may override properties believed to be inherited. For example, consider a situation where the following two rules are set:

```
table { font: bold 100%/1.3em "Times New Roman", Times, serif; }
td { font: 95% Arial, Helvetica, sans-serif; }
```

You might reasonably believe that table cells in this situation would be bold with a line-height of 1.3 em, which would certainly be the case normally, as they are both properties that are inherited. However, the use of font in the td declaration changes this. Because the font property in the td rule does not expressly set either font-weight or line-height, they are both set to their defaults of normal and 1 em, respectively. Oddly, while there is no way to set it in the font shorthand, this property also sets the font-stretch to its defaults as well, so if you wish to control font-stretch while using font, you must first give the font property, and then set font-stretch.

Add Background Colors to Elements on a Page

U

sing CSS, you can set the background color of any element on the page by using the background-color property and an appropriate color value. Just as with color, background-color can take as its value a named color, an RGB (red, green, blue) value, or a hexadecimal value.

```
h1 { background-color: #3F6; }
```

By default, background-color is set to none, which allows the color of the parent element to be seen through the current element. CSS also supports a value of transparent, which gives the same result as none. Either of these values can be used to override a background color that is being inherited from a parent element.

Setting the background-color of the body alleviates the need to use the deprecated bgcolor attribute and sets

the background of the entire page. Likewise, you can discontinue use of bgcolor for the table, tr, and td elements and replace it with this property.

```
body {background-color: #FFF; }
```

Note that in the previous example, the background color is being explicitly set to white, its default. This is a recommended best practice to ensure a white background when that is desired, as there is no guarantee that all browsers will always stick with a white default background. In fact, very early browsers defaulted to gray.

Inline as well as block elements can take a background color, so it is possible to create highlighting effects within text.

Add Background Colors to Elements on a Page

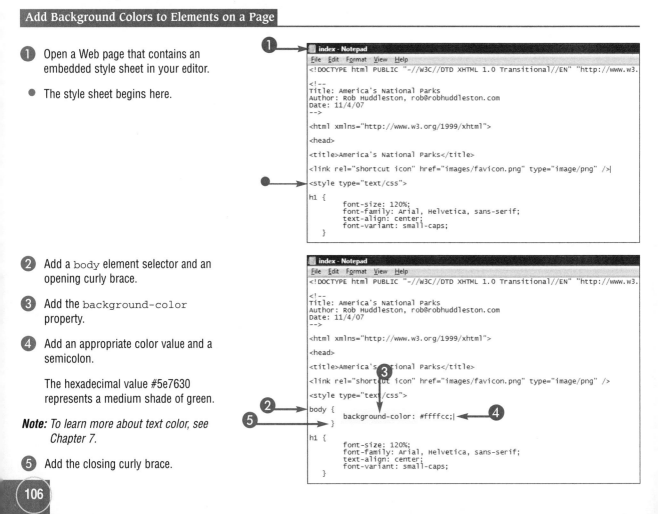

1 Open a Web page that contains an embedded style sheet in your editor.

● The style sheet begins here.

2 Add a body element selector and an opening curly brace.

3 Add the background-color property.

4 Add an appropriate color value and a semicolon.

The hexadecimal value #5e7630 represents a medium shade of green.

Note: To learn more about text color, see Chapter 7.

5 Add the closing curly brace.

6 Add the `background-color` property to an existing declaration.

7 Add an appropriate color value and a semicolon.

8 Save the document.

9 Open the page in a browser.

The page opens, showing the new background colors.

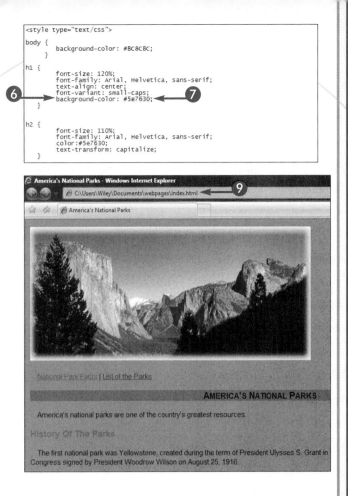

Extra

You need to take care to ensure that you maintain good contrast between the foreground and background colors. Too little contrast will make your text difficult if not impossible to read, and will almost certainly cause users to leave your page. Color-blind users in particular have problems seeing text or other elements against colored backgrounds with insufficient contrast. Further, the background color of your page should enhance rather than detract from your design, so for most sites very bright or very dark background colors will be inappropriate.

Background colors cannot be semitransparent, so if you apply a color to an element that is contained within another element, the nested element's background color will completely obscure the parent element's background. The CSS3 specification is supposed to provide for semitransparency, but as of the time of this writing, the specification is still years from completion, and full browser support for it will take years beyond that.

Add Background Images to Elements on a Page

Rather than using a solid color as the background of an element, you can use an image. You can use a GIF (Graphics Interchange Format), JPEG (Joint Photographic Experts Group), or PNG (Portable Network Graphics). You apply an image to the background of an element with the `background-image` property. As with `background-color`, you can use images as the background of any element.

The `background-image` property takes as its value a path to the image, set in parentheses and preceded by `url`. You can use a relative, site-root relative, or absolute path.

```
h1 { background-image: url(images/
bkgrnd.jpg); }
```

By default, the image will tile both horizontally and vertically within the background of the element, but you can control this with the `background-repeat` property. Possible values are `repeat`, which is the default and

causes tiling; `no-repeat`, which results in the image only appearing once; `repeat-x`, which causes the image to tile only along the x-axis; and `repeat-y`, which tiles only along the y-axis.

```
h1 { background-image: url(images/
bkgrnd.jpg); background-repeat:no-repeat; }
```

If your background image is a transparent GIF or PNG, or possibly a semitransparent PNG, then the background color of the element will be visible through the transparent areas of the image. It is considered a best practice to always set a background color along with the image, as the browser will act as though no background image has been set if it cannot find the image. This is particularly important if the text will not be visible if the image does not appear when you set a text to be a very light color (assuming that a dark image in the background would make it readable). Setting a dark background color in this case will maintain readability.

Add Background Images to Elements on a Page

1. Open a Web page that contains an embedded style sheet in your editor.

2. Add a `body` element selector and an opening curly brace.

3. Add the `background-image` property.

4. Type `url`, an opening parenthesis, a path to an image, a closing parenthesis, and a semicolon.

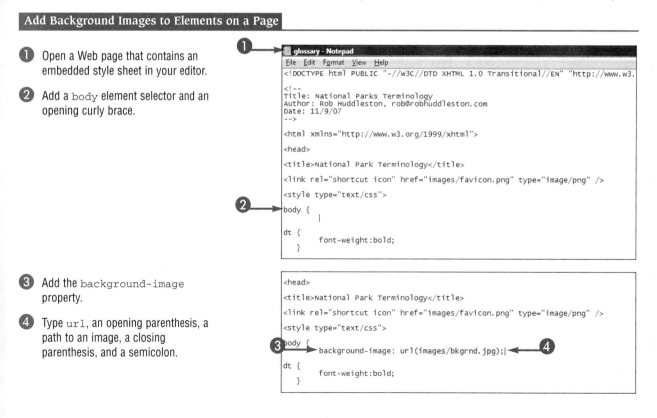

⑤ Add a `background-repeat` property.

⑥ Add a value of `repeat-x` and a semicolon.

⑦ Add the closing curly brace.

⑧ Save the document.

⑨ Open the page in a browser.

● The page opens, showing the new background colors.

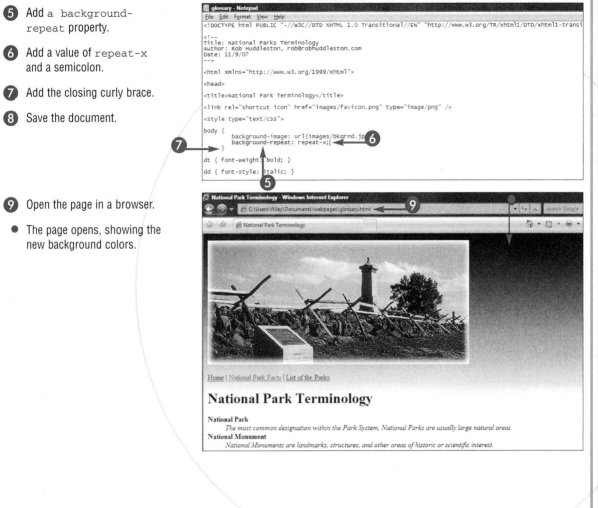

Extra

Even more so than with background colors, you need to be sure that your background image enhances rather than detracts from your design. If the image is going to tile, make sure that it tiles gracefully. Images that will serve as backgrounds to elements with text need to be fairly consistent in their color and contrast, as it will be difficult or impossible to set the text to a color that will be readable across an image with both very bright and very dark areas.

Screen readers and search engines ignore images in your CSS, so do not use the `background-image` property to place images on your page that are important to the content of your page. You need to add them to your XHTML via the `img` element. You should place images that exist solely to add visual impact to the page, but do not add to its content, via CSS.

Control the Position of Background Images

You can use the `background-position` property to control where the image appears within an element. You can prevent a background image from scrolling with the rest of the page through the `background-attachment` property as well.

The default position of a background image is the top-left corner of the element. You can control this by providing values to the `background-position` property, and can set this several ways. You can use a pair of percentages to reference a relative distance from the top-left corner, so `background-position: 50% 50%;` will center the image within the element. You can also use specific length measurements, where `background-position: 25px 50px;` will position the top-left corner of the image 25 pixels from the left edge of the element and 50 pixels

from the top edge. You can mix percentage and length values, so `background-position: 25px 100%;` will position the image 25 pixels from the left edge of the element and at the bottom of the element.

CSS also provides a set of keywords to use in positioning background images. The `top` keyword positions the top of the image with the top of the element. Other keywords are `left`, `right`, `bottom`, and `center`. You can use the keywords by themselves, so `background-position: right;` sets the image along the right edge of the element, with the vertical position being set to the default (`top`). You can also use them together: `background-position: bottom right;` aligns the image in the lower-right corner of the element. Keywords and percentage or length values may not be combined.

Control the Position of Background Images

① Open a Web page that contains an embedded style sheet in your editor.

② If necessary, add a `body` element selector and an opening curly brace.

③ Add the `background-image` property.

④ Type `url`, an opening parenthesis, a path to an image, a closing parenthesis, and a semicolon.

⑤ Add a `background-repeat:no-repeat;` rule.

6 Add a background-position property.

7 Type bottom right as the value of the property.

8 If necessary, add the closing curly brace.

9 Save the document.

10 Open the page in a browser.

● The page opens, showing the new background image.

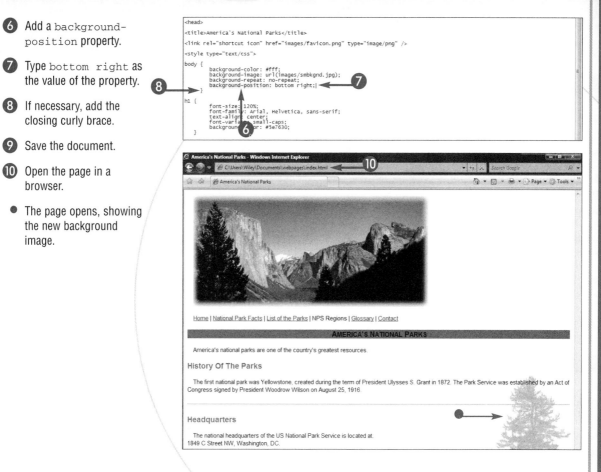

Apply It

You can prevent the page's background image from scrolling with the page content by using the background-attachment property and setting its value to fixed.

```
body {
    background-image: url(images/bkgrd.jpg);
    background-repeat: no-repeat;
    background-position: center;
    background-attachment: fixed;
}
```

While the CSS specification supports adding a fixed background to any element, many browsers do not and will only correctly render this property when applied to the body.

The other possible value for background-attachment is scroll, which is the default: The image will scroll with the page.

Using the Background Shorthand Property

I f you plan to apply a background color and background image, as well as set the `repeat`, `position`, and `attachment` properties of the image, you can use the `background` shorthand property instead, condensing the declarations from a potential of five lines to one.

Unlike many other shorthand properties, `background` has no set order in which the properties must be presented. In addition, any or all of them may be used, so some designers will choose to write `background: #fcc;` instead of `background-color: #fcc;`, or `background: url(images/bkg.jpg);` instead of `background-image: url(images/bkg.jpg);`. The first and second instances in each case are functionally equivalent, although the argument could be made that the latter makes for clearer, more readily understandable

code. Also, certain CSS editors will not provide proper code hinting when using this or other shorthand properties, although this is a limitation of the editor, not the language. As it makes no logical sense to use `background-attachment`, `background-repeat`, and `background-position` without a `background-image`, those properties would not normally appear alone or even together without the image; however, it is nonetheless legal and you may do it if the background image, for whatever reason, is being set by its own property elsewhere.

It must be noted that, as with other shorthand properties, if you choose to omit a particular value when using the background shorthand, the undeclared values will be set back to their default values. As few of the background properties inherit to child elements, or are inherited from parent elements, this is rarely an issue in practice.

Using the Background Shorthand Property

① Open a Web page that contains an embedded style sheet in your editor.

② If necessary, add a `body` element selector and an opening curly brace.

③ Add the `background` property.

④ Type a color value.

⑤ Type `url`, and open parenthesis, a path to a background image, and a closing parenthesis.

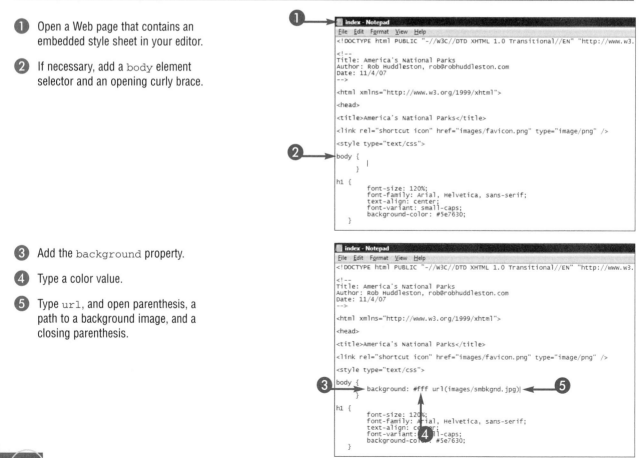

6 Type values for `background-repeat` and `background-position`.

7 Type a semicolon.

8 If necessary, add the closing curly brace.

9 Save the document.

10 Open the page in a browser.

● The page opens, showing the background image.

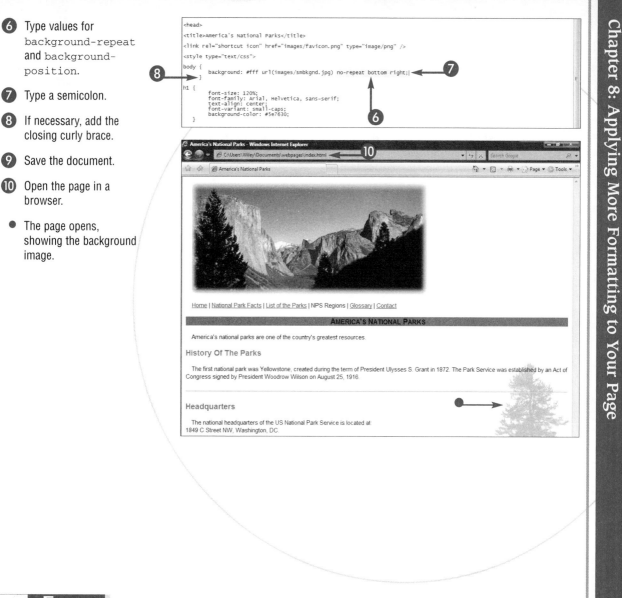

Extra

One potential source of confusion when using the shorthand property is in implementing the `background-position` property, given that it, by itself, can take a space-separated list of values. So long as those values are presented together, the browser should have no issues resolving the rule, regardless of where in the rule the values appear.

```
body { background: #fcc url(images/bkg.jpg) 100px 150px fixed no-repeat; }
```

Add Padding to Elements on a Page

Every block-level element exists within a box that is made up of four key sections: the content, padding, borders, and margins. Each section, except the content, has a series of CSS properties that you can use to adjust the appearance for each of the four sides of the box. The innermost section of the box is the content: the area defined by the actual display of the element. For most elements, the content will be the text in the element, although some elements may define it based on one or more nested elements' contents.

The area immediately surrounding the content of the box is padding. Padding defines the space that will exist between the content section and the border. Because the `background-color` and `background-image` properties fill both the content and the padding, controlling the padding allows you to adjust the position of the content relative to the edge of the padding.

Four properties exist in CSS to allow you to set padding for each side individually: `padding-top`, `padding-right`, `padding-bottom`, and `padding-left`. Values for each are most often set in either pixels or percents, but any valid CSS unit of measurement is allowed.

```
p          { padding-top: 15px; padding-bottom:
15px; padding-right: 10px; padding-left:
10px;  }
```

Remember that you must always provide a unit for the measurement, except when setting the value to 0. As each of the properties is specific to an edge of the box, the properties can be presented in any order. Also, you do not need to provide values for each of the sides if you do not want to set padding on one or more side.

---

① Open a Web page that contains an embedded style sheet in your editor.

● The style sheet begins here.

② Add the `background-color` property to an existing rule.

③ Add an appropriate color value and a semicolon.

4 Add a `padding-top` property, a value, and a semicolon.

5 Add a `padding-bottom` property, a value, and a semicolon.

6 Add a `padding-left` property, a value, and a semicolon.

7 Add a `padding-right` property, a value, and a semicolon.

8 Save the document.

9 Open the page in a browser.

● The page opens, showing the padding around the heading.

```
<head>
<title>National Park Terminology</title>
<link rel="shortcut icon" href="images/favicon.png" type="image/png" />
<style type="text/css">
body {
        background: #fff url(images/smbkgnd.jpg) no-repeat bottom right;
    }
h1 {
        font-size: 120%;
        font-family: Arial, Helvetica, sans-serif;
        font-variant: small-caps;
        background-color: #5e7630;
        padding-top: 5px;
        padding-bottom: 5px;
        padding-left: 10px;
        padding-right: 10px;|
    }
```

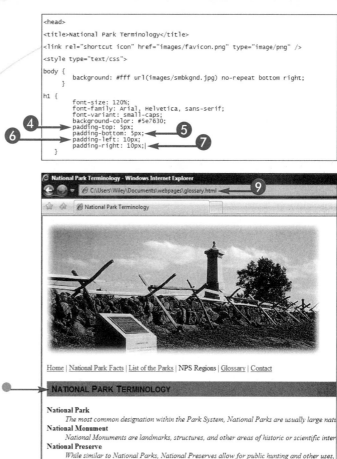

Home | National Park Facts | List of the Parks | NPS Regions | Glossary | Contact

NATIONAL PARK TERMINOLOGY

National Park
    The most common designation within the Park System, National Parks are usually large nati
National Monument
    National Monuments are landmarks, structures, and other areas of historic or scientific inter
National Preserve
    While similar to National Parks, National Preserves allow for public hunting and other uses,

---

Extra

All elements are defined as being either block or inline. Most XHTML elements are block elements, which means that they occupy their own space on the page. When you wrap text in a paragraph tag, for example, that paragraph creates space above and below it, separating itself from other elements on the page. Headings, tables, lists, and horizontal rules are a few other block elements that have been discussed so far.

However, when you wrap an anchor tag around text, it does not cause the line to break as it is an inline element. Inline elements are those that can exist within a larger block of text and do not need to define their own space. In addition to anchors, the `strong` and em elements for making text bold or italic are inline elements.

Thinking logically, this distinction makes sense. You want to be able to set a single word or set of words within a line in a bold or italic typeface or make them a link, so those elements must be inline. On the other hand, a paragraph by definition needs to exist in its own space, and thus must be a block.

Add Borders to Elements on a Page

S urrounding the padding of the box is its border. The border is invisible by default for most elements, but many interesting visual effects can be achieved by manipulating the border. The border essentially defines the interior area of the box: Background colors fill to the outer edge of the border, and background images are positioned relative to it.

Each border in CSS has three distinct properties: `border-color`, `border-width`, and `border-style`. The `border-color` is any valid color value, and the `border-width` is set in any valid unit, although pixels are used most often. The `border-style` is set by keywords: `dotted`, `dashed`, `double`, `groove`, `inset`, `outset`, `ridge`, and `solid`. For those border styles that contain gaps, such as `dotted` and `dashed`, the `background-color` will show through as it fills to the outside edge of the border. Styles that contain shading, including

`groove`, `inset` and `outset`, use browser-determined shades of the `border-color`. The exact distance between gaps in the `dotted` and `dashed` styles and the distance between lines in the `double` style are also determined by the browser.

Two additional styles will effectively remove the border: `none` and `hidden`. For most elements, they will render in exactly the same way. The only exception is with tables, where a value of `hidden` will cause the cells to collapse into one another, eliminating the default `cellspacing`, while a value of `none` will not.

Each side of the box can have its border set individually. Therefore, the top border of the box can be set by `border-top-color`, `border-top-style`, and `border-top-width` properties. The same applies to the other sides, where `top` in the property name is simply replaced with the appropriate side.

Add Borders to Elements on a Page

① Open a Web page that contains an embedded style sheet in your editor.

● The style sheet begins here.

① ──▶

```
index - Notepad
File  Edit  Format  View  Help
<!DOCTYPE html PUBLIC "-//W3C//DTD XHTML 1.0 Transitional//EN" "http://www.w3.

<!--
Title: America's National Parks
Author: Rob Huddleston, rob@robhuddleston.com
Date: 11/4/07
-->

<html xmlns="http://www.w3.org/1999/xhtml">

<head>

<title>America's National Parks</title>

<link rel="shortcut icon" href="images/favicon.png" type="image/png" />

<style type="text/css">

body {
        background: #fff url(images/smbkgnd.jpg) no-repeat bottom right;
      }

h1 {
        font-size: 120%;
        font-family: Arial, Helvetica, sans-serif;
        text-align: center;
        font-variant: small-caps;
        color: #fff;|
        background-color: #5e7630;
      }
```

② Add a `border-bottom-color` property with an appropriate value to an existing declaration.

③ Add a `border-bottom-style` property with an appropriate value.

```
<style type="text/css">

body {
        background: #fff url(images/smbkgnd.jpg) no-repeat bottom right;
      }

h1 {
        font-size: 120%;
        font-family: Arial, Helvetica, sans-serif;
        text-align: center;
        font-variant: small-caps;
        color: #fff;
        background-color: #5e7630;
      }

h2 {
        font-size: 120%;
        font-family: Arial, Helvetica, sans-serif;
        color: #5e7630;
        text-transform: capitalize;
        border-bottom-color: #5e7630;
        border-bottom-style: solid;
      }
```

② ──▶   ③ ◀──

4 Add a `border-bottom-width` property with an appropriate value.

5 Save the page.

```
<style type="text/css">
body {
        background: #fff url(images/smbkgnd.jpg) no-repeat bottom right;
    }
h1 {
        font-size: 120%;
        font-family: Arial, Helvetica, sans-serif;
        text-align: center;
        font-variant: small-caps;
        color: #fff;
        background-color: #5e7630;
    }
h2 {
        font-size: 120%;
        font-family: Arial, Helvetica, sans-serif;
        color: #5e7630;
        text-transform: capitalize;
        border-bottom-color: #5e7630;
        border-bottom-style: solid;
        border-bottom-width: 2px;|
    }
```

4 ➞

6 Open the page in a browser.

● The page opens in the browser, showing the borders below the headings.

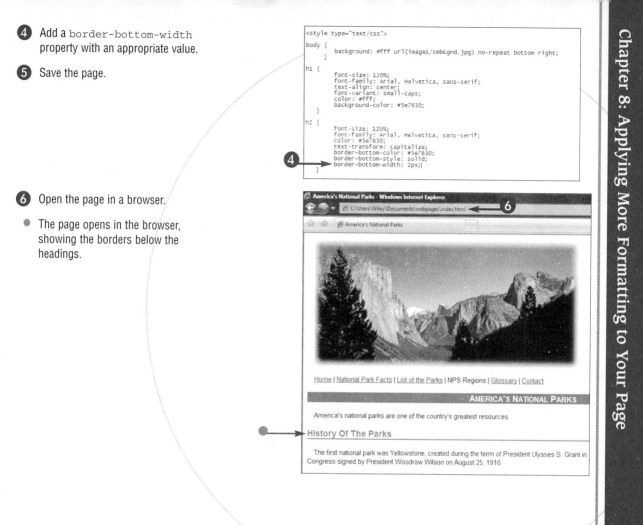

6 ➞

● ➞ History Of The Parks

You can reduce the amount of code needed to set borders by specifying the color, width, and style of each side of the border in one line:

```
h1      {
border-top: 1px solid #369;
border-bottom: 1px solid #369;
border-right: 2px dashed #9cc;
border-left: 2px dashed #9cc;
}
```

Add Margins to Elements on a Page

The final piece of the box model is the margin, which defines the area outside of the box and effectively separates elements from one another on the page. Many new Web designers are frustrated by the space created by default between paragraphs. Prior to the advent of CSS, there was no way to reduce or eliminate this space, but today, it can be controlled with precision using the `margin` property.

Adjacent vertical margins collapse into one another. Therefore, the space between two paragraphs is both the top margin of the lower paragraph, and the bottom margin of the upper paragraph. Simply reducing one without modifying the other will not reduce the space; instead, it is necessary to work with both. Many designers prefer to completely eliminate either the top or

bottom margin of the element by setting it to `0`, freeing them to only adjust the other to control the spacing.

Margins are set for each side of the box using the `margin-top`, `margin-bottom`, `margin-left`, and `margin-right` properties. Like padding, margins can be set using any unit of measurement, although pixels are most often used. Remember that you must always provide a unit of measurement, except when setting the value to `0`.

While it is technically legal to apply top and bottom margins to inline elements, they will have no visual effect. Left and right margins, however, will apply to inline elements and can be useful to offset hyperlinks or other pieces of a line that should have more space before or after them.

Add Margins to Elements on a Page

① Open a Web page that contains an embedded style sheet in your editor.

● The style sheet begins here.

② Add a `margin-top` property with an appropriate value to an existing rule.

③ Add a `margin-bottom` property with an appropriate value.

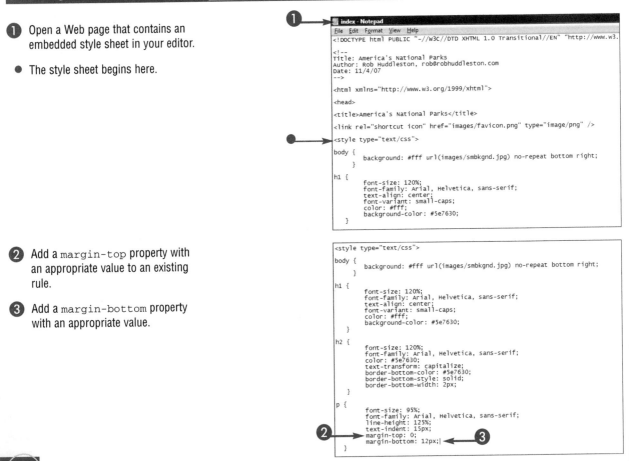

118

4 Add a `margin-left` property with an appropriate value.

5 Add a `margin-right` property with an appropriate value.

6 Save the page.

 7 Open the page in a browser.

● The page opens, showing the revised margins.

```
p {
        font-size: 95%;
        font-family: Arial, Helvetica, sans-serif;
        line-height:125%;
        text-indent: 15px;
        margin-top: 0;
        margin-bottom: 12px;
        margin-left: 20px;|
        margin-right: 20px;
    }

</style>

</head>

<body>
```

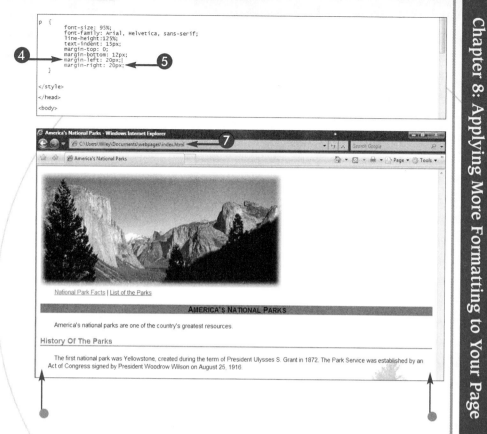

Apply It

You can center content using left and right margin values of `auto`, so long as the element in question also has a width set to a specific length:

```
h1      {
        width: 100%;
        margin-right: auto;
        margin-left: auto;
        }
```

Set the Width and Height of Elements

Most block elements, by default, are set to a width of 100% of their parent element. Therefore, an element that is the direct child of the body will have a width of 100% of the body, which in effect means that it will stretch across the entire browser window. Table cells, on the other hand, are set to a width that is a calculation of the minimum width needed to display the cell's content and the width needed by that cell to make up its part of the width of the table's row.

The CSS `width` property allows designers to override this default setting and specify a width to be used by the element. As with other size-related properties, all of the valid units of measurement are allowed. Most often, designers will use pixel-based measurements to set exact widths, or use percentages to allow the element the

flexibility to expand or collapse based on the width of the browser window.

Element heights are usually exactly as big as they need to be to fit the contents, but CSS does provide for a `height` property to allow more control. However, care should be taken when setting the height of an element, as it can create undesired results. If you use a percentage for the width of an element, the exact height of text within the element will vary depending on the browser's width; however, if you also set a height, you can end up with a large empty space at the bottom of the element's block if the page is being viewed on a much wider screen than you anticipated. Because of these types of issues, many designers prefer to always avoid setting the height on elements.

Set the Width and Height of Elements

1 Open a Web page that contains an embedded style sheet in your editor.

● The style sheet begins here.

2 Add the `width` property to an existing rule.

3 Add a value.

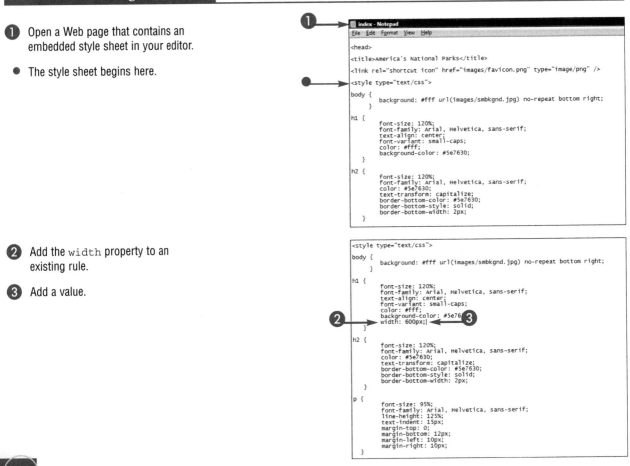

④ Repeat Steps 2 and 3 for any other elements on which you wish to set the width.

⑤ Save the page.

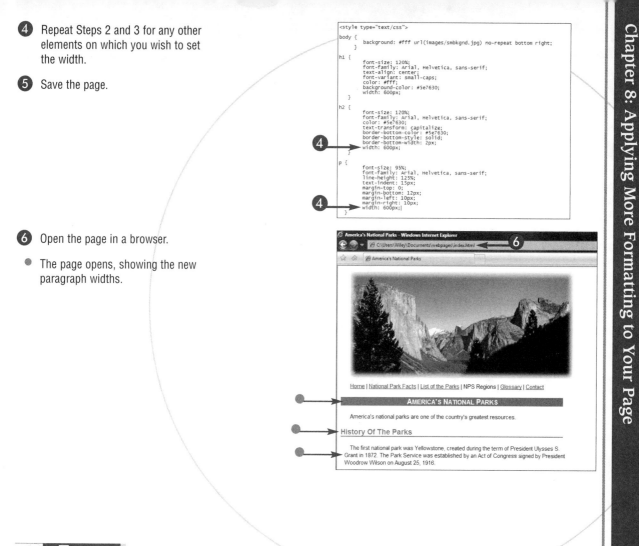

```
<style type="text/css">
body {
        background: #fff url(images/smbkgnd.jpg) no-repeat bottom right;
    }

h1 {
        font-size: 120%;
        font-family: Arial, Helvetica, sans-serif;
        text-align: center;
        font-variant: small-caps;
        color: #fff;
        background-color: #5e7630;
        width: 600px;
    }

h2 {
        font-size: 120%;
        font-family: Arial, Helvetica, sans-serif;
        color: #5e7630;
        text-transform: capitalize;
        border-bottom-color: #5e7630;
        border-bottom-style: solid;
        border-bottom-width: 2px;
        width: 600px;
    }

p {
        font-size: 95%;
        font-family: Arial, Helvetica, sans-serif;
        line-height: 125%;
        text-indent: 15px;
        margin-top: 0;
        margin-bottom: 12px;
        margin-left: 10px;
        margin-right: 10px;
        width: 600px;|
    }
```

⑥ Open the page in a browser.

● The page opens, showing the new paragraph widths.

America's National Parks — Windows Internet Explorer

C:\Users\Wiley\Documents\webpages\index.html ◄ ⑥

America's National Parks

Home | National Park Facts | List of the Parks | NPS Regions | Glossary | Contact

AMERICA'S NATIONAL PARKS

America's national parks are one of the country's greatest resources.

History Of The Parks

The first national park was Yellowstone, created during the term of President Ulysses S. Grant in 1872. The Park Service was established by an Act of Congress signed by President Woodrow Wilson on August 25, 1916.

Extra

According to the CSS specification, the total width of an element is supposed to be calculated by adding together the width of the content, left and right padding, left and right border widths, and left and right margins. Unfortunately, Microsoft took a different approach in their implementation for Internet Explorer, which instead uses only the width of the content. So, while other browsers include the padding, border, and margin values within the width, they are added to the width in Internet Explorer.

Microsoft fixed this issue in Internet Explorer 7, released in 2006. Internet Explorer 6 had a "standards" mode that correctly calculated the width and a default "quirks" mode that did not, but it would only use standards mode on pages with a valid XHTML Strict DOCTYPE. Tantek Çelik, a developer who helped build the rendering engine behind Internet Explorer for the Macintosh, developed the "box model hack," which provides a workaround to the problem. It's an odd combination of properties that essentially confuses Internet Explorer into using the correct width:

```
h1 { width: 400px; voice-family: "\"}\""; voice-family: inherit; width: 300px; }
```

Using CSS Shorthand Properties for the Box Model

Several common CSS properties require a lot of code to implement. Setting margins or padding around all four sides of an element each require four lines of code each, while setting the color, width, and style of all four borders of an element can take twelve each. Therefore, a series of shorthand properties exist to allow you to set related properties together at once.

Whenever you wish to set a value for all four margins on a page, you can use the `margin` shorthand property instead of the individual properties of `margin-top`, `margin-left`, and so on. You can provide one, two, or four values for the property. If you provide one, it will be used for each of the four sides; if you provide two, the first will be used for the top and bottom, and the second for the left and right; four values lets you set the margins individually. Note that if you give four values, they *must* be in the order `top`, `right`, `bottom`, `left`: You work

clockwise around the box. Therefore, `margin-top: 5px; margin-right:10px; margin-bottom: 5px; margin-left: 10px;` could be instead given as `margin: 5px 10px`. The same rules apply to the `padding` shorthand.

Borders have a series of shorthand properties. If you wish to use the same width, style, or color for all four borders, you can use `border-width`, `border-style`, or `border-color` respectively. Note that you can use the same rules as described previously for `margins` or `padding`, proving one, two, or four values for each. You can set the width, style, and color for each side using the `border-top`, `border-bottom`, `border-left`, or `border-right` properties. Here, you provide a value for the `width`, `style`, and `color` as a space-separated list. Because there can be no confusion as to which property each value represents, they can be in any order.

Using CSS Shorthand Properties for the Box Model

1 Open a Web page that contains an embedded style sheet in your editor.

2 Add a `margin` property to an existing declaration.

3 Add two values, separated by a space, to set the margins.

```
<style type="text/css">
body {
        background: #fff url(images/smbkgnd.jpg) no-repeat bottom right;
    }
h1 {
        font-size: 120%;
        font-family: Arial, Helvetica, sans-serif;
        text-align: center;
        font-variant: small-caps;
        color: #fff;
        background-color: #5e7630;
        width: 600px;
    }
h2 {
        font-size: 120%;
        font-family: Arial, Helvetica, sans-serif;
        color: #5e7630;
        text-transform: capitalize;
        border-bottom-color: #5e7630;
        border-bottom-style: solid;
        border-bottom-width: 2px;
        width: 600px;
    }
p {
        font-size: 95%;
        font-family: Arial, Helvetica, sans-serif;
        line-height: 125%;
        text-indent: 15px;
        width: 600px;
        margin: 10px 0;|
    }
```

4 Add a `padding` property.

5 Add a single value to apply equal amounts of padding to all four sides.

```
<style type="text/css">
body {
        background: #fff url(images/smbkgnd.jpg) no-repeat bottom right;
    }
h1 {
        font-size: 120%;
        font-family: Arial, Helvetica, sans-serif;
        text-align: center;
        font-variant: small-caps;
        color: #fff;
        background-color: #5e7630;
        width: 600px;
    }
h2 {
        font-size: 120%;
        font-family: Arial, Helvetica, sans-serif;
        color: #5e7630;
        text-transform: capitalize;
        border-bottom-color: #5e7630;
        border-bottom-style: solid;
        border-bottom-width: 2px;
        width: 600px;
    }
p {
        font-size: 95%;
        font-family: Arial, Helvetica, sans-serif;
        line-height: 125%;
        text-indent: 15px;
        width: 600px;
        margin: 10px 0;
        padding: 0;|
    }
```

6 Add a `border-top` property to an existing declaration.

7 Add values for the color, width, and style.

8 Repeat Steps 6 and 7 for the other sides on which you wish to add a border.

9 Save the page.

10 Open the page in a browser.

● The page opens, showing the border around the main heading.

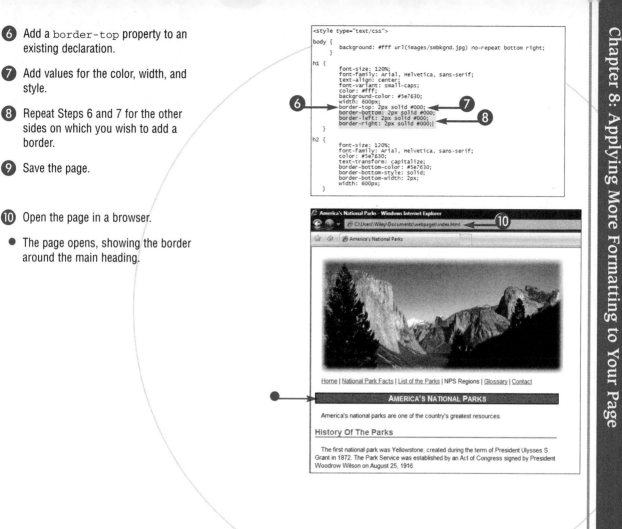

```
<style type="text/css">
body {
        background: #fff url(images/smbkgnd.jpg) no-repeat bottom right;
     }
h1 {
        font-size: 120%;
        font-family: Arial, Helvetica, sans-serif;
        text-align: center;
        font-variant: small-caps;
        color: #fff;
        background-color: #5e7630;
        width: 600px;
        border-top: 2px solid #000;
        border-bottom: 2px solid #000;
        border-left: 2px solid #000;
        border-right: 2px solid #000;
     }
h2 {
        font-size: 120%;
        font-family: Arial, Helvetica, sans-serif;
        color: #5e7630;
        text-transform: capitalize;
        border-bottom-color: #5e7630;
        border-bottom-style: solid;
        border-bottom-width: 2px;
        width: 600px;
     }
```

Home | National Park Facts | List of the Parks | NPS Regions | Glossary | Contact

AMERICA'S NATIONAL PARKS

America's national parks are one of the country's greatest resources.

History Of The Parks

The first national park was Yellowstone, created during the term of President Ulysses S. Grant in 1872. The Park Service was established by an Act of Congress signed by President Woodrow Wilson on August 25, 1916.

Apply It

You can also condense the border properties into a single line using `border`, which takes a `style`, `color`, and `width` property to be applied to all four sides. The exact order in which you present these values is irrelevant. Therefore, the following code, which uses twelve properties to set the border:

```
h1      {
border-top-style: solid; border-top-width:1px; border-top-color: #ccc;
border-bottom-style: solid; border-top-width:1px; border-top-color: #ccc;
border-right-style: solid; border-top-width:1px; border-top-color: #ccc;
border-left-style: solid; border-top-width:1px; border-top-color: #ccc;
}
```

can be written as:

```
h1      {
border: solid 1px #ccc;
}
```

Style
Links

Hyperlinks present a unique design challenge. It is absolutely necessary that hyperlinks provided within a block of text, such as a paragraph, be obviously different from the surrounding text. Without this difference, the user will have no way of knowing that a hyperlink is even present.

In addition to the need to maintain a distinct visual appearance for links, hyperlinks also exist is different "states": when a page is first visited, when the link has already been clicked, when it is being moused over, and when it is being clicked. In CSS, each of these is available through a special selector known as a *pseudo-class*. Four primary pseudo-classes exist for styling links, representing in order of the "states" noted previously: `link`, `visited`, `hover`, and `active`. The syntax for using these pseudo-classes is to provide the element in question, a colon, and the pseudo-class, as in `a:link`,

`a:visited`, `a:hover`, and `a:active`. Note that the specification provides for other elements to support the pseudo-classes, in particular hover, but many browsers do not in practice recognize them when used with anything other than the anchor element.

Any property that is valid for the content of the link can be used with the pseudo-classes. One property that is particularly useful in styling links is `text-decoration`. The possible values are `none`, `underline`, `overline`, and `line-through`. By far the two most commonly used are `none`, which hides the default underline on the links, and `underline`, which brings it back. A popular technique is to set `text-decoration:none` for `a:link` and `a:visited`, and then `text-decoration: underline` for `a:hover`, causing the underline to only appear when the user mouses over the link.

Style Links

1 Open a Web page that contains an embedded style sheet in your editor.

● The style sheet begins here.

2 Add an `a:link` pseudo-class selector and an opening curly brace.

3 Set properties for the link.

4 Add the closing curly brace.

5 Add an `a:visited` pseudo-class selector and an opening curly brace.

6 Set properties for the link.

7 Add the closing curly brace.

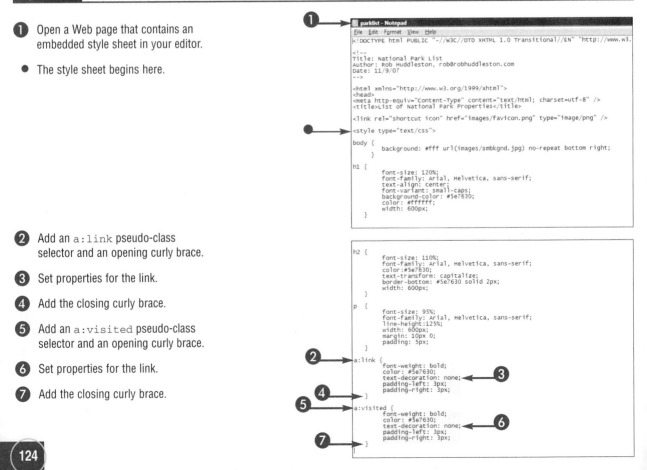

8. Add an `a:hover` pseudo-class selector and an opening curly brace.

9. Set properties for the link.

10. Add the closing curly brace.

11. Add an `a:active` pseudo-class selector and an opening curly brace.

12. Set properties for the link.

13. Add the closing curly brace.

14. Save the page.

15. Open the page in a browser.

● The page opens, showing the link styles. When you mouse over a link, the hover style will appear.

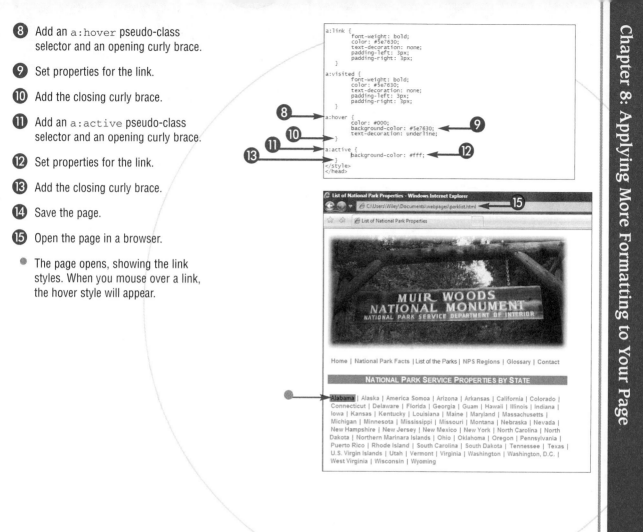

You do not need to use all four pseudo-classes together. If, for example, you wish to have a different color for the default state of the link and for visited links, but not have them change when moused over, you can simply style `a:link` and `a:visited`. However, it must be noted that should you choose to use more than one of the pseudo-classes, they *must* be given in the order `link`, `visited`, `hover`, `active`. The properties inherit from one pseudo-class to the next, but the inheritance will not work properly if they are given in any other order. A simple mnemonic device to help remember the order is "LoVe-HAte." It is also valid, and at times helpful, to style the `a` element directly, without the pseudo-classes. If you do this, be sure to list it before any pseudo-class selectors, for the reason stated previously.

When applying effects on hover, you should take care to avoid properties that may change the size of text, such as `font-size`, `font-family`, `font-weight`, and `font-style`, as doing so may force the browser to change how the text wraps on the page, causing a kind of flickering effect.

Style Tables

C SS styling relies on applying rules to elements on the page. Due to the number of elements involved in rendering tables, designers are given a rich set of possibilities when styling tables. With some creativity, tables can become some of the most visually exciting elements on a page.

Perhaps the most important thing to keep in mind when styling tables is inheritance. Every table is made up of, at a minimum, a `table`, `tr`, and `td` element. As the `tr` must by definition be nested within the `table`, most properties set on the latter will apply to the former. The same applies to the `td`, although it will inherit not only from the `table`, but also from the `tr`. Add in `thead`, `tfoot`, and `tbody` elements, and the fact that most, but not all properties will inherit, and the potential for

inheritance can become quite confusing. Practice and careful testing of the page will reveal which properties are being inherited and which are not and how they work together.

At a minimum, you will most likely want to set borders on the table. Note that borders are a property that does not inherit to the children elements in a table, so setting a border on the table element itself will draw the border only around the outside of the table. You must set borders on the cells themselves — the `th` and `td` elements — to draw the borders around the cells.

You can also achieve nice visual effects by setting background colors or images on the table itself or on cells, and controlling the appearance of the fonts for the text within the table.

Style Tables

1. Open a Web page that contains an embedded style sheet and a table in your editor.

2. Add a `table` element selector and an opening curly brace.

3. Add a `border` property with appropriate values for width, color and style.

4. Add a closing curly brace.

5. Add a `th` element selector and an opening curly brace.

6. Add a `background-color` property with an appropriate value.

7. Add a `border` property with appropriate values for color, width and style.

8. Add a closing curly brace.

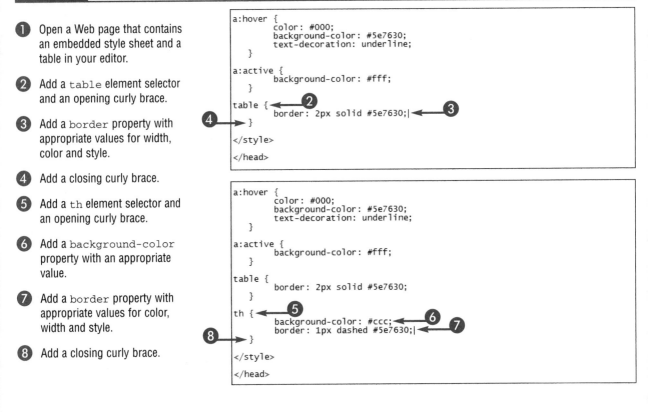

```
a:hover {
        color: #000;
        background-color: #5e7630;
        text-decoration: underline;
    }
a:active {
        background-color: #fff;
    }
table {
        border: 2px solid #5e7630;|
    }
</style>
</head>
```

```
a:hover {
        color: #000;
        background-color: #5e7630;
        text-decoration: underline;
    }
a:active {
        background-color: #fff;
    }
table {
        border: 2px solid #5e7630;
    }
th {
        background-color: #ccc;
        border: 1px dashed #5e7630;|
    }
</style>
</head>
```

⑨ Add a `td` element selector and an opening curly brace.

⑩ Add a `border` property with appropriate values for color, width and style.

⑪ Add a closing curly brace.

⑫ Save the page.

⑬ Open the page in a browser.

● The page opens, showing the table.

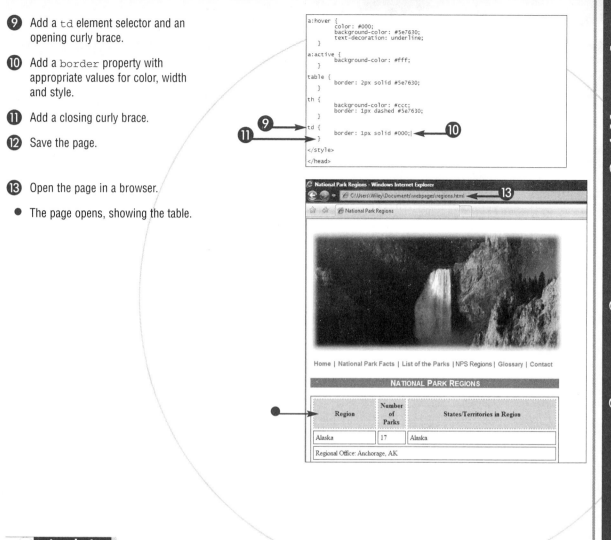

```
a:hover {
        color: #000;
        background-color: #5e7630;
        text-decoration: underline;
    }
a:active {
        background-color: #fff;
    }
table {
        border: 2px solid #5e7630;
    }
th {

        background-color: #ccc;
        border: 1px dashed #5e7630;
    }
td {

        border: 1px solid #000;|
    }
</style>
</head>
```

Apply It

You can use the `border-collapse` property to determine whether adjacent cell borders are drawn as separate lines with space in-between or not. The `border-collapse` property takes as its value either `collapse` or `separate`, with the latter being the default. It can only be used on the table element, as it must logically apply to the entire table.

```
table {
      border: 1px solid #ccc;
      border-collapse: collapse;
}
td {
      border: 1px solid #333;
}
```

Replace the Bullets on a List

Lists in XHTML provide many styling options as well. CSS provides several list styling properties. One, `list-style-type`, allows you to change the default appearance of the bullet, while a another, `list-style-image`, lets you replace the bullet with a custom image.

Possible values for the `list-style-type` property are: `none`, `disc`, `circle`, `square`, `decimal`, `decimal-leading-zero`, `lower-roman`, `upper-roman`, `lower-alpha`, `upper-alpha`, `lower-greek`, `lower-latin`, `upper-latin`, `hebrew`, `armenian`, `georgian`, `cjk-ideographic`, `hiragana`, `katakana`, `hiragana-iroha`, and `katakana-iroh`. Clearly, most of these values are more logically applied to ordered lists rather than unordered ones. The logical unordered values — `none`, `disc`, `circle`, and `square` — are the most commonly used. The default is `disc`. Of the options that apply most logically to ordered lists, `decimal`, `decimal-leading-zero`, `lower-roman`, and `upper-roman` are most

common. It should be noted that while it does not make sense logically to apply a number-based item to an unordered list, that behavior is technically allowed.

You can also create your own image to use in place of the bullets or numbers on a list by applying the `list-style-image` property, which takes a path to an image as its value. While any image can be used, it is generally preferable if the image is fairly small, as the list item's line height will have to increase to accommodate a large image. There is no way to specify that the browser should attempt to resize the image. An image being inherited by a list item from a parent list, as can happen with nested lists, can be overridden by setting `list-style-image` to `none`.

While the `list-style-image` setting will override any setting from `list-style-type`, many designers choose to specify both. This way, the desired type will display as a fallback in case the image fails to display for some reason.

Replace the Bullets on a List

1 Open a Web page that contains an embedded style sheet and a list in your editor.

2 Add a `ul` element selector and an opening curly brace.

3 Add the `list-style-type` property.

4 Add an appropriate value.

5 Add the closing curly brace.

6 Save the page.

7 Open the page in a browser.

● The page opens, showing the square bullets.

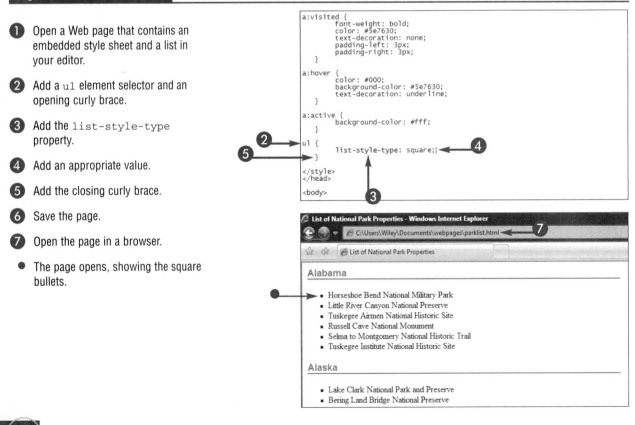

8 Return to your editor.

9 Add a `list-style-image` property.

10 Add a `url`, a parenthesis, a path to an image, and a closing parenthesis.

11 Save the page.

```
a:visited {
        font-weight: bold;
        color: #5e7630;
        text-decoration: none;
        padding-left: 3px;
        padding-right: 3px;
    }

a:hover {
        color: #000;
        background-color: #5e7630;
        text-decoration: underline;
    }

a:active {
        background-color: #fff;
    }

ul {
        list-style-type: square;
        list-style-image: url(images/treebullet.gif);|
    }

</style>
</head>

<body>
```

12 Open the page in a browser.

● The page opens, showing an image used as a bullet.

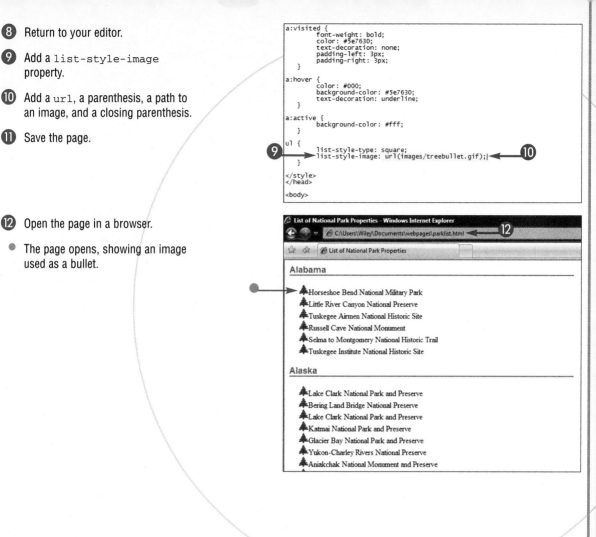

Alabama

🌲Horseshoe Bend National Military Park
🌲Little River Canyon National Preserve
🌲Tuskegee Airmen National Historic Site
🌲Russell Cave National Monument
🌲Selma to Montgomery National Historic Trail
🌲Tuskegee Institute National Historic Site

Alaska

🌲Lake Clark National Park and Preserve
🌲Bering Land Bridge National Preserve
🌲Lake Clark National Park and Preserve
🌲Katmai National Park and Preserve
🌲Glacier Bay National Park and Preserve
🌲Yukon-Charley Rivers National Preserve
🌲Aniakchak National Monument and Preserve

Extra

Ordered lists always increment the counter numerically, even when the `list-style-type` is set to an alphabetic type. The browser takes the next highest number for the list and converts it to the equivalent value in the alphabet being used. In other words, if the next item of the list is number 5, and the type is set to `lower-alpha`, the browser will use e; if it set to `lower-greek`, it uses epsilon (ε).

The CSS specification does not provide for the ability for the counting to continue beyond the letters in the desired alphabet, so there is, for example, no definition for what follows z. Modern browsers seem to agree that the item following z when using `lower-alpha` is aa, but as this is undocumented there is no guarantee for consistent display.

Technically, the list counter should not increment for unordered lists given ordered types, but in practice this will occur. If the list is defined with a counting type that the browser does not support, it will default to decimal.

Control the Indentation of Lists

By default, both unordered and ordered lists indent the individual items. As the `li` element, used by both to define the items, is a block element in XHTML, controlling the amount of indentation should be simple by setting either the padding or margin of the items.

There is no agreement amongst browser developers as to why, exactly, list items indent. The bullets or numbers for the list actually exist *outside* the box for the list item itself. This means that the bullet or number will actually appear outside any borders applied to list items as well, except on Internet Explorer, which chooses to draw the border to include the item. Browser developers, essentially given the choice between applying the indentation through a left `margin` of the `ul` or `ol`, or left `padding`, unfortunately choose both; Internet Explorer and Opera use `margin`, while all Gecko-based browsers

such as Firefox use `padding`. For this reason, it is necessary to set both `margin-left` and `padding-left` to the same value to achieve consistency across browsers. Note that both of these are properties of the list itself, not the individual items, and thus need to be set at the `ul` or `ol` level.

The other behavior regarding indentation that is fortunately consistent is whether or not the lists use a hanging indent. That is, when a list item is long enough to wrap to more than one line, by default the additional lines will align with the top item, and not the bullet or number. The `list-style-position` property can change this by setting it to inside. This actually sets the number or bullet as an inline element within the list item. As this property will inherit to nested lists, you may need to override it later by setting `list-style-position` back to the default value of `outside`.

Control the Indentation of Lists

① Open a Web page that contains an embedded style sheet and a list in your editor.

● The `ul` selector begins the list in this example.

② Add the `margin-left: 10px;` declaration to an existing `ul` declaration.

③ Add `padding-left: 10px;` to the declaration.

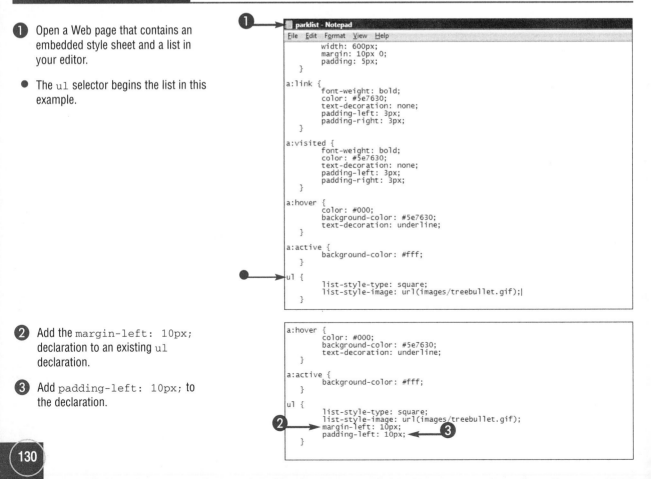

130

4 Add a `list-style-position: inside;` property.

5 Save the page.

```
a:hover {
        color: #000;
        background-color: #5e7630;
        text-decoration: underline;
}

a:active {
        background-color: #fff;
}

ul {

        list-style-type: square;
        list-style-image: url(images/treebullet.gif);
        margin-left: 10px;
        padding-left: 10px;
        list-style-position: inside;|
}
```

4 →

6 Open the page in a browser.

● The page opens, showing the indented text.

List of National Park Properties - Windows Internet Explorer

C:\Users\Wiley\Documents\webpages\parklist.html ← **6**

List of National Park Properties

Whiskeytown National Recreation Area
Redwood National and State Parks
John Muir National Historic Site
AIDS Memorial Grove National Memorial
Lava Beds National Monument
Santa Monica Mountains National Recreation Area
Kings Canyon National Park
Fort Point National Historic Site
Muir Woods National Monument
Devils Postpile National Monument
Mojave National Preserve
Sequoia National Park
Rosie the Riveter/World War II Home Front National Historical Park
Cabrillo National Monument
Joshua Tree National Park
Golden Gate National Recreation Area
→ Alcatraz Island
Presidio of San Francisco
San Francisco Maritime National Historical Park

Apply It

You can set the three list style properties at once using the `list-style` shorthand. Therefore, instead of writing three separate lines to set the type, image, and position of a list:

```
ul      {
        list-style-type: square;
        list-style-image: url(images/smbullet.jpg);
        list-style-position: inside;
}
```

you could instead combine them as a single line:

```
ul      {
        list-style: square url(images/smbullet.jpg) inside;
        }
```

Because there is no possibility for confusing the property's values, they can be presented in any order. All three do not need to be present, so you could use `list-style` to just set the image if you wish, but be aware that doing so sets the position to its default of `outside` and the type to its default of `disc`, even for ordered lists.

Customize Cursors

As you move your mouse around a page, the appearance of the mouse cursor changes to give you a visual idea of the actions you can perform. Normally, the cursor is an arrow, but the most obvious indication of change is the appearance of a hand with a pointer finger when you mouse over a link. Even if the link is not underlined, most users will recognize that they can click on the item if they see the pointer finger. Less noticeable but nonetheless important is the I-beam cursor that appears when you mouse over selectable text or over a form field.

Using CSS, it is possible to provide your own set of cursors. Several additional cursors are defined in the language, such as a `help` cursor that shows a large question mark next to the arrow. You may also create your own cursors to use that fit with the overall branding of the site.

The CSS `cursor` property allows you to define which cursor should be used. Possible values are a `url` to your own image; `auto` and `default`, which let the browser decide; `crosshair`, which looks like a large plus sign; `pointer`, the hand normally used on hyperlinks; `move`, usually represented by an cross with four arrow heads; `e-resize`, `ne-resize`, `nw-resize`, `n-resize`, `se-resize`, `sw-resize`, `s-resize`, and `w-resize`, which are usually two-way arrows pointing in the appropriate direction on a compass; `text`, the I-beam cursor; `wait`, usually an hourglass; and `help`.

You should at all times avoid using a cursor property that will confuse your user. Never, for example, use a value of `pointer` on something that is not clickable, or create your own custom cursor that does not have an obvious relation to its purpose on the page.

You may provide a space-separated list so that the browser has an alternative cursor to use in case the one provided is not supported.

Customize Cursors

1. Open a Web page that contains an embedded style sheet in your editor.

● The style sheet begins here.

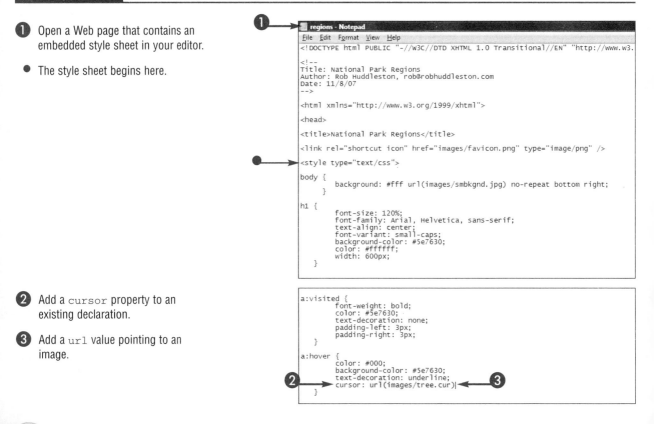

2. Add a `cursor` property to an existing declaration.

3. Add a `url` value pointing to an image.

④ Add a second value to use in case the browser does not support the custom cursor.

⑤ Save the page.

⑥ Open the page in a browser.

⑦ Mouse over the element to which you applied the cursor style.

The custom cursor appears.

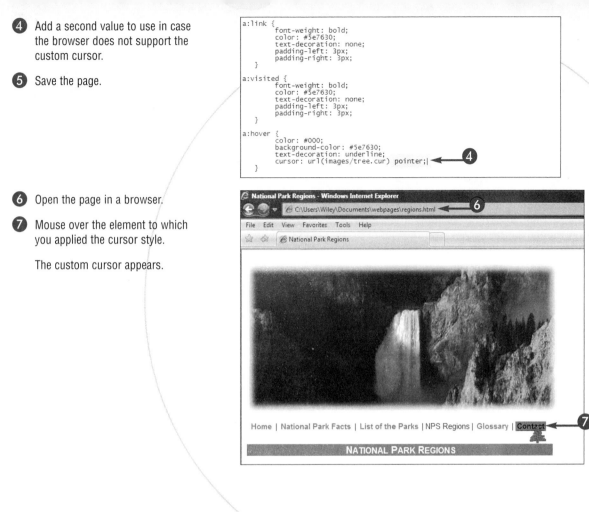

```
a:link {
        font-weight: bold;
        color: #5e7630;
        text-decoration: none;
        padding-left: 3px;
        padding-right: 3px;
    }

a:visited {
        font-weight: bold;
        color: #5e7630;
        text-decoration: none;
        padding-left: 3px;
        padding-right: 3px;
    }

a:hover {
        color: #000;
        background-color: #5e7630;
        text-decoration: underline;
        cursor: url(images/tree.cur) pointer;|
    }
```

Extra

Browser support for custom cursors is far from satisfactory. Some browsers let you use almost any image file type, while others, in particular Internet Explorer, require that the cursor be of a file type .cur, which requires special cursor-creating software. You can find many freeware cursor creation programs through a search engine.

In addition to the standardized values listed in the previous text, many browser-specific values exist for the cursor property. Early versions of Internet Explorer used hand instead of pointer. Internet Explorer as of version 6 will also support progress, a combination of the normal arrow and an hourglass; all-scroll, which is a modification of the move cursor that shows the heads of the arrows but not the lines of the cross; col-resize, two separated bars with arrows pointing left and right; and row-resize, the same cursor as col-resize rotated ninety degrees. It also supports no-drop, a pointer hand with a "no" symbol (⊘) and the closely-related not-allowed, which is just the "no" symbol, and vertical-text, the normal text cursor rotated ninety degrees.

Apply Styles to More than One Element at a Time

Often, you will have several elements to which you want to apply the same style. Writing separate declarations for these elements is not only needlessly redundant, but it also makes updating the styles difficult. For example, say you wished to apply a text color to paragraphs and first- and second-level headings. It would work to write three separate declarations, setting the color in each, but if you later decided you wanted a different color, you would need to change all three to retain consistency.

To solve this issue, CSS allows you to create declarations that contain multiple selectors. So long as you plan to apply the exact same style rules to each of the selectors, you can group the rules into a single declaration by

providing a comma-separated list of the elements to which you wish to apply the rule; for example:

```
p, h1, h2 { color: #f66; }
```

It is legal in CSS to have multiple declarations that affect a single element, so some designers choose to group as many rules into single declarations as they can, and then have additional declarations to apply element-specific rules. For example, you may have a group declaration that applies the same color and font family to paragraphs, headings, and table cells, and then another group selector that applies the same font size to the paragraphs and cells, while using individual declarations to set unique font sizes for each of the headings.

Apply Styles to More than One Element at a Time

① Open a Web page that contains an embedded style sheet in your editor.

● The style sheet begins here.

② Add a group element selector by typing a comma-separated list of elements and the opening curly brace.

③ Add the `font-family` property.

④ Add an appropriate list of fonts and a semicolon.

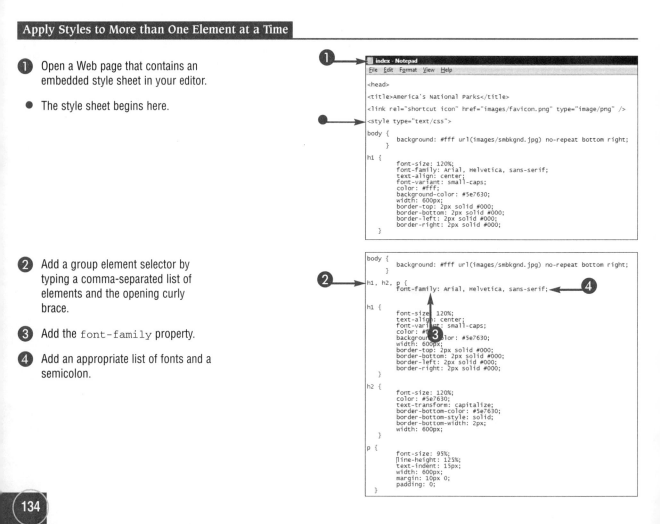

⑤ Add a `width` property.

⑥ Add an appropriate value.

⑦ Add the closing curly brace.

⑧ Save the document.

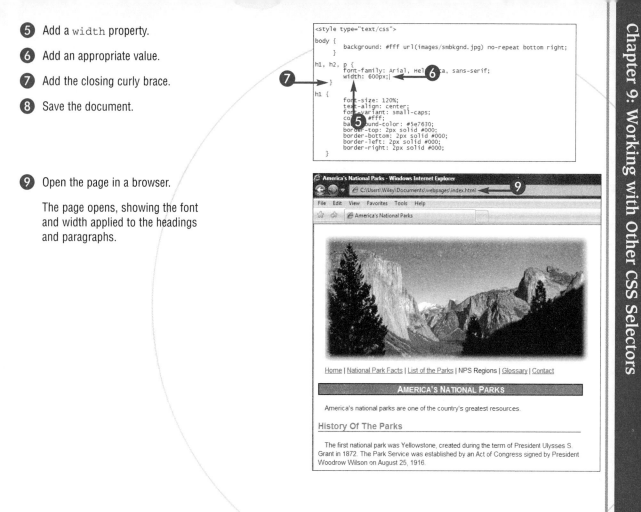

⑨ Open the page in a browser.

The page opens, showing the font and width applied to the headings and paragraphs.

Extra

Be careful when using shorthand properties with group selectors. You need to keep in mind that undeclared properties within the shorthands are not ignored, but are instead reset to their defaults. Consider an example where you use a group selector to set the `color` and `font-family` of several elements:

```
p, h1, h2, td, th { color: #c3F; font-family: Arial, Helvetica, sans-serif; }
```

Then, you use the `font` shorthand in an individual rule for the paragraph to only set the `font-size` and `line-height`:

```
p { font: 90%/1.4 em; }
```

You may not end up with the desired `font-family` in this case, as according to the CSS specification the `font` shorthand should reset undeclared properties, such as `font-family`, to their default, which on most browsers is Times New Roman. The good news here is that many browsers will ignore the specification and use the `font-family` set in the group selector, but you cannot be certain that this will always occur.

CSS applies its styles to text by altering the appearance of the nearest element containing the text. For most work on your page, you can simply style whatever element already exists, such as the paragraph. However, there will be times when you need to style a group of words or letters within a bigger block, and in particular style a portion of text that has no other XHTML element around it. Take, for example, the following piece of code:

```
<p>America's National Parks are
administered by the National Park Service,
a division of the Department of the
Interior.</p>
```

What if you wanted to make the words "National Park Service" stand out on the page by applying a bold or italic typeface to them? In this case, it would not be appropriate to use the XHTML strong or em elements, as you are applying the type face for purely aesthetic reasons, and not for emphasis, so you need to apply a CSS rule to the text. The problem is that those words are not wrapped in an element, and applying the rule to the p would, of course, render the entire paragraph in bold or italic.

The span element was added to XHTML to solve this issue. Unlike most other elements, span does not have any default formatting properties, so simply adding a span to your page will not change its appearance in the browser. It truly exists solely to provide you with an inline element to which you can apply styles.

Using the Span Element

1 Open a Web page that contains an embedded style sheet in your editor.

2 In the body of the document, wrap a span tag around the text you wish to format.

```
hr {
        width: 600px;
        text-align: left;
    }
</style>

</head>

<body>

<p><img src="images/yosemitevalley.jpg" alt="Yosemite Valley" /></p>

<p><a href="index.html" title="Home Page">Home</a> | <a href="facts.html"
Facts</a> | <a href="parklist.html" title="List of the National Parks">Lis
href="glossary.html" title="Glossary of Park Service Terms">Glossary</a> |
Page">Contact</a></p>

<h1>America's National Parks</h1>

<p>America's national parks are one of the country's greatest resources.</

<h2>History of the Parks</h2>

<p>The first national park was <span>Yellowstone</span>, created during th
Park Service
was established by an Act of Congress signed by President Woodrow Wilson o

<hr />

<h2>Headquarters</h2>

<p>The national headquarters of the US National Park Service is located at
```

3 In the style sheet, add a span element selector and an opening curly brace.

```
hr {
        width: 600px;
        text-align: left;
    }
span {

</style>

</head>

<body>

<p><img src="images/yosemitevalley.jpg" alt="Yosemite Valley" /></p>

<p><a href="index.html" title="Home Page">Home</a> | <a href="facts.html"
Facts</a> | <a href="parklist.html" title="List of the National Parks">Lis
href="glossary.html" title="Glossary of Park Service Terms">Glossary</a> |
Page">Contact</a></p>

<h1>America's National Parks</h1>

<p>America's national parks are one of the country's greatest resources.</

<h2>History of the Parks</h2>

<p>The first national park was <span>Yellowstone</span>, created during th
Park Service was established by an Act of Congress signed by President Woo
```

④ Add style rules you wish to apply to the span.

⑤ Add the closing curly brace.

⑥ Save the document.

⑦ Open the page in a browser.

● The page opens, showing the changes.

In this example, the word *Yellowstone* is formatted in bold, green type.

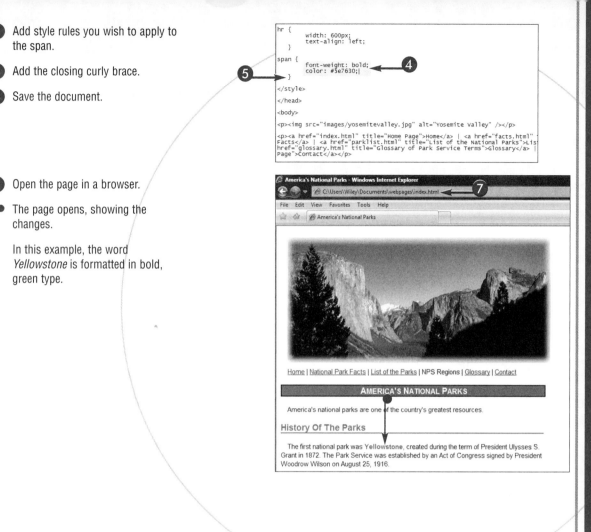

Structure the Page with the Div Element

Most Web pages can be divided into logical sections. At or near the top, there is often a banner with the logo and primary navigation. Below that, there may be one or more columns of content and secondary navigation. At the bottom of the page, you will generally find a footer with copyright notices, addresses, and the like. While each of these sections needs to be coded with the appropriate elements, you also need to define the section itself.

The div element exists in XHTML to allow you to define these sections. Like the span element, div does not have any default formatting properties, and exists to allow you to logically group other elements into sections and then apply styles accordingly. The difference between div and span is that the latter is an inline element, while the former is a block element, so it creates its own space; that is, content wrapped in a div will exist on its own line, separate from other content.

The div is designed to be a generic structural element, used when no other element makes sense. In the previous examples, there is a banner section containing an image for a logo and a set of navigational links. Together, these do not represent a paragraph, nor are they a heading on the page, a list, or a table. However, they do represent a logical part of the structure of the page — one of its sections. This is the purpose of the div: providing a structural element whose logic to the page is determined by the designer.

Structure the Page with the Div Element

① Open a Web page that contains an embedded style sheet in your editor.

② Immediately following the body element's opening tag, add a div element's opening tag.

③ Immediately before the closing body tag, close the div tag.

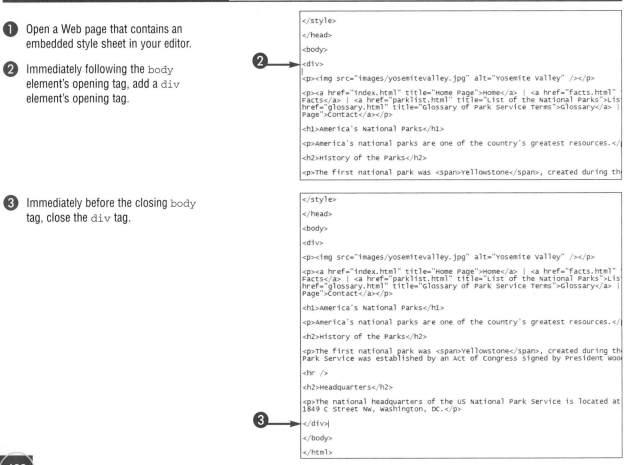

138

④ In the style sheet, add a `div` selector and an opening curly brace.

⑤ Add a `width` property.

⑥ Set the value of the width.

⑦ Add `margin-left: auto;`.

⑧ Add `margin-right:auto;`.

⑨ Add the closing curly brace.

⑩ Save the document.

⑪ Open the page in a browser.

The page opens, showing the changes.

In this example, the content within the `div` is centered in the browser window.

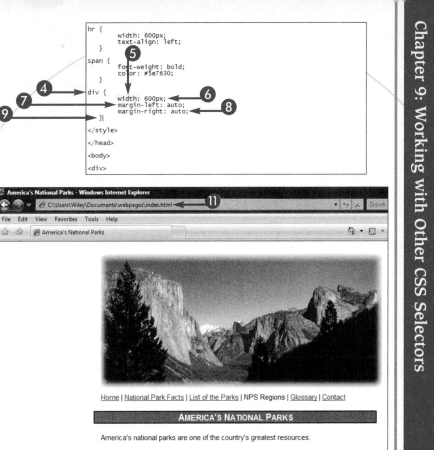

Extra

You can contain any other elements within a `div`. While it is not legal to nest a paragraph within a heading or another paragraph, both can be wrapped within a `div`. In fact, it is not only legal but also it is fairly common to nest `div` elements within other `div` elements. As its primary purpose is to create sections of the page, it only makes sense that any other elements can appear within it.

The name `div` is derived from division: In the overly technical specifications, content sections are thought of as divisions of the page.

The `div` element was actually introduced in HTML 3.2, where its most common use was centering content by applying the `align="center"` attribute. Today, the `align` attribute has been deprecated, so centered content should be applied through the appropriate CSS property, as shown previously.

Like `span`, `div` is often overused. It should only be applied in those cases where no other element would work logically. Do not use it and CSS in place of the header elements, paragraphs, or, as is seen too often, proper list markup.

Control Styles with Classes

So far, all of the styling you have seen has been done at the element level. Most style sheets will begin with a section of element-level declarations to set some basic defaults for the page, but this will only take you so far. Fairly quickly, you will discover the need for more control over exactly when and how your styles apply.

Take as an example a large table. To enhance the readability of the table, you may want to alternate the background color of every other row. Table rows are defined using the `tr` element, but in this case, it is necessary to apply the color to only some of the rows. To this end, CSS and XHTML define a class selector.

You need two things to use classes on your page. Your

CSS will declare styles using a class selector. However, the class selector is generic. Unlike element selectors, the browser will not automatically know to what it should apply a style declared with a class. Therefore, you also need to add a `class` attribute to the XHTML to associate that particular instance of an element with the style.

Classes are defined in the CSS by providing a logical name for the class, preceded by a period, as in this example:

```
.firstrow { background-color: #ccc; }
```

When applied in the XHTML through the attribute, you drop the period from the name:

```
<tr class="firstrow">
```

Control Styles with Classes

① Open a Web page that contains an embedded style sheet in your editor.

② Add a class selector and an opening curly brace.

Note: *Remember that class names need to begin with a period.*

③ Add the rules to format the class.

④ Add the closing curly brace.

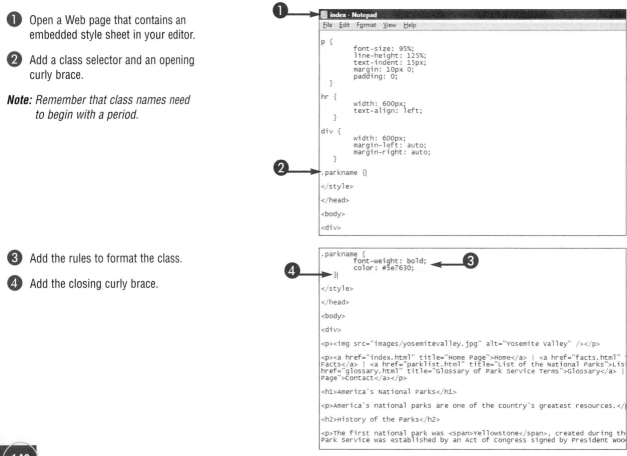

⑤ In the XHTML, add a `class` attribute to an existing element's opening tag.

⑥ Set the value of the attribute to the class you defined in the CSS.

Note: Do not include the period as part of the class name.

⑦ Save the document.

⑧ Open the page in a browser.

● The page opens, showing the changes.

In this example, the word *Yellowstone* is formatted in bold, green type.

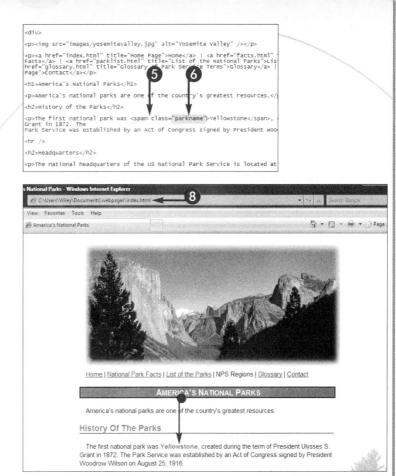

Extra

According to the specification, any XHTML element that causes content to be rendered to the screen can take a `class` attribute. In real terms, this means that any element that can legally exist within the body of the document, including `body` itself, can take class.

Web standards guru Jeffrey Zeldman cautions against something he refers to as "classitis." This is the tendency of new designers to begin using classes almost exclusively as a way to apply styles. It is unfortunately not uncommon to see situations where designers forget that they can use element selectors and instead apply a class to a heading element, or even go so far as to apply a class to every single paragraph or table cell on the page. While the class selector is a powerful tool, you should only use it where necessary. Anytime you are applying the same class to multiple consecutive elements, you should pause and see if there is a way that the style could be applied without the class.

Style Specific Elements with IDs

In defining sections of your page with the `div` element, you quickly encounter a logical conundrum. If each section is to be marked up with the same element — `div` — how can those sections have different styles? If you want one section to have a different background color or image, font properties, padding or margin, or any other style from another section, it will obviously not work to style the `div` element directly. Instead, you need some mechanism to apply styles to individual elements on the page.

The solution to this problem is the ID selector. Like class, the ID selector is generic, so while its styles are declared in the style sheet, it also needs to be referenced in the XHTML, this time by adding an `id` attribute to an

element's opening tag. Like the `class` attribute, the `id` attribute can be used on any element that can legally appear with the `body`, including `body`.

Whereas class selectors are defined in the CSS by a name beginning with a period, IDs are defined by names beginning with a pound sign (#). Both of these designations are designed to avoid confusion with element selectors. It is actually possible to have a class called, for example, "table," or an ID called "table," as the class would be in the CSS as `.table`, and the ID as `#table`, and the regular element selector would simply be `table`. For the sake of clarity and your own sanity, you should avoid this practice, but it is legal.

Style Specific Elements with IDs

① Open a Web page that contains an embedded style sheet in your editor.

② Add an ID selector and an opening curly brace.

Note: *Remember that ID names need to begin with a period.*

③ Add rules to format the ID.

④ Add a closing curly brace.

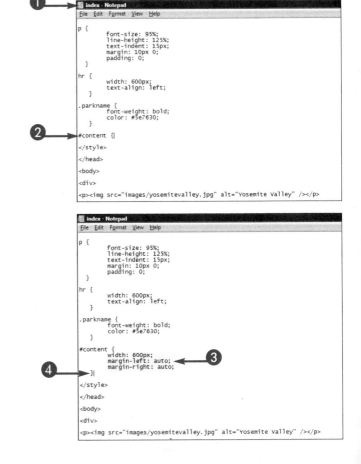

142

⑤ In the XHTML, add an `id` attribute to an existing element's opening tag.

⑥ Set the value of the attribute to the ID you defined in the CSS.

Note: *Do not include the pound sign as part of the ID name.*

⑦ Save the document.

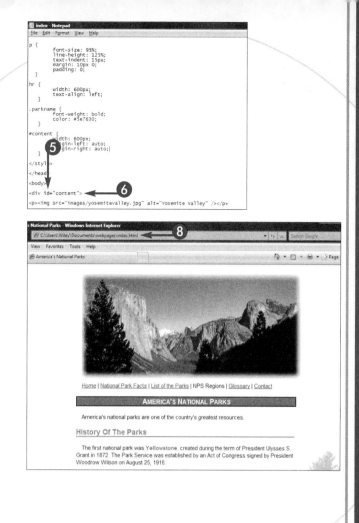

⑧ Open the page in a browser.

The page opens, showing the content centered in the browser window.

There is an understandable amount of confusion amongst beginners as to when it is best to use an ID versus a class. The simple difference between the two is that while a class can be used repeatedly on a page, an ID must only be used once per page. Therefore, it is appropriate to use an ID on the `div` element that is marking up the main content on the page, as there will only be one main content section. In contrast, you must use a class to set up alternating row colors on a table, as they are by definition going to be used more than once.

IDs are an incredibly powerful tool. While they are being presented here as a way to apply styles to specific elements, they actually give you much more functionality. An element with an ID can be the target of a piece of JavaScript that manipulates the element or its contents in some way. The ID attribute can be used as the target of an internal link, replacing anchor tags with `name` attributes. Finally, if you make your IDs clear and logical, they can serve as a sort of "self documentation" within the document. For example, you do not necessarily need to add a comment before a block stating that a block of code will contain the main content if the opening tag of the block has an ID of, say, "maincontent."

Apply Styles with Contextual Selectors

Most of your styles will need to target specific elements within the page. While you will have a certain amount of generic settings, such as applying a `font-family` to the `body`, most of your work will be along the lines of saying, "I need this specific paragraph to be this color, different from the rest of the paragraphs on the page." You have already seen that you can achieve this through the use of ID or class selectors, but there are times when this can become needlessly cumbersome. For example, if you have several tables within a section of your page that you wish to style, you might think it necessary to add a class to each table.

Fortunately, neither of these is necessary, as CSS provides a method by which you can reference an

element based on its context, or where it appears in relation to other elements on the page. In the previous example, you can say that the tables and cells in question are already uniquely identified, assuming that they exist within some other element, most likely a `div`, that has its own ID. Therefore, you can reference the table based on its location within the ID.

For the sake of example, suppose that you have two tables within a `div` with `id` of `sidebar`. A CSS contextual selector for the table might look like `#sidebar table`, while the cells can be selected with `#sidebar td`. Note here that you use a space-separated list for the selectors, which are read right to left: select the table or cells within the element of `id sidebar`.

Apply Styles with Contextual Selectors

① Open a Web page that contains an embedded style sheet in your editor.

② Add a contextual selector and an opening curly brace.

③ Add a rule to the declaration.

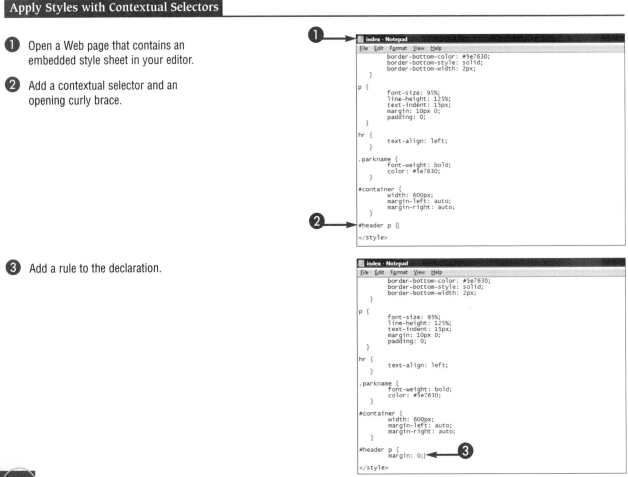

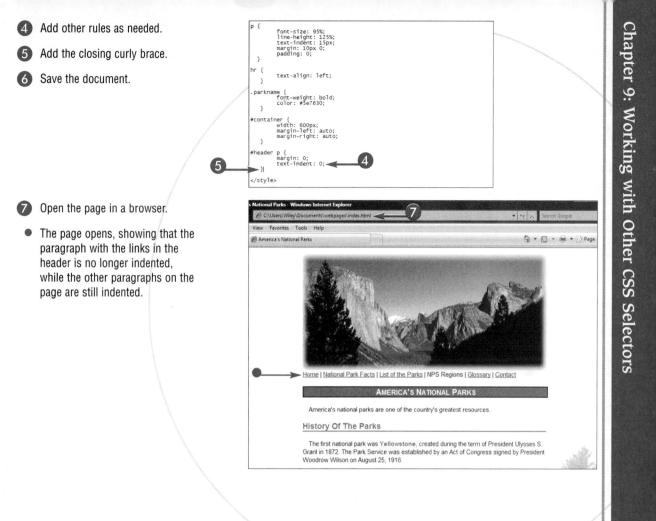

4 Add other rules as needed.

5 Add the closing curly brace.

6 Save the document.

```
p {
    font-size: 95%;
    line-height: 125%;
    text-indent: 15px;
    margin: 10px 0;
    padding: 0;
}

hr {
    text-align: left;
}

.parkname {
    font-weight: bold;
    color: #5e7630;
}

#container {
    width: 600px;
    margin-left: auto;
    margin-right: auto;
}

#header p {
    margin: 0;
    text-indent: 0;    ◄── 4
5 ──► }
}
</style>
```

7 Open the page in a browser.

● The page opens, showing that the paragraph with the links in the header is no longer indented, while the other paragraphs on the page are still indented.

Home | National Park Facts | List of the Parks | NPS Regions | Glossary | Contact

AMERICA'S NATIONAL PARKS

America's national parks are one of the country's greatest resources.

History Of The Parks

The first national park was Yellowstone, created during the term of President Ulysses S. Grant in 1872. The Park Service was established by an Act of Congress signed by President Woodrow Wilson on August 25, 1916.

Extra

You can reference as many levels of your page's hierarchy as needed. Therefore, a link within a paragraph within a table cell within a table that has an ID of #contactnumbers can be referenced as #contactnumbers td p a. You may also find it necessary to reference classes or IDs at multiple levels of the selector, such as #contactnumbers #sales p .numbers, which references some element that has a class of numbers, which is, in turn, nested within a paragraph inside an element with an id of sales, which is in some element with an id contactnumbers.

The only important aspect of the contextual selector is that you provide enough selectors to make it clear which element you wish to style. Technically, the example given in the text of a table cell within a div of ID sidebar could be written body #sidebar table tr td, given the cell is directly nested within a table row, which is in the table, which is in the div that is, of course, nested within the body. While there is nothing technically wrong with this level of detail, it is unnecessary.

Apply Other Selectors

You will do most of your work using class, ID, or contextual selectors, but the CSS specification provides for several other selector types. Browser support for these additional selectors varies, so be sure to test them thoroughly to ensure that you get the desired results.

The CSS child selector can be used to designate elements that are the direct descendent of another. For example, `body > div` would select only those `div`s that are directly nested within the `body`, not `div`s that are children of other `div`s. Note that the child selector uses a greater than symbol (>) to separate the elements in question.

The adjacent sibling selector allows you to select an element that immediately follows another element. If you wanted to style paragraphs that immediately followed an

`h2`, you could write `h2 + p`. Note that unmarked text between the elements in question will not affect the selector, but other elements will, so if there is a `div` between the `h2` and the paragraph, the paragraph would not be styled.

The CSS specification also allows you to select elements based on an attribute. Therefore, `a[name]` will select any anchor tag that contains a name attribute. You can also select based on the value of the attribute, so `input[type="text"]` will select input elements so long as the type is set to text. Finally, you can select based on a partial value match, so `img[alt~="Fig"]` will select any image whose alternate text contains the letters "fig" at any point. Note the tilde between the attribute and equal sign in this example.

Apply Other Selectors

① Open a Web page that contains an embedded style sheet in your editor.

② Add a child selector.

③ Add appropriate rules to the declaration.

④ Add an attribute selector.

⑤ Add appropriate rules to the declaration.

⑥ Save the document.

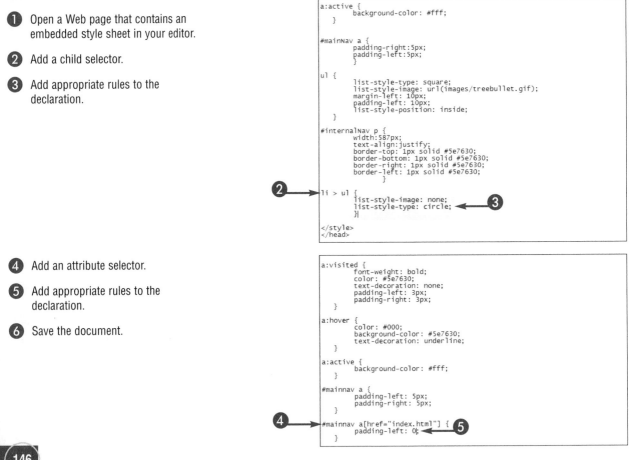

⑦ Open the page in a browser.

The page opens, showing that the styles are applied.

● In this example, the left padding on the links at the top of the page is not applied to the Home link.

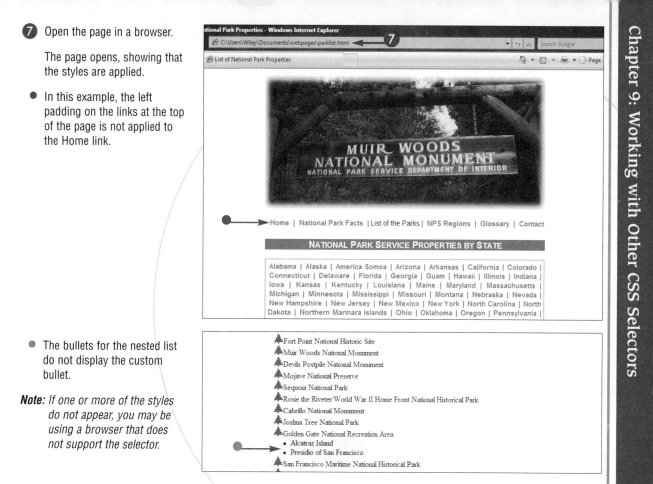

● The bullets for the nested list do not display the custom bullet.

Note: *If one or more of the styles do not appear, you may be using a browser that does not support the selector.*

Extra

The child selector and contextual selector serve similar purposes, but have a fundamental difference. Using `#sidebar td` will select a table cell *at any level* below the element with the sidebar ID, whereas `#sidebar > td` will only select a cell if it is nested directly below the element with the ID. In this example, that effectively restricts the `#sidebar` to a `tr` element, as it is the only element under which the `td` can be legally nested. This can be one of the child selector's most useful features, as the more general nature of the contextual selector can often lead to unexpected elements being styled.

Microsoft Internet Explorer, in particular, has problems with many of these selectors, which has led to them being widely ignored. Internet Explorer only began supporting the selectors listed in this task as of version 7, released in 2007. Any version prior to that will either simply ignore the style declaration, as is the case with attribute selectors, or will implement them incorrectly, as with child selectors, in which the browser will select the last element listed as if it was a regular element selector.

Create Effects with Pseudo-Elements

Pseudo-elements are a special type of selector in which the browser acts as if an element was present for styling when one in fact does not exist. The four pseudo-elements supported in CSS are `first-letter`, `first-line`, `before`, and `after`. All are denoted by a normal element selector, a colon, and the pseudo-element, as in `h1:first-letter` or `p:first-line`.

The `first-letter` pseudo-element allows you to style only the first character within an element's content. Often, this is used to create a drop-cap effect on text by applying `font-size` and possibly `font-weight`, `font-family`, or `color` properties to the element. The `first-line` pseudo-element allows you to create the common effect from print of rendering the first line of a block of text in bold or italic or a different color. For practical reasons, this is almost always applied to paragraphs and table cells, as

headings and list items rarely contain more than one line of text, although it is valid on any block element.

Not all CSS properties may be applied to the `first-letter` and `first-line` pseudo-elements. The only allowed properties for both are `font-variant`, `font-style`, `font-weight`, `font-size`, `font-family`, `font`, `color`, `background-color`, `background-image`, `background-repeat`, `background`, `vertical-align`, `line-height`, `text-decoration`, `text-transform`, `word-spacing`, `letter-spacing`, and `clear`. The `background-attachment` property is also supported for the `first-line` pseudo-element, while all of the `margin` and `padding` properties are also allowed with `first-letter`.

You can use class and ID selectors with the pseudo-elements, so `#sidebar:first-line` is a legal selector. You may also use contextual selectors, as in `#maincontent p:first-letter`, or any other selector.

Create Effects with Pseudo-Elements

1 Open a Web page that contains an embedded style sheet in your editor.

2 Add a `first-letter` pseudo-element selector.

3 Add rules to the declaration to format the first letter.

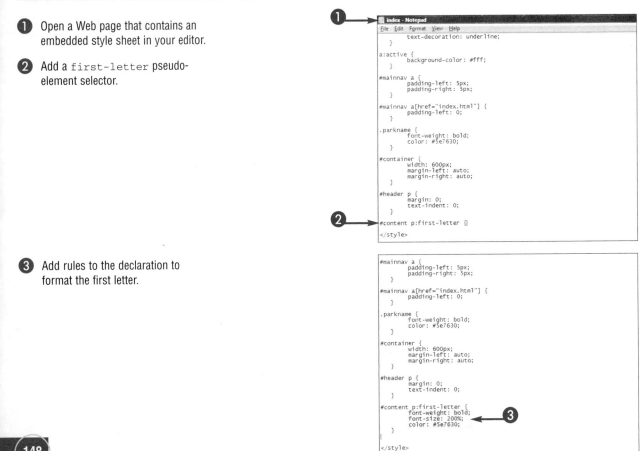

④ Add a `first-line` pseudo-element selector.

⑤ Add rules to the declaration to format the first line.

⑥ Save the document.

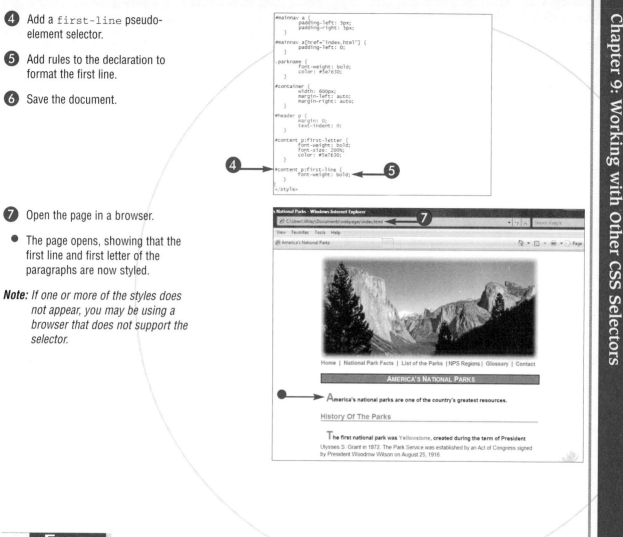

⑦ Open the page in a browser.

● The page opens, showing that the first line and first letter of the paragraphs are now styled.

Note: *If one or more of the styles does not appear, you may be using a browser that does not support the selector.*

Two additional pseudo-elements exist: `before` and `after`. These pseudo-elements are used with the CSS `content` property, which allows you to place generated content either immediately before or immediately after the content of the element. This content can either be literal text or an image, so it can, for example, be used to place an icon identifying the file type before a link to a downloadable file. An example of generated literal text might look like this:

```
p:before {content: "Fig: "; }
```

Internet Explorer, even as of version 7, does not support the `content` property, so the `before` and `after` pseudo-elements are essentially worthless for most developers and are rarely used.

While the `before` and `after` pseudo-elements are designed to work with `content`, you can apply additional rules to the declaration. These styles will be used on the generated `content` itself, so you can, for example, designate the `font-family` and `color` to be used if you are generating literal text. Any CSS properties that can be inherited from the parent element will be.

Apply Additional Styles through Pseudo-Classes

In print, a common practice is to style the first paragraph of a block of text differently from the rest, perhaps rendering it in bold or a different color. A contextual selector in this case will not work, as it is not specific enough to only select the first paragraph in a series.

Instead, CSS provides for a `first-child` pseudo-class. Pseudo-classes function very similarly to pseudo-elements. Technically, the only difference is that browsers behave as if an additional element exists with pseudo-elements; with pseudo-classes, they behave as though you had added a `class` attribute to an element that is already present.

The four most common pseudo-classes are `link`, `visited`, `hover`, and `active` — the pseudo-classes used to style hyperlinks. There is, however, one additional pseudo-class that can be useful for styling the example given previously. When you wish to apply a style to the first instance of an element after another element, you can use the `first-child` pseudo-class. For example, if you have a level 2 heading followed by a paragraph, and you want to make that paragraph blue and bold, you could write:

```
h2:first-child { font-weight: bold; color:
#00F; }
```

Note that the style is applied in this case to the heading, as you are attempting to style the element immediately following that heading. The danger here is that the style will be applied to whatever element immediately follows the heading; this syntax does not allow you to target a paragraph specifically.

Apply Additional Styles through Pseudo-Classes

① Open a Web page that contains an embedded style sheet in your editor.

② Add an element selector with the `first-child` pseudo-class.

③ Add rules to the declaration.

④ Save the document.

⑤ Open the page in a browser.

● The page opens, showing the style applied to the first child of the selected element.

In this example, the bottom margin is applied to the image, which is the first child of the paragraph element within the header.

Specify Rules as Important

There may be times when you need to ensure that a particular rule will apply at all times, particularly if the rule is in an external style sheet and there is a chance that an embedded style sheet may attempt to override it. For example, if you have a policy within your organization that all headings must be in all capital letters, you can use the `text-transform` property in your external sheet. However, it would be possible for another designer to add an embedded style sheet to a page and set `text-transform` for the headings to another value, thereby overriding your preference.

The `!important` command in CSS is designed to solve this issue. By setting a rule as `!important`, you force the browser to use that rule and its setting,

regardless of any other declarations that might change it. In the previous example, you might set:

```
h1 { font-family: "Times New Roman",
Times, serif; color: #9F9; text-
transform: uppercase !important; }
```

Note that the `!important` command is part of a particular rule, and not the entire declaration. If you wanted to force the headings to always be Times New Roman and the color #9F9, you would need `!important` declarations on each of those:

```
h1 { font-family: "Times New Roman",
Times, serif !important; color: #9F9
!important; text-transform: uppercase
!important; }
```

Specify Rules as Important

① Open a web page that contains an embedded style sheet in your editor.

② Add an `!important` declaration to a rule.

③ Save the document.

④ Open the page in a browser.

The page opens, showing that the `!important` rule is over-riding the other rules.

```
body {
        background-color: #fff;
        background-image: url(images/smbkgnd.jpg);
        background-repeat: no-repeat;
        background-position: bottom right;
        }

#container {
        width:600px;
        margin: 0 auto;
                }

h1 {
        font-size: 120%;
        font-family: Arial, Helvetica, sans-serif;
        text-align: center;
        font-variant: small-caps;
        background-color: #5e7630 !important;    ◄── ②
        color: #ffffff;
        width: 600px;
        }
```

America's National Parks - Windows Internet Explorer

C:\Users\Wiley\Documents\webpages\index.html ◄── ④

America's National Parks

Home | National Park Facts | List of the Parks | NPS Regions | Glossary | Contact

AMERICA'S NATIONAL PARKS

America's national parks are one of the country's greatest resources.

History Of The Parks

The first national park was Yellowstone, created during the term of President
Ulysses S. Grant in 1872. The Park Service was established by an Act of Congress signed by President Woodrow Wilson on August 25, 1916.

Create an External Style Sheet

One of the most powerful features of CSS is the ability to define styles that are independent of a particular document. By separating your content and presentation into distinct documents, you can apply the styles to as many XHTML documents as you wish. This both ensures that you can maintain a consistent look and feel to your entire site as well as makes it quite simple to modify your design site-wide, as changes to the external styles document will be reflected throughout all of the pages.

Creating an external style sheet is a fairly simple process. First, you need to move your existing styles into a new empty document. Save this document inside your Web folder using a `.css` extension. The exact filename is unimportant, but it must follow normal Web page file-naming rules.

Then, on every page on which you wish to apply the styles, you will add a `link` element to the head. The `link` element takes three required attributes: `rel`, `type`, and `href`. The `rel` attribute specifies the relationship between this page and the style sheet, and will most often be set to a value of `stylesheet`. The `type` informs the browser as to which type of file it can expect when it requests the style sheet from the server, and will always be `text/css`. Finally, the `href` attribute sets the path to the style sheet document itself. An example of a complete link tag might be:

```
<link rel="stylesheet" type="text/css"
href="styles/mainstyles.css" />
```

Create an External Style Sheet

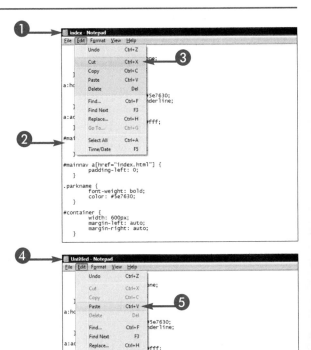

① Open a Web page that contains an embedded style sheet in your editor.

② Select all of the declarations in the style sheet.

③ Cut the styles.

④ Open a new, blank document in your editor.

⑤ Paste the styles into the new document.

● The styles are pasted in.

⑥ Save the document.

Note: *Be sure to save this file with a .css extension.*

7. Open the document from which you cut the styles.

8. If necessary, delete the opening and closing `style` tags.

9. Add a `link` tag.

10. Add the `rel` attribute, with a value of `stylesheet`.

11. Add the `type` attribute set to `text/css`.

12. Add the `href` attribute, with its value set to the path to the document you created in Step 6.

13. Save the document.

14. Open the page in a browser.

    The page opens.

Note: It should look just as it did before.

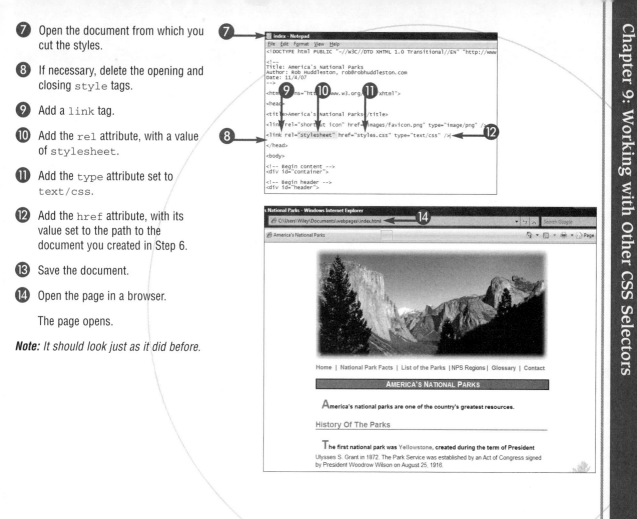

Apply It

Instead of linking to the external document, you can import it using the `@import` command in an embedded style sheet.

```
<style type="text/css">
@import url(styles/mainstyles.css);
</style>
```

The end result will be the same: The document will derive its style instructions from the external style sheet. Importing has one primary advantage over linking styles, which is that imported styles will have a higher precedence than linked styles. The disadvantage to importing, however, is that many older browsers do not recognize imported styles, so you need to be sure to test.

Override Styles Using the Cascade

I t is possible to have CSS declarations in both an external style sheet and an embedded style sheet. In this case, the order of the cascade specifies that the embedded styles will override conflicts with the external styles. This can be used to your advantage, as it allows you to have page-specific formatting for select elements while still maintaining the overall look and feel of the site.

It is important to understand that only those styles that are in direct conflict will be overridden. As much as possible, the browser will attempt to use both the external and embedded styles together. For example, say you have the following declaration in your external style sheet:

```
p { font-family: Arial, Helvetica, sans-
serif; color: #00F; font-size: 90%; line-
height: 1.4em; }
```

Then, in an embedded style sheet on a page linked to that external sheet, you have:

```
p { font-weight: bold; line-height: 1.2
em; }
```

The resulting paragraph text on the page would be displayed in bold, blue Arial at 90% with a line height of 1.2 em. As the embedded style sheet is silent on the font-family, color, and size, those properties are not overridden.

Override Styles Using the Cascade

① Open a Web page that contains a link to an external style sheet.

● The style sheet link code appears here.

② In the head of the document, add a style element's opening tag.

③ Set the type attribute to text/css.

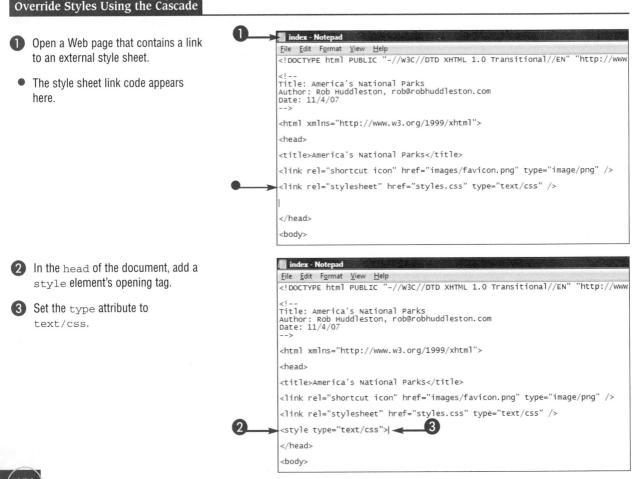

4 Add a declaration to the embedded style sheet.

5 Save the document.

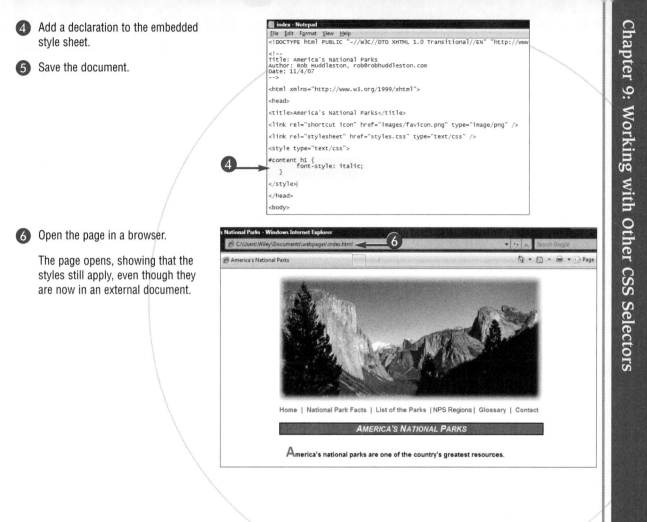

6 Open the page in a browser.

The page opens, showing that the styles still apply, even though they are now in an external document.

The most important factor in determining whether a style will override another is specificity. That is, a declaration with a more specific selector will override one with a less specific selector. ID selectors, for example, are very specific: They target one distinct element on a page. Class selectors are less specific, and element selectors less still.

The relative proximity of a style declaration to its affected element is another factor in determining whether a particular rule will be overridden. Because external styles are in a separate document while embedded styles are present in the same page, embedded styles have precedence. Where two declarations exist at the same level, their relative position within the style sheet will come into play, with declarations lower in the sheet overriding ones that are higher.

Imported styles are considered to exist within an embedded style sheet, even though they technically exist in an external document. If you have a link to one style sheet and import another, the imported sheet's styles will override those in the linked sheet. Because the @import command will be at the top of the embedded style sheet, its styles will be overridden by other declarations in the embedded sheet simply because they will appear lower in the document.

Lay Out Your Page Using Floated Elements

Prior to the advent of Cascading Style Sheets (CSS), the only method of creating multicolumn layouts was to use Hypertext Markup Language (HTML) tables. This resulted in bloated, mostly inaccessible code that was difficult to maintain. As an alternative, CSS introduced several properties to assist in laying out pages. One of the most commonly used is `float`.

Normally, XHTML block elements will be left-aligned and stacked on top of one another in the order in which they appear in the code. The `float` property allows you to take these elements and enables them to appear horizontally next to one another. The three possible values for float are `left`, `right`, and `none`, with the last one being the default.

If you have two elements that you wish to appear next to one another, you can apply `float:left` to the first. This in essence tells the browser to allow this element to appear to the left of elements that follow it, and causes the second element to move into the space to the right of the floated element. It is important to understand, however, that the second element can only float to the right of the first if there is sufficient space. As all elements by default have a `width` of 100%, floating will not work at all unless both elements are given an explicit `width`, and the total widths of the elements must be less than or equal to the total width of the window or parent element.

The most common element to which you will apply a float is a `div` with an `id` attribute. The `div` allows you to group logical sets of elements that should be laid out together, and the `id` allows you to float to that particular element.

Lay Out Your Page Using Floated Elements

1 Open a Web page that contains a link to an external style sheet.

2 If necessary, wrap the content you wish to float in a `div` tag with an `id` attribute.

```
<h1>America's National Parks</h1>
<p>America's national parks are one of the country's greatest resources.</p>
<div id="maincol">
<h2>History of the Parks</h2>
<p>The first national park was <span class="parkname">Yellowstone</span>, created during
Grant in 1872. The Park Service was established by an Act of Congress signed by President
1916.</p>
</div>|
<h2>Headquarters</h2>
<p>The national headquarters of the US National Park Service is located at:<br />
1849 C Street NW, Washington, DC.</p>

<!-- End content -->
</div>

</body>

</html>
```

3 Repeat Step 2 for any additional elements you wish to float.

4 Save the page.

```
<h1>America's National Parks</h1>
<p>America's national parks are one of the country's greatest resources.</p>
<div id="maincol">
<h2>History of the Parks</h2>
<p>The first national park was <span class="parkname">Yellowstone</span>, created during
Grant in 1872. The Park Service was established by an Act of Congress signed by President
1916.</p>
</div>
<div id="sidebar">
<h2>Headquarters</h2>
<p>The national headquarters of the US National Park Service is located at:<br />
1849 C Street NW, Washington, DC.</p>
</div>|
<!-- End content -->
</div>
```

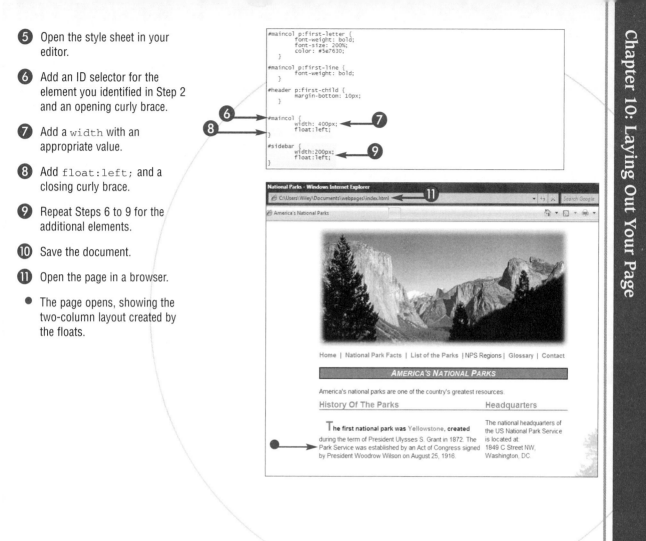

5 Open the style sheet in your editor.

6 Add an ID selector for the element you identified in Step 2 and an opening curly brace.

7 Add a `width` with an appropriate value.

8 Add `float:left;` and a closing curly brace.

9 Repeat Steps 6 to 9 for the additional elements.

10 Save the document.

11 Open the page in a browser.

● The page opens, showing the two-column layout created by the floats.

```
#maincol p:first-letter {
        font-weight: bold;
        font-size: 200%;
        color: #5e7630;
}

#maincol p:first-line {
        font-weight: bold;
}

#header p:first-child {
        margin-bottom: 10px;
}

#maincol {
        width: 400px;
        float:left;
}

#sidebar {
        width:200px;
        float:left;
}
```

Extra

Internet Explorer has a well-documented bug known as the "double float margin bug." If you float an element, and then use a margin to create space between the floated element and the element next to it, Internet Explorer will double the margin. This only occurs in cases where the float and the margin are on the same side; for example, if you have `float:left` and `margin-left` set for the same element. Also, only the first `float` within a given row will be affected by the bug. The solution to the bug is odd, but works well: Add `display:inline` to the element in question, and the bug disappears. The `display` property will be discussed in more detail later in this chapter, but this is one of those instances where adding the fix for Internet Explorer does not affect the display in any other browser, given all other browsers treat floated elements as block elements, regardless of any other setting. The bug also only occurs in Internet Explorer for Windows, and not Internet Explorer for Macintosh. When applying this fix, be sure to add a comment to your code to remind yourself why the extra seemingly meaningless rule is in your style sheet.

Clear Floats

All elements that follow a floated element will attempt to move into the next horizontal available space. You can prevent this behavior by applying the `clear` property to elements that you wish to ignore the `float` on a previous element. Possible values for clear are `left`, to ignore a prior `float:left`; `right`, which tells the element to ignore a previous elements' `float:right`, and `both`, to ignore either right or left `float`.

A common layout for Web pages is to have a banner stretch across the top of the page with the logo and primary navigation, and then two or three columns for the main page, generally with the left column containing secondary navigation, the middle column containing the content, and, if present, the right column containing

additional information or links. This layout can be easily achieved by floating the left, middle, and right columns.

However, another common piece of this layout is a footer that stretches across the bottom of the page. If the elements — most likely `divs` — that make up the columns each have `float:left` applied, then the footer element will end up trying to float to the right of the last column. If the layout does not allow enough room for it, most browsers will show it below the final column, but only as wide as the column. You can solve this issue easily by applying the `clear` property to the footer, which will break it from the floats above and place it where you would expect. In this case, either `clear:left` or `clear:both` will work.

Clear Floats

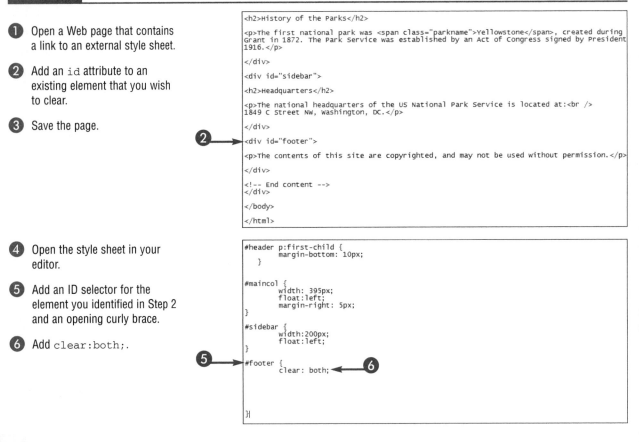

① Open a Web page that contains a link to an external style sheet.

② Add an `id` attribute to an existing element that you wish to clear.

③ Save the page.

```
<h2>History of the Parks</h2>

<p>The first national park was <span class="parkname">Yellowstone</span>, created during
Grant in 1872. The Park Service was established by an Act of Congress signed by President
1916.</p>

</div>

<div id="sidebar">

<h2>Headquarters</h2>

<p>The national headquarters of the US National Park Service is located at:<br />
1849 C Street NW, Washington, DC.</p>

</div>

<div id="footer">

<p>The contents of this site are copyrighted, and may not be used without permission.</p>

</div>

<!-- End content -->
</div>

</body>

</html>
```

④ Open the style sheet in your editor.

⑤ Add an ID selector for the element you identified in Step 2 and an opening curly brace.

⑥ Add `clear:both;`.

```
#header p:first-child {
        margin-bottom: 10px;
    }

#maincol {
        width: 395px;
        float:left;
        margin-right: 5px;
}
#sidebar {
        width:200px;
        float:left;
}
#footer {
        clear: both;



}
```

7 Add any additional properties you wish to set for the element and a closing curly brace.

8 Save the document.

9 Open the page in a browser.

● The page opens, showing a footer.

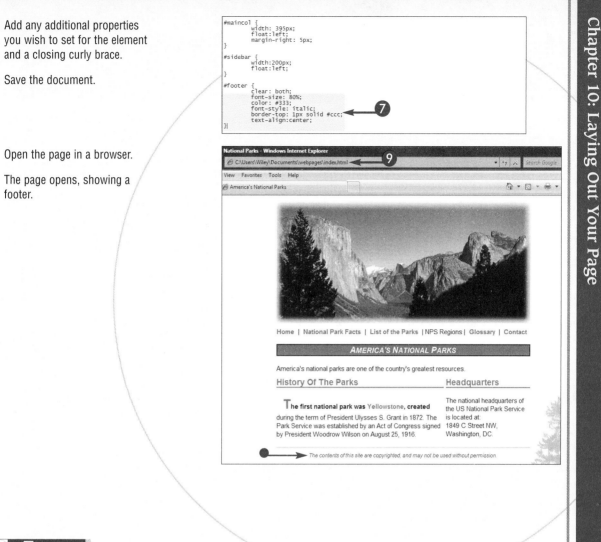

```
#maincol {
        width: 395px;
        float:left;
        margin-right: 5px;
}

#sidebar {
        width:200px;
        float:left;
}

#footer {
        clear: both;
        font-size: 80%;
        color: #333;
        font-style: italic;
        border-top: 1px solid #ccc;
        text-align:center;
}|
```

C:\Users\Wiley\Documents\webpages\index.html

America's National Parks

Home | National Park Facts | List of the Parks | NPS Regions | Glossary | Contact

AMERICA'S NATIONAL PARKS

America's national parks are one of the country's greatest resources.

History Of The Parks

The first national park was Yellowstone, created during the term of President Ulysses S. Grant in 1872. The Park Service was established by an Act of Congress signed by President Woodrow Wilson on August 25, 1916.

Headquarters

The national headquarters of the US National Park Service is located at: 1849 C Street NW, Washington, DC.

The contents of this site are copyrighted, and may not be used without permission.

Extra

There may be times when you need to clear a float for everything following a particular block on the page. In this case, you need to add an element to the page solely for the purpose of holding the `clear` property. There is a considerable amount of debate online as to the value of adding this element, as ideally there will be nothing in your XHTML that exists for pure stylistic purposes, but esoteric debates aside, the reality is that it is necessary at times. So if you accept its necessity, the next debate begins as to the appropriate element to use. The three most common elements used are the `br`, the `hr`, and the `div`. Each has its supporters and detractors, and to the impartial observer, all make good points on both sides. In the end, you should decide which makes the most sense to you and use it, but be aware that you will likely encounter all three at times.

Lay Out Your Page Using Absolute Positioning

There may be times when you wish to have an element appear in an exact position on the page, regardless of the position of any other elements. The CSS `position:absolute` property allows you to achieve this effect. In addition to setting the `position` property itself to `absolute`, you must also provide a location for the element using some combination of the `top`, `left`, `bottom`, and `right` properties. Their values will be set to some unit, usually either a pixel or percent, measured from the corresponding corner of the browser window.

In the normal layout of the page, every element exists within the "flow" of the page. That is, each element is aware of the size and position of each other element, and so each positions itself so as to not overlap with the others. When using `position:absolute`, the element in question is removed from the flow. Therefore, it is not aware of other elements, nor are other elements aware of

it. This can result in elements overlapping one another, so care should be taken to make sure that absolutely positioned elements will remain out of the way of non-absolute elements, unless the overlapping is a desired effect.

Absolute positioning is perhaps the easiest of the CSS layout properties to grasp for beginners. Many who are new to CSS design will attempt to build pages where every element is absolutely positioned, as this behavior to some extent mimics the design capabilities of page layout software. However, because absolutely positioned elements are out of the flow of the page, the layout cannot adjust as the size of the content changes. Some simple static layouts will work this way, but most pages will have content that changes frequently, and purely absolute layouts will quickly become problematic. Therefore, you should only use this property for certain select elements on the page, and not the entire layout.

Lay Out Your Page Using Absolute Positioning

① Open a Web page that contains a link to an external style sheet.

② Add an `id` attribute to an existing element that you wish to position.

③ Save the page.

④ Open the style sheet in your editor.

⑤ Add an ID selector for the element you identified in Step 2 and an opening curly brace.

⑥ Add a `width` with an appropriate value.

⑦ Add `position:absolute`.

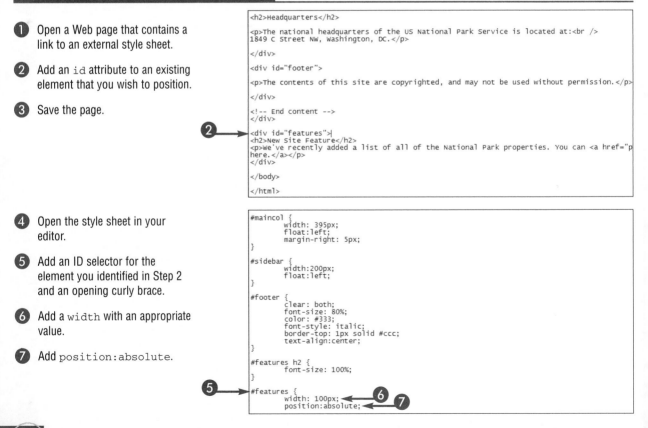

```
<h2>Headquarters</h2>

<p>The national headquarters of the US National Park Service is located at:<br />
1849 C Street NW, Washington, DC.</p>

</div>

<div id="footer">

<p>The contents of this site are copyrighted, and may not be used without permission.</p>

</div>

<!-- End content -->
</div>

<div id="features">
<h2>New Site Feature</h2>
<p>We've recently added a list of all of the National Park properties. You can <a href="p
here.</a></p>
</div>

</body>

</html>
```

```
#maincol {
        width: 395px;
        float:left;
        margin-right: 5px;
}

#sidebar {
        width:200px;
        float:left;
}

#footer {
        clear: both;
        font-size: 80%;
        color: #333;
        font-style: italic;
        border-top: 1px solid #ccc;
        text-align:center;
}

#features h2 {
        font-size: 100%;
}

#features {
        width: 100px;
        position:absolute;
}
```

8 Add a `top` property with a value for the number of pixels from the top corner of the browser window.

9 Add a `left` property with a value for the number of pixels from the left corner of the browser window and a closing curly brace.

10 Save the document.

11 Open the page in a browser.

● The page opens, showing the positioned content.

In this example, the sidebar discussing the new content is absolutely positioned.

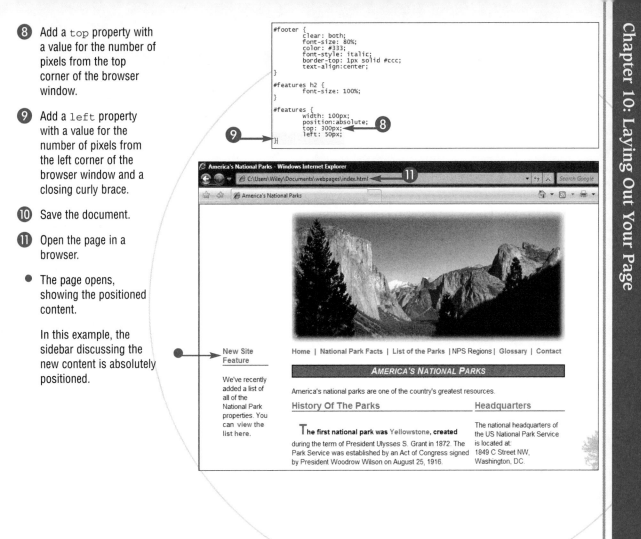

```
#footer {
        clear: both;
        font-size: 80%;
        color: #333;
        font-style: italic;
        border-top: 1px solid #ccc;
        text-align:center;
}

#features h2 {
        font-size: 100%;
}

#features {
        width: 100px;
        position:absolute;
        top: 300px;
        left: 50px;
}
```

As was noted previously, pages that rely solely on absolute positioning will rarely be flexible enough to suit the needs of an ever-changing Web site. Unfortunately, because it is the easiest of the CSS layout properties to use, many visual design tools provide tools that make creating an absolutely positioned layout very easy. For example, Adobe Dreamweaver CS3 has a set of so-called AP Elements tools — short for Absolutely Positioned Elements. Prior versions of the program called these "layers." Designers can simply click-and-drag to create the `divs` at exact locations on the screen, and can reposition them at will by simply dragging. Dreamweaver creates the necessary CSS code with the `position`, `top` and `left`, and `width` properties. Although many beginners find that creating pages this way is extremely simple, the pages too quickly become inflexible and require a redesign using some other CSS technique later.

The concept of positioning elements was initially developed by Netscape, which introduced a proprietary `layer` element for this purpose. The `div` element was determined to be more robust, so no browser, not even those from Netscape, currently supports `layer`. However, some legacy tutorials and even programs still make reference to it on occasion.

Lay Out Your Page Using Relative Positioning

A nother possible value for the `position` property in CSS is `relative`. Like `position:absolute`, `position:relative` removes an element from its normal spot in the document and places it in a new location. However, relative positioning differs from absolute positioning in two key ways.

First, you use the `top`, `left`, `right`, or `bottom` properties to specify the new location, just as you do with absolute positioning. However, the values for those properties when using relative positioning are based on the element's original location, not a corner of the window. Therefore, you can move an element down and to the right from where it would have been originally by giving `bottom` and `right` values. Negative values are allowed for these properties, so you can also move an element up on the page by providing a negative measurement for the `top` property.

The second key difference between absolute and relative positioning is that while both remove the element from

the normal flow of the page and can, thus, result in overlapping, other elements on the page will still be placed according to the relatively positioned element's original location. So, if you move an element up and to the left using relative positioning, there will be an empty space in the layout where the element would have originally appeared.

For this reason, relative positioning is not normally used to actually relocate elements on the page. Rather, you will often find designers using `position:relative` and `position:absolute` together. Absolutely positioned elements that are nested within a relatively positioned element will be placed based on the corner of the relative element, rather than the browser window. In creating this setup, you will use `position:relative` on the parent element, but not provide any location properties. You can then use `position:absolute` on nested elements, providing `top`, `bottom`, `left`, or `right` values as needed.

Lay Out Your Page Using Relative Positioning

① Open a Web page that contains a link to an external style sheet.

② Add an `id` attribute to an existing element that you wish to position.

③ Add an `id` to an element nested within the element used in Step 2.

④ Save the page.

```
<p><a href="http://www.nps.gov" title="National Park Service Home Page">National Park Ser

<div id="factcontainer">
<h1>National Park Facts</h1>

<ul id="factlist">
        <li>Parks by Size
            <ul>
                <li>The largest national park is the <strong>Wrangell-St. Elias N
in Alaska at 13.2 million acres, or 20,625 square miles.</li>
                <li>The smallest national park by area is the <strong>Thaddeus Ko
in Pennsylvania, at just .02 acres, or about 871 square feet.</li>
            </ul>
        </li>
        <li><a href="mostvisited.html" title="Most Visited Parks">Most Visited Parks</a><
</ul>

</div>

</div>

</div>
```

⑤ Open the style sheet in your editor.

⑥ Add an ID selector for the element you identified in Step 2 and an opening curly brace.

⑦ Add `position:relative` and a closing curly brace.

```
#features h2 {
        font-size: 100%;
}

#features {
        width: 100px;
        position:absolute;
        top: 300px;
        left: 50px;
}

#factcontainer {
        position: relative;
}

#factlist {
        width: 400px;
        position: absolute;
        top: 50px;
        left: 30px;
}
```

8. Add an ID selector for the element you identified in Step 3 and an opening curly brace.

9. Add a `width` with an appropriate value.

10. Add `position: absolute;`.

11. Add a `top` property with a value for the number of pixels from the top corner of the parent element.

12. Add a `left` property with a value for the number of pixels from the left corner of the parent element and a closing curly brace.

13. Save the document.

14. Open the page in a browser.

- The page opens, showing the positioned content.

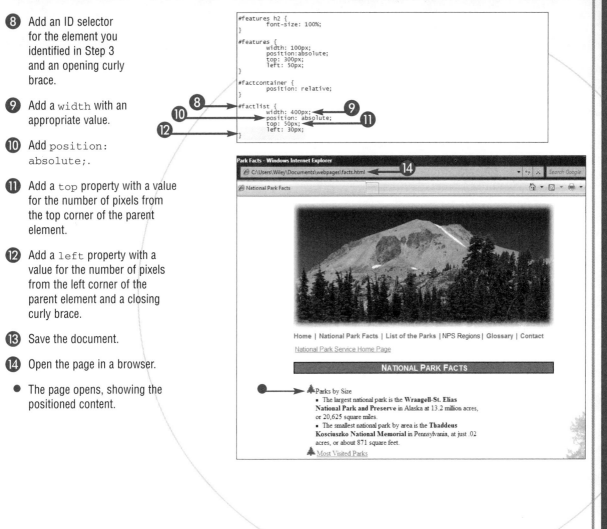

Lay Out Your Page Using Fixed Positioning

The `position` property in CSS also supports a value of `fixed`. A fixed position element will act almost exactly like an absolutely positioned element. You must, therefore, provide `top`, `bottom`, `left`, or `right` values to specify its location, and it will be removed from the flow of the document.

However, `position:fixed` has one interesting variance from `position:absolute`. Absolutely positioned elements are placed in a precise location on the page, but they will continue to scroll with the page, while fixed elements will remain in place as the user scrolls. This can create the effect of allowing elements to scroll over or under other elements, and is sometimes used to create a banner that remains in place. Because the fixed element is removed from the page's flow, you will need to adjust the margin of elements that follow it to prevent them from overlapping.

Anytime elements overlap, their stacking order is defined by their position in the code, with elements that appear earlier in the code stacking below elements that appear later. Therefore, if you wish to create the effect mentioned previously of a banner that remains in place with the content scrolling below it, you must reset the stacking order. Because fixed position elements are removed from the flow, you could in theory simply place the XHTML code for the banner at the top of the page, thereby assuring that the rest of the code will come first and that it will be the highest element. Doing this might detract from the accessibility of the page, however, unless the section of the box would logically occur first in the document. Instead, you can apply the `z-index` property in CSS. The `z-index` lets you specify an integer as its value, whereby elements with higher integers will be stacked higher than those with lower values. Elements with no `z-index` are stacked in their normal order, which will be below any elements that are given a `z-index`.

Lay Out Your Page Using Fixed Positioning

① Open a Web page that contains a link to an external style sheet.

② If necessary, add an `id` attribute to an existing element to which you wish to apply the fixed position.

③ Add an embedded style sheet to the page.

④ Add an ID selector for the element you identified in Step 2 and an opening curly brace.

⑤ Add `position:fixed`.

⑥ Add a `top` property with a value for the number of pixels from the top corner of the browser window.

⑦ Add any additional properties you wish to set on the element and a closing curly brace.

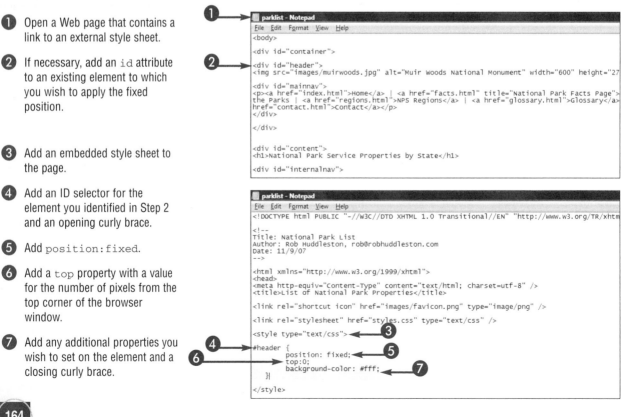

8 Add an ID selector for the element that follows the fixed element.

9 Add a `margin-top` property with a value to move the following element below the fixed element.

10 Save the document.

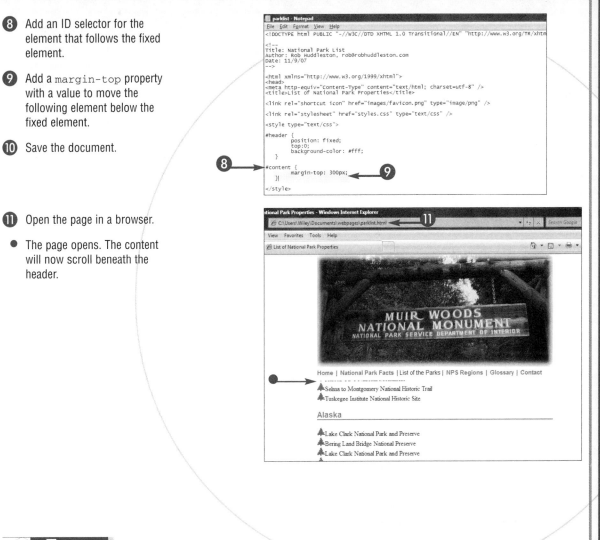

11 Open the page in a browser.

● The page opens. The content will now scroll beneath the header.

Extra

Unfortunately, Internet Explorer only adopted support for `position:fixed` as of version 7. If you need to support an older version, a Web search will reveal JavaScript implementations that can simulate the effect, but as more people adopt version 7, these will become increasingly unnecessary.

When you apply `z-index`, you do not need to use consecutive numbers. In fact, if you are applying it to several elements, it is recommended that you set it in intervals of 5 or 10, simply so that you can add other elements later and place them into the stacking order without needing to renumber anything else. In theory, any large number can be used to set the `z-index`, so to ensure that a particular element always exists on top of every other element on the page, you might choose to assign a `z-index` of something like 1000.

Work with Element Overflow

For the most part, it is best to not explicitly set a height on any element, and instead allow the browser to set the element's height to whatever is necessary to fit the content. There will be times, however, that explicit heights are necessary. A common, if not recommended, situation is on a page that uses all absolute positioning. In order to place an element below another element, you need to know exactly how high the one on top will be.

Unfortunately, browsers are very inconsistent when dealing with content that will not fit in an element's given height. Some will enforce the height and simply clip the extra content, while others, including Internet Explorer 7 and Firefox 2, will enforce the height with regard to drawing the border and background color, but allow additional content to flow out of the box and down the page, which may cause it to overlap content below.

To solve problems such as these and ensure that the browsers all behave the same, you can set the `overflow` property in CSS. The property's allowed values are `visible`, `hidden`, `scroll`, and `auto`. Setting it to `visible` is the same as the current implementation in Internet Explorer and Firefox: The border and background color will be constrained by the height, but not the content. `Hidden` causes the browser to clip the content, so the box height is always observed and additional content will be invisible. A value of `scroll` will clip the content, but provide the user with a scrollbar to enable them to see the rest of the content. `Auto` has the same effect in most browsers as `scroll`, with the exception that `scroll` will display the scrollbar whether it is needed or not, while `auto` will only show it if needed.

Work with Element Overflow

① Open a Web page that contains an embedded style sheet in your editor.

● The style sheet begins here.

② Add an ID selector for the element on which you wish to add scrolling.

③ Add a `height` property to an existing declaration with an appropriate value.

④ Add an `overflow:auto` rule to the declaration.

⑤ Save the page.

```
<style type="text/css">
table {
        border: 2px solid #5e7630;
        border-collapse: collapse;
    }
th {

        background-color: #ccc;
        border: 1px dashed #5e7630;
        padding: 5px;
    }
td {

        border: 1px solid #000;
        padding: 5px;
    }
#content {
        height: 300px;
        overflow: auto;|          ④
    }
</style>
```

⑥ Open a Web page linked to the style sheet in a browser.

● The page opens, showing scrollbars on the element if needed.

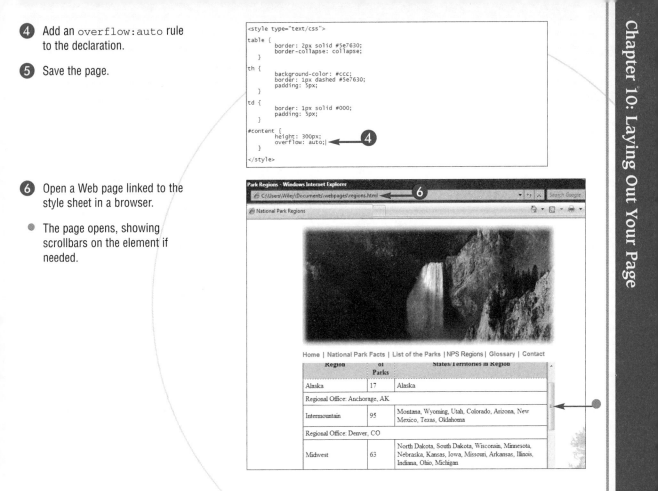

Extra

The `overflow` property will have no effect at all on elements with no height, or elements where the height is greater than the content. Note that when the scrollbar is present, it should be drawn between the outer edge of the padding and the inner edge of the border, and its width will effect the calculation for the `width` of the box.

Internet Explorer supports a set of properties that allow you to change the color of the scrollbar and its various components. The properties are `scrollbar-face-color`, `scrollbar-shadow-color`, `scrollbar-highlight-color`, `scrollbar-3dlight-color`, `scrollbar-darkshadow-color`, `scrollbar-track-color`, and `scrollbar-arrow-color`. All of these properties take valid colors as their values. You can apply these properties to the body element to change the browser's scrollbar, or to any element on the page that might have a scrollbar. Very few other browsers support these properties, although other browsers fail gracefully by simply ignoring them. They are officially considered "invalid" according to the CSS specification and many users may be annoyed by them, so use them with caution.

Set Minimum and Maximum Widths and Heights

The content on many pages will need to constantly change. You may have a news or blog site that is being frequently updated throughout the day, or a products page with a varying number of items for sale. The content may be entered manually by you or others in your organization, or it may be populated dynamically from a database. In either case, you will have no way of knowing in advance how wide or tall a particular element box needs to be, so it may be impossible to set a specific width or height.

Using the `overflow` property is one solution to this issue, but many designers and users do not like having to scroll through content. Instead, you can use the `min-width`, `min-height`, `max-width`, and `max-height` properties. These allow you the flexibility to build a design around certain parameters.

The `min-width` and `min-height` properties allow you to set the lower boundary of the size of the box. The browser will calculate the `width` or `height` of the box using its normal methods, and then compare that `width` or `height` to the given minimum. If the calculated box is smaller than the minimum, the minimum will be used. A similar process is involved in calculating the maximums.

These minimums and maximums can be used in conjunction with the `height` and `width` properties. While it obviously makes no logical sense to use them when height or width is set to a number of pixels, as the box will by definition always be exactly that tall or wide, you can use them to constrain either dimension when percents are used. A `max-width`, for example, can prevent a box with a width set to 75% from becoming too wide for users with widescreen or unusually large monitors.

Set Minimum and Maximum Widths and Heights

① Open a style sheet in your editor.

```
styles - Notepad
File  Edit  Format  View  Help

a:active {
        background-color: #fff;
    }

#mainnav a {
        padding-left: 3px;
        padding-right: 3px;
    }

#mainnav a[href="index.html"] {
        padding-left: 0;
    }

.parkname {
        font-weight: bold;
        color: #5e7630;
    }

#container {
        margin-left: auto;
        margin-right: auto;|
    }
```

② Add a `min-width` property to an existing declaration with an appropriate value.

```
styles - Notepad
File  Edit  Format  View  Help

a:active {
        background-color: #fff;
    }

#mainnav a {
        padding-left: 3px;
        padding-right: 3px;
    }

#mainnav a[href="index.html"] {
        padding-left: 0;
    }

.parkname {
        font-weight: bold;
        color: #5e7630;
    }

#container {
        margin-left: auto;
        margin-right: auto;
        min-width: 500px;|
    }
```

③ Add a `max-width` property to the declaration with an appropriate value.

④ Save the page.

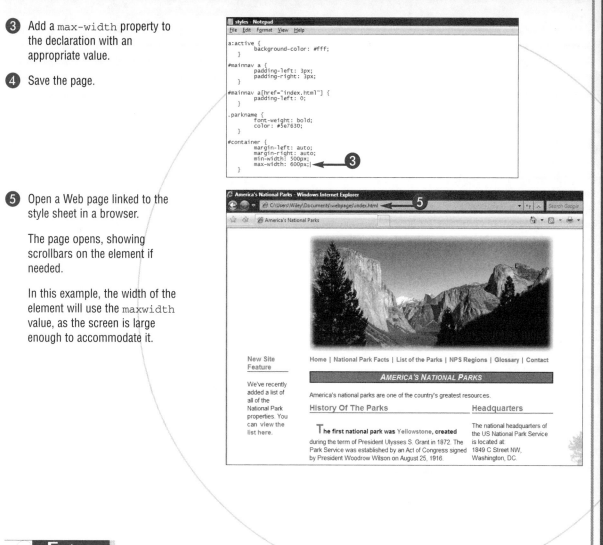

⑤ Open a Web page linked to the style sheet in a browser.

The page opens, showing scrollbars on the element if needed.

In this example, the width of the element will use the `maxwidth` value, as the screen is large enough to accommodate it.

Extra

There is no effective way to force an element to always have a height of 100 percent of the height of the browser window. This means in essence that it is difficult to fill a column with a background color and get that color to extend to the bottom of the screen, even if the content does not. The reason is because the height is calculated using, in part, the height of the content. Nowhere in the calculation is the height of the window taken into account. Many designers, not unreasonably, think that a setting of `min-height:100%` will work, but all this does is ensure that the box will be at least as big as its content. There are several solutions on the Web for achieving the appearance of equal column heights, but all of them involve significant hacks in both the XHTML and the CSS.

None of these properties have been widely used in the past due to the lack of support from Internet Explorer, the world's most popular browser. Fortunately, all are now supported by version 7 of the browser.

Apply the
Display Property

A ll elements in XHTML are defined as being either block or inline. Block elements define their own space, while inline do not. CSS provides the display property that allows you to alter the default behavior causing normally block elements to display inline or vice versa.

The anchor tag is an inline element. One implication of this is that the clickable region of the anchor is only as wide as the actual text. For hyperlinks in a paragraph, this is fine, but if you have a column down the side of your page for your navigation, it can be useful to have the clickable region extend to the width of the column so your user does not need to be directly over the text of the link to activate it. You would need to set the anchor's width to 100% to achieve this result, but inline elements cannot take a width, so you also need to set its display to block.

The display property's value can also be set to none, which effectively removes the element from the page, a common technique in creating print style sheets that will be discussed later in this chapter.

The display property actually has a host of other possible values, although none of them are commonly used. The list-item value lets you treat a non-list element as a list, and marker sets an element to act like the counter in an ordered list. A set of values allows you to treat non-table elements as tables: table, inline-table, table-row-group, table-header-group, table-footer-group, table-row, table-column-group, table-column, table-cell, and table-caption.

Apply the Display Property

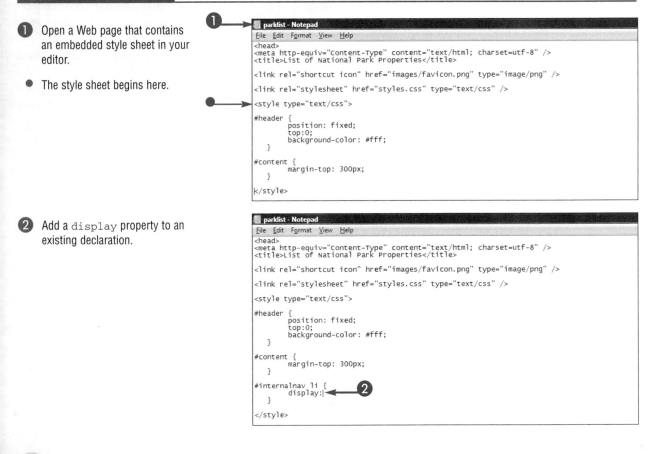

① Open a Web page that contains an embedded style sheet in your editor.

● The style sheet begins here.

② Add a display property to an existing declaration.

③ Set the value to `inline` if the element being styled is a `block`, or `block` if it is `inline`.

④ Save the page.

⑤ Open a Web page linked to the style sheet in a browser.

● The page opens, showing the list for the navigation on a single line.

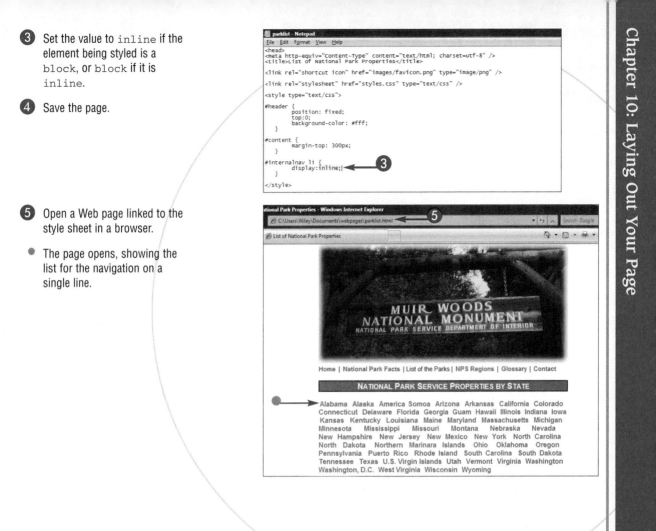

Extra

Closely related to the `display` property is `visibility`, which has commonly used values of `visible` and `hidden`. Obviously, the default is `visible`, but elements can be set to `hidden` so that they do not show up on the page. While it may seem at first that `display:none` and `visibility:hidden` are the same, they have an important difference. Setting an element to `display:none` removes it from the page entirely, while with `visibility:hidden`, it is merely not showing. This is crucial in determining the layout of the page. Elements with `display:none` will not affect other elements on the page as they are treated as if they were not present, while elements with `visibility:hidden` will still be considered as being part of the flow of the page and thus may impact the placement of other elements. `Visibility` also accepts a value of `collapse`, which only applies in tables and causes the cells, rows, or columns to which it is applied to be hidden in the document but still affects the overall layout of the table; for example, a width set on a column with `visibility:collapse` would still be used in calculating the width of the table.

Replace a Header with an Image

Even given the rich formatting possibilities available in CSS, many designers would prefer to design images to use in place of headers. Unfortunately, using an `img` tag instead of `h1`, `h2`, or other header tags severely impacts the accessibility and searchability of your site, as both accessible devices and search engines rely heavily on the presence of header elements. However, you do not have to sacrifice the visual appearance of your page in the name of making a site search engine friendly and accessible. CSS gives you the ability to use its background image property, along with a few tricks, to get the best of both.

The header replacement technique involves starting with normal header text, marked up with the appropriate heading element and an ID: `<h1 id="mainheader"> Welcome to our site</h1>`.

Then you can use CSS to place an image in the background of the header by setting the `background-image`, `background-repeat`, and `background-position` properties. Finally, you need to hide the text. You cannot use the `display:none` or `visibility:hidden` properties, as both have the effect of removing or hiding the entire element, including its background. Instead, most designers rely on the `text-indent` property. You will recall that `text-indent` indents the first line of a block of text. However, this property, like most others in CSS, allows for a negative value, so you simply add a very large negative indent to the heading, and your text is hidden off-screen for your sighted users, leaving only your image, while search engines and accessible devices continue to read it.

```
#mainheader { background-image:
url(images/mainhead.jpg); background-
repeat:no-repeat; background-position: top
left; text-indent: -9999px;}
```

Replace a Header with an Image

① Open a Web page with an embedded style sheet in your editor.

● The style sheet begins here.

② Add a declaration for the heading you will replace.

③ Add a `background` property with a value pointing to the image you wish to use for your heading, `no-repeat`, and `top left`.

4. Add a `text-indent` property with a value set to `-9999px`.

5. Add a `height` property equal to the height of the image.

6. Add any additional rules you need.

7. Save the page.

8. Open the Web page in a browser.

● The page opens, showing the header image.

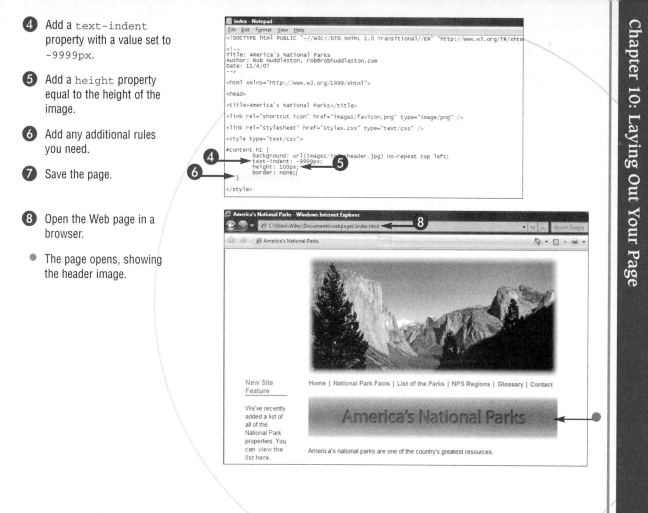

Apply It

If the text that you are replacing is hyperlinked, the browser will draw a thin dotted outline around the text if users tab to the link or if they click the link and then use the browser's Back button to return to the page. Because of the negative `text-indent`, this outline will appear to have started somewhere off the page, and come all the way across to end where the text would have ended. You can prevent this outline from showing up by adding the `outline:none` property to your style declaration:

```
#mainheader {
background-image: url(images/mainhead.jpg);
background-repeat:no-repeat;
background-position: top left;
text-indent: -9999px;
outline: none;
}
```

Create Tabbed Navigation

Most sites place their *main navigation* — the links to the primary sections of the site — in a row somewhere near the top of the page. A look originally popularized by Amazon.com, but now used with increasing frequency throughout the Web, is tabbed navigation, whereby these main links are presented as a series of individual tabs. In the early days of the Web, including Amazon.com's original implementation, tabbed navigation required that the designer create a series of images for the links. Unfortunately, this reduced the accessibility and searchability of the page, as well as dramatically increased the development time required to maintain the page, as even minor changes to the navigation required reworking images.

Today, the same look can be achieved on pure text links via CSS. Using a simple unordered list and normal, text-based anchor tags, along with a few simple images, you can create visually stunning navigation that is accessible, search-engine friendly, and extremely simple to maintain.

To implement this technique, you will combine a series of CSS properties. First, you need to make a few modifications to the list. It needs to be rendered horizontally, which you can achieve either by setting its `display` property to `inline` or by `floating` the items. While either will work, it is a little easier to control the list through floats. Also, you need to eliminate the default list indentation and the marker. Then you need to set the `display` property of the anchor to `block`, so that you can control the `height` and `width` using the block box model, rather than the inline model. Next, you need to set a `width` of `100%` and `float` the container for the element, which ensures that the links appear as a stand-alone block on the page. You can also set basic `font` properties for the links and a `background-color` for the container.

Create Tabbed Navigation

CREATE THE NAVIGATION LIST

1. Open a Web page that contains a link to a style sheet and a list of main links in your editor.

2. If necessary, add an `id` attribute and appropriate value to the container around the navigation.

3. Save the page.

4. Open the style sheet in your editor.

5. Add a declaration for the container element.

6. Add a `width` rule, `float:left`, and any other desired properties to the declaration.

7. Use a contextual selector to create a declaration for the `ul` in the container.

8. Add `margin:0`, `padding:0`, `list-style-type:none` and, if necessary, `list-style-image:none` rules.

9. Use a contextual selector to create a declaration for the `li` elements in the container.

10. Add a `float:left` rule.

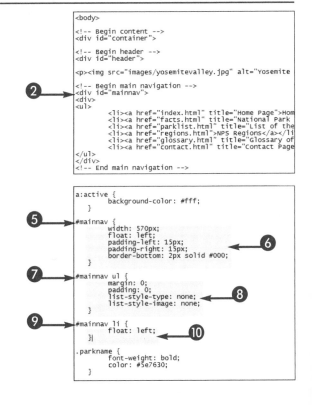

```
<body>

<!-- Begin content -->
<div id="container">

<!-- Begin header -->
<div id="header">

<p><img src="images/yosemitevalley.jpg" alt="Yosemite

<!-- Begin main navigation -->
<div id="mainnav">
<div>
<ul>
        <li><a href="index.html" title="Home Page">Hom
        <li><a href="facts.html" title="National Park
        <li><a href="parklist.html" title="List of the
        <li><a href="regions.html">NPS Regions</a></li
        <li><a href="glossary.html" title="Glossary of
        <li><a href="contact.html" title="Contact Page
</ul>
</div>
<!-- End main navigation -->
```

```
a:active {
        background-color: #fff;
    }
#mainnav {
        width: 570px;
        float: left;
        padding-left: 15px;
        padding-right: 15px;
        border-bottom: 2px solid #000;
    }
#mainnav ul {
        margin: 0;
        padding: 0;
        list-style-type: none;
        list-style-image: none;
    }
#mainnav li {
        float: left;
    }
.parkname {
        font-weight: bold;
        color: #5e7630;
    }
```

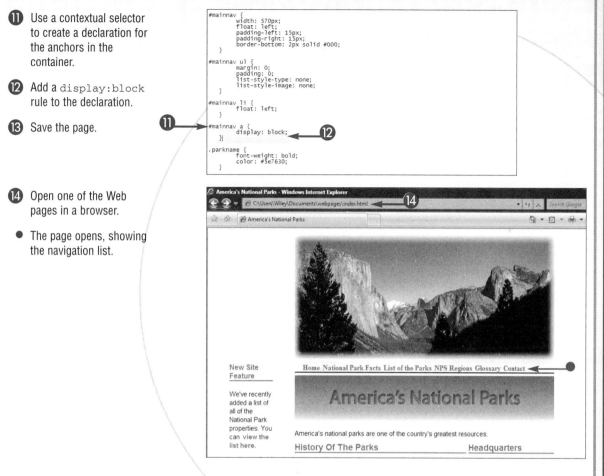

⑪ Use a contextual selector to create a declaration for the anchors in the container.

⑫ Add a `display:block` rule to the declaration.

⑬ Save the page.

⑭ Open one of the Web pages in a browser.

● The page opens, showing the navigation list.

Extra

Several bugs exist in older browsers that can cause problems with this technique. Internet Explorer 5 for Macintosh, for example, does not correctly implement floats. In this case, that browser shows your tabs stacked on top of one another and extending the length of the page. Fortunately, you can fix this problem by setting a `float` for the anchors, which causes the browser to render the effect correctly, and then use the "IE5/Mac backslash hack" technique to reset the `float` to `none` to prevent the fix from breaking the effect in other browsers. This and other hacks will be discussed later in this chapter.

Internet Explorer 6 and earlier for Windows suffer from another issue. This implementation should allow the user to click anywhere within the tab area to activate a link, but older versions of Internet Explorer only allow clicking on the text area of a link, even if it is rendered as a block. The fix to this issue is to give the anchor a tiny `width` of perhaps 1%. Unfortunately, while this fixes the issue for those browsers, it creates unclickable links on every other browser, which will apply the tiny width. Therefore, it will be necessary to use a child selector — not supported by Internet Explorer for Windows until version 7 — to reset the `width` to `auto`.

continued ➡

O nce you have the basic list styles in place, you can add the images to complete the tabbed navigation effect. To allow the tabs to expand as much as needed to fit different lengths of text, you will need at least two images: one for the left edge of the tab, and another for the right edge.

CSS only supports placing one image in the background of each element. Fortunately, however, you have two elements in place for each link: the list item and the anchor. Therefore, you can create the effect of combining the two images for your effect. A fortunate side effect of CSS is that background images on nested elements will overlap, so you can have the left edge image be only wide enough for the curved top effect, and the right edge image actually contain both that edge and the background for the rest of the tab. By making the right

edge image much longer than necessary, and then placing it on the anchor, it will slide beneath the left edge image, allowing your tab to expand and contract as needed — thus, the creator of this technique, Douglas Bowman, dubbed it "sliding doors."

It is perhaps easiest to create the tab as a single image in your editor. Most graphics programs allow you to "slice" an image into pieces, so you can take the single tab image and save it as the two you need.

You might also decide to create a "current" image that represents some visual modification of the normal image to place on the link to the page on which the user is currently visiting. You can use the "You Are Here" technique outlined in the next task to apply the image to the current page.

Create Tabbed Navigation (continued)

CREATE THE TABS

1 In the style sheet, add a background property to the declaration for the li in the container.

2 Set the url value to the path for the image that will be the right side of the tab.

3 Add no-repeat right top to the rule.

4 Add left and right margins to create space between each tab.

5 Add a background property to the declaration for the anchors.

6 Set the url value to the path for the image that will be the left side of the tab.

7 Add no-repeat left top to the rule.

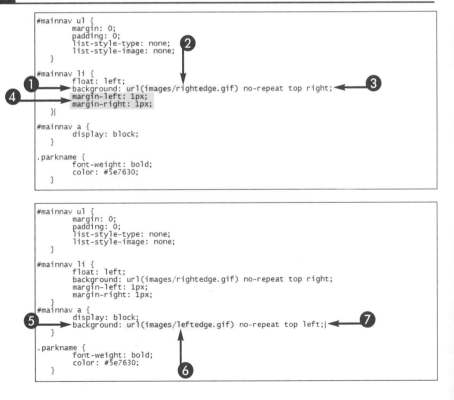

```
#mainnav ul {
        margin: 0;
        padding: 0;
        list-style-type: none;
        list-style-image: none;
}

#mainnav li {
        float: left;
        background: url(images/rightedge.gif) no-repeat top right;
        margin-left: 1px;
        margin-right: 1px;
}

#mainnav a {
        display: block;
}

.parkname {
        font-weight: bold;
        color: #5e7630;
}
```

```
#mainnav ul {
        margin: 0;
        padding: 0;
        list-style-type: none;
        list-style-image: none;
}

#mainnav li {
        float: left;
        background: url(images/rightedge.gif) no-repeat top right;
        margin-left: 1px;
        margin-right: 1px;
}
#mainnav a {
        display: block;
        background: url(images/leftedge.gif) no-repeat top left;|
}

.parkname {
        font-weight: bold;
        color: #5e7630;
}
```

8 Add `padding` to position the link text within the tab.

9 If necessary, change the `color` of the anchor text so that it will be readable against the image.

10 Save the page.

11 Open one of the web pages in a browser.

- The page opens, showing the tabbed navigation.

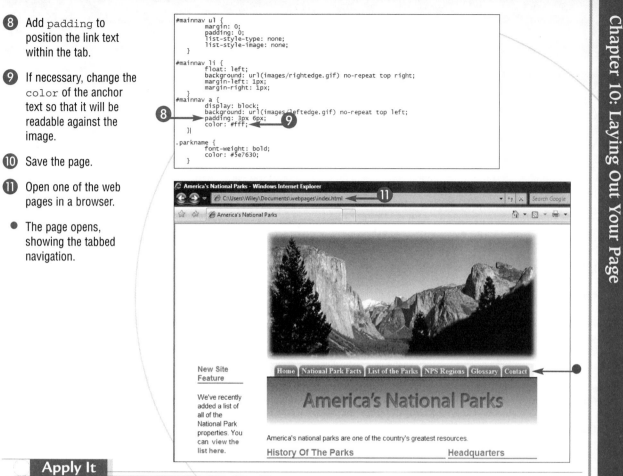

```
#mainnav ul {
        margin: 0;
        padding: 0;
        list-style-type: none;
        list-style-image: none;
    }
#mainnav li {
        float: left;
        background: url(images/rightedge.gif) no-repeat top right;
        margin-left: 1px;
        margin-right: 1px;
    }
#mainnav a {
        display: block;
        background: url(images/leftedge.gif) no-repeat top left;
        padding: 3px 6px;
        color: #fff;
    }

.parkname {
        font-weight: bold;
        color: #5e7630;
    }
```

Apply It

Often, you will want a border along the bottom of the navigation bar, but also want the current link to "bleed through" this border. You can achieve this by adding a background image that includes the bottom border to the container element, and then ensuring that the current link has an additional pixel of bottom padding so that it overlaps the container's background.

```
#header {
    background:#DAE0D2 url("bg.gif") repeat-x bottom;
    /* other styles omitted for space */
    }
  #header ul {
    padding:10px 10px 0 10px;
    /* other styles omitted for space */
    }
#header a {
    padding:5px 15px 4px 15px;
    /* other styles omitted for space */
    }
  #header #current a {
    padding-bottom:5px;
    /* other styles omitted for space */
    }
```

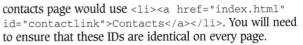
An important aspect of usability is letting your users know which page they are on currently. On sites with tabbed navigation, this might involve changing the color of the tab. Sites with traditional text links will often change the text or background color of the link to the current page. However you accomplish it, you need to do something to give your users a visual indicator of their location. Normally, adding this kind of indicator would require that you modify the XHTML pages themselves. However, it is possible to use CSS contextual selectors to achieve the same effect without modifying the individual pages at all.

To begin this process, you need to add unique identifiers to each link. For example, your link to your home page, assuming that you are using an unordered list for your navigation, might be `<li><a href="index.html" id="homelink">Home</a></li>`, while your link to the contacts page would use `<li><a href="index.html" id="contactlink">Contacts</a></li>`. You will need to ensure that these IDs are identical on every page.

The real "magic" of this technique involves uniquely identifying each of the actual pages, which you can accomplish by adding the ID attribute to the body element: `<body id="homepage">` or `<body id="contactpage">`.

Now that your elements are identified, you can simply create a declaration that uses a contextual selector to style the `homelink` only when it appears within the `homepage`, and the `contactlink` only when it appears within the `contactpage`:

```
#homepage #homelink, #contactpage
#contactlink {

    /* unique current page style here */ }
```

Create "You Are Here" Navigation

① Open a Web page that contains a link to a style sheet in your editor.

② Add an `id` attribute and appropriate value to each element containing a link in the navigation section.

③ Add an `id` attribute and appropriate value to the `body` element's opening tag.

④ Save the page.

⑤ Repeat Steps 1 to 4 for each additional page in your site.

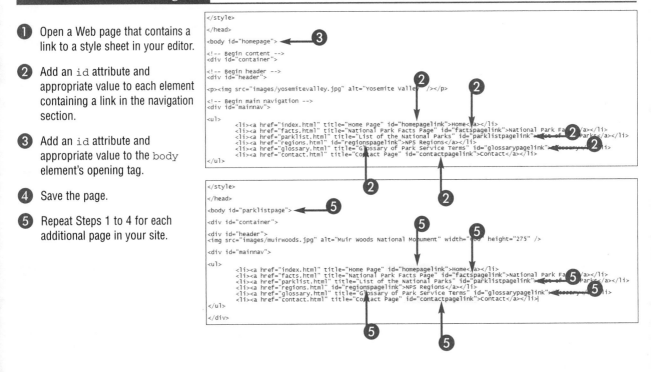

⑥ Open the style sheet in your editor.

⑦ Add a declaration using a contextual group selector for each page/link ID combination.

⑧ Add rules for the links.

⑨ If necessary, add other declarations to further style the links.

⑩ Save the page.

⑪ Open one of the Web pages in a browser.

⑫ Click one of the links in the navigation.

● The new page opens, showing the changed link.

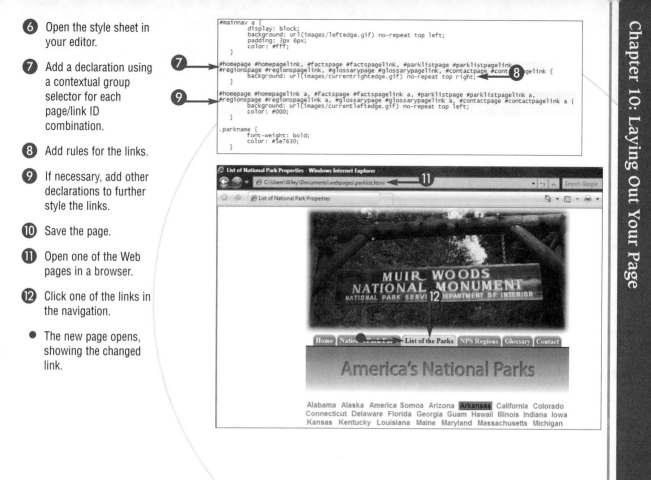

```
#mainnav a {
        display: block;
        background: url(images/leftedge.gif) no-repeat top left;
        padding: 3px 6px;
        color: #fff;
}

#homepage #homepagelink, #factspage #factspagelink, #parklistpage #parklistpagelink,
#regionspage #regionspagelink, #glossarypage #glossarypagelink, #contactpage #contactpagelink {
        background: url(images/currentrightedge.gif) no-repeat top right;
}

#homepage #homepagelink a, #factspage #factspagelink a, #parklistpage #parklistpagelink a,
#regionspage #regionspagelink a, #glossarypage #glossarypagelink a, #contactpage #contactpagelink a {
        background: url(images/currentleftedge.gif) no-repeat top left;
        color: #000;
}

.parkname {
        font-weight: bold;
        color: #5e7630;
}
```

Extra

This technique is particularly helpful if you use Adobe Dreamweaver, Adobe Contribute, or Microsoft Expression Web for your editing. All three of those applications can rely on a templating system, originally developed for Dreamweaver, whereby the designer can create a template for pages and then designate that only certain areas of the document can be modified in pages created from the template. As the main navigation is almost always not in the editable area of the page, it is not generally possible to make page-by-page modifications to create the "You Are Here" links. You can accomplish the technique outlined previously almost entirely from the template itself, where you would set up the links and their IDs, and the style sheet. The only modification that you need to make to the individual pages is to add the ID to the body element; and the programs make it possible to make a particular attribute of an element — in this case, the ID of the body — editable.

Create a Print Style Sheet

The Web and print are fundamentally different media, and designs that work well for one will not work well for the other. Anyone who has ever tried to print a Web page knows that it rarely works as expected.

Rather than maintaining a separate print-friendly version of each page, or converting the document into an overly large, unwieldy PDF, or ignoring the issue altogether, you can use CSS to create printer-friendly pages. One of the biggest advantages to creating standards-based pages that separate content from presentation is that the presentation layer can then change based on the current needs, without having to modify the underlying content.

Creating a print style sheet is a fairly straightforward process. You simply create a new CSS document that will contain the style declarations to be used when printing.

This style sheet will be used in conjunction with the main style sheet, so most of the work in the print CSS will be overriding properties from the main style sheet that will not apply. You might, for example, want to set all of your `font-size` properties to use points instead of percentages. You can also use the `display:none` rule to remove elements, such as navigation, that would not be necessary in print, and reposition and resize other elements accordingly to create an entirely new layout for the page.

Once the new style sheet has been created, you can add another `link` element to your document. In addition to the `rel`, `href`, and `type` attributes, you will now add a `media` attribute, set to `print`. With this present, the browser automatically applies the print styles — but only when printing.

Create a Print Style Sheet

① Create a new style sheet document in your editor.

② Add a comment at the top of the document that this is a print style sheet.

③ Add declarations for each element you wish to style.

④ Save the page.

5 Open a Web page in your editor.

6 In the head section, add a link element.

7 Add appropriate rel, href, and type attributes.

8 Add a media attribute with a value of print.

9 Save the page.

10 Open the Web page in a browser.

11 Click File → Print Preview.

● The Print Preview displays.

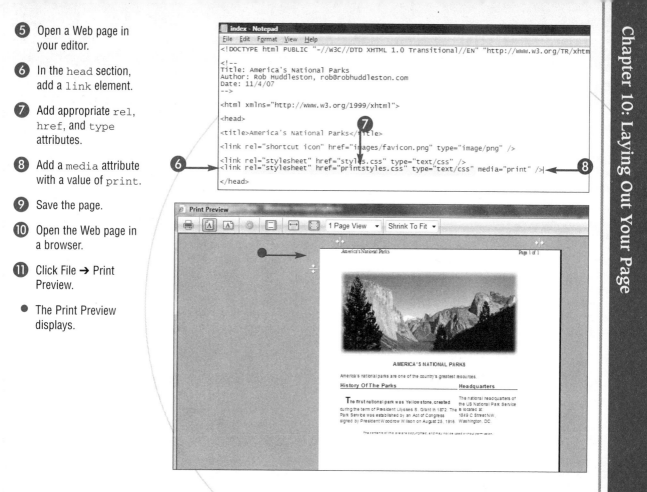

Apply It

You can specify the media type if you are importing style sheets by adding the media property following the path to the imported style sheet:

```
<style type="text/css">
@import url(mainstyles.css);
@import url(printstyles.css) print;
 </style>
```

You can also add the media attribute to the style element's opening tag if you wish to add media-specific embedded styles:

```
<style type="text/css" media="print">
@import url(printstyles.css);
p { font-size: 12pt; }
</style>
```

Understanding Common CSS Hacks

One of the common criticisms of CSS is that while the language itself is fairly well developed, browser implementation lags far behind. Microsoft Internet Explorer, by far the most commonly used browser, has long been a source of frustration by designers due to its many incorrect or missing implementations of aspects of the language. Over the years, many hacks have been developed to overcome browser limitations.

To Hack or Not to Hack

Before utilizing a CSS hack, you should ask yourself whether you really need it. The problem with all of these hacks is that they are just that: hacks. By definition, they are not supported features of the language, and therefore needlessly clutter your code. Also, the possibility exists that a future version of a browser may solve the problem by itself, thereby breaking the very page you were attempting to fix. This actually occurred in 2006, when Microsoft released Internet Explorer 7, which vastly improved the browser's support for CSS but in the process broke many pages that were using Internet Explorer-specific hacks targeted at older versions.

Internet Explorer Conditional Comments

Internet Explorer supports the use of conditional comments to make available sections of code — usually, browser-specific CSS work-arounds — to certain versions of the browser. While not technically hacks as they are formally documented in the browser, conditional comments only apply to one particular browser, and while officially supported by Microsoft, are not part of the actual CSS specification.

Conditional comments are expressed in the code through the use of a normal XHTML comment syntax, with an added conditional statement:

```
<!--[if IE6]
<style type="text/css">
/* IE 6 specific code here
</style>
-->
```

The Phantom html Parent Element

Many of the hacks employed by designers are targeted at one set of browsers: Internet Explorer 6 and earlier for Windows. While most of the fixes to Internet Explorer CSS bugs are fairly simple, most will unfortunately cause other browsers to read the fixes as valid CSS and actually break their display.

While many hacks rely on conditional comments, another way to hide Internet Explorer-specific hacks is through the use of a strange artifact in the early Internet Explorer CSS implementation. CSS relies on the fact that every XHTML element is nested within some other element, up to the root html element. Internet Explorer, however, saw a mystical "wrapper" element that was a container for html, and represented by an asterisk. Because no other browser saw this phantom parent element, styles applied to it would only affect Internet Explorer.

```
* html #container { /* IE 6 and earlier hacks
*/ }
```

It is important to note that Internet Explorer 7 no longer recognizes this element, so hacks targeted at it through this method will not work.

The IE5/Mac Backslash Hack

Another common problem browser is Internet Explorer 5 for the Macintosh. Oddly, this version of the browser was fundamentally different from its Windows counterpart, so while it had a host of CSS rendering problems, they were for the most part different from the problems suffered by Internet Explorer for Windows, and required different hacks. However, like the Windows version, the hacks centered around solving problems on the Macintosh version required that they be hidden from supporting browsers.

This issue was solved through the Backslash Hack. This odd little solution became available when it was discovered that if a CSS comment contained a backslash, the Macintosh browser would ignore whatever declaration followed. Therefore, the following block of code hides the width assignment from the browser.

```
/* hide from IE5/Mac \ */
height: 1%;
/* end IE5/Mac hiding */
```

It is worth noting that Microsoft has discontinued support and development of Internet Explorer for Macintosh, so its use has been steadily declining and should disappear altogether in the near future.

The Holly Hack

The Holly Hack, named for the hack's inventor, Holly Bergevin, is one of the best-known CSS hacks. It was developed to solve the "Expanding Box Problem" in Internet Explorer for Windows and Macintosh. Basically, when the browser encounters a floated box with a given dimension in either width or height, but the contents of the box are too large for the stated dimension, the browser incorrectly expands the box to fit. This is most obvious in boxes with a stated height that have too much content. In other browsers, the content will overflow the box, but its height in regards to the drawing of borders and placement of other elements will adhere to the stated height. Internet Explorer 6 and earlier actually resize the box.

The Holly Hack solves this problem by giving the floated box a very small height — usually, 1%. This causes the browser to behave correctly.

```
/* hide this from IE5/Mac \ */
* html #problemBox { height: 1%; }
/* end hide */
```

The Box Model Hack

One of the best known issues with Internet Explorer is that it incorrectly calculates the dimensions of boxes. According to the CSS specification, the stated width of a box is the width of the content, so the total horizontal dimension is the width plus the left and right padding, plus the size of the left and right borders, plus the left and right margins. Unfortunately, Internet Explorer calculated the box differently, applying the width to the total horizontal dimension, making it necessary to calculate the actual size of the content by *subtracting* the margins, borders, and padding from it. The height of a box is calculated in the same way.

Developer Tantek Çelik created an odd but functional workaround that involves setting the width or height to the size expected by Internet Explorer, and then essentially confusing the browser into giving up on the rest of the declaration, at which point a "correct" dimension can be given.

```
#container {
    width: 150px; /* incorrect IE width */
    voice-family: "\"}\"";
    voice-family: inherit;
    width: 130px; /* corrected width */
}
```

The voice-family lines are CSS rules that the browser does not understand. Note the closing curly brace in the first line: Standards-based browsers ignore it, while the problem browser sees it as the end of the declaration, and thus it never sees the new width.

Internet Explorer 6 and 7 both introduced a new fix to this solution: Both will correctly calculate dimensions if they are in "standards" mode, which occurs whenever they are given a correct HTML Strict or XHTML Strict DOCTYPE; therefore, this hack is unnecessary if you use either of those.

Create a Form

X HTML provides for a host of form controls to accept different types of data. Which controls you use depends on the needs of your site, but regardless of what kind of information you need to collect or what you plan to do with it, you will always begin with the `form` element to define the form itself. All of the form controls will be wrapped within this element's tags.

The `form` tag takes two required attributes. The easier attribute to understand is `action`, which is simply the path to the page on the server that will process the form — that is, the page to which you need to send the data. The second attribute, `method`, instructs the browser as to how it should send the data, and it accepts two possible values:

`get` and `post`. When using `get`, the data from the form is sent as part of the URL as a query string. The URL visible in the browser on the action page will consist of the address of the page, followed by a question mark, and then the form data.

Unfortunately, there are many disadvantages to using `get`, not the least of which is that the URL has a limited length. When attempting to send large amounts of data, as from a long form, you should use `post`, in which the browser sends the form data in the HTTP headers: the information it sends to the server when it connects. In theory, any amount of data can be sent in a `post` request. While `get` is the default method, it is recommended that you always use `post`.

Create a Form

① Open a Web page in your editor.

② Within the `body`, add a `form` element's opening tag.

```
<!-- End main navigation -->
</div>

<!-- End header -->
</div>

<!-- begin main content -->
<div id="content">

<h1>Contact Us</h1>

<form |          ← ②

<div id="footer">

<p>The contents of this site are copyrighted, and may not be used without permission.</p>

</div>

<!-- End content -->
</div>

</body>

</html>
```

③ Add the `action` attribute.

④ Set the attribute's value to a path to a file on the server.

```
<!-- End main navigation -->
</div>

<!-- End header -->
</div>

<!-- begin main content -->
<div id="content">

<h1>Contact Us</h1>

<form action="contact_action"|     ← ④

<div id="footer">

<p>The contents of this site are copyrighted, and may not be used without permission.</p>

</div>   ③

<!-- End content -->
</div>

</body>

</html>
```

5 Add the `method` attribute.

6 Set the value to `post`.

```
<!-- End main navigation -->
</div>

<!-- End header -->
</div>

<!-- begin main content -->
<div id="content">

<h1>Contact Us</h1>

<form action="contact_action" method="post">  ←——— 6

<div id="footer">

<p>The contents of this site are copyrighted, and may not be used without permission.</p>

</div>

<!-- End content -->
</div>

</body>

</html>
```

5

7 Add the closing `form` tag.

8 Save the page.

The file is saved.

```
<!-- End main navigation -->
</div>

<!-- End header -->
</div>

<!-- begin main content -->
<div id="content">

<h1>Contact Us</h1>

<form action="contact_action" method="post">

</form>  ←——— 7

<div id="footer">

<p>The contents of this site are copyrighted, and may not be used without permission.</p>

</div>

<!-- End content -->
</div>

</body>
```

Extra

Because the form values are visible on the browser's title bar when using `get`, many designers perceive it as less secure. In fact, none of the data sent by the browser, regardless of the method used, is secured in a normal Web transaction. Securing the data involves encrypting the data stream itself through SSL, or Secure Sockets Layer. This is an issue that has nothing to do with XHTML or the design of the Web page, and is best handled by a server administrator trained in security.

Using the `get` method presents several other disadvantages in addition to the length issue mentioned previously. Because the information is visible on the browser's address bar, it can be altered by the user without the user actually going through the form itself. In addition, you cannot send binary data with `get`, so you cannot allow for file uploads, whereas you can with `post`. The data in a `post` request is more effectively hidden from the user, and thus more difficult to send without the form. The biggest advantage of `get`, however, is that the results page can be saved as a Favorite or Bookmark in the browser, which is the reason why search engines use it instead of `post`.

Add a
Text Box

The most common form control by far is the single-line text field. Search engines use it to provide entry for search terms; registration systems use it for names, addresses, and credit card numbers; log-in systems rely on it for usernames.

Single-line text fields can be created in XHTML through the use of the `input` element. Somewhat unfortunately, `input` is actually used by almost every form control, and as such, it has a required `type` attribute that allows it to distinguish precisely which control is desired. For text fields, `type` will be set, logically, to `text`.

When the browser sends the information to the server, it needs to associate the user-entered data with the form control into which it was entered, and thus every form control has a required `name` attribute. The `name` may

consist only of letters, numbers, dashes, and underscores. As it will most likely become a variable in the programming language that processes the form, it will need to follow variable naming conventions for that language. While those rules vary, most languages require that the `name` begin with a letter and not a number. Also, depending on the language used, the `name` may be case-sensitive. Note that these are requirements of the processing language, and not XHTML. You will need to check with the developer who is creating the processing script or the documentation for the language to see if these or additional rules apply, but to be safe you should at least always begin with a letter.

The `input` tag will always be empty, so you should remember to put the trailing slash on the tag to close it.

Add a Text Box

① Open a Web page that contains a form in your editor.

② Within the form, add an `input` element's opening tag.

```
<!-- End main navigation -->
</div>

<!-- End header -->
</div>

<!-- begin main content -->
<div id="content">

<h1>Contact Us</h1>

<form action="contact_action" method="post">

<input |     ←——② 

</form>

<div id="footer">

<p>The contents of this site are copyrighted, and may not be used without permission.</p>

</div>

<!-- End content -->
</div>
```

③ Add the `type` attribute.

④ Set the attribute's value to `text`.

```
<!-- End main navigation -->
</div>

<!-- End header -->
</div>

<!-- begin main content -->
<div id="content">

<h1>Contact Us</h1>

<form action="contact_action" method="post">

<input type="text"|   ←——④

</form>

<div id="footer">

<p>The contents of this site are copyrighted, and may not be used without permission.</p>

</div>

<!-- End content -->
</div>
```

⑤ Add the `name` attribute.

⑥ Set the value to a name for the field.

⑦ Add a closing slash to the tag.

⑧ Save the page.

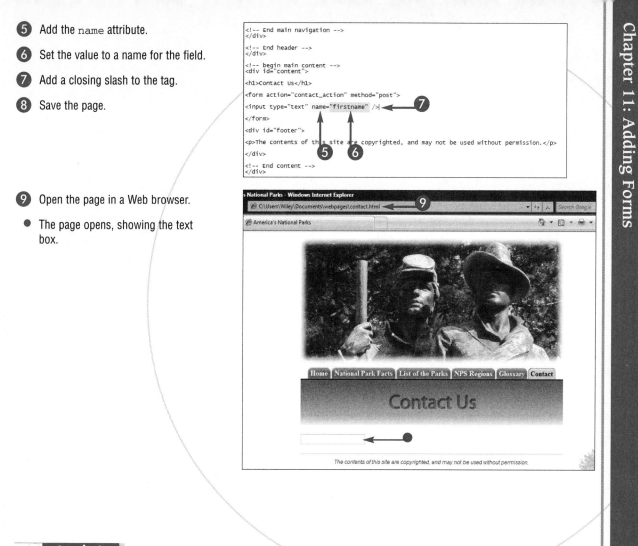

```
<!-- End main navigation -->
</div>

<!-- End header -->
</div>

<!-- begin main content -->
<div id="content">

<h1>Contact Us</h1>

<form action="contact_action" method="post">

<input type="text" name="firstname" />    ⑦

</form>

<div id="footer">

<p>The contents of this site are copyrighted, and may not be used without permission.</p>

</div>

<!-- End content -->
</div>
```

⑤ ⑥

⑨ Open the page in a Web browser.

● The page opens, showing the text box.

```
s National Parks - Windows Internet Explorer
C:\Users\Wiley\Documents\webpages\contact.html    ⑨
America's National Parks
```

Home | National Park Facts | List of the Parks | NPS Regions | Glossary | Contact

Contact Us

The contents of this site are copyrighted, and may not be used without permission.

Apply It

You can set the visible width of the field by adding the `size` attribute to the `input` tag:

```
<input type="text" name="custname" size="30" />
```

`Size` will not limit the number of characters the user may enter. Instead, the limit can be set with the `maxlength` attribute, which need not be the same as `size`:

```
<input type="text" name="custname" size="30" maxlength="20" />
```

You can also prefill data into the field through the `value` attribute:

```
<input type="text" name="custname" size="30" maxlength="20" value="Please enter a name" />
```

Add
Labels

A form that consists solely of form controls will be useless: How will users know what data to put in which fields if all they see are text fields? It is therefore necessary to add labels to the form.

Many designers simply label fields by placing text near the field: `<p>First Name: <input type="text" name="fname" /></p>`. While this approach will work, it unfortunately lacks any association between the text and the field. Sighted visitors will have no problem understanding that the text "First Name" is labeling the field, but screen readers for the blind may not be able to make that guess, particularly if other XHTML tags separate the items. Therefore, it is better to use the `label` element to explicitly create the association.

You can apply the label to the field in one of two ways. If no other code will separate the label from the field, then you can wrap the label text and the `input` tag in the `label` tag:

```
<label>First Name: <input type="text" name="fname" /></label>
```

If, however, other code needs to appear between the label and the control, you can associate one with the other by adding an `id` attribute to the form field, and then setting the `label` element's `for` attribute to a value matching the `id`:

```
<td><label for="fname">First Name</label></td><td><input type="text" name="fname" id="fname" /></td>
```

Add Labels

1 Open a Web page that contains a form in your editor.

2 Within the form, add a block element such as a paragraph.

```
<!-- begin main content -->
<div id="content">

<h1>Contact Us</h1>

<form action="contact_action" method="post">

<p>|

</form>

<div id="footer">

<p>The contents of this site are copyrighted, and may not be used without permission.</p>

</div>

<!-- End content -->
</div>

</body>

</html>
```

3 Add a `label` element's opening tag.

4 Add a descriptive label.

5 Add an `input` element's opening tag.

6 Add the `type` attribute.

7 Set the attribute's value to `text`.

```
<!-- begin main content -->
<div id="content">

<h1>Contact Us</h1>

<form action="contact_action" method="post">

<p>
<label>First Name: <input type="text"|

</form>

<div id="footer">

<p>The contents of this site are copyrighted, and may not be used without permission.</p>

</div>

<!-- End content -->
</div>

</body>
```

8. Add the `name` attribute.

9. Set the value to a name for the field.

10. Add a closing slash to the tag.

11. Add a closing label tag.

12. Add the closing paragraph tag.

13. Save the page.

14. Open the page in a Web browser.

- The page opens, showing the text field and its label.

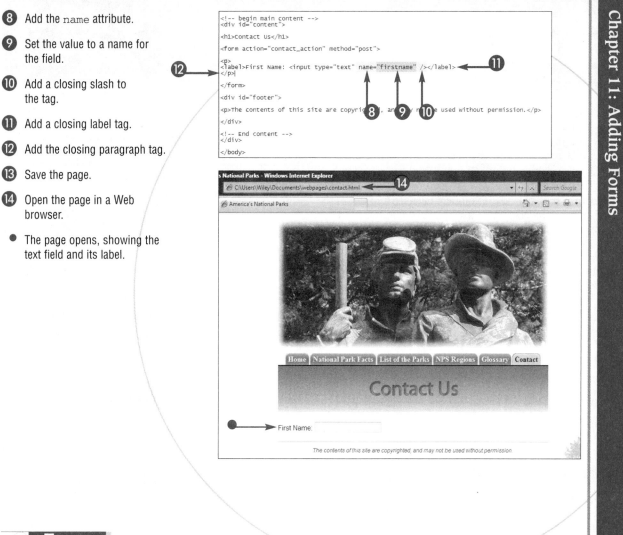

Extra

Several other advantages exist for using the `label` element beyond accessibility. For one, having the element gives you something to style: If you want to make all of the labels on the form bold and a particular color, you can do so through CSS by styling the `label` element.

Browsers also allow the user to click the label to give the form field focus. While this may not be necessary for text fields, it is particularly useful for smaller form controls such as radio buttons and check boxes. Be aware, however, that Internet Explorer from Windows suffers from a strange bug whereby it only allows the user to click the label to give the field focus if the `label` tag is using the `for` attribute, even if the tag wraps around the `input`. Therefore, many designers will use the `for` attribute at all times, even when wrapping the tag, to ensure proper behavior by Internet Explorer.

```
<label for="fname">First Name: <input type="text" name="fname" id="fname" /></label>
```

Add Check Boxes and Radio Buttons

Many times, you will not want your user to enter information, but rather select it from a preset list. While you cannot predict a user's name, and so must allow the user to enter it, you may have a set of additional offers you would like to present to your user.

Three form controls exist to allow your user to choose items from a predetermined list: check boxes, radio buttons, and select lists. Check boxes and radio buttons are useful when you have a fairly limited set of choices or when you need to present additional information about each choice. They differ in that check boxes allow the user to select zero or more of the choices, while radio buttons restrict the user to a single choice.

Like text fields, both check boxes and radio buttons use the input element. The only difference between the two in code is the type, which will be either checkbox or radio. Like all other form controls, both require a name. However, unlike text fields, which should always have unique names, all of the check boxes or radio buttons within a group need to have identical names. This way, the data can be handled as a logical set. If you do not use the same name on a set of radio buttons, the browser will not restrict the user to a single selection.

Finally, both check boxes and radio buttons require a value, which should be unique to each button. As there is no way for the user to enter a value, the value attribute allows you to set the meaning of the check box or radio button.

Add Check Boxes and Radio Buttons

1 Open a Web page that contains a form in your editor.

2 Within the form, add a block element such as a paragraph and some text to describe the group of check boxes.

3 Add a `label` element's opening tag followed by a descriptive label.

4 Add an `input` element's opening tag, with a `type` attribute with a value of `checkbox` and a `name` attribute with an appropriate value.

5 Add a `value` attribute with an appropriate value.

6 Add a closing slash to the tag and a closing label tag.

7 Repeat Steps 3 to 6 to add additional check boxes.

Note: Be sure that each check box has the same name, but a different value.

8 Add a closing paragraph tag.

9 Add a block element such as a paragraph and some text to describe the group of radio buttons.

10 Add a `label` element's opening tag followed by a descriptive label.

```
<p>
<label>Email: <input type="text" name="email" /></label>
</p>

<p>
How did you hear about our site (check all that apply):
<label>Search Engine
<input type="checkbox" name="referrer" value="searchengine" /></label>
<label>Print Ad
<input type="checkbox" name="referrer" value="printad" /></label>
<label>Radio Ad
<input type="checkbox" name="referrer" value="radioad" /></label>
</p>

</form>

<div id="footer">
```

```
<p>
<label>Email: <input type="text" name="email" /></label>
</p>

<p>
How did you hear about our site (check all that apply):
<label>Search Engine
<input type="checkbox" name="referrer" value="searchengine" /></label>
<label>Print Ad
<input type="checkbox" name="referrer" value="printad" /></label>
<label>Radio Ad
<input type="checkbox" name="referrer" value="radioad" /></label>
</p>

<p>
Please select your preferred method of contact:
<label>Email
<input type="radio" name="contact" value="email" /></label>
</p>

</form>

<div id="footer">
```

① Add an `input` element's opening tag with a `type` attribute with a value of `radio` and a `name` attribute with an appropriate value.

② Add a `value` attribute with an appropriate value.

③ Add a closing slash to the tag and a closing label tag.

④ Repeat Steps 9 to 13 to add additional radio buttons.

Note: Be sure that each radio button has the same name, but a different value.

⑤ Add a closing paragraph tag.

⑥ Save the page.

The file is saved.

⑦ Open the page in a Web browser.

● The page opens, showing the check boxes and radio buttons.

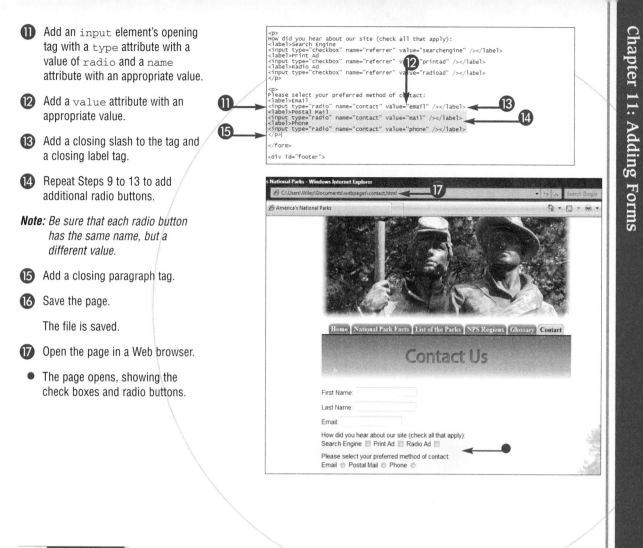

Apply It

You can pre-select a check box or radio button by adding the `checked="checked"` attribute to the tag:

```
<input type="checkbox" name="offers" value="1" checked="checked" />
<input type="radio" name="accept" value="yes" checked="checked" />
```

The attribute is oddly redundant because HTML did not require that attributes have a value, and thus in HTML using simply `checked` is legal. A value is required for all attributes in XHTML, and it was decided to simply use the name of the attribute as its only possible value.

Build a Drop-Down List

C heck boxes and radio buttons, by their nature, take a significant amount of space to implement. Therefore, if you have a lot of options from which you would like your user to choose, such as a list of the states in the United States or countries in the world, you can instead present the options as a drop-down list.

Drop-down lists in XHTML rely on two primary elements: select and option. The select element defines the list as a whole and provides its name. Within the select tags, you will have a series of option tags. Each option will contain a value, which is the data to be sent to the server. Between the opening and closing option tags will be the text that the user will see in the browser.

```
<select name="states">

        <option value="AL">Alabama</option>

        <option value="AK">Alaska</option>

</select>
```

Select lists with only a name attribute function equivalently to radio buttons: The user can only make a single selection. However, you can add two additional attributes to the select element to mimic the multiple-select action of check boxes. The multiple attribute, which will always have a value of multiple, instructs the browser that it should allow more than one selection, while the size attribute determines the number of options visible on the screen. Additional options can be accessed through a scroll bar the browser automatically adds.

Build a Drop-Down List

1. Open a Web page that contains a form in your editor.

2. Within the form, add a block element such as a paragraph.

3. Add a label element's opening tag followed by a descriptive label.

4. Add a select element's opening tag.

5. Add the name attribute with an appropriate value.

6. Add an option element's opening tag.

7. Add a value attribute and an appropriate value.

8. After the tag, add the text to display.

9. Add the closing option tag.

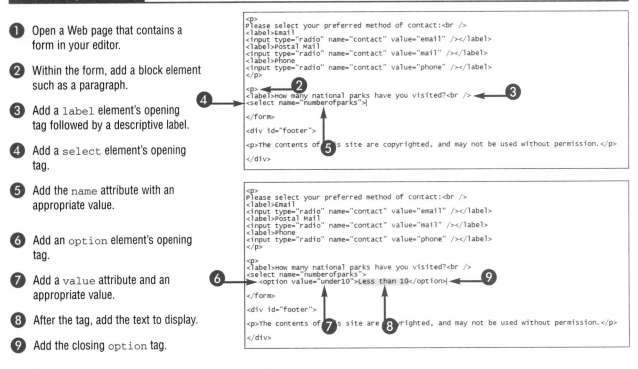

⑩ Repeat Steps 6 to 9 to add additional options.

⑪ Add a closing `select` tag, a closing `label` tag, and a closing paragraph tag.

⑫ Save the page.

⑬ Open the page in a Web browser.

● The page opens, showing the drop-down menu.

```
<p>
<label>How many national parks have you visited?<br />
<select name="numberofparks">
    <option value="under10">Less than 10</option>
    <option value="10-50">Between 10 and 50</option>
    <option value="51-100">Between 50 and 100</option>
    <option value="over100">More than 100</option>
</select>
</label>
</p>

</form>

<div id="footer">

<p>The contents of this site are copyrighted, and may not be used without permission.</p>

</div>
```

Extra

Your users can choose multiple adjacent options when using `multiple="multiple"` by pressing and holding the shift key while they make their choices. They can press and hold the Control key on Windows or the Command Key on the Macintosh to select more than one non-adjacent item. While many computer professionals will guess at this, as it is fairly standard on other applications, you can safely assume that most casual users will not. Therefore, it is always a good idea to add some helper text near the field to explain the use: "To choose more than one item, press and hold the Control key (Windows) or Command key (Macintosh)." Many designers simply place this instruction next to the field in question. Do not worry about making the distinction between holding the Shift key and holding Control. As the latter will work in all situations, it is simpler to just give your users the single option.

Like its counterpart in check boxes and radio buttons, the multiple attribute predates the XHTML required value rule, and thus was originally just `multiple`. XHTML uses the redundant but necessary `multiple="multiple"`.

Group Drop-Down Options

Some drop-down lists may contain many items. XHTML places no limit on the number of options that can be placed within a `select` list. However, users can find it intimidating to be faced with a very long list. Fortunately, you have the ability to group items into logical categories within the same list using the `optgroup` element. This element must be placed within a `select` tag, and will wrap around a set of `option` elements.

The `optgroup` element takes a required `label` attribute, which allows you to insert a description of the group of options that follows. On most browsers, the `label` text will be displayed with that group's options nested and slightly indented below it. Most browsers on Windows display the label using a bold, italic typeface, while

Macintosh browsers tend to use the regular typeface; however, you can change this through styles to ensure consistency across platforms. You should note that the `optgroup`'s label will not in itself be selectable.

Just as XHTML does not limit the number of options that may occur within `select`, it does not limit the number of `optgroups` either. However, XHTML does not currently provide the capability of nesting `optgroups`, so you cannot have subcategories. While future versions of the language may permit it, it is currently invalid and browser display of nested `optgroups` will vary from simply ignoring the nested group to possibly failing to render the options, so you must avoid this. Further, your pages will not validate, the importance of which will be discussed in Chapter 17.

Group Drop-Down Options

① Open a Web page that contains a form in your editor.

② Within the form, add a block element such as a paragraph.

③ Add a `label` element's opening tag followed by a descriptive label.

④ Add a `select` element's opening tag with an appropriate `name` attribute.

⑤ Add an `optgroup` element's opening tag.

⑥ Add a `label` attribute with an appropriate value.

⑦ Add an `option` element's opening tag with a `value` attribute and an appropriate value.

⑧ Add text to display for the option.

⑨ Add the closing `option` tag.

⑩ Add a closing `optgroup` tag.

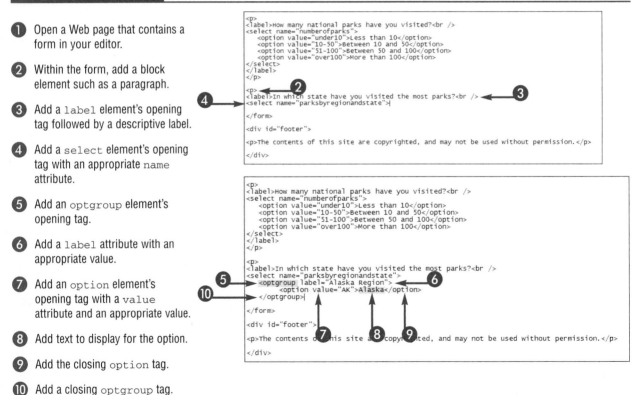

⑪ Repeat Steps 5 to 10 to add additional grouped options.

⑫ Save the page.

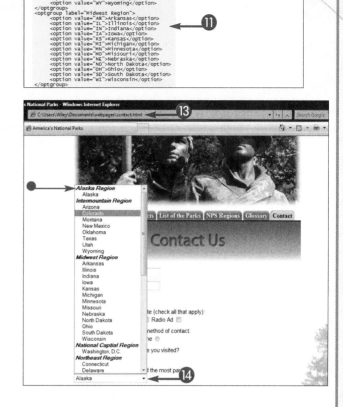

```
<select name="parksbyregionandstate">
   <optgroup label="Alaska Region">
      <option value="AK">Alaska</option>
   </optgroup>
   <optgroup label="Intermountain Region">
      <option value="AZ">Arizona</option>
      <option value="CO">Colorado</option>
      <option value="MT">Montana</option>
      <option value="NM">New Mexico</option>
      <option value="OK">Oklahoma</option>
      <option value="TX">Texas</option>
      <option value="UT">Utah</option>
      <option value="WY">Wyoming</option>
   </optgroup>
   <optgroup label="Midwest Region">
      <option value="AR">Arkansas</option>
      <option value="IL">Illinois</option>
      <option value="IN">Indiana</option>
      <option value="IA">Iowa</option>
      <option value="KS">Kansas</option>
      <option value="MI">Michigan</option>
      <option value="MN">Minnesota</option>
      <option value="MO">Missouri</option>
      <option value="NE">Nebraska</option>
      <option value="ND">North Dakota</option>
      <option value="OH">Ohio</option>
      <option value="SD">South Dakota</option>
      <option value="WI">Wisconsin</option>
   </optgroup>
```

⑬ Open the page in a Web browser.

⑭ Click the select list to see the grouped options.

● The list displays.

Extra

While modern browsers seem to have some of an agreement as to the display of `optgroup`, Internet Explorer 5 for the Macintosh — a browser no longer in development but still in use in many cases — takes a different and very visually interesting approach. Rather than simply listing the `optgroup`'s label and then placing the options below it, this browser actually creates a submenu system, whereby the initial display of the select list shows only the `optgroup` labels. When the user mouses over the label (●), a submenu appears with the options.

Insert a Text Area

Single-line text fields are fine for most text input, but there will be times when you need to encourage or allow your user to input large blocks of text. For example, social networking sites such as MySpace.com and online dating sites such as Match.com will have a field when you register in which you can write a short biography of yourself. E-commerce sites may provide a space in which customers can write a message to be printed on a greeting card for gifts. Online classified advertising sites like Craigslist.org must provide a space for the text of the ad.

XHTML provides for these scenarios through the use of the `textarea` element. Like every other form control, `textarea` takes a required `name` attribute. The default display size of the field varies between browsers, but the element also accepts `rows` and `cols` attributes to set the size, where the former sets the field's height and the latter its width.

Unlike the `input` element used for single-line fields, `textarea` is a container element, and thus has a required closing tag. If you wish to prepopulate the field with some default text, it will appear between the opening and closing tags. Interestingly, the `textarea` element violates the normal whitespace insensitivity of XHTML, as any whitespace between the opening and closing tags will be respected by the browser. For example, if you place the closing tag on a line below the opening tag and indent it, the initial cursor in the `textarea` will appear indented on the second row of the field.

Without JavaScript, there is no way to limit the amount of information the user can enter into a `textarea`. Some browsers restrict the data entry to 65,536 characters, but this cannot be guaranteed.

Insert a Text Area

1. Open a Web page that contains a form in your editor.

2. Within the form, add a block element such as a paragraph.

3. Add a `label` element's opening tag followed by a descriptive label.

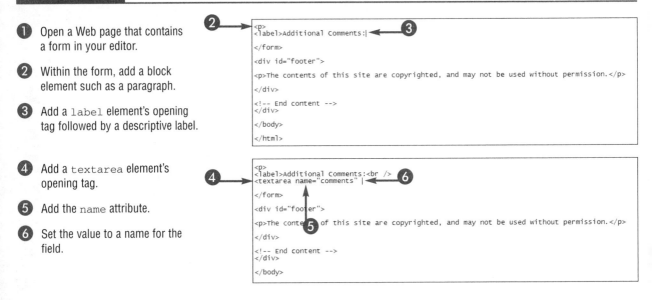

4. Add a `textarea` element's opening tag.

5. Add the `name` attribute.

6. Set the value to a name for the field.

7. Add a `rows` attribute and an appropriate value.

8. Add a `cols` attribute and an appropriate value.

9. Add the closing `textarea` tag.

10. Add the closing `label` tag and the closing paragraph tag.

11. Save the page.

12. Open the page in a Web browser.

• The page opens, showing the text area.

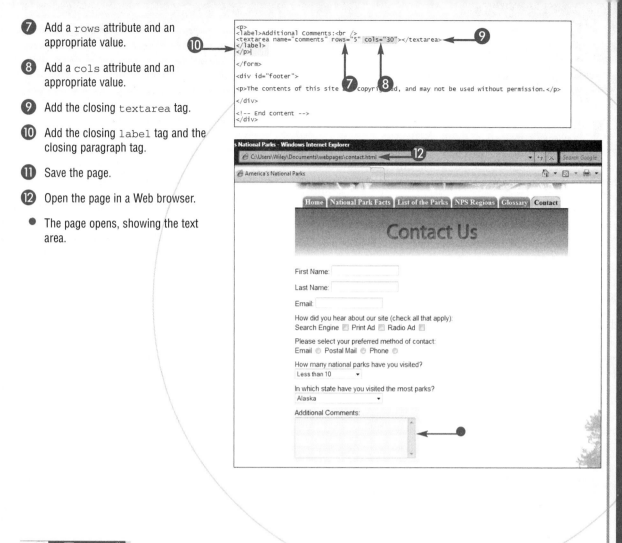

XHTML does not have a control for a rich text form field that provides a toolbar to allow the user to set the font and typeface properties such as bold, italic, and size. However, several implementations of rich text editors exist, and most are free to use.

One of the most robust and popular rich text fields is the FCKEditor. It can be downloaded free of charge from www.fckeditor.net. Implemented through a combination of XHTML and JavaScript, it includes a full feature set that allows you to set which tools will appear. It then takes the formatted text and translates it to XHTML for submission to the server. For example, if the user selects some text and clicks the bold button, the editor will wrap the text with a `strong` element. The editor even allows users to create hyperlinks within their text block. FCKEditor is also highly customizable, allowing you to choose which buttons will appear on its toolbars.

Add a
Hidden Field

Most form controls are, by definition, designed to allow your users to input the data they wish to send. However, there may be times on a form that you need to embed data to be sent that should not be editable by, or even visible to, users.

A good example of the use of hidden fields can be found on Google. When you visit the home page at www.google.com, you are presented with three visible form controls: a single-line input for the search term, and two buttons for performing the search. However, when you enter a search term and click one of the buttons, you will see that the address bar on the results page will look something like this:
www.google.com/search?q=xhtml&hl=en&btnG=Search+ Google. In this case, www.google.com/search is the form's action; q=xhtml is the data from the text field,

which Google somewhat oddly simply named "q"; and btnG=Search+Google is the name and value of the button. However, note that a third option exists from the form: hl=en. Google allows its users to translate its home and results pages into any one of several dozen real and fictional languages. The user's preference for the language is then embedded on the pages in a hidden field named hl.

Hidden fields are implemented through the use of input, this time setting the type attribute to hidden. The name attribute is as usual required. However, as the user obviously cannot enter information into the field, you must also provide a value attribute representing the data that is being embedded. No other attributes are needed or allowed with the hidden field, as settings such as size or maxlength obviously have no logical meaning.

Add a Hidden Field

① Open a Web page that contains a form in your editor.

② Within a block-level element in the form, add an input element's opening tag.

```
<p>
<label>Additional Comments:<br />
<textarea name="comments" rows="5" cols="30"></textarea>
</label>

<input |          ②
</p>

</form>

<div id="footer">

<p>The contents of this site are copyrighted, and may not be used without permission.</p>

</div>

<!-- End content -->
</div>
```

③ Add the type attribute.

④ Set the attribute's value to hidden.

⑤ Add the name attribute with an appropriate value.

```
<p>
<label>Additional Comments:<br />
<textarea name="comments" rows="5" cols="30"></textarea>
</label>

<input type="hidden" name="ref" |     ⑤
</p>

</form>

<div id="③ter" ④

<p>The contents of this site are copyrighted, and may not be used without permission.</p>

</div>

<!-- End content -->
</div>
```

6 Add a `value` attribute with an appropriate value.

7 Add a closing slash to the tag.

8 Save the page.

```
<p>
<label>Additional Comments:<br />
<textarea name="comments" rows="5" cols="30"></textarea>
</label>

<input type="hidden" name="ref" value="1" />
</p>

</form>

<div id="footer">

<p>The contents of this site are copyrighted, and may not be used without permission.</p>

</div>

<!-- End content -->
</div>
```

7

6

9 Open the page in a Web browser.

The page opens, but the hidden field does not appear.

9 C:\Users\Wiley\Documents\webpages\contact.html

s National Parks - Windows Internet Explorer

America's National Parks

| Home | National Park Facts | List of the Parks | NPS Regions | Glossary | Contact |

Contact Us

First Name:

Last Name:

Email:

How did you hear about our site (check all that apply):
Search Engine ☐ Print Ad ☐ Radio Ad ☐

Please select your preferred method of contact:
Email ◉ Postal Mail ◉ Phone ◉

How many national parks have you visited?
Less than 10 ▾

In which state have you visited the most parks?
Alaska ▾

Additional Comments:

Extra

E-commerce sites often use a multiple-page checkout system, where one page collects basic information from the customer such as name and address; and another page collects payment information, most often a credit card number; and yet another page displays the customer's shopping cart and a total for the transaction, allowing the user to confirm the order before placing it. The problem faced in creating such a form is the need to get the data collected on the first two pages to persist through to the third. Many beginning developers will attempt to use hidden fields for this purpose, whereby they take the data from page one and place it in hidden fields on page two, and then pass the combined pages one and two data as hidden fields on page three.

You need to keep in mind that while hidden fields do not appear in the browser window, they still exist in the underlying code and can be read using the browser's View Source command. Therefore, you should never store sensitive data in a hidden field, including passwords or, in the case mentioned previously, credit card numbers. Rather, the information should be stored on the server and looked up as needed.

Add a Password Field

Many Web sites need to be able to identify the user. Whether they are social networking sites that allow pages to be personalized for individuals, e-commerce sites that retain per-user order histories, or intranet sites that simply require users to be securely logged in before they can access information, you are likely to encounter many cases where you wish to require that your user enter a username and password.

In most cases, the username will be entered via a single-line text field, although situations may exist where the user can select his ID from a drop-down list or other control. The password, however, will always be entered via a field that masks the input. The XHTML password field is created using the `input` element with a `type` of `password`. Nothing more is required of the designer: The

browser will automatically replace the text being inserted into the field with a bullet or asterisk.

Like its text counterpart, the password `input` field accepts a `size` attribute to set the physical width of the field and a `maxlength` attribute to restrict the number of characters being input. Unlike the text field, however, the `value` attribute is not supported; for security reasons, the browser will not allow the password field to be pre-filled when the form loads. You will still need to provide a descriptive label for the field, which should be enclosed in a `label` tag.

You should note that the password field is only being masked by the browser, and is not at all secure. You will need to secure the transmission of the data to the server, as otherwise the password, along with all of the other data from the form, is sent in plain text and can be easily intercepted and read.

Add a Password Field

① Open a Web page that contains a form in your editor.

② Within the form, add a block element such as a paragraph.

③ Add a `label` element's opening tag, followed by a descriptive label.

④ Add an `input` element's opening tag.

⑤ Add the `type` attribute with a value of `password`.

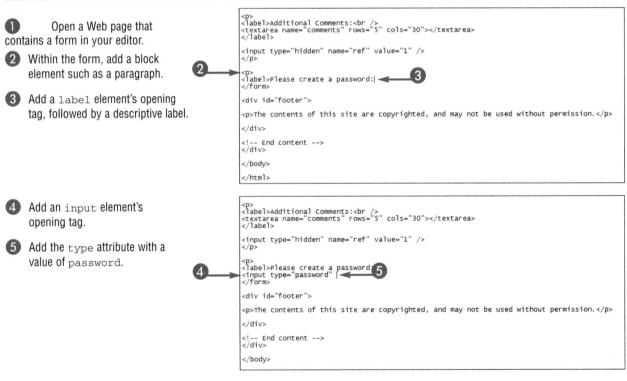

6 Add the `name` attribute with an appropriate value.

7 Add a closing slash to the tag.

8 Add a closing `label` tag and a closing paragraph tag.

9 Save the page.

10 Open the page in a Web browser.

● The page opens, showing the password field.

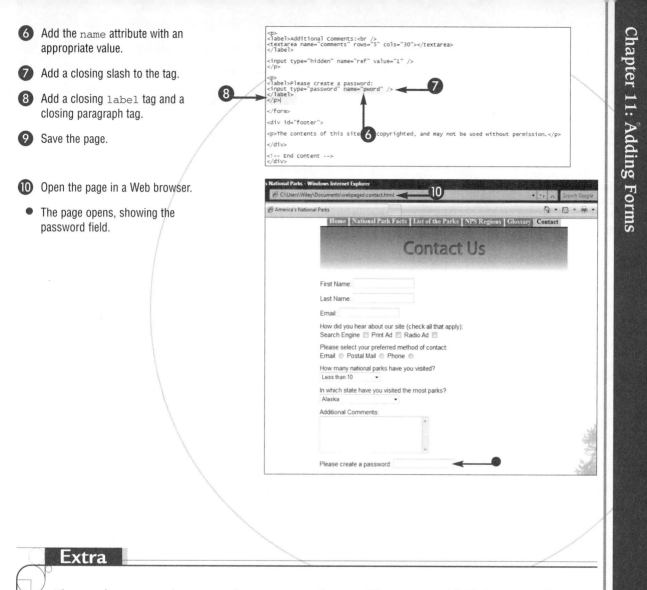

Add a File Upload Field

An increasingly popular use of the Web in the corporate world is for content management systems (CMS): Web sites, often housed and accessible only internally, that provide for information sharing throughout the company. CMS rely heavily on file uploads to allow employees to share documents. This way, a person in one section of the company can create a file using Microsoft Word or Excel or any other program and then use the CMS to upload to a central repository, making that document available to others in the company.

A file upload field on a Web page will consist of two parts: a text field for the path to the file and a button that allows the user to browse her computer's hard drive for the file. Both are implemented in XHTML through the `input` field with the `type` set to `file`. As always, a `name` is required on the field.

While you should still use an appropriate `label` for the field, the `size` and `maxlength` attributes are not supported. The latter makes no logical sense, as the field must in the end contain a complete path to the file being uploaded, and you as the designer will neither know nor care how long that path will be. Non-support for size is another issue, as many designers prefer the clean look of similarly sized fields, and this is simply an unfortunate oversight in the implementation of XHTML. Some browsers will allow the use of CSS to size the field, while others will not. You also do not have control over the size or placement of, or the text on, the Browse button.

Browsers, also unfortunately, do not allow for more than one file to be uploaded per field, so if you need to permit your users to upload multiple files, you will need to provide multiple fields, one per file.

Add a File Upload Field

① Open a Web page that contains a form in your editor.

② Within the form, add a block element such as a paragraph.

③ Add a `label` element's opening tag followed by a descriptive label.

④ Add an `input` element's opening tag.

⑤ Add the `type` attribute with a value of `file`.

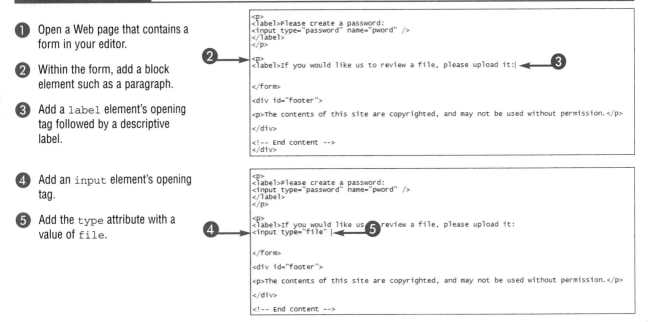

⑥ Add the `name` attribute with an appropriate value.

⑦ Add a closing slash to the tag.

⑧ Add a closing `label` tag and a closing paragraph tag.

⑨ Save the page.

⑩ Open the page in a Web browser.

● The page opens, showing the upload field.

```
<p>
<label>Please create a password:
<input type="password" name="pword" />
</label>
</p>

<p>
<label>If you would like us to review a file, please upload it:
<input type="file" name="upload" />
</label>
</p>

</form>

<div id="footer">

<p>The contents of this site are copyrighted, and may not be used without permission.</p>

</div>
```

s National Parks - Windows Internet Explorer

C:\Users\Wiley\Documents\webpages\contact.html

America's National Parks

Contact Us

First Name:

Last Name:

Email:

How did you hear about our site (check all that apply):
Search Engine ☐ Print Ad ☐ Radio Ad ☐

Please select your preferred method of contact:
Email ○ Postal Mail ○ Phone ○

How many national parks have you visited?
Less than 10

In which state have you visited the most parks?
Alaska

Additional Comments:

Please create a password:

If you would like us to review a file, please upload it: [Browse...]

Extra

In order for the file upload to succeed, you need to add an additional attribute to the `form` tag itself, `enctype`. The default `enctype` is `application/x-www-form-urlencoded`, in which the browser sends all of the data as text. When using file uploads, the file needs to be sent as binary data, while the rest of the information can still transmit as text, so you will need to add the `enctype` attribute and set its value to `multipart/form-data`. Also, you must set the `method` to `post` when using uploads.

```
<form method="post" action="form_action" enctype=" multipart/form-data">
<label>Select a file to upload: <input type="file" name="upload" /></label>
</form>
```

Add a Submit Button

After filling out the form, the user needs a way to instruct the browser that he is done and that it should send the data to the server for processing. This is most often accomplished via a submit button.

Buttons on forms most often use, like many other controls, the `input` element, this time with a `type` set to `submit`. Valid XHTML requires a `name` for the button. Browsers vary on the default text they use for buttons. You can overcome this and ensure consistency by providing a `value` attribute, which will be used as the text that appears on the button itself. For example, this allows you to have the button on a contact form say "Contact Us" rather than "Submit." The size of the button is determined by the length of the text provided in the `value` attribute, but it can be more precisely controlled via CSS.

Unfortunately, browsers are inconsistent in their handling of the user pressing the Return or Enter key instead of clicking the button with their mouse. So long as the form only contains a single button, all browsers will submit the form when the Enter or Return key is pressed; however, most but not all will not submit the button's `name` and `value` to the server if it is not clicked.

Multiple submit buttons are allowed on forms, but obviously only one may ever be clicked. A simple online calculator needs at a minimum four buttons, one for each of the basic mathematical operations. In this case, you need to be sure to provide a unique `name` for each, and use your server processing script to determine which button was clicked and then perform the necessary processing.

Add a Submit Button

① Open a Web page that contains a form in your editor.

② Within the form, add a block element such as a paragraph.

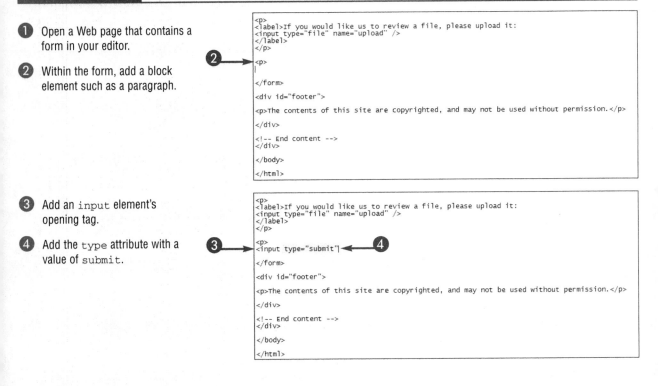

③ Add an `input` element's opening tag.

④ Add the `type` attribute with a value of `submit`.

⑤ Add the `value` attribute with an appropriate value.

⑥ Add a closing slash to the tag.

⑦ Add a closing paragraph tag.

⑧ Save the page.

⑨ Open the page in a Web browser.

● The page opens, showing the submit button.

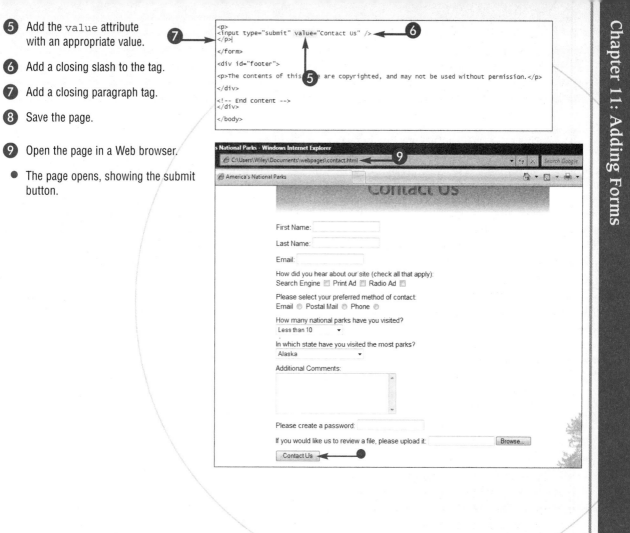

Make an Image into a Button

The `input` element can also have its `type` set to `image`. This somewhat confusing value in fact creates a submit button, but the browser will place an image on the page in place of the normal grey button with text.

Image buttons allow you, as the designer, to create submit buttons that more closely match the overall look of your site. The image path is set using the `src` attribute of input, and just as in using regular images, you should also use `alt` to set alternate text. If the image is not the proper size, it should ideally be resized in an image editor, but you can use the `width` and `height` attributes here to set the size if you wish. You can see that this is a particularly well-thought-out part of the XHTML implementation: In combining the `input` and `img`

elements, all of the relevant attributes from each were retained.

The main disadvantage is that, without JavaScript, there is no way to get an image button to do anything other than submit the form.

A somewhat strange side effect of using the image type for `input` is that the browser will automatically transmit the x and y coordinates of the spot on the image that was actually clicked. In theory, this data, sent as `field_name.x` and `field_name.y` variables, where `field_name` is the `name` specified in the `input` tag, could allow the developer to respond differently depending on the area of the button that was clicked. The origin point of the coordinates is the top-left corner of the image.

Make an Image into a Button

① Open a Web page that contains a form in your editor.

② Within the form, add a block element such as a paragraph.

③ Add an `input` element's opening tag.

④ Add the `type` attribute with a value of `image`.

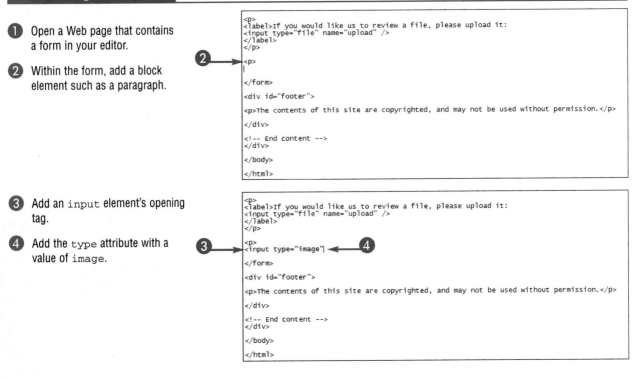

⑤ Add a `src` attribute with a path to an image that you plan to use for the button.

⑥ Add an `alt` attribute with an appropriate value.

⑦ Add a closing slash to the tag.

⑧ Add a closing paragraph tag.

⑨ Save the page.

⑩ Open the page in a Web browser.

● The page opens, showing the image button.

```
<p>
<input type="image" src="images/contactbtn.gif" alt="Contact Us" />
</p>

</form>

<div id="footer">

<p>The contents of this site are copyrighted, and may not be used without permission.</p>

</div>

<!-- End content -->
</div>

</body>
```

C:\Users\Wiley\Documents\webpages\contact.html

America's National Parks

Contact Us

First Name:

Last Name:

Email:

How did you hear about our site (check all that apply):
Search Engine ☐ Print Ad ☐ Radio Ad ☐

Please select your preferred method of contact:
Email ◉ Postal Mail ◉ Phone ◉

How many national parks have you visited?
Less than 10 ▾

In which state have you visited the most parks?
Alaska ▾

Additional Comments:

Please create a password:

If you would like us to review a file, please upload it: [Browse...]

Contact

Extra

Many designers are tempted to try new and unusual things on their pages to make them stand out from others. While this is fine, it should only be done to a point. In the case of using images as buttons, it is absolutely vital that the image still look mostly button-like. If the image you are using for the button looks too little like something that should be clicked, then your users are likely to become frustrated and may potentially leave the site for one that does not confuse them.

As with any image, appropriate alternate text is required for image buttons. Any time you have an image that contains text, the alternate text should match the words on the image, and this will almost always be the case with image buttons. In the example above, the image says "Contact," so the alternate text should simply be "contact" as well. There is no need to describe the appearance of the image any further.

Create a Button with the Button Element

O ne of the challenges of visually designing forms is that too many of the form controls rely on the same element. Text, password, and file upload fields; check boxes and radio buttons; and submit, reset and generic buttons all use input, so any CSS styles applied to that element will affect all of them. Attribute selectors can be used to more specifically target particular controls, but as this selector was not supported by Internet Explorer until version 7, it has not been one that can be relied upon.

Of particular concern is the desire to have the buttons be visually different from the other controls. Although many designers prefer to stick with white backgrounds for text fields, the default grey of a button does not fit many designs. As there was no reliable way to target buttons until recently, many designers resorted to adding class attributes to the buttons for styling.

Fortunately, there is a better way: the button element. While the element has long existed within HTML, few

designers seem to be aware of its existence. Like its input counterpart, button takes a required type attribute, set to either submit, reset, or button. All other valid attributes of the input element when using one of those types apply as well. However, the button element has one big advantage over input: It is a container element. Therefore, rather than setting the text on the button with the value attribute, you can set it as text: <button type="submit" name="submitbtn">Place Order</button>. The text can be further marked up with other elements, so, for example, it could be strongly emphasized: <button type="text" name="submitbtn">Place Order</button>.

It can also replace the input type="image" construct by simply placing an XHTML image element within the button: <button type="submit"><img src="images/submitbtn" alt="Place Order" /></button>.

Create a Button with the Button Element

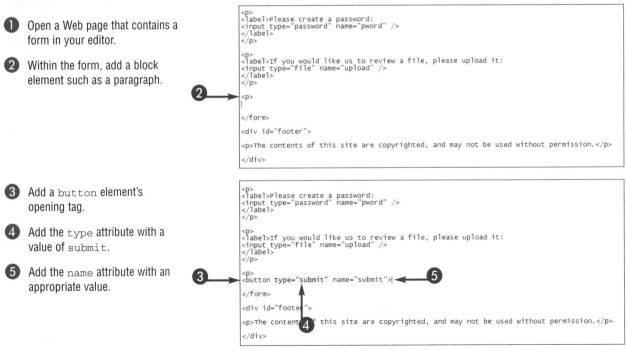

① Open a Web page that contains a form in your editor.

② Within the form, add a block element such as a paragraph.

```
<p>
<label>Please create a password:
<input type="password" name="pword" />
</label>
</p>

<p>
<label>If you would like us to review a file, please upload it:
<input type="file" name="upload" />
</label>
</p>

<p>
|
</form>

<div id="footer">

<p>The contents of this site are copyrighted, and may not be used without permission.</p>

</div>
```

③ Add a button element's opening tag.

④ Add the type attribute with a value of submit.

⑤ Add the name attribute with an appropriate value.

```
<p>
<label>Please create a password:
<input type="password" name="pword" />
</label>
</p>

<p>
<label>If you would like us to review a file, please upload it:
<input type="file" name="upload" />
</label>
</p>

<p>
<button type="submit" name="submit">|
</form>

<div id="footer">

<p>The contents of this site are copyrighted, and may not be used without permission.</p>

</div>
```

6 Add text to be displayed on the button, or an `img` tag.

7 Add a closing `button` tag.

8 Add the closing paragraph tag.

9 Save the page.

10 Open the page in a Web browser.

● The page opens, showing the button.

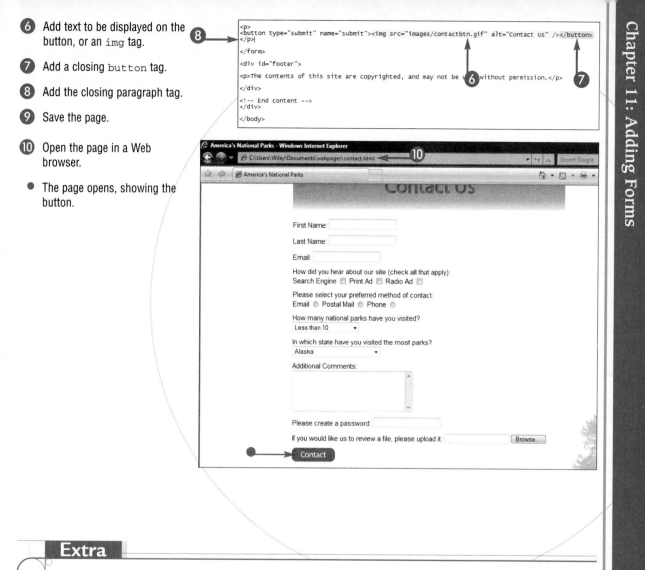

```
<p>
<button type="submit" name="submit"><img src="images/contactbtn.gif" alt="Contact Us" /></button>
</p>

</form>

<div id="footer">
<p>The contents of this site are copyrighted, and may not be u    without permission.</p>
</div>

<!-- End content -->
</div>

</body>
```

Extra

You can use both text and images inside the button element to create buttons that appear to have an icon.

```
<button type="submit" name="submitbtn"><img src="images/btnimage.gif" alt="" />Submit
Information</button>
```

It should be noted that in this case, the alternate text of the image can be left empty, as the image is not terribly important by itself because the button's text adequately describes its purpose. In fact, visually impaired users will get more meaning in this case from having empty alternate text, as the screen reader will simply ignore the image, which will most likely be less confusing for your users.

Group Related Form Elements

large forms can be difficult for users to navigate and even intimidating when first loaded. Disabled users in particular can find long, unorganized forms hard to use. Fortunately, XHTML provides a set of elements that can group form controls into logical blocks and even provide an attractive visual interface.

The `fieldset` element is used to group a collection of presumably related fields. By default, the browser will draw a border around the elements. Some browsers will slightly vary the color of the opposite edges of the border, creating a raised effect. Microsoft Internet Explorer on Windows will also round the corners of the border if certain display themes are enabled in Windows XP or Windows Vista. Regardless, you can use CSS to set the width, style, and color of the border to make its appearance more universal; unfortunately, applying any

styling to the border of a `fieldset` on Windows will cause it to lose the rounded corners.

Simply using the `fieldset` to wrap form fields assists in both usability and accessibility, but you should further provide a `legend`. The `legend` will appear near the top-left corner of the `fieldset`, bisecting the border. This unique display of the `legend` — no other element exists by default in the border of another element — is part of why using `fieldset`s and `legend`s can greatly enhance the overall appearance of the form.

It is legal in XHTML to nest `fieldset`s, so, for example, you can have a "user data" `fieldset`, and within that, add a "personal information" set with name, address, and phone fields and a "site data" set with username and password fields.

Group Related Form Elements

① Open a Web page that contains a form in your editor.

② Following the `form` element's opening tag, add a `fieldset` element's opening tag.

③ Add a `legend` element's opening tag.

④ Add an appropriate legend.

⑤ Add a closing `legend` tag.

⑥ Add the closing `fieldset` tag after a set of form elements.

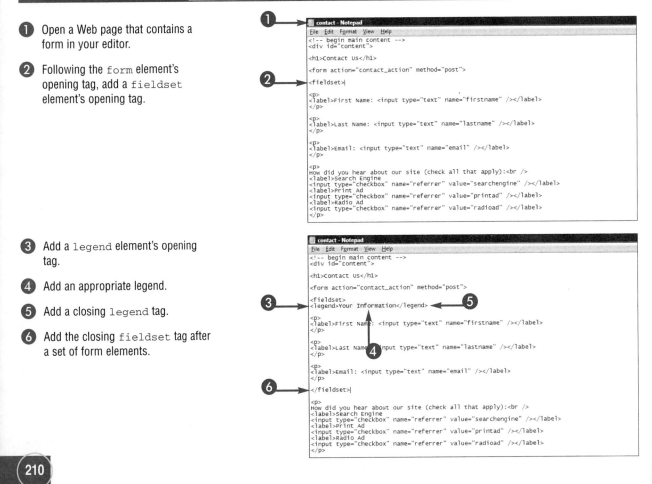

7 Repeat Steps 2 to 6 to complete the form.

8 Save the page.

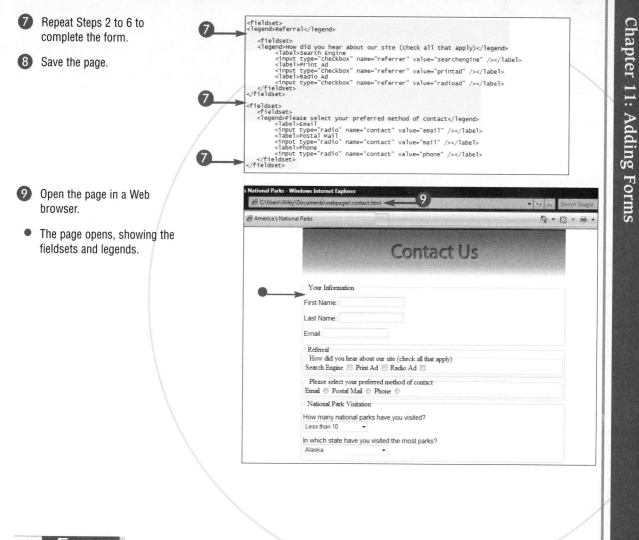

```
<fieldset>
<legend>Referral</legend>

    <fieldset>
    <legend>How did you hear about our site (check all that apply)</legend>
        <label>Search Engine
        <input type="checkbox" name="referrer" value="searchengine" /></label>
        <label>Print Ad
        <input type="checkbox" name="referrer" value="printad" /></label>
        <label>Radio Ad
        <input type="checkbox" name="referrer" value="radioad" /></label>
    </fieldset>
</fieldset>

<fieldset>
    <fieldset>
    <legend>Please select your preferred method of contact</legend>
        <label>Email
        <input type="radio" name="contact" value="email" /></label>
        <label>Postal Mail
        <input type="radio" name="contact" value="mail" /></label>
        <label>Phone
        <input type="radio" name="contact" value="phone" /></label>
    </fieldset>
</fieldset>
```

9 Open the page in a Web browser.

● The page opens, showing the fieldsets and legends.

Extra

Browsers seem to disagree quite a bit as to how to style the backgrounds of the fieldset and legend. If you add a background-color property to the fieldset, and set a different background-color on the legend, Firefox will display the colors as expected, with the legend's background color forming a sort of tab on the fieldset. However, Internet Explorer will extend the background-color of the fieldset to the height of the legend's text, above the fieldset's top border.

You can manage this behavior through a slight hack. Using the html > fieldset child selector, you can set the fieldeset to position:relative, and then add position:absolute with a negative top position on the legend, again using the html > legend selector. As these selectors are not seen by Internet Explorer 6 and earlier, they effectively correct the problem. Unfortunately, Internet Explorer 7 will see these rules but still has the fieldset display issue, so you will also need to work with the fieldset's padding to keep the elements within it from coming into contact with the border, as happens with elements inside a relatively positioned element.

Control the Tab Order

Many users prefer to navigate through forms using the Tab key on their keyboard. It is generally faster to simply enter data into a form field, and then press Tab to move to the next field rather than stop, grab the mouse, move it into position, and then click in the field.

By default, the tab order of form fields is determined by the order in which they appear in the code. However, any hyperlinks also exist within the same tab order, so a user who first encounters the form may have to press tab dozens of times in order to reach the form fields. A popular movie-related Web site routinely requires pressing Tab over twenty times to reach the main search field on the page, despite this being the most logical starting point for using the site. Many designers overlook this aspect of their sites, assuming that users can simply

click in the form field but ignoring the fact that many disabled users cannot physically use the mouse and must navigate with Tab.

All of these issues can be remedied very easily by adding the `tabindex` attribute to form fields and anchors. The value of the attribute is an integer between 1 and 36,768. The lower the number given, the earlier in the tab order the element will appear, so in the previous example of the movie site, simply adding `tabindex="1"` to the search field would eliminate the problem.

Any anchor or form field not given a `tabindex` attribute will appear in its normal order on the page, from top to bottom in the code, but after all elements given the attribute. Care should be taken to avoid duplicate entries, but if any are given, the control that appears first in the XHTML will take precedence.

Control the Tab Order

① Open a Web page that contains a form in your editor.

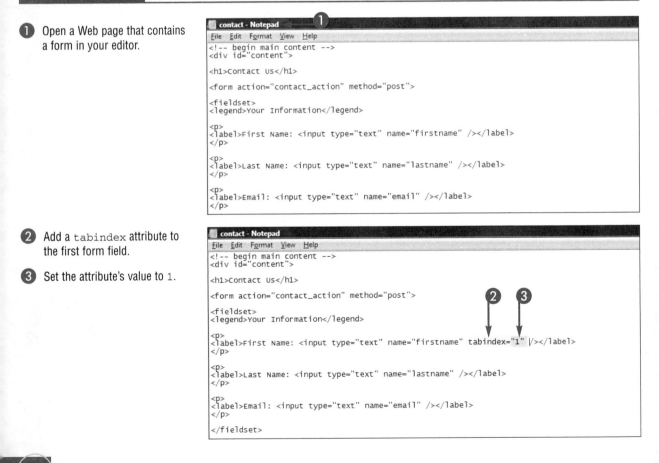

② Add a `tabindex` attribute to the first form field.

③ Set the attribute's value to `1`.

④ Repeat Steps 2 to 3 for each other form field, incrementing the value with each.

⑤ Save the page.

```html
<p>
<label>First Name: <input type="text" name="firstname" tabindex="1" /></label>
</p>

<p>
<label>Last Name: <input type="text" name="lastname" tabindex="10"></label>
</p>

<p>
<label>Email: <input type="text" name="email" tabindex="20"></label>
</p>

</fieldset>

<fieldset>
<legend>Referral</legend>

    <fieldset>
    <legend>How did you hear about our site (check all that apply)</legend>
        <label>Search Engine
        <input type="checkbox" name="referrer" value="searchengine" tabindex="30"></label>
        <label>Print Ad
        <input type="checkbox" name="referrer" value="printad" /></label>
        <label>Radio Ad
        <input type="checkbox" name="referrer" value="radioad" /></label>
    </fieldset>
</fieldset>

<fieldset>
    <fieldset>
    <legend>Please select your preferred method of contact</legend>
        <label>Email
        <input type="radio" name="contact" value="email" tabindex="40"></label>
        <label>Postal Mail
        <input type="radio" name="contact" value="mail" /></label>
        <label>Phone
        <input type="radio" name="contact" value="phone" /></label>
    </fieldset>
</fieldset>
```

④ ④ ④ ④

⑥ Open the page in a Web browser.

The page opens.

⑦ Press the tab key to move through the form fields.

s National Parks - Windows Internet Explorer

C:\Users\Wiley\Documents\webpages\contact.html ⑥ ▾ | ✦₊ | ✕ | Search Google

America's National Parks

Contact Us

Your Information

First Name: | ← ⑦

Last Name:

Email:

Referral
How did you hear about our site (check all that apply)
Search Engine ☐ Print Ad ☐ Radio Ad ☐

Please select your preferred method of contact
Email ◉ Postal Mail ◉ Phone ◉

Extra

The value of `tabindex` need not be consecutive, and, in fact, it probably should not be. If you set the values of fields to, for example, 1, 2, 3, 4, and 5, and then later add a new field between the first and second fields, you will then need to renumber all of the others. Instead, if you numbered them 1, 10, 20, 30, and 40, you could add another field and set its `tabindex` to 5, ensuring that it will appear in the correct order without needing to reset any other values. With more than 32,000 valid values, you should not need to worry about conserving numbers.

Check boxes and radio buttons most often appear within a group of like-named fields. These buttons cannot be individually tabbed to, so the `tabindex` will only affect the first field. Users can choose which button or check box to select by using their left and right arrow keys.

Process Form Data

O nce the user fills out the form and presses Submit, the browser will collect all of the data and transmit it to the page set in the form's `action` attribute, using the `method`. At that point, a script on the server will need to execute to actually process the form data.

Many server scripting languages exist to allow you to process the form. Each has specific advantages and disadvantages. Following is an overview of the most popular modern languages.

Server Technologies

Following is a brief summary of the primary server technologies used on Web sites.

Adobe ColdFusion

Adobe ColdFusion was the first server scripting language developed. In the fall of 2007, Adobe released version 8. The biggest advantage of ColdFusion is that it is designed as a rapid development language. Many processes that require complex code in other languages are implied in ColdFusion. It relies on a tag-based markup language and looks and acts very similar to HTML, so it also has one of the lowest learning curves.

ColdFusion also enjoys close integration with other Adobe technologies. For example, it features the capability to generate PDF documents dynamically, it can create Adobe Flash-based forms, and version 8 introduced image manipulation. The language is built on Java, and has access to server-side Java code so that advanced developers can further expand its capabilities. Further, it is database-agnostic, so it can communicate with almost any relational database.

Microsoft Active Server Pages

Now popularly referred to as Active Server Pages (ASP) Classic, Microsoft's older server scripting technology is still in widespread use, despite having been officially discontinued by Microsoft in 2002. ASP is tightly bundled with Microsoft's Web server, Internet Information Services, and thus installs automatically on Windows servers. It can also access other Windows services such as user account control.

ASP pages can technically be written either in JScript, Microsoft's implementation of JavaScript, or VBScript, a scripting version of its Visual Basic programming language; however, almost all are written in VBScript. While technically database agnostic, most ASP pages use Microsoft's SQL Server as the database backend.

Besides being discontinued, ASP's other main disadvantage is the fact that it only works in Windows environments without a significant additional cost.

Microsoft ASP.NET

In 2002, Microsoft officially replaced ASP with ASP.NET, part of the bigger .NET technology. So-called classic ASP and ASP.NET share very little in common, other than the acronym of their name and the fact that both only officially run on Windows servers.

Most .NET pages are written either in VB.NET, the newest version of the Visual Basic language, or C# (pronounced "C-Sharp"). As both are full object-oriented programming languages, .NET is considerably more powerful than its predecessor. ASP.NET is currently in version 3. Like ColdFusion, its goal is to simplify many of the redundant tasks that consume too much of a Web developer's time, such as building database update forms.

PHP Hypertext Preprocessor

Most developers who are looking for an open-source alternative to Web development languages turn to PHP (PHP Hypertext Preprocessor). Originally developed as an alternative to Perl, PHP now enjoys an extremely active and robust development community and is used on tens of thousands of sites around the Internet.

PHP uses a fairly simple yet robust scripting language. While it can function with any relational database, it is most often implemented with MySQL, the open-source, enterprise-grade database system. PHP has many functions developed specifically with MySQL in mind, making the transition easier.

PHP can be run on any platform, using almost any Web server. Many PHP applications run on the free Apache Web server, and many of those are installed on open source, Unix-based operating systems, although PHP, Apache, and MySQL all run on Windows.

Ruby on Rails

Many developers who want to work in an open source environment but, for various reasons, dislike PHP are turning to Ruby on Rails (RoR). RoR is a framework that uses the Ruby programming language to implement dynamic Web sites. As a framework, RoR sets forth specific file structures, naming conventions, and application structures that free the developer from worrying about minutiae. It takes the ideal espoused by languages such as ColdFusion and ASP.NET of reducing or eliminating the need to create redundant Web forms and the like to an extreme.

RoR requires a slightly different approach to development that is familiar to experienced programmers but can quickly overwhelm those less experienced.

Perl

Most early Web applications relied on Perl, a programming language developed in the early days of the Web. While ColdFusion was technically created first, the wider Web audience first became aware of dynamic applications due in large part to Perl.

Perl is open source and easy to install, but relies on an, at times, obtuse programming syntax that makes it difficult to learn. However, many older Web applications are still running at least in part in Perl, and some of the best-known free scripts, such as Matt Wright's FormMail, are written using it. You can download FormMail from www.scriptarchive.com/formmail.html.

Creating and Uploading Scripts

Once you have selected the server technology you wish to use, you will need to create the scripts to process your form data. Most scripts can be written in any text editor, although just as with XHTML, you will find it much faster and easier to use an editor specifically designed for the task. Most XHTML editors have some support for scripting languages. For example, Microsoft Expression Web is designed to make the creation of ASP.NET pages easier, and version 3 of the program is due to introduce PHP support. Adobe Dreamweaver not only supports code hinting for ASP, ASP.NET, ColdFusion, and PHP but it also contains a series of so-called "Server Behaviors" that can write much of the necessary code for you through dialog boxes and other selections in the visual interface.

The completed script will be uploaded to your server along with the other XHTML and CSS files. In most cases, the scripts will reside alongside the other files in your site, although some technologies, such as Perl, may require that the files be placed in specific directories with special permissions in order to run.

Setting Up the Server

In order to process any scripts, the appropriate technology will need to be configured on your Web server's computer. The precise steps required will vary depending on the technology. You can download PHP, Perl, and ColdFusion from their respective Web sites and install them on the server just as you would for any other application. The installation will automatically detect the Web server software on the machine and add the necessary settings so that the Web server and the server scripting technology can communicate with one another.

If you are on a Windows server using Microsoft's Internet Information Services, then you do not need to perform any additional steps to run ASP Classic. So long as you are using at least Windows 2003 or Windows Vista, you will also not need to specifically set up the server to run ASP.NET scripts. Third-party software to allow ASP or ASP.NET pages in non-Windows environments does exist, and will require additional setup.

Add JavaScript to Your Page

J avaScript was originally developed by the Netscape Corporation to allow for greater interactivity between Web pages and users. Today, it is widely supported across all major browsers. In fact, the language is now a recognized Internet standard, technically called ECMAScript, although few people like or use that name.

Early implementations of JavaScript ranged from very useful functions such as validating forms to less useful, more fanciful animations. While both of those implementations are still found on the Web, the language is enjoying a resurgence in popularity today, thanks in large part to the ever-increasing popularity of Ajax, or Asynchronous JavaScript and XML.

Many uses of JavaScript rely on the code being embedded in a Web page. You can embed JavaScript on your page using the XHTML `script` element. The element takes

one required attribute, `type`, which will always be set to `text/javascript`. Anything between the opening and closing `script` tags will be interpreted by the browser's JavaScript engine.

JavaScript is a fairly simple scripting language. It uses an object-based model, meaning that it can identify and manipulate most of the elements on the page by seeing them as objects. Almost every XHTML element that you place in a Web page can be treated as an object in your script. Most often, you will need to add an `id` attribute to an element in order for the script to differentiate it on the page.

JavaScript provides a rich library of functions, methods, and properties that allow you to perform the tasks you need. One common built-in function is `alert`, which causes the browser to display a pop-up dialog box.

Add JavaScript to Your Page

① Open a Web page in your editor.

② In the head section of your page, add a `script` element's opening tag.

③ Add a `type` attribute.

④ Set the attribute's value to `text/javascript`.

5 Type `alert(""Hello, world!");`.

6 Add the closing `script` tag.

7 Save the page.

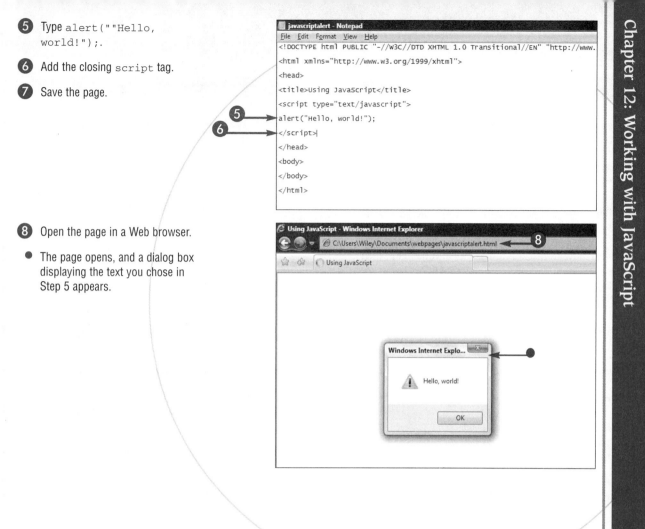

8 Open the page in a Web browser.

● The page opens, and a dialog box displaying the text you chose in Step 5 appears.

Extra

JavaScript is case-sensitive. Keywords and phrases in the language use all lowercase letters or mixed case. Variables you create can be in any case, but you should try to be consistent. References to elements from your Web page must match the case in which they exist in the code; this is less a problem today with XHTML as it requires that elements be all lowercase. However, attribute values must match case when referenced in JavaScript as well, so pay close attention to the casing when you create values for attributes, such as `id`, that are commonly used by the script.

Each statement in JavaScript should end in a semicolon. While this is technically required by the language, most browsers will ignore the rule and properly run scripts without the semicolon, but it is considered a best practice to use it, regardless.

The `script` element is unique in XHTML in that it may legally appear in either the `head` or the `body` of the document. If placed in the `head`, the `script` will attempt to execute when the page first loads, although this can be controlled through the use of functions. Scripts included in the body will execute when the browser reaches that portion of the page.

Add Event Handlers

Javascript is known as an event-driven language. That is, nothing in JavaScript can execute without the user triggering some sort of event. The user loading a page in his browser is an event, as is the user clicking a button or hyperlink or moving his mouse over an image.

JavaScript events can be triggered by adding an event handler to an XHTML element. Most elements support `onclick`, `ondblclick`, `onkeydown`, `onkeypress`, `onkeyup`, `onmousedown`, `onmousemove`, `onmouseout`, `onmouseover`, and `onmouseup`. Form controls and the anchor element also support `onblur` and `onfocus` events, and the `input`, `select`, and `textarea` elements also support `onchange`. The `input` and `textarea` elements further support an `onselect` event, while the `form` element itself supports `onreset` and `onsubmit`. Finally, `onload` and `onunload` are legal on the `body` element.

Scripts to be triggered by an event will need to be written as functions in the script. JavaScript follows the common convention of writing functions by using the keyword `function`, followed by the function's name and a set of parentheses that include the function's arguments. A pair of curly braces will enclose the code for the function.

```
function showalert() {

        alert("Hello, world");

}
```

The function will most likely be included in a script block in the head of the document, and can be called by using its name as the value of the appropriate event handler:

```
<button name="triggerevent"
onclick="showalert();">Show dialog</button>.
```

Add Event Handlers

1. Open a Web page in your editor.

2. In the head section of your page, add a `script` element's opening tag.

3. Add a `type` attribute with a value of `text/javascript`.

4. Type `function showalert()` and an opening curly brace.

5. Type `alert("Hello, world!");`.

6. Add the closing curly brace.

7. Add the closing `script` tag.

8 In the body of the document, add a `form` element's opening tag. Set the `method` attribute to `post`, and add an `action` with an empty string.

9 Add a paragraph element's opening tag and a `button` element's opening tag.

10 Add `type="button"` and an appropriate `name` attribute.

11 Add an `onclick` event with a value of `showalert();`.

12 Add text to the button.

13 Add the closing `button` tag and the closing paragraph tag.

14 Add the closing `form` tag.

15 Save the page.

16 Open the page in a Web browser.

17 Click the button.

● A dialog box appears.

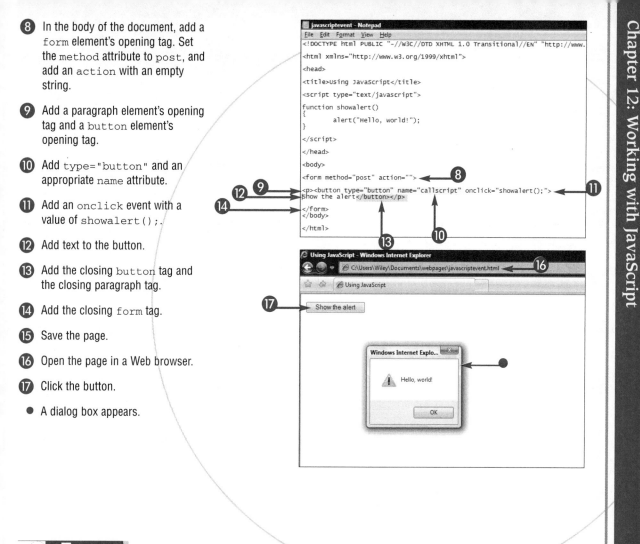

Extra

As with any programming, you should get in the habit of commenting your code to document the actions you are performing. JavaScript supports two forms of comments. A single-line comment, which can stand alone on its own line or be added to the end of a line of script, is denoted by two forward slashes:

```
function showMe() {
    alert("Hello"); //displays a dialog
}
```

Comments that span more than one line begin with a slash and an asterisk, and end with an asterisk and a slash:

```
function add() {
/* A function to add numbers.
Written 12/12/07. */
}
```

Validate
a Form

While XHTML forms provide for inputs to cover most types of data you may want to collect from your users, they do not give you a way to ensure that the data entered is appropriate. For example, XHTML has text fields, but no concept of data typing to require numeric input. While you can use `maxlength` to set an upper limit on the number of characters entered, there is no equivalent to set a minimum.

Using JavaScript, you can write a function that verifies the input from your users to make sure that the data being entered matches what you expect or need for the processing code.

Any form that you plan to validate should have a `name` attribute. The form exists as an object in JavaScript that is a child of the `document` object. Each form control is a child of the `form`. As with other modern programming languages, JavaScript uses *dot notation* to reference child

objects, so, for example, a `firstname` input field in a `signup` form can be called as `document.signup.firstname`, and its value can be accessed via `document.signup.firstname.value`. Keep in mind that JavaScript is case-sensitive, so `document` will always be lowercase, and the names of controls must match those given in the XHTML.

You will rely heavily on JavaScript `if` statements to validate the controls. The `if` syntax is similar to other languages, whereby you provide a logical test within parentheses following the `if`, and the code to execute if the statement is true in curly braces. You can use an `else` statement to set code to execute if the statement is false.

JavaScript uses a double equal sign (`==`) to test for equality, and an exclamation point followed by an equal sign (`!=`) to test for inequality. You can test to see if a field was left empty by comparing its value to an empty string, or two double quotation marks.

Validate a Form

① Open a Web page that contains a form in your editor.

② Add a `name` attribute with an appropriate value to the `form` element's opening tag.

③ In the head section of your page, add a `script` element's opening tag with a `type="text/javascript"` attribute.

④ Type `function validateform()` and an opening curly brace.

⑤ Type `if(document.contactform.firstname.value == "") {`.

Note: *You will need to replace* `contactform` *with the name of your form, and* `firstname` *with the name of your first text field.*

⑥ Add the closing curly brace for the `if` statement.

7 Repeat Steps 5 and 6 to add tests for each other field in the form that you wish to validate.

8 Add the closing curly brace for the function.

9 Add the closing `script` tag.

10 Save the page.

11 Open the page in a Web browser.

The page opens. If the browser returns any JavaScript errors, you will need to fix them.

Note: *Refer to the task "Debug JavaScript" later in this chapter for help on troubleshooting the error.*

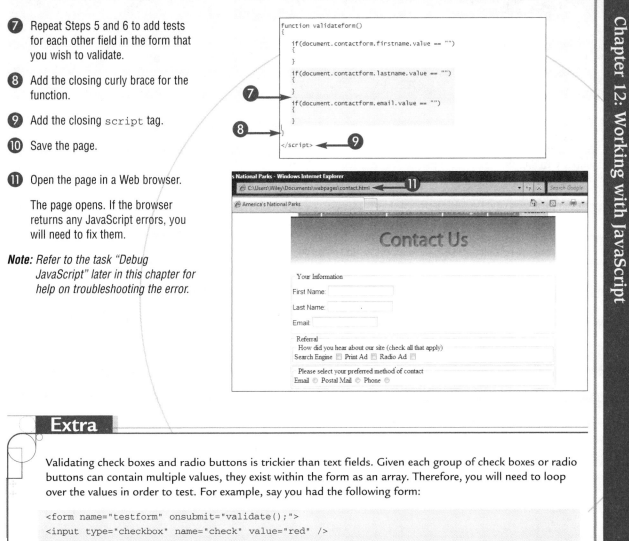

```
function validateform()
{
    if(document.contactform.firstname.value == "")
    {
    }
    if(document.contactform.lastname.value == "")
    {
    }
    if(document.contactform.email.value == "")
    {
    }
}
</script>
```

Extra

Validating check boxes and radio buttons is trickier than text fields. Given each group of check boxes or radio buttons can contain multiple values, they exist within the form as an array. Therefore, you will need to loop over the values in order to test. For example, say you had the following form:

```
<form name="testform" onsubmit="validate();">
<input type="checkbox" name="check" value="red" />
<input type="checkbox" name="check" value="blue" />
<input type="checkbox" name="check" value="green" />
<input type="submit" />
</form>
```

You would need your validation function to read:

```
function validate() {
    for(i=0; i<document.testform.check.length; i++) {
        if(document.testform.check[i].value == "red") {
            alert(true);
        }else{
            break;
        }
    }
}
```

continued ➡

221

As with all other JavaScript, your validation function will need to be triggered by an event. You can validate your form field by field as your user enters data by calling the `onblur` event, but this can be somewhat annoying, particularly if you are triggering `alert` dialog boxes for errors. Instead, it is often better to wait until the form is complete, and then call the validation function using the `onsubmit` event of the form itself.

In order to prevent the browser from sending the data until the validation is complete, you will need the function to return either a `true` value if the validation is okay, or `false` if it fails. The `return` statement needs to be the final line in the function. You will also need to include `return` as part of the event trigger so that the browser knows it needs to wait for the JavaScript to finish.

Generally, you will want to create a variable in which you will store the validation error messages, and then display the variable once the validation completes. Variables are created in JavaScript using the `var` keyword, followed by the name of the variable and a value. For validation, you can set the variable to an empty string. Then, you can add a value to the variable each time a validation error occurs. At the end of the function, you can see if the variable is still empty, in which case there were no errors, or you can output any errors that may have been triggered.

Many designers display the errors in an `alert` dialog box. You should add the newline character — `\n` — to indicate a carriage return after each error message so that it will appear on a separate line in the dialog box.

Validate a Form *(continued)*

⑫ Open a web page in your editor.

⑬ At the top of the function, create an `error` variable.

⑭ Within each `if` statement, add an appropriate message to the `error` variable.

⑮ After all of the form value `if` statements, add another `if` statement.

⑯ Test the `error` variable to see if it is blank.

⑰ Within the curly braces, add `return true;`.

⑱ Add an `else` statement.

⑲ Within the curly braces, add an alert message that displays the values in the `error` variable and type `return false;`.

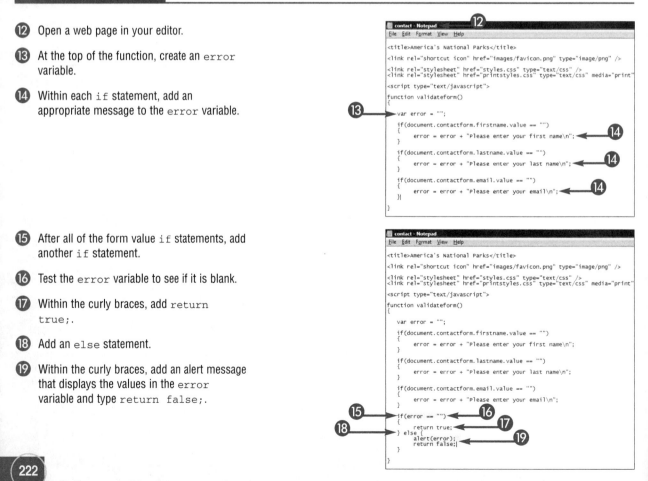

20 In the form element's opening tag, add `onsubmit="return validateform();"`.

21 Save the page.

20

22 Open the page in a Web browser.

23 Without entering any information, click the submit button.

● A dialog box appears showing that the fields are required.

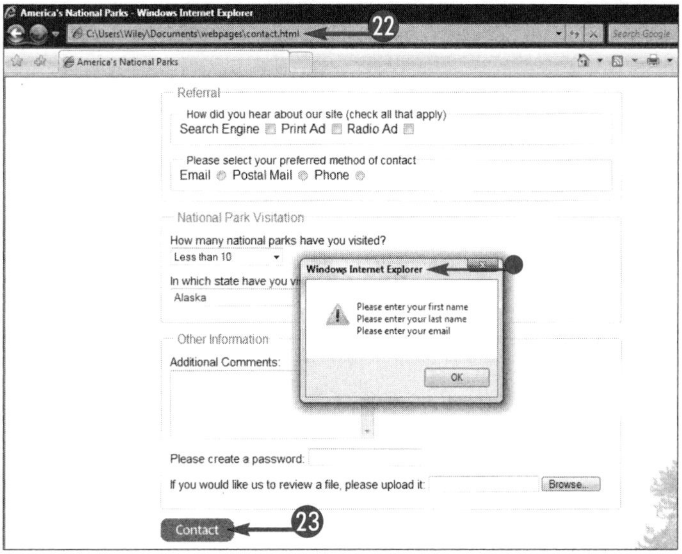

Apply It

You can display the errors in line with the form fields, rather than in a dialog box, by combining the JavaScript `getElementById` function, its `innerHTML` property, and an empty `span` element.

The following form:

```
<form name="testform" onsubmit="return validate();">
First name: <input type="text" name="firstname" />
<span id="firstnameerror"></span><br />
<input type="submit" />
```

could be validated with this function:

```
function validate() {
if(document.testform.firstname.value == "") {
    document.getElementById("firstnameerror").innerHTML = "You must enter a first name";
        return false;
    }
}
```

The error message, "You must enter a first name", would appear next to the form field. You could further add a class to the span, `<span id="firstnameerror" class="error">`, and then use CSS to format the message.

Open a New Window

Early in its development, JavaScript gained the ability to open a new browser window. This functionality, it was hoped, would enable Web sites to allow users to open helper pages or pages that provided additional details about products or services while still leaving the original document open.

Unfortunately, an abuse of this capability quickly spread. As any JavaScript code can be triggered by any event, Web designers began using the new window functionality coupled with the `body` element's `onload` event, which is triggered when the page first loads, to open advertising windows every time a user visited a page. These pop-up advertisements eventually became so widespread — and so hated by users — that a cottage industry was born developing software to block them. Later, the browser

companies stepped in, and today every major browser contains a pop-up blocker.

Abuses aside, pop-ups can still be helpful when used appropriately and for their original intent. If, for example, you have a form that contains a field whose purpose may not be clear, you can include a link near the field that opens a pop-up window with details as to the meaning of the field and the data that should be entered in it. Browser pop-up blockers are designed to allow pop-ups that are triggered by a specific user-initiated action, such as clicking a link or a button, but block those generated by `onload` and `onunload`.

The JavaScript function to generate a new window is simply `open`. The function takes a series of arguments. The first is the only required argument: The URL to the page that will be opened in the window. The second, optional argument lets you set a name for the window.

Open a New Window

1. Open a Web page that contains a form in your editor.

2. Add a `name` attribute with a value of `myform` to the form element's opening tag.

3. In the head section of your page, add a `script` element's opening tag with a `type="text/javascript"` attribute.

4. Type `function openwin()` and an opening curly brace.

5. Type `open` and an opening parenthesis.

6. Type the path to the document that will open in the window, followed by a comma.

7. Type a name for the new window and a closing parenthesis.

Note: *Both the URL and the name need to be enclosed within single quotation marks.*

8. Type a closing curly brace.

9. Add the closing `script` tag.

① **javascriptnewwin - Notepad**
File Edit Format View Help
```
<!DOCTYPE html PUBLIC "-//W3C//DTD XHTML 1.0 Transitional//EN" "http://www.
<html xmlns="http://www.w3.org/1999/xhtml">
<head>
<title>Opening a New Window</title>
<script type="text/javascript">   ③
function openwin()
{
    |

</head>
<body>
<form action="" method="post" name="myform" >   ②
```

④ → function openwin()

② **javascriptnewwin - Notepad**
File Edit Format View Help
```
<!DOCTYPE html PUBLIC "-//W3C//DTD XHTML 1.0 Transitional//EN" "http://www.
<html xmlns="http://www.w3.org/1999/xhtml">
<head>
<title>Opening a New Window</title>
<script type="te  ⑥ /javascript">
function openwin()
{
    open('details.html', 'newwin');   ⑦
}
</script>|   ⑨
</head>
<body>
<form action="" method="post" name="myform" >
```

⑤ → open
⑧ → }

10. In the form, add a `button` element's opening tag with a `type="button"` attribute and an appropriate name.

11. Add text to display on the button and the closing tag.

12. Add an `onclick` event to the button's opening tag that calls the function.

13. Save the page.

14. Open the page in a Web browser.

15. Click the button.

● A new window appears.

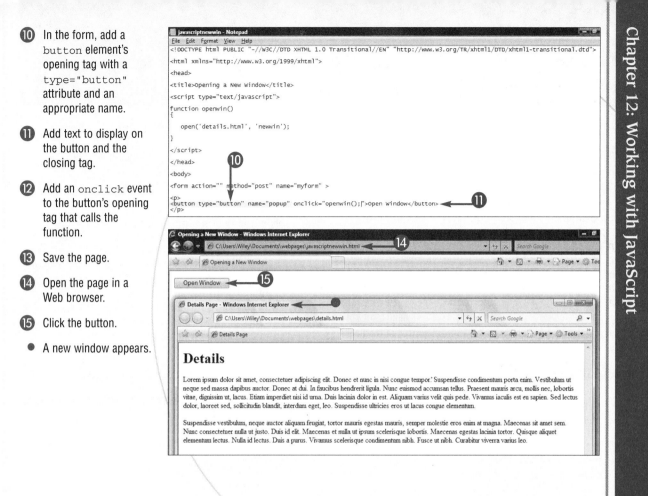

Apply It

You can determine what the browser window that opens looks like by adding an optional third argument to the open function. In the argument, you can specify whether or not toolbars, the location or address bar, the status bar, menu bar, and scrollbars appear by setting each to a value of `true`. You can also set whether or not the window will be resizable by adding it as `true` as well. Finally, you can add `width` and `height` values to size the window, and `top` and `left` values to position it relative to the top-left corner of the user's monitor.

```
function openwin() {

open('somepage.html','mywin','toolbars=yes,location='yes',status=yes,menubar=yes,scrollbars=yes
,resizable=yes,width=300,height=300,top=150,left=250');
}
```

Hide and Show Elements

Modern implementations of JavaScript include the capability for the language to dynamically manipulate CSS properties on the page. While this presents many possibilities for dynamic rendering, one of the most common uses is changing the value of the `visibility` property to show or hide content.

A good example of this technique can be found on the home page of the city of Juneau, the capital of Alaska. When you visit the site at www.juneau.org, the center of the page is dominated by an image. In the lower-left corner of the image is a small button labeled "Info." If you mouse over the button, a light yellow box appears over the image, displaying information about the city.

To achieve this effect, Juneau's Web designers placed the information in a `div` element, and then used CSS to set the element's `position` over the picture and its `visibility` to `hidden`. Following that, they added a simple JavaScript function call, relying on the JavaScript style property to set visibility to `visible`:

```
document.getElementById('showme').style.
visibility = 'visible';
```

The information box is hidden again by setting the property back to `hidden`. Both events are triggered by mouse movement, with the visibility turned on using the `onmouseover` event and hidden or turned back off using `onmouseout`. While these events could in theory be triggered by text within a `div`, it is safer to either use a hyperlink in the `div` or a form button, as not all browsers support mouse events on other elements.

Hide and Show Elements

1. Open a Web page that contains an embedded style sheet in your editor.

2. In the document, add a `div` element's opening tag with an `id` attribute and an appropriate value.

3. Add an anchor tag's opening element with an `href` set to `javascript:;`.

4. Add `onmouseover="showinfo();"`.

5. Add `onmouseout="hideinfo();"`.

6. Add the text to the link and a closing anchor tag.

7. Add a closing `div` tag.

8. Add another `div` element's opening tag with an `id` of showme.

9. Add content to the `div`.

10. Add the closing `div` tag.

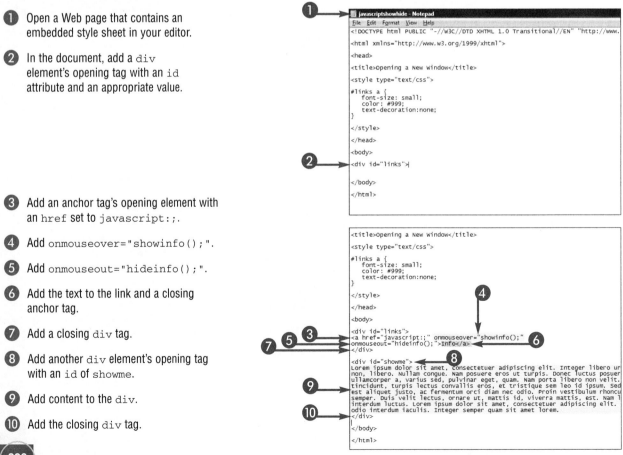

⑪ In the head section of your page, add a `script` element's opening tag with a `type="text/javascript"` attribute.

⑫ Type `function showinfo()` and an opening curly brace.

⑬ Type `document.getElement ById('showme')style. visibility = 'visible'`.

⑭ Type a closing curly brace.

⑮ Type `function hideinfo()` and an opening curly brace.

⑯ Type `document.getElement ById('showme').style. visibility = 'hidden'`.

⑰ Type a closing curly brace.

⑱ Add the closing script tag.

⑲ In the style sheet, add a declaration for the `showme` div. Add a `visibility: hidden` rule and any other desired formatting.

⑳ Save the page.

㉑ Open the Web page in a browser.

㉒ Mouse over the link.

● The info box appears.

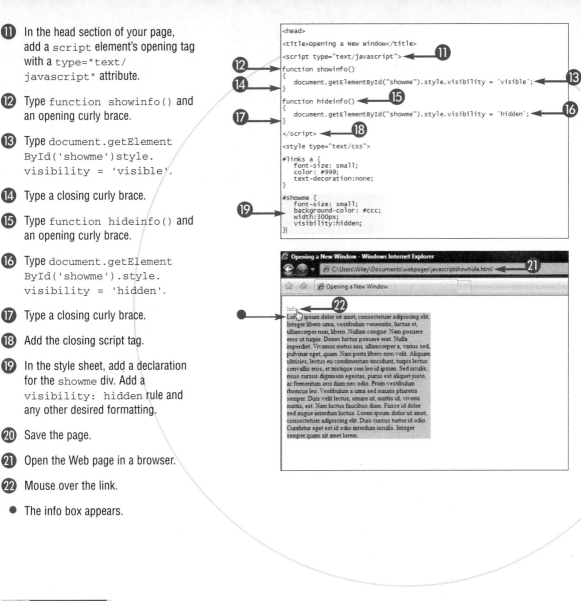

In this example, JavaScript is used to change the `visibility` property from `hidden` to `visible` and back. At first glance, it might seem that you could achieve the same effect by changing the `display` property from `none` to `block` and vice versa. However, the two are not the same, and one factor in particular makes `visibility` the better property here, which is simply that that property makes the page more accessible. Ideally, screen readers for the blind would completely ignore anything you may set in your style sheet, but unfortunately they do not, and in particular, many readers will ignore contents set in an element with `display:none`. As a blind user will not be able to move her mouse over a link to trigger the JavaScript to show the element, she will not be able to access its contents. Using `visibility:hidden` removes this consideration, as the screen reader will present the contents as if they were visible on the page.

Swap Images

You can make your pages more usable by providing your user with a visual indicator that he has moved over a hyperlink. A common technique for this is to use an *image rollover*: an image that changes when the mouse is moved over it.

To create this effect, you first need two images: the original and the rollover. Care should be taken to make sure that the pixel dimensions of the images match, as otherwise the browser may have to move the rest of the contents of the page on rollover, creating an undesirable flickering effect.

Place the original image on the page as normal, using the `img` element and being sure to include an `id`, and then wrap it in an anchor tag. Set the anchor's `href` to a JavaScript call using `javascript:;`, and add `onmouseover` and `onmouseout` event calls.

The JavaScript required is fairly simple. In the function being called `onmouseover`, you get the element using `document.getElementById`, referencing the image's `id`, and then set its `src` to the second image. The `onmouseout` function merely reverses this, setting the `src` back to the original.

If you have multiple images, you can simplify your code by passing a reference to the image as an argument in the function, and then using that reference as the value for `getElementById`. You would want to pass a second argument with the desired source of the image. This technique allows you to use a single pair of functions regardless of the number of images, as well as makes your code more portable, as the values for the images do not need to be hard-coded in the script.

Swap Images

① Open a Web page in your editor.

② Add an image with an `id`.

③ Wrap an anchor tag around the image.

④ Add an `onmouseover` event handler to the anchor's opening tag.

⑤ Call a `swap()` function, and add the `id` of the image and the path to the new image in the parentheses.

⑥ Add an `onmouseout` event handler to the anchor's opening tag.

⑦ Call a `restore()` function, and add the `id` of the image and the path to the original image in the parentheses.

Note: *In both cases, the `id` of the image and the path need to be enclosed within single quotation marks.*

```
javascriptswapimage - Notepad
File Edit Format View Help
<!DOCTYPE html PUBLIC "-//W3C//DTD XHTML 1.0 Transitional//EN" "http://www.
<html xmlns="http://www.w3.org/1999/xhtml">
<head>
<title>Swapping Images</title>

<style type="text/css">
img { border:0; }
</style>
</head>
<body>
<div id="images">
<a href="index.html">
<img src="images/home_up.gif" alt="Home" id="homeimage"/>
</a>
</div>
</body>
</html>
```

```
javascriptswapimage - Notepad
File Edit Format View Help
<!DOCTYPE html PUBLIC "-//W3C//DTD XHTML 1.0 Transitional//EN" "http://www.w3.org/TR/
<html xmlns="http://www.w3.org/1999/xhtml">
<head>
<title>Swapping Images</title>

<style type="text/css">
img { border:0; }
</style>
</head>
<body>
<div id="images">
<a href="index.html" onmouseover="swap('homeimage','images/home_down.gif');"
onmouseout="restore('homeimage', 'images/home_up.gif');">
<img src="images/home_up.gif" alt="Home" id="homeimage"/>
</a>
</div>
</body>
</html>
```

⑧ In the head section of your page, add a `script` element's opening tag with a `type="text/javascript"` attribute.

⑨ Type `function swap(image, source)` and an opening curly brace.

⑩ Type `document.get ElementById(image) .src = source;` and the closing curly brace.

⑪ Repeat Steps 9 to 10, but name the function `restore`.

⑫ Save the page.

⑬ Open the page in a Web browser.

⑭ Mouse over the image.

● The new image appears.

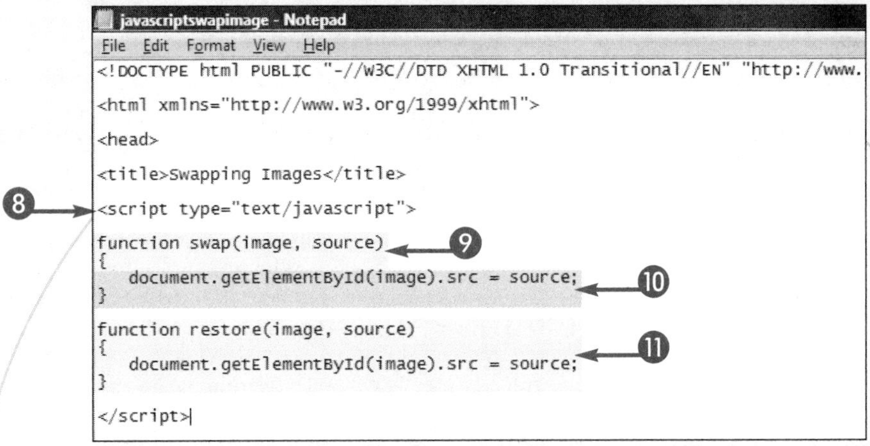

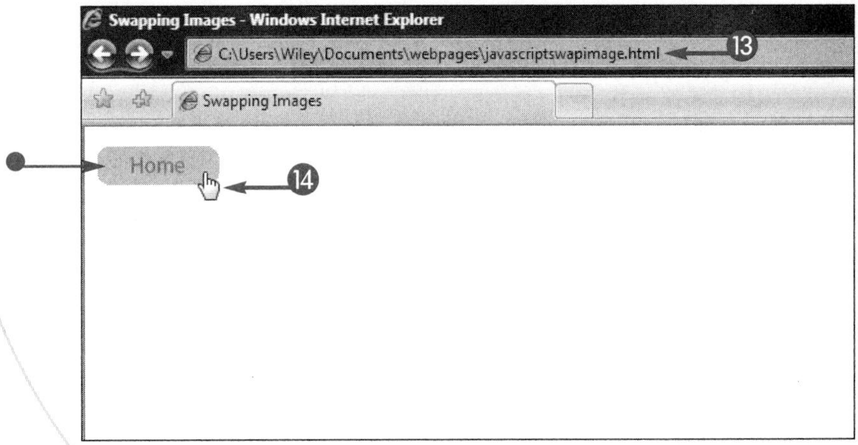

```
javascriptswapimage - Notepad
File  Edit  Format  View  Help
<!DOCTYPE html PUBLIC "-//W3C//DTD XHTML 1.0 Transitional//EN" "http://www.
<html xmlns="http://www.w3.org/1999/xhtml">
<head>
<title>Swapping Images</title>
<script type="text/javascript">          ⑧
function swap(image, source)          ⑨
{
    document.getElementById(image).src = source;          ⑩
}
function restore(image, source)
{
    document.getElementById(image).src = source;          ⑪
}
</script>
```

```
Swapping Images - Windows Internet Explorer
C:\Users\Wiley\Documents\webpages\javascriptswapimage.html          ⑬
Swapping Images

Home          ⑭
```

This example demonstrates an important best practice in writing functions. Ideally, functions should maintain independence from the code that calls them. If you were to write the functions shown here by hard-coding the `id` of the image and the path to the source in the JavaScript, then not only is that script only useful for that image, but it is only useful for this page. By instead passing the `id` and `source` as arguments, you could in theory take this code and add it to any other page and have it continue to work as before. While it is not always possible to make functions independent of the page, it can be done most of the time, and should be done whenever possible.

Any time you need to use a hyperlink to call a function, you should set the value of the `href` to `javascript:;`. Many beginning designers use the pound or hash symbol (#) instead, as that symbol in a hyperlink references the page on which the link is located. However, when such a link is clicked, the browser actually reloads the page, which most of time causes it to scroll back to the top. If the page has a form, clicking such a link may clear the form. Using `javascript:;` instead prevents these problems.

Debug JavaScript

Any time you write in a programming language, you are bound to make mistakes, from simple syntax errors such as using the wrong capitalization to major mistakes such as creating infinite loops. You will need to be sure to fix these errors before you take your site live.

Debugging JavaScript in the browser alone can be difficult. All major browsers will stop executing script when they encounter an error, but to the casual observer, most of these errors will go unnoticed, and it will appear instead that the browser simply did not execute the script. However, a closer look at the browser window should reveal some sort of indication of an error. Most often, there will be a small icon in one of the lower corners of the browser window. In Internet Explorer for Windows, the error will appear as a page icon with a yellow warning triangle that contains an exclamation

mark. The icon appears in the lower-left corner. Firefox indicates JavaScript errors with a white "x" in a red circle and a text indication of the number of errors, which will appear in the lower-right corner.

Depending on the browser, you will need to either click the icon once or twice to bring up the error details. Unfortunately, the text of the error will rarely be helpful without an in-depth knowledge of JavaScript. For example, if you try to call `getElement`, rather than the correct `getElementById`, the error in Internet Explorer simply says "Object doesn't support this property or method" — without saying *which* object or *which* property or method is the problem. While the text might not help, the browser should at least indicate the line on which the error occurred to give you a starting point for troubleshooting. You can also generally find solutions by using a search engine such as Google to look up the error message.

Debug JavaScript

① Open a Web page that contains JavaScript in your editor.

② Add an error to the code, such as removing the quotes around the word in the parentheses.

③ Save the page.

④ Open the page in a Web browser.

⑤ Double-click the error icon.

Note: *In Internet Explorer, you will also need to click Show Details to see the actual error.*

⑥ Note the error message and the line number.

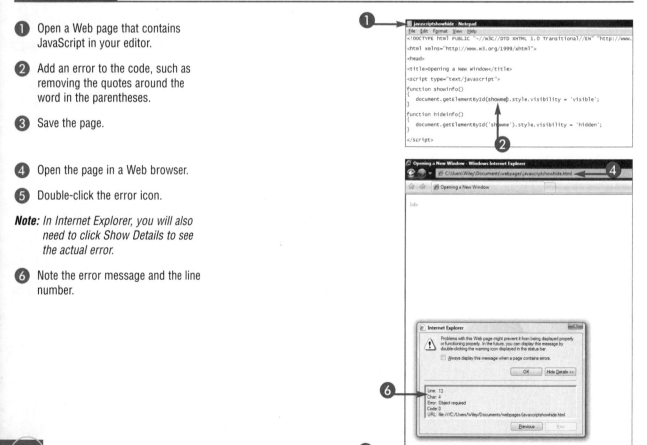

⑦ Return to your editor.

⑧ Fix the problem.

⑨ Save the page.

⑦

```
javascriptshowhide - Notepad
File Edit Format View Help
<!DOCTYPE html PUBLIC "-//W3C//DTD XHTML 1.0 Transitional//EN" "http://www.
<html xmlns="http://www.w3.org/1999/xhtml">

<head>

<title>Opening a New Window</title>

<script type="text/javascript">

function showinfo()
{
    document.getElementById('showme').style.visibility = 'visible';
}

function hideinfo()
{
    document.getElementById('showme').style.visibility = 'hidden';
}

</script>
```
⑧

⑩ Return to the Web browser.

⑪ Refresh the page.

⑫ Mouse over the text to trigger the event.

● The page opens and no error displays.

⑩

⑪

⑫

```
Opening a New Window - Windows Internet Explorer
C:\Users\Wiley\Documents\webpages\javascriptshowhide.html
Opening a New Window

Info
Lorem ipsum dolor sit amet, consectetuer adipiscing elit.
Integer libero urna, vestibulum venenatis, luctus et,
ullamcorper non, libero. Nullam congue. Nam posuere
eros ut turpis. Donec luctus posuere erat. Nulla
imperdiet. Vivamus metus nisi, ullamcorper a, varius sed,
pulvinar eget, quam. Nam porta libero non velit. Aliquam
ultricies, lectus eu condimentum tincidunt, turpis lectus
convallis eros, et tristique sem leo id ipsum. Sed iaculis,
risus cursus dignissim egestas, purus est aliquet justo,
ac fermentum orci diam nec odio. Proin vestibulum
rhoncus leo. Vestibulum a urna sed mauris pharetra
semper. Duis velit lectus, ornare ut, mattis id, viverra
mattis, est. Nam luctus faucibus diam. Fusce id dolor
sed augue interdum luctus. Lorem ipsum dolor sit amet,
consectetuer adipiscing elit. Duis cursus tortor id odio.
Curabitur eget est id odio interdum iaculis. Integer
semper quam sit amet lorem.
```

Extra

If you use Firefox, you have access to a much better debugger. Firebug is a free extension to the browser that gives you a rich, interactive debugging window.

Using Firefox, go to www.firebug.org to download the extension, which should install automatically. Restart the browser; then click Tools → Firebug → Open Firebug. The extension will appear along the bottom of the browser window. You will need to click the link to enable the extension. Then, from the tabs along the top of the Firebug panel, click Script. The source code of your page should appear, showing the JavaScript.

One of the nicest features of Firebug is that you can set *breakpoints*, or spots in your script where you would like the code to stop executing. You can set a breakpoint by clicking the line number to the left of the desired line.

More details on the features of Firebug can be found on its Web site, along with a support forum should you encounter problems when using it.

Understanding Web Accessibility

To reach the widest possible audience for your site, take into consideration those users who may have physical or cognitive disabilities that would impede their ability to effectively use your site.

Primary Disabilities that Affect Web Usage

Following is a brief overview of the common disabilities that you need to consider when creating your Web sites.

Visual Impairment

As the Web is a primarily visual medium, visual impairment is perhaps the most important disability to consider when building your site. From total blindness to very poor eyesight, those with visual impairments use software applications called *screen readers* to navigate on their computers. Screen readers do precisely what they say: All of the content on the page, including text within applications, menus, and dialog boxes, are read to the user. Visually impaired users rely almost exclusively on their keyboards to navigate within their machine, as they obviously cannot use a mouse or other pointer device. The two most popular screen readers are JAWS, made by Freedom Scientific, and WindowEyes, made by GW Micro.

Color Blindness

A very significant percentage of people, mostly men, suffer from some degree of color blindness. Many believe that being color-blind means that one cannot see color at all. While extreme cases involve the complete inability to see color, most people suffer from some lesser degree of color blindness whereby they are simply unable to distinguish between certain shades of color, or see differences between colors if they lack sufficient contrast. If you have ever had an eye exam, one of the tests presents circles made up of splotches of colors and containing an embedded number or letter. This is a color blind test, and if you cannot see the number or letter, you are at least partially color blind.

Mobility Impairment

While a lot of Web professionals now understand, and take into consideration, visual impairment, many still ignore mobility impairments. They mistakenly believe that so long as a person can see, they can use any Web site. However, many people with mobility impairments lack the full use of their hands, which in turn means that they cannot use a mouse. If your site does not take this into consideration and provide alternatives for mouse-based navigation, your site is not accessible.

Hearing Impairment

Hearing disabilities will of course only affect your site if you have audio content, usually in videos. You need to ensure that any content delivered through audio channels is also available in a non-audio format, either through closed captioning or similar technologies or through a text transcript of the audio. You should also consider that many of your users who can hear may be visiting your site either on a computer without speakers or with the volume turned off, so considering hearing impairments in your design will assist those users as well.

Cognitive Disabilities

Those with cognitive disabilities, such as learning disorders or dyslexia, will have a difficult time understanding your site's content unless you take these disabilities into consideration and be sure to create content that can be easily understood.

Web Accessibility Guidelines

While the Access Board has established a set of accessibility guidelines for the United States government, the World Wide Web Consortium, or W3C, the Web standards body, created a Web Accessibility Initiative (WAI) that, in turn, devised the Web Content Accessibility Guidelines (WCAG). These guidelines, considered by many to be the standards by which designers should attempt to create their sites, set forth three priority levels. Priority 1 guidelines outline those issues that would make it impossible for disabled persons to successfully use a site. Priority 2 guidelines cover those areas that cause difficulties for the disabled, and Priority 3 are optional guidelines that mostly cover specific use-case scenarios. To be considered "accessible" under the WAI, sites must at least pass all Priority 1 guidelines. Appendix C of this book outlines these guidelines in detail.

Accessibility Myths

Many myths exist around the issue of Web accessibility.

Creating Accessible Pages Is Difficult or Costly

Modifying an existing page that was created with no regard for accessibility can indeed involve an enormous commitment of both time and effort, but creating a site from the beginning with accessibility in mind takes very little extra time and effort.

Making Accessible Pages Is a Lot of Effort for a Few People

Current estimates are that as much as 10 percent of the population suffers from one or more of the major disabilities listed previously, and this does not include color blindness. Most businesses would not consider 10 percent of their potential customer base insignificant, and would consider it a high enough number to make the effort worthwhile.

Accessible Web Sites Are Ugly

If done correctly, accessible sites can be every bit as visually attractive as their non-accessible counterparts. In fact, for the most part, non-disabled users should be unaware that they are visiting an accessible site.

Accessibility Means Providing the Exact Same Experience

Making your site accessible means that disabled users will be able to successfully visit and navigate the site and that they will be able to gain the same information as the non-disabled. It does not mean that they have to have the exact same experience at the site. Obviously, the hearing impaired cannot listen to music on a Web site, but if the site exists to sell CDs of the music, they should be able to navigate in the site and make purchases with the same relative ease as anyone else.

Accessible Sites Have Benefits for All Users

This one is true. Forms that use labels allow the user to click the label, as well as in the form control, to give the form field focus. Everyone benefits when the clickable area of a form control is bigger and easier to click. Sites that present content in a logical, easy-to-use manner are easier for all. Also, because most search engines read your code in a manner very similar to that of screen readers, accessible sites, in general, will receive higher rankings than their non-accessible counterparts.

Legal Considerations

Many governmental bodies around the world have established laws requiring Web accessibility.

Section 508

In the United States, the primary legal requirement for Web accessibility is the Workforce Investment Act of 1998, which added Section 508 to the Rehabilitation Act, 29 U.S.C. 794d. Popularly referred to as Section 508 or, at times, simply 508, the act states in part that it is a requirement for "individuals with disabilities who are members of the public seeking information or services from a Federal department or agency to have access to and use of information and data that is comparable to the access to and use of the information and data by such members of the public who are not individuals with disabilities." The law applies to all United States government agencies. The act established that an Access Board would meet and determine the specific requirements for making sites accessible under the law, and this board established a set of 17 checkpoints that Web developers are to follow under the law.

The Americans with Disabilities Act

The Americans with Disabilities Act, or ADA, does not specifically cover Web accessibility because it was written and signed into law before the Web existed. However, disability advocacy groups have sued companies under the law to attempt to force them to make their sites accessible. While no final decision has been reached, and the matter will ultimately need to be settled by either a specific amendment to the law or a clear decision by the Supreme Court, most of the decisions to date have leaned in favor of those bringing the cases and against the companies that feel that making their sites accessible places is too great a burden on them.

Other National Laws

Outside of the United States, many other countries have passed legislation requiring that Web sites be accessible. While details vary from one nation to the next, the basic principals are the same. In Australia, Web accessibility is covered under the Disability Discrimination Act of 1992. Canada's Human Rights Act of 1977 has been interpreted as covering Web sites in that nation. The Disability Discrimination Act of 1995 in the United Kingdom and the Disability Act of 2005 in Ireland cover it as well. Denmark, Finland, France, Germany, Hong Kong, India, Israel, Italy, Japan, New Zealand, Portugal, Spain, and Switzerland have similar laws.

Add a Caption and Summary to a Table

Data tables present a particular challenge for accessibility. Sighted users can fairly easily scan a table to get an idea about the information it contains and how it is organized. Non-sighted users, on the other hand, must just listen to their screen reader, and if the table is not carefully constructed, can quickly become lost.

As XHTML defines tables by rows and cells, screen readers will present the data in the same way. When encountering a table constructed with no concern for accessibility, the screen reader simply reads the contents of the first cell, then the second, and so forth. Some may indicate when they begin a new row, but not all will.

Some of the difficulties around tables can be alleviated by adding a summary of a table's contents and a caption to

provide a title for it. The summary is added through the use of the summary attribute of the table element. The summary should present a brief description of the purpose of the table, along with a summary of the table's contents and organization. For example, a table on a page that is being used to display a company's phone list might have the following summary: "This table presents the company phone list. It contains columns for the employee's name, department, and telephone extension."

The caption element, which must appear as the first child element of the table, can be used to display a block of text immediately above the table. This helps with accessibility because it provides an additional clue as to the purpose of the table. Unlike the summary, however, which will only ever be encountered by screen readers, the caption will be visible on the page.

Add a Caption and Summary to a Table

① Open a Web page that contains a table in your editor.

```
regions - Notepad                          ①
File  Edit  Format  View  Help
<div id="content">

<h1>National Park Regions</h1>

<table>

        <col width="150" />
        <col width="50" />
        <col width="400" />

        <thead>
        <tr>
                <th>Region</th>
                <th>Number of Parks</th>
                <th>States/Territories in Region</th>
        </tr>
        </thead>

        <tfoot>
        <tr>
                <td colspan="3">Total Regions: 7; Total Parks: 482</td>
        </tr>
        </tfoot>
```

② In the table element's opening tag, add a summary attribute.

③ Type a descriptive summary of the table.

```
regions - Notepad
File  Edit ②ormat  View  Help
<div id="content">

<h1>National Park Regions</h1>

<table summary="This table lists the National Park Service regions. It conta     ③
column with the number of parks in the region, and a column with a list of t
region. Following each region is a row that lists the regional office locati

        <col width="150" />
        <col width="50" />
        <col width="400" />

        <thead>
        <tr>
                <th>Region</th>
                <th>Number of Parks</th>
                <th>States/Territories in Region</th>
        </tr>
        </thead>
```

④ Immediately following the opening `table` tag, add a `caption` element's opening tag.

⑤ Add a descriptive caption.

⑥ Add a closing `caption` tag.

⑦ Save the page.

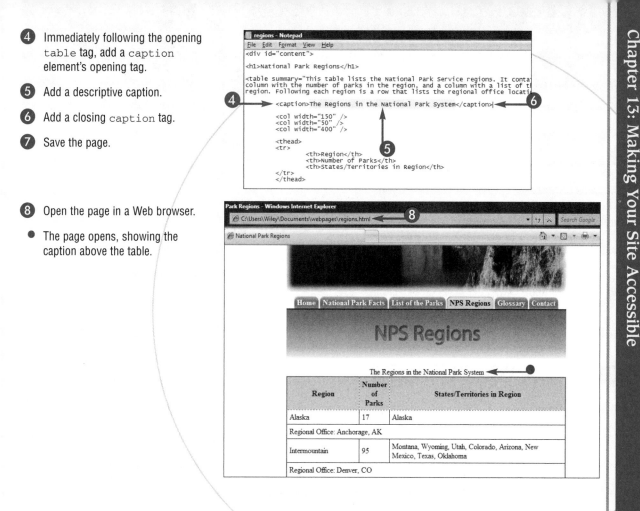

⑧ Open the page in a Web browser.

● The page opens, showing the caption above the table.

Extra

The `caption` element has a deprecated `align` attribute to place it somewhere other than centered above the table. Rather than use `align`, you can apply styles to the caption to not only change its position above the table but to also style it to fit the overall look and feel of your site.

```css
caption {
    text-align: left;
    font-weight: bold;
    font-style: italic;
    font-size: larger;
}
```

Using Additional Header Markup in Your Tables

Screen readers *linearize* data tables; that is, they read the table as if it were a solid string of text. Each cell is read immediately following the one previous to it, row by row. If not designed with this in mind, tables can quickly become one of the least usable aspects of your site.

You must do several things to ensure that your table is understandable when it is read for your visually impaired users. First and foremost, be sure to always include a header row, a column, or both, and properly mark up the header content with the th element. Some screen readers will repeat the contents of header text before reading each cell. For example, a product table may be read: "Product Name: Green Widget; Product Price: $14.50; Product Name: Blue Widget; Product Price: $29.95." As

the repetitiveness of long header text can become tedious, you can provide a shorter form by using the abbr attribute of th. In the previous example, you might code the headers as <th abbr="name">Product Name</th><th abbr="price">Product Price</th>. In this case, the full text of the header will only be read for the first row, while the abbreviated version will be used for other cells.

You should also include the scope attribute in the th, specifying whether the header corresponds to the row or column. This is of particular importance for complex tables with more than one header, such as data charts that may contain both a header row along the top as well as additional header information in the left-most column.

Using Additional Header Markup in Your Tables

1 Open a Web page that contains a table in your editor.

2 If necessary, replace td elements with th elements in the header row.

3 Add descriptive, abbreviated text for long headers by adding abbr attributes.

④ Add a `scope` attribute to each header with an appropriate value.

⑤ Save the page.

```
regions - Notepad
File  Edit  Format  View  Help
<div id="content">

<h1>National Park Regions</h1>

<table summary="This table lists the National Park Service regions. It contains a column
column with the number of parks in the region, and a column with a list of the states or
Following each region is a row that lists the regional office location.">

        <caption>The Regions in the National Park System</caption>

        <col width="150" />
        <col width="50" />
        <col width="400" />

        <thead>
        <tr>
                <th scope="col">Region</th>
                <th scope="col" abbr="Num Parks">Number of Parks</th>
                <th scope="col" abbr="State List">States/Territories in Region</th>
        </tr>
        </thead>

        <tfoot>
        <tr>
                <td colspan="3">Total Regions: 7; Total Parks: 482</td>
        </tr>
        </tfoot>
```

④

⑥ Open the page in a Web browser.

The page opens, showing the headers. Note that the changes you made do not affect the page visually.

Park Regions - Windows Internet Explorer

C:\Users\Wiley\Documents\webpages\regions.html ◄────── ⑥

National Park Regions

Home | National Park Facts | List of the Parks | NPS Regions | Glossary | Contact

NPS Regions

The Regions in the National Park System

Region	Number of Parks	States/Territories in Region
Alaska	17	Alaska
Regional Office: Anchorage, AK		
Intermountain	95	Montana, Wyoming, Utah, Colorado, Arizona, New Mexico, Texas, Oklahoma
Regional Office: Denver, CO		

Extra

Proper use of the table section elements `thead`, `tfoot`, and `tbody` will further improve the readability of your table. All three further enhance the underlying logic of the table code, and thus its accessibility.

While you should always avoid tables for layout, you will likely encounter legacy pages that still rely on them as they were the standard method of creating multicolumn layouts on Web pages for many years. One of the primary challenges for making a page that uses tables for layouts accessible is that content in layout tables is rarely presented in a logical order when the table is linearized. Layout tables should ideally be removed and replaced by appropriate CSS, leaving only data tables behind. In the meantime, however, you should not use headers or captions on layout tables, as neither makes logical sense when the table is not being used to simply display data.

Make Complex Tables Accessible

A common data layout in spreadsheets, such as those created in Microsoft Excel, is to have dual headers, most often a header row along the top of a table to describe each column and a header column along the left edge to describe each row.

Tables such as these will have `th` elements for both the header row and the column. However, simply adding the `scope` attribute will not suffice to make the table accessible, as each cell will actually have two headers. In this case, you will need to give each header an `id` attribute, which, as usual, must be unique for that page. Then, each `td` element for the cell will have a `headers` attribute added, which will contain a space-separated list of the headers that apply to that cell.

```
<table>

    <tr><td></td><th
id="2006">2006</th><th
id="2007">2007</th></tr>

    <tr><th id="income">Income</th><td
headers="2006 income">$245,000</td><td
headers="2007 income">$360,000</td></tr>

    <tr><th
id="expenses">Expenses</th><td
headers="2006 expenses">$152,000</td><td
headers="2007 expenses">$300,000</td></tr>

</table>
```

Make Complex Tables Accessible

1 Open a Web page that contains a table in your editor.

```
<table summary="A table of the most and least visited parks by region.">

    <caption>Largest and Smallest Parks by Region</caption>

    <tr>
        <td></td>
        <th abbr="Largest">Most Visited Park</th>
        <th abbr="Smallest">Least Visited Park</th>
    </tr>
    <tr>
        <th abbr="Alaska">Alaska Region</th>
        <td>Glacier Bay National Park and Preserve</td>
        <td>Aniakchak National Monument and Preserve</td>
    </tr>
    <tr>
        <th abbr="Intermountain">Intermountain Region</th>
        <td>Grand Canyon National Park</td>
        <td>Rio Grande Wild and Scenic River</td>
    </tr>
    <tr>
        <th abbr="Midwest">Midwest Region</th>
        <td>Jefferson National Monument</td>
        <td>William Howard Taft National Monument</td>
    </tr>
    <tr>
        <th abbr="Capital">National Capital Region</th>
        <td>Lincoln Memorial</td>
        <td>Mary McLeod Bethune Council House National Historic Site </td>
    </tr>
```

2 Add an `id` attribute to each header cell.

3 Add an appropriate, unique identifier as the value.

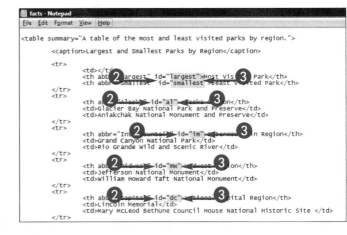

④ Add a `headers` attribute to each cell with an appropriate value.

⑤ Save the page.

```
<tr>
    <td></td>
    <th abbr="Largest" id="largest">Most Visited Park</th>
    <th abbr="Smallest" id="smallest">Least Visited Park</th>
</tr>
<tr>
    <th abbr="Alaska" id="al">Alaska Region</th>
    <td headers="largest al">Glacier ❹ National Park and Preserve</td>
    <td headers="smallest al">Aniakchak National Monument and Preserve</td>
</tr>
<tr>
    <th abbr="Intermountain" id="im">Intermountain Region</th>
    <td headers="largest im">Grand Can ❹ National Park</td>
    <td headers="smallest im">Rio Grande Wild and Scenic River</td>
</tr>
<tr>
    <th abbr="Midwest" id="mw">Midwest Region</th>
    <td headers="largest mw">Jefferso ❹ ional Monument</td>
    <td headers="smallest mw">William Howard Taft National Monument</td>
</tr>
<tr>
    <th abbr="Capital" id="dc">National Capital Region</th>
    <td headers="largest dc">Lincoln ❹ ial</td>
    <td headers="smallest dc">Mary McLeod Bethune Council House National Historic Site </td>
</tr>
```

⑥ Open the page in a Web browser.

The page opens, showing that the changes above have not altered the visual appearance of the table.

Park Facts - Windows Internet Explorer

C:\Users\Wiley\Documents\webpages\facts.html ← ⑥

View   Favorites   Tools   Help

National Park Facts

NPS Facts

National Park Service Home Page

Parks by Size
- The largest national park is the **Wrangell-St. Elias National Park and Preserve** in Alaska at 13.2 million acres, or 20,625 square miles.
- The smallest national park by area is the **Thaddeus Kosciuszko National Memorial** in Pennsylvania, at just .02 acres, or about 871 square feet.

Largest and Smallest Parks by Region

	Most Visited Park	Least Visited Park
Alaska Region	Glacier Bay National Park and Preserve	Aniakchak National Monument and Preserve
Intermountain Region	Grand Canyon National Park	Rio Grande Wild and Scenic River
Midwest Region	Jefferson National Monument	William Howard Taft National Monument
National Capital Region	Lincoln Memorial	Mary McLeod Bethune Council House National Historic Site

Extra

Like the summary attribute, the `scope` and `headers` attributes will never be visible on the Web page unless your user views the page source. These are often what are in people's minds when they complain that making a page accessible requires a lot of extra work that will only benefit disabled users. However, adding these attributes while you initially code the table is not an inordinate amount of work, and, in fact, it has the added benefit of forcing you to think about the table's structure more carefully from the beginning. You can also use them as a sort of self-documentation, as the `ids` in each header should clearly identify their purpose, while the `headers` attributes further describe each cell's place in the table and can make reading the code for very large tables easier.

While manufacturers of visual design tools have made great strides recently to produce programs that aid in making standards-compliant, accessible pages, they still occasionally fall short. For example, neither Microsoft Expression Web nor Adobe Dreamweaver provides any tools in their visual interface to add or work with scope or header information, so you will be required to add and maintain these aspects of your table in code view.

Add a Long Description to an Image

All images require alternate text, unless they are backgrounds placed via CSS. Images that exist for pure visual flair and do nothing to add to the actual page content should ideally be added as CSS backgrounds, but if they are not, they should be given empty alternate text by setting the `alt` attribute to an empty string: `alt=""`. Alternate text is an important accessibility feature of XHTML, but as it is also a required attribute, it is discussed in detail in Chapter 4.

For most images, descriptive alternate text will suffice. While in theory there is no limit as to the length of alternate text, it should be kept fairly short and to the point. However, you may occasionally encounter images that cannot be easily summed up in alternate text. For example, it is impossible to describe a chart or graph in a short alternate description. For these types of images, XHTML provides the ability to add a long description to the page.

Long descriptions should be written in plain, descriptive text in a separate document. This document is then referenced via the `longdesc` attribute of the `img` element. Unlike `alt`, `longdesc` is optional, and should only be used for those images that cannot be adequately described in alternate text.

As these pages will only ever be accessed by screen readers, you do not need to provide any visual enhancement to the page. Navigation is also not necessary; the screen reader will inform the user that a long description is available, and should the user choose to go to the page, the reader will recite the text on it and then return the user to the original document.

Add a Long Description to an Image

① Open a new document in your editor.

② Add an appropriate `DOCTYPE`.

③ Add the basic XHTML structure elements.

④ Within the body, add a paragraph element's opening tag.

⑤ Add a description of the image.

⑥ Add the closing paragraph tag.

⑦ Save the document.

8 Open a Web page that contains an image needing a long description in your editor.

9 In the `img` tag, add a `longdesc` attribute.

10 Set its value to the path to the page saved in Step 6.

11 Save the page.

12 Open the page in a Web browser.

The page opens, showing that the changes you made do not show in the browser.

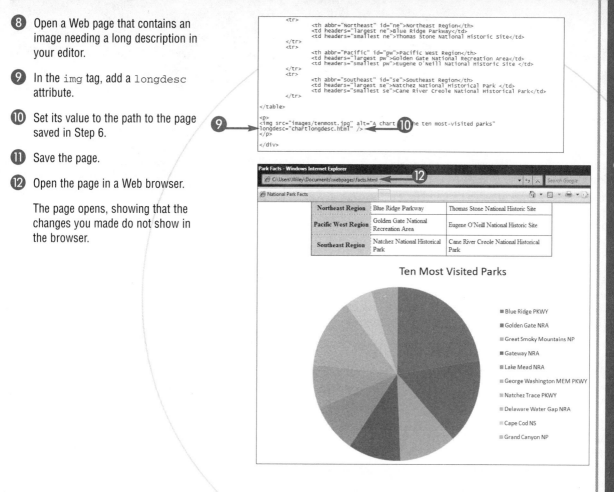

Extra

There is considerable debate in the online community about the practical value of `longdesc`. Unfortunately, studies have shown that very few visually impaired users ever bother to follow the link to the long description page, which is why it is only recommended for those very few images for which it is absolutely necessary.

Screen readers, like visual browsers, are inconsistent in many regards, not the least of which is dealing with `longdesc` pages. JAWS opens the page in a new window, which can be confusing to its users who may not be aware that the new window is open or who can become disoriented by having multiple browser windows open. Providing a link on the page that uses JavaScript to close the window unfortunately causes problems with many of the competitors of JAWS, which open the `longdesc` page in the same window as the original. Due to these issues, some online accessibility advocates have suggested placing the `longdesc` in a block on the same page as the image, and using internal page link references to locate it and CSS to hide it from visual browsers.

Make Navigation Accessible

ood navigation is one of the most important elements of any Web site, and if not done properly, it can become one of the biggest hindrances to the site's accessibility. Fortunately, implementing accessible navigation is not very difficult.

There are a few simple rules you should follow for your navigation. First, do not use images alone for navigation. In addition to being more difficult to maintain, image-based navigation is much less accessible, even with appropriate alternate text. You can use CSS to achieve a visual effect that is similar to most image-based links. Second, be sure that your navigation can be successfully accessed without the mouse. Many site designers use complex JavaScript solutions to create drop-down menus for their site, never considering that many of those

implementations require the mouse to navigate. If your user cannot use a mouse due to visual or motor skills impairment, he will be unable to go anywhere in the site. Third, you need to provide a user with some means of skipping the navigation. Under normal circumstances, the screen reader will read through the page chronologically. As most sites have the main navigation at or near the top of the document, above the main content, blind users will have to endure having all of the links read to them for each and every page, which can quickly become annoying.

The skip navigation link is simple to implement. Add a descriptive id attribute to the main content, and provide a link just before the navigation to that spot on the page. Do not get creative here: The wording on the link should just be "skip navigation," so that there is no doubt as to the link's purpose.

Make Navigation Accessible

① Open a Web page in your editor.

② In the element that wraps around the main content, or the main content's first element, add a descriptive id attribute if one does not already exist.

③ Just before the main navigation, add an anchor element's opening tag.

④ Add the href attribute, with a value of a pound sign and the id referenced in Step 2.

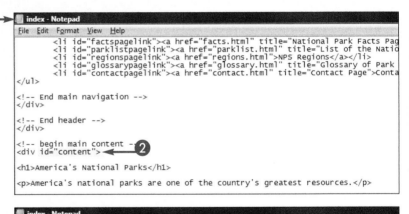

⑤ Type **Skip Navigation** as the link text.

⑥ Add the closing anchor tag.

⑦ Save the page.

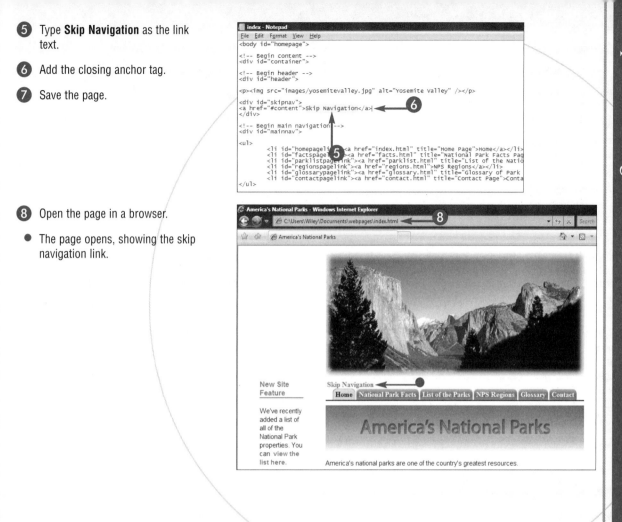

⑧ Open the page in a browser.

● The page opens, showing the skip navigation link.

Extra

Many designers use one of several techniques to hide the skip navigation link on the page, believing that it somehow destroys the visual layout. Some use CSS, positioning the link off the page through a negative text-indent property or absolute positioning. Others place the link on a tiny, one-pixel image that is effectively hidden from view but will still be read by a screen reader.

However, many accessible advocates point out that the link can add not just to the accessibility of the page, but also to its usability. There are some users who simply prefer to use their keyboards instead of their mouses, and face the same problem of having to repeatedly tab through the navigation on pages to reach the content. If the skip navigation link is hidden, they will be unaware of its existence. It should also be pointed out that the link can be easily integrated into the page design so that it does not negatively impact the layout.

Make Forms Accessible

Forms are becoming an increasingly popular and necessary tool on Web pages. Fortunately, they are one of the easier parts of a page to make accessible.

Accessible Elements and Attributes

The elements needed for accessible forms are covered in Chapter 11. For your form to be accessible, you need to be sure that you include a label tag around each label in your form. Although not required, you can make your forms easier to use by grouping related fields using the `fieldset` and `legend` elements.

Visually impaired and other disabled users must rely on the Tab key to move from one field to the next, so be sure that the tab order of the fields is logical. If your fields are presented logically, this should not be an issue, but you should add the `tabindex` attribute to fields if you have any doubt as to the tab order.

Groups of check boxes and radio buttons can be made more accessible by using nested `fieldsets`. The `label` element should be used to mark up the text labeling each individual check box or radio button, and not the label of the group as a whole. In the nested `fieldset`, the label for the group as a whole would most likely become the `fieldset`'s legend.

You should also use the `optgroup` element to group options in a large select list to make it easier to follow.

If you use an image for the button, be sure that the alternate text clearly describes the button's purpose.

Form Layout and Organization

More important than any specific group of elements, however, is the organization and layout of your form. To make a form accessible, you need to be sure that the fields are presented in a logical order. For example, if you have two sets of fields for addresses, one for shipping and another for billing, do not lay them out side by side in a table so that the shipping name is followed by the billing name rather than the shipping street address. Make sure that the shipping fields all follow one another, and that the billing fields follow those as a group. You can still lay them out visually side by side using floats or some other CSS positioning technique.

Make Your Form Easy to Understand

Making sure that your form is easily understood benefits all of your users, not just those who are disabled. Be sure to include clear instructions on your form.

Include Obvious Required Fields

In particular, many sites fail to indicate which fields on the form are required. Instead, they make the user guess which fields are needed, only waiting until the form has been submitted to return a validation error that states required fields.

Provide Instructions for Required Formats

Increasingly, Web sites are requiring the use of strong passwords for user registration. A strong password is one that contains some combination of lower- and uppercase letters, numbers, and special characters. Sites may also require that passwords be at least a certain length. If your site has these requirements, spell them out clearly on the form. One of the most popular social networking sites on the Web fails in this regard, and only informs you that you need a strong password after the form has been submitted and returns a validation error.

Remind Users to Refill Passwords

Password fields cannot be prefilled with data, and if the form is reloaded, they will not be refilled. Particularly if you are using server-side validation that requires that the browser reload the form page in the case of validation errors, be sure to remind users that they need to re-enter data into any password fields.

Do Not Use Color Alone

Do not use color alone to indicate required fields. An instruction such as "required fields are indicated in red below" is useless to visually impaired users and quite possibly color blind users as well. Instead, add a symbol such as an asterisk to indicate that a field is required, or perhaps best of all, simply write "required" next to the field. As with many other accessibility additions to your page, this helps not only your disabled users, but also anyone who attempts to fill out the form. This is not, by the way, to say that you cannot *also* use color to indicate a required field, but rather that you should not do it without some descriptive text as well.

Use Tables Appropriately

Forms are not data, and thus you should not lay out your form using a table. Unfortunately, however, many designers insist on form fields being perfectly lined up, and tables are without question an easy way to accomplish this. Many times, you can accomplish nicer layouts by using CSS and a little creativity instead of the table, but if you must lay out your form in a table, there are some guidelines you need to follow.

Place Labels Next To, Not Above, Fields

Some designers have attempted to create tables where they have a row of labels, followed by a row of fields, so that each label sits in a cell above its field. Because this causes the label text to be separated from the field by a considerable amount of code, screen readers will find it very difficult to properly describe the form. Using the `label` element with appropriate `for` attributes will alleviate much of this issue, but if you want your labels to appear above the field, place them in the same cell, using a break element, instead of different rows.

Each Fieldset Needs a New Table

One of the reasons why the `fieldset` element was not widely used until fairly recently was that a `fieldset` cannot wrap around a portion of a table. If you use a single table for your entire form, then you could only use a single `fieldset`. Therefore, to properly organize your form, you need to create separate tables within each `fieldset`.

Test
Accessibility

Perhaps the most difficult aspect of building accessible Web pages is testing to be sure that your efforts will succeed. Clearly, the best method of testing to be sure that your page can be used by the visually impaired would be to acquire a screen reader, so that you could use your site in much the same way as your users. Unfortunately, none of the developers of the leading screen reading applications have made an affordable developer edition available, and at close to $1,000, purchasing such software is cost-prohibitive for many designers. These same applications do offer trial versions, but most require that you reboot your computer frequently, as often as every 20 to 40 minutes, in order to use them.

The next best thing then is to use software that will analyze your page against the accessibility checkpoints developed by the Access Board for Section 508 and the WAI for the WCAG. A free online service to test accessibility is Cynthia Says at www.cynthiasays.com.

Cynthia Says will generate reports indicating errors, or items on your page that fail against the checkpoints and must be corrected, and warnings, which indicate items on the page that need to be double-checked but may be fine. The service allows you to choose whether you want a WCAG or 508 report.

It does not provide the capability of uploading local files to be checked, so you will need to run it against pages that have already been uploaded to a Web server.

Test Accessibility

TEST FOR SECTION 508 COMPLIANCE

1 Open www.cynthiasays.com in your browser.

2 Enter the URL of the page you wish to test.

3 Select Section 508 from the Accessibility Report Mode drop-down.

4 Click Test Your Site.

● The results page opens.

5 Review the report to note any errors or warnings.

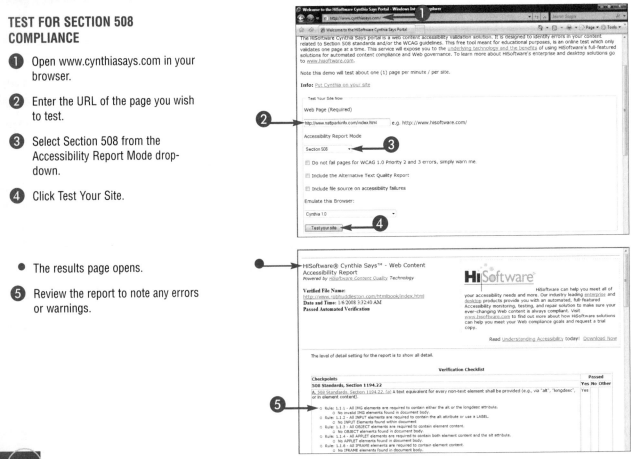

TEST FOR WCAG COMPLIANCE

① Click your browser's Back button to return to the Cynthia Says homepage.

② Select WCAG Priority 1,2,3 from the Accessibility Report Mode drop-down.

Note: *The URL you entered before should still be in the text box.*

③ Click Test Your Site.

● The results page opens.

④ Review the report to note any errors or warnings.

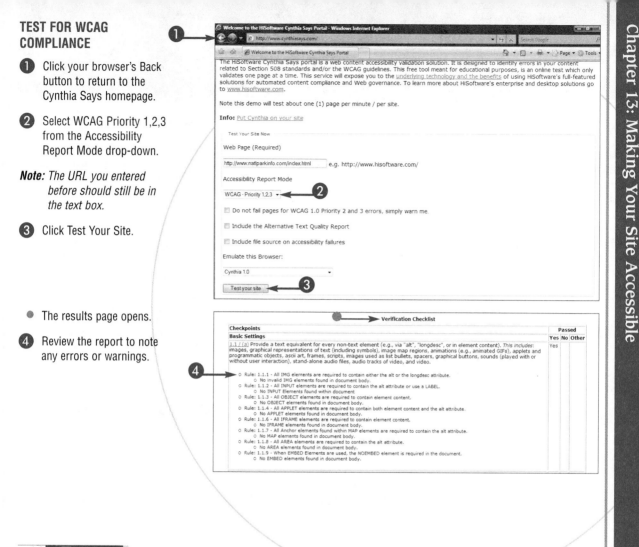

Extra

Warnings generated by the reports are often misunderstood and can be a source of frustration, because very few pages will ever fail to generate warnings. Leaving alternate text off an image entirely will generate an error. However, no computer can check that the alternate text you have on an image adequately describes it; thus, the accessibility reports will always generate a warning for every image on the page, which serves as a reminder that you need to look at the image and the alternate text and be sure it is accurate.

The same will apply to the warnings you see about the use of color on the page. They are not saying that you cannot use color, but rather that you need to be sure that you are not relying on color alone to convey information and that you are maintaining sufficient contrast between the foreground and background.

Pages can be said to have "passed" an accessibility report so long as they do not generate errors. They do not have to be free of warnings.

Add Special Characters to Your Page

X HTML supports a set of *character entities*, which are codes that represent special characters that will be interpreted by the browser to display non-standard characters. The syntax to create any of these entities is to use an ampersand, followed by the code for the character, followed by a semicolon.

These entities fall into three main categories. The first contains a single entity, , which represents a non-breaking space. As browsers will ignore consecutive whitespace characters, this entity lets you force additional space as needed. The second category contains four characters which, if typed in directly, would potentially confuse the browser. They are the two angle brackets, < and >, the double quotation mark and the apostrophe, and the ampersand. The first two are represented by the < and > entities. The double quotation mark is ". The apostrophe is ', although it is valid

only in XHTML, not HTML. The ampersand is represented by &. Consider creating a page that discussed basic math concepts. You might wish to have a statement such as 5 < 10. If typed directly, the browser would believe that the less-than symbol was actually the beginning of an XHTML tag and would ignore everything until it encountered the opposite bracket, which it would interpret as the end of the tag. Instead, you can use the entity for the less-than symbol and write 5 < 10. This results in the correct display in the browser.

The final category is by far the largest, and represents the group of characters that cannot be directly typed on a keyboard. For example, © is the copyright symbol. Keyboards have a dollar sign, but lack a key for the British pound, euro, or yen, but each can be encoded using £, €, and ¥, respectively. See Appendix A for a complete list of the entities.

Add Special Characters to Your Page

① Open a Web page in your editor.

```
index2 - Notepad                    ①
File  Edit  Format  View  Help
</div>

<!-- begin main content -->
<div id="content">

<h1>America's National Parks</h1>

<p>America's national parks are one of the country's greatest

<div id="maincol">

<h2>History of the Parks</h2>

<p>The first national park was <span class="parkname">Yellowst
Grant in 1872. The Park Service was established by an Act of C
1916.</p>

</div>

<div id="footer">
```

② Add a character entity to the page.

③ Save the page.

```
<h2>History of the Parks</h2>

<p>The first national park was <span class="parkname">Yellowst
Grant in 1872. The Park Service was established by an Act of C
1916.</p>

</div>

<div id="sidebar">

<h2>Headquarters</h2>

<p>The national headquarters of the US National Park Service i
1849 C Street NW, Washington, DC.</p>

</div>           ②

<div id="footer">

<p>&copy; 2008, all rights reserved.</p>

</div>
```

④ Open the page in a Web browser.

● The page opens, showing the character represented by the entity.

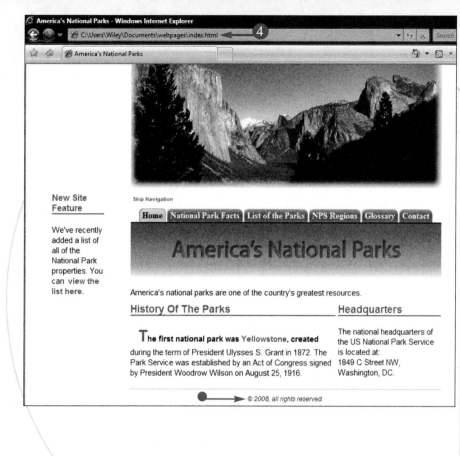

Extra

Many designers are careful to use entities in place of the angle brackets, but fail to use the quotation mark and apostrophe entities. While browsers will have no trouble correctly displaying pages that use these characters directly, an XHTML Strict document will not validate if you do not encode them.

The same is true of the ampersand, which is most frequently used within long, complex URLs to separate pairs of variables that are being passed to server-side scripts. Here again, browsers will not have any trouble correctly rendering pages that use unencoded ampersands, but your document will fail to validate. This can cause problems with content that you may be including from other sources, such as advertising or RSS feeds. While some developers create complicated scripts to parse these incoming URLs and properly encode the ampersands, others take the approach of being careful to write their code as XHTML Strict, but rely on the XHTML Transitional DOCTYPE so that their pages will still validate.

Add an Address to a Page

ompanies establishing an online presence will often wish to place their physical addresses on their sites. Doing so establishes a sense of legitimacy, as many people may be uncomfortable doing business with a company that seems to have no physical presence.

XHTML provides the address element for this purpose. You can also use the element to mark the section of your page that shows contact information, such as the e-mail address of the Web master or the phone numbers for customer support. If you have an online form that you intend for the user to print and mail to you, you should use this element to mark the mailing address:

```
<address>123 Main St., Someplace,
12345</address>
```

The address element is a block-level element, so it should not be placed within a paragraph or heading, although it can reside within a div or other similar block. For some obscure reason, browsers traditionally display the contents of address in italic, but this behavior can be overridden through a simple style sheet declaration:

```
address { font-style: normal; }
```

Traditionally the address is used in either the header or the footer of the document. The element takes no unique attributes, although like other basic structure elements it does support id, class, style, lang, title, and the JavaScript event handlers.

Add an Address to a Page

① Open a Web page that contains a link to a style sheet in your editor.

② Near the bottom of the page, add an address element's opening tag.

```
<div id="sidebar">
<h2>Headquarters</h2>
<p>The national headquarters of the US National Park Service i
1849 C Street NW, Washington, DC.</p>
</div>
<div id="footer">
<p>&copy; 2008, all rights reserved.</p>
<address>|
</div>
<!-- End content -->
</div>
```

② ➞

③ Enter the address of the Web site's company.

④ Add a closing address tag.

⑤ Save the page.

```
<div id="sidebar">
<h2>Headquarters</h2>
<p>The national headquarters of the US National Park Service i
1849 C Street NW, Washington, DC.</p>
</div>
<div id="footer">
<p>&copy; 2008, all rights reserved.</p>
<address>
123 Some St., Somewhere, 12345   ◀── ③
</address>|
</div>
```

④ ➞

6 Open the style sheet in your editor.

7 Add an `address` selector and an opening curly brace.

8 Add `font-style:normal;`.

9 Add a closing curly brace.

10 Save the page.

11 Open the Web page in your browser.

• The page opens, showing the address block.

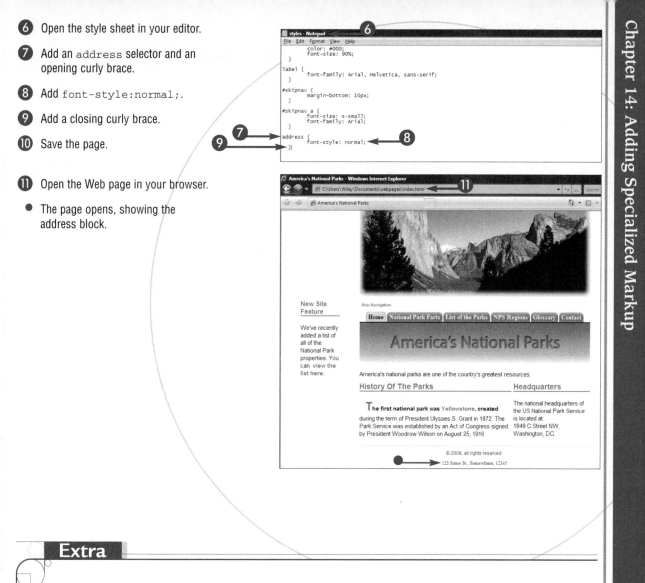

Extra

According to the actual HTML 4.0 specification, "The address element may be used by authors to supply contact information for a document or a major part of a document such as a form." This wording has led some to argue that the element is not properly used to provide a physical mailing address, but should rather be used solely to provide contact information for a particular page, such as an e-mail address for the Web master.

As one of a half dozen or so elements that will by default cause their contents to render in italics, the `address` element had on occasion been misused simply to create italicized text. Obviously, it is better to use the `em` element when italicizing for emphasis and CSS when italicizing for mere visual effect and reserve the `address` for its intended purpose.

Using Quoted Text

Sometimes, you may wish to quote others in the content of your page. Many companies, for example, have a testimonials section of the Web site with quotes from satisfied customers. Blogs will often include quotes from famous authors or celebrities.

XHTML provides two elements for marking up quotations: `q` and `blockquote`. The `q` element is an inline element, intended for short quotes that will be included within a block of text such as a paragraph. The `title` attribute is often used to provide a reference to the source of the citation:

```
<q>We have done the impossible, and that
makes us mighty.</q>
```

The browser will automatically add quotation marks at the beginning and end of the included text, so the previous line would render as "We have done the impossible, and that makes us mighty."

You can use the `cite` element to provide a reference to the author of the quote. Following the previous example, you might, for example, have `<cite>Malcolm Reynolds</cite>`. Browsers will, for the most part, display the contents of `cite` using an italic typeface, but, again, you can easily override this through CSS.

Longer quotes should more properly be set apart from the text and indented. Both of these are provided by the `blockquote` element. Unlike `q` and `cite`, `blockquote` is a block element, and so it creates space above and below the block, and also indents the text from both the left and right margins.

```
<blockquote> Love. You can learn all the
math in the 'verse, but you take a boat in
the air that you don't love, she'll shake
you off just as sure as the turning of
worlds. And love keeps her in the air when
she oughtta fall down, tells ya she's
hurtin' 'fore she keens, makes her a home.
- Malcolm Reynolds </blockquote>
```

Using Quoted Text

① Open a Web page in your editor.

② Add a `q` element's opening tag.

③ Add a short quote.

④ Add a closing `q` tag.

```
<!-- End main navigation -->
</div>

<!-- End header -->
</div>

<!-- begin main content -->
<div id="content">

<h1>About Us</h1>

<p>Our website has been called <q>the best on the web</q> by .</p>

<div id="footer">

<p>&copy; 2008, all rights reserved.</p>

<address>
123 Some St., Somewhere, 12345
</address>

</div>
```

⑤ Add a `cite` element's opening tag.

⑥ Add a citation for the quote's author.

⑦ Add the closing `cite` tag.

```
<!-- End main navigation -->
</div>

<!-- End header -->
</div>

<!-- begin main content -->
<div id="content">

<h1>About Us</h1>

<p>Our website has been called <q>the best on the web</q> by <cite>National Park Travel</cite>. </p>

<div id="footer">

<p>&copy; 2008, all rights reserved.</p>

<address>
123 Some St., Somewhere, 12345
</address>

</div>
```

⑧ Add a `blockquote`'s opening tag.

⑨ Add a longer quotation.

⑩ Add the closing `blockquote`.

⑪ Save the page.

⑫ Open the page in a browser.

● The page opens, showing the quote.

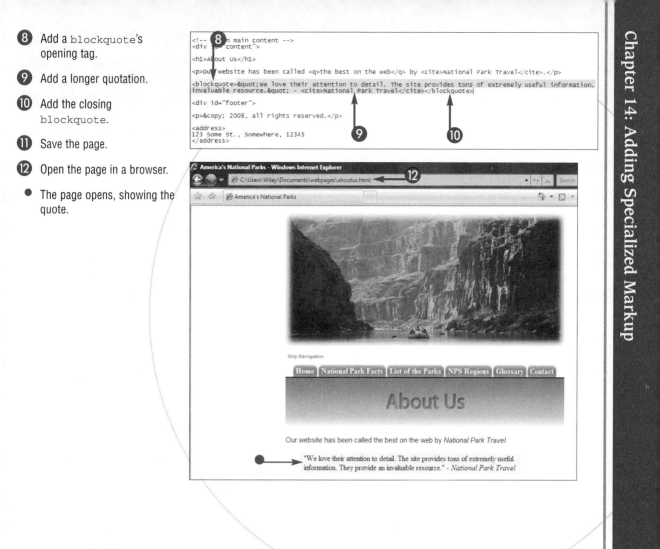

If the source of the `blockquote` is another Web page, you can provide a path to that page using the `cite` attribute, but unfortunately, modern browsers do not provide any visual indication that such a citation is present, nor do they provide a way to move to the page indicated. Therefore, you should be sure to include a proper citation either within the quote itself or immediately following.

Prior to the advent of CSS, a common practice was to use `blockquote` as a method of indenting text on a page. This practice should now be avoided, as CSS provides more control over indentation without sacrificing the structural meaning of the document.

Because browsers automatically add the quotation marks when using `q`, you should not provide them yourself. `Blockquotes` may or may not be quoted depending on the context, so browsers will not add the quotation marks, leaving you to do it instead. Keep in mind that you must escape the marks using the `&quot;` character entity in order to produce valid XHTML.

Using Abbreviations and Acronyms on a Page

Many industries rely heavily on abbreviations and acronyms, some to the point that the abbreviations and acronyms are adopted by the population at large and enter the general lexicon. Many acronyms, such as laser and radar, have become so widely used that they have lost their original meanings.

In XHTML documents, you can use the `abbr` element for abbreviations and `acronym` for acronyms. While many online tutorials attempt to provide a differentiation between the two, stating that abbreviations are shorter forms of words, such as "in" for "inch," while acronyms are constructed from the first letter of the words in a phrase such as laser, the XHTML specification makes no such distinction. In fact, it provides WWW as an example of the use of `abbr`, even though it is technically an

acronym. In practice, therefore, it is proper to use either element interchangeably.

When using either of these elements, you should provide a `title` attribute with the full meaning of the abbreviation or acronym. For example: `<acronym title="North Atlantic Treaty Organization">NATO</acronym>`. As every modern browser provides a pop-up tooltip when it encounters an element with a title attribute, this usage provides a convenient way for users to find the meaning of unfamiliar abbreviations and acronyms. Many authors will also use CSS to provide some sort of visual clue that additional information is available, such as using the border-bottom property to draw a light dashed or dotted line below the element.

Using Abbreviations and Acronyms on a Page

1. Open a Web page in your editor.

2. Add an `abbr` element's opening tag.

3. Add a `title` attribute.

4. Set the value of the attribute to the full form of the abbreviation.

5. Add the abbreviation.

6. Add the closing tag.

7. Save the page.

8. Open the page in a browser.

● The page opens, showing the abbreviation.

Display Code on a Page

Web sites that provide technical information or support, or tutorials on programming or markup languages, will often need a way to display blocks of code on a page. Traditionally, these code blocks will be rendered in a different typeface, often a monospace font such as Courier.

XHTML includes four elements for this purpose: code, kbd, samp, and var. The first three will be rendered by default in a monospaced font, while var is most often displayed using italics.

```
<p>Headings in XHTML are marked up using
the <code>&lt;h1&gt;</code> through
<code>&lt;h6&gt;</code> tags.</p>
```

The specification does not provide any details as to how these should be used. Presumably, code is for short passages of sample code, such as those provided throughout this book in the introductions. The kbd element is used to designate code that should be entered as is by the user, and would logically appear in step-by-step tutorials. The samp element designates sample output from programs, and implies simple text output from older programs such as DOS commands. As few modern applications are going to have monospaced output, this would likely be the least used of these elements.

The var element should indicate the presence of a variable in the code. This will again rarely be used outside of programming tutorials. You might, for example, write the following:

```
<p>In your JavaScript code, increment
the value of <var>i</var> by entering
<kbd>i++</kbd>.</p>
```

Display Code on a Page

1. Open a Web page in your editor.

2. Add a code element's opening tag.

3. Add sample code.

4. Close the tag.

5. Save the page.

6. Open the file in a Web browser.

● The page opens, showing the code sample.

```
<h1>About Us</h1>
<p>Our website has been called <q>the best on the web</q> by <cite>National Park Travel</cite>.</p>
<blockquote>&quot;We love their attention to detail. The site provides tons of extremely useful informat
invaluable resource.&quot; - <cite>National Park Travel</cite></blockquote>
<h2>Link To Us</h2>
<p>If you would like to link to us from your website, simply copy the code below into your web editor:<
<code>
&lt;a href=&quot;http://www.nationalparkinfo.org&quot;&gt;National Park Information Site&lt;/a&gt;
</code>
<div id="footer">
```

Denote Inserted and Deleted Text

Often, authors of documents will need to specify text that has either been added or removed since the last revision. In print, these are most often represented by underlined text for insertions and text with strikethrough for deletions.

The XHTML `ins` and `del` elements allow designers to replicate this display in browsers. Text marked with `ins` will generally be underlined, while text within `del` will usually display using strikethrough.

Both elements can take a `datetime` attribute, allowing you to specify exactly when the change was made. Assuming that you are working in a group environment if you are using these elements on your page, you should determine some standard way to denote the date and time in this attribute.

Both elements can also take a `cite` attribute, wherein you can provide a path to a document that describes the

reasons for the change or provides more information about the revision of the document in general. Unfortunately, however, browsers will do nothing to render or indicate the presence of the `cite` attribute or its target page, so you might also provide pertinent information regarding the document's changes in the `title` attribute.

The `ins` and `del` elements are unique in XHTML in that they can exist as either block or inline elements. It is therefore legal to place them within another block element, such as a paragraph:

```
<p>There were <del>10</del><ins>13</ins>
episodes of <span
class="showtitle">Firefly</span></p>
```

Likewise, they can be placed as the parent element of a block:

```
<ins><p>The new policies will go into
effect on January 1.</p></ins>
```

Denote Inserted and Deleted Text

① Open a Web page in your editor.

② Add a `del` element's opening tag before text that is to be marked as deleted.

③ Add a `datetime` attribute with the date of the deletion.

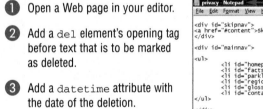

④ Add a `title` attribute with a description of the reason for the change.

⑤ Add the closing `del` tag after the text.

⑥ Add an `ins` element's opening tag.

⑦ Add a `datetime` attribute with an appropriate value.

⑧ Add a `title` attribute describing the change.

⑨ Add the closing `ins` tag after the text.

⑩ Save the page.

⑪ Open the page in a Web browser.

● The page opens, showing the text revisions.

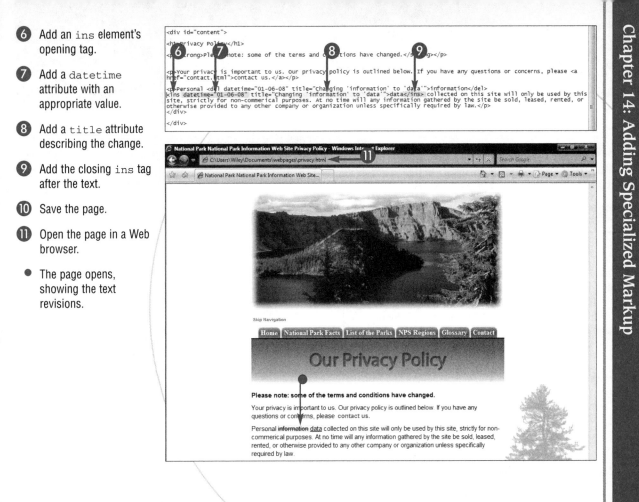

While the print world long ago established underlining as the standard for the display of inserted text, it presents a problem on Web pages as most users automatically assume that underlined text will be a hyperlink. This was not originally considered a problem as hyperlinks are designed to display as a different color from surrounding text, while `ins` text will not. However, as it is now common to use CSS to change the color of links, users cannot rely on thinking that blue underlined text is a link while black underlined text is not. Therefore, you may wish to use CSS to alter the display of the `ins` text somewhat, possibly by removing the default underline and replacing it with a dashed or dotted border. Should you decide to change the color of the `ins` text, you must ensure that it is a sufficiently different color from the hyperlinks on the page so as to avoid confusion.

An example of CSS to alter the underline follows:

```
ins { text-decoration:none; /* removes the underline */
     border-bottom: 1px dashed #333333; /* dark grey dashed border to replace the underline
*/
}
```

Understanding XML

HTML and XHTML are both effective languages for describing the structure of content on a Web page. CSS is useful for describing the formatting of the page. At times, however, you may need a language to describe the actual content of the page. The Extensible Markup Language, or XML, was created for this purpose.

Background of XML

Search engines have consistently become more powerful and better at returning relevant results, but the very nature of XHTML still presents limitations for them. Because XHTML does not give developers a way to define the underlying data on a page, search engines have no effective way to differentiate between uses of common words. For example, a search for the term *firefly* brings up pages that discuss the insect, products with that name, and the television show.

The World Wide Web Consortium, or W3C, created XML in part to combat this issue. Using XML, developers can specify that they are using the previous term to reference the TV show, and that can, in theory, provide better search results.

Today, one common use of XML is to create RSS documents that allow pages to share content with other pages.

XML Does Not Replace HTML

A common myth about XML is that it was designed to replace HTML. In fact, these two languages are entirely different with entirely different purposes. HTML is for structure and presentation, while XML is for data. Neither is intended to replace the other, but instead, each can be used to complement the other.

Some Web sites might benefit from being entirely XML based, but most would not, as the logical structure of the page and how it appears in a browser are more important in most cases.

Writing XML

XHTML provides a defined set of elements with specific purposes. XML, on the other hand, does not. When you write XML documents, you invent the set of elements you need for that document's purposes. You can also create your own attributes and entities. While many XML documents can share the same structure, others will not — and that is part of the design of the language. It is, in fact, what is meant when it is called "extensible."

XML follows a much more strict syntax than HTML. XML tags are case-sensitive, although you can choose which casing scheme you wish to use. XML attributes must always have a value, and that value must always be quoted. Finally, all XML tags must always be closed.

These syntax rules may sound similar to the syntax rules for XHTML. XHTML derives its syntax from XML, so it follows the same rules. Technically, XHMTL documents are, in fact, XML documents.

XML and HTML Similarities

While XML does not rely on a fixed set of tags, it is still tag-based. XML documents look similar to HTML documents. Both are simple text documents that can be created in almost any editor.

Also, neither XML nor HTML can actually "do" anything as they are not programming languages. Both require some other application to parse and interpret them and respond accordingly. In the case of HTML, the helper application is most often a Web browser. XML can be parsed and interpreted by browsers, but there are many other applications available today capable of using XML.

XML was originally developed as a Web technology. Its growth and development is still governed by the W3C. Books on XML are invariably located in the same section of the bookstore next to other Web development titles. However, much of the use of XML today is not Web based.

Microsoft has taken a great interest in XML for its operating system and desktop applications. For example, the latest version of its popular Office suite, Office 2007, relies extensively on XML. The core Office 2007 programs — Word, Excel, and PowerPoint — now use a new file format when saving files, dubbed Open Office XML. Documents saved in this format are in fact ZIP files that contain a series of XML files to describe the content, structure, styling, and other aspects of the document. This way, the programs can more easily share data with one another.

Because XML is completely open and very easy to implement, many other businesses have begun adopting it in many different situations. Large food and beverage manufacturers have converted to XML-based ordering systems that allow them to process orders with retailers who may have otherwise incompatible ordering systems. Government agencies around the world have started using it for similar reasons.

XML Technologies

XML documents describe the data itself, but there are other, related technologies that may be needed to assist in creating an application.

DTD and XSD

XML allows developers to create their own set of tags. However, in order for other users or applications to read or understand the XML, the developer must define the structure of the document, which tags are required or optional, the relationships between tags, what attributes may exist, and other information.

When XML was originally created, the only way to define these details about XML applications was an older system derived from XML's parent language, the Standard Generalized Markup Language, or SGML. This method relies on Document Type Definition documents, or DTDs. HTML itself is actually defined through a DTD.

DTDs have several distinct disadvantages. First, they are not written in XML, so developers must learn a completely separate syntax. Second, they are limited as to what they can define. Data types and specific limits as to the number of instances of elements are two examples of common limits developers need to set on elements but cannot in DTDs. Therefore, the W3C developed an XML-based language for defining XML documents, called the Extensible Schema Definition language, or XSD.

XSLT

While increasing numbers of Web designers today try to separate the structure and content of a site from its presentation by adhering to Web standards and using CSS, with XML, this separation must be maintained. Browsers have predefined rules for basic formatting with XHTML elements, such as defining all elements as either block or inline and rendering headings in bold.

Obviously, browsers cannot have predefined formats for XML elements, as the elements themselves are not predefined. Therefore, XML documents will always be solely data, with no presentation layer at all.

The Extensible Stylesheet Language – Transformations, or XSLT, was designed as an XML-based formatting solution. Through XSLT, designers can use XML parsers to transform XML documents into other formats such as HTML, which then allows them to access the formatting possibilities of HTML or CSS to render their documents.

Namespaces

It is possible, and at times probable, that two developers may develop related XML documents in which they use the same element names for different purposes. For example, one developer of an XML document to store address information might use a contact element as a container element, nesting name, address, and phone elements within it. Another developer might choose to use the contact element in place of name.

So long as these two documents are used in separate applications, no conflict will occur. However, if these two companies merged, and they attempted to use the XML documents in the same application, they would have a problem programming their parser to understand the conflicting contact element.

To avoid these problems, XML provides the ability to define a *namespace*, which is in essence a way for a single application to access XML elements from more than one schema. Most established XML applications use a namespace to increase potential flexibility.

Understanding RSS

Many sites have content that will be constantly updated. News sites, content management systems, and blogs all rely on frequent content changes. It can be daunting for users to keep abreast of even daily changes, and even more difficult to follow content that is seemingly in constant flux.

RSS, which stands for *Really Simple Syndication,* enables users to subscribe to sites with these types of updates and either read them through a dedicated application or publish them on their own Web sites. RSS feeds are defined as an XML document, using a standardized schema.

The History of RSS

Ramanathan V. Guha, an engineer for Netscape, created the first version of RSS, which then stood for *RDF Site Summary*, in 1999 as an extension for the My Netscape portal, an early attempt at creating a news and information Web site that users could personalize. Another developer named Dan Libby revised the RSS standard shortly thereafter, renaming it in the process as *Rich Site Summary*.

In 2002, the meaning of the acronym was formally changed to *Really Simple Syndication*, and a version 2 was released after several years of open development. Another group continues to develop a slightly different standard based on the original RDF format, which is currently in version 1. That same year, the *New York Times* began offering an RSS feed of its headlines, and the technology took off from there.

Today, most major news sites have followed the *New York Times's* lead and offer RSS feeds, as do almost all blogs, many e-commerce sites, and others.

Subscribing to and Reading RSS Feeds

In the early days of its adoption, several specialized RSS readers or aggregators were available. An RSS reader is merely an application that understands and can correctly parse a document written to the RSS schema. As the technology has become more widespread and popular, the ability to read RSS has been integrated into more and more applications, including most major browsers, many major e-mail clients, and other applications. Microsoft Windows Vista, the latest incarnation of the Windows operating system, includes an RSS reader in its Sidebar, a set of gadgets always visible on the side of the user's screen. Each of these programs gives users the ability to subscribe to the feed, allowing them to receive updates to the feed's data automatically as it is made available.

Atom

Atom represents the third branch of RSS development and was developed in an attempt to reconcile several issues with the RSS 2 specification. This group is now a part of the Internet Engineering Task Force, one of the major Internet standards organizations. Atom is generally considered to be more extensible than the RSS formats, but as the newer format, it is not as widely supported by aggregators.

As a developer, you simply need to decide which standard you will use. Most RSS readers have sidestepped the standards issue altogether and simply support all three, so the problems of having three competing versions are transparent to the end users and most developers.

Note that Atom is not an acronym but is instead merely the name of the standard.

Regardless of which RSS standard you choose to rely on, you will be creating an XML document. The only real differences between the three standards are in the actual elements used.

RSS 1 Syntax

RSS 1 documents use a root `rdf` element with, confusingly, an `rdf` namespace. The first child element will be `channel`, used to describe the basic information about your feed, including a title and a link to the home page from the site serving the feed. An optional `image` element for a feed logo follows, and then a series of `item` elements. Each `item` element will contain a `title` element for the specific item, a `link` element with the path to the item's page, and a `description` element that provides a brief summary of the item. These `item` elements will make up the bulk of your feed.

RSS 2 Syntax

RSS 2 uses a root `rss` element. Its first child will, like RSS 1, be a `channel` element, but unlike the version 1 standard, the `channel` element on most feeds will actually contain the rest of the feed, almost becoming a second, nested root element, although it exists for this reason because advanced users can create separate channels within the same document. The `channel` element will contain a `title` element for the feed, a `link` element to the feed's main page, a `description` or `summary` of the feed, a `language` to define the base language used in the feed, a `pubDate` and `last BuildDate`, which are used by aggregators to know if the feed has been updated, and then some general information such as `docs`, `generator`, `managing Editor`, and `webMaster` elements. Following these elements, RSS 2, like version 1, has a series of `item` elements for the actual data. These `item` elements will contain a `title`, `link`, and `description`, along with a `pubDate` and `guid` element, the latter providing a unique identifier for the item.

Atom Syntax

Atom uses a very different syntax from the two RSS formats. The root element of an Atom document is `feed`. Its child elements are `title`, `subtitle`, `link`, `updated`, `author`, and `id`, which describe the feed as a whole, just as in RSS 1 and 2. The main body of the document will be a series of `entry` elements, which will contain `title`, `link`, `id`, `updated`, and `summary` elements.

The RSS Logo

When Mozilla first added RSS feeds to their Firefox browser, they developed a logo to represent feeds and released the logo under the GNU General Public License. The logo is a small orange square with white radio waves radiating from the bottom-left corner. In 2005, Microsoft announced that they were adopting the logo to represent RSS feeds in Internet Explorer and Outlook. Opera soon followed, making the little orange square the recognized standard for RSS. Web developer Matt Brett developed a Web site, Feed Icons at www.feedicons.com, to provide the logo in a variety of formats and colors and help facilitate its widespread use.

File Extensions

There is no agreed-upon file extension for RSS feeds. The most commonly used are .rdf, .rss, .atom, or .xml.

Create an RSS Feed

Creating an RSS feed for your site involves setting up an XML file to hold the information for your feed. You first need to decide on which standard you will use. This task uses RSS 2, as it is generally the easiest syntax to work with.

As an XML document, your RSS feed must follow the syntax rules of the language. As such, it needs to begin with an XML prolog, which tells the parser which version of XML you will be using and the character encoding set that is appropriate for the document. A standard XML prolog looks like this:

```
<?xml version="1.0" encoding="UTF-8" ?>
```

In your XML document, remember after the opening channel to add title, description, and link elements that will describe your feed as a whole. As you add item elements, make sure that each item element also contains, at a minimum, a title, a description, and a link to the page for the item.

After you have created the file, you will need to save it with an appropriate extension. For RSS 2, you should use either .rss or .xml. Then you will upload the file to your server — the exact location is unimportant.

You will want to validate your feed to make sure that you used the proper format. The free Feed Validator at www.feedvalidator.org will do this for you.

Create an RSS Feed

1 Create a new XML document in your editor.

2 Type an XML prolog.

3 Type an opening rss element.

4 Type **version="2.0"**.

5 Type an opening channel element.

```
Untitled - Notepad
File  Edit  Format  View  Help
<?xml version="1.0" encoding="UTF-8" ?>
<rss version="2.0">
        <channel>
```

6 Type a title element's opening tag.

7 Type an appropriate title for your feed and a closing title tag.

8 Type a description element's opening tag.

9 Type an appropriate description and a closing description tag.

10 Type a link element's opening tag.

11 Type the path to your home page and a closing link tag.

```
Untitled - Notepad
File  Edit  Format  View  Help
<?xml version="1.0" encoding="UTF-8" ?>
<rss version="2.0">
        <channel>
                <title>National Park Information</title>
                <description>All the latest information on
                America's National Parks.</description>
                <link>http://www.natlparkinfo.com</link>
```

⑫ Type an `item` element's opening tag.

⑬ Type a `title` element's opening tag.

⑭ Type an appropriate title for the item and a closing `title` tag.

⑮ Type a `description` element's opening tag.

⑯ Type an appropriate description for the item and a closing `description` tag.

⑰ Type a `link` element's opening tag.

⑱ Type a path to the page for the item and a closing `link` tag.

⑲ Close the item element.

⑳ Repeat Steps 12 to 19 to add more items.

㉑ Add a closing `channel` tag and a closing `rss` tag.

㉒ Save the document.

The file is saved, and the RSS feed has been created.

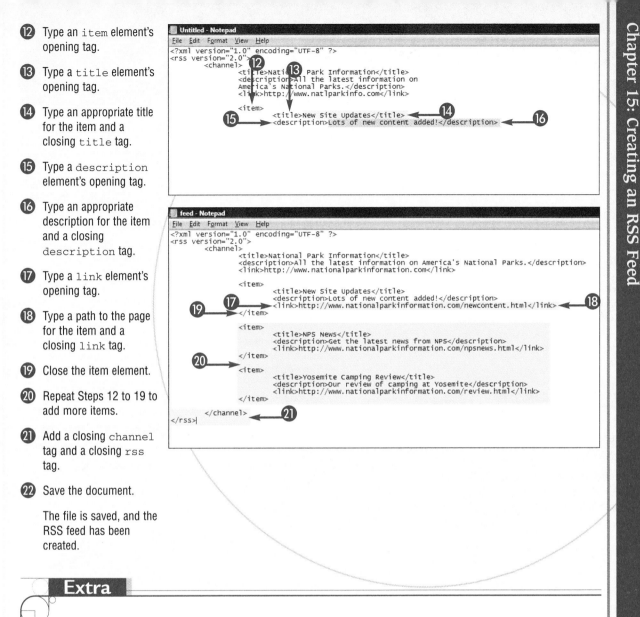

Extra

To have your RSS feed update automatically as your site's content changes, you will need to use server-side scripting. The exact syntax that you will need to use will vary depending on the language, but you need something that will scan your Web pages for changes, read through those pages, and generate the appropriate XML.

Most Web blogging software includes the ability to automatically generate RSS feeds every time that you update your blog. RSS is in fact one of the reasons why blogging has become so popular, as blogs on related topics can be easily aggregated, and it is possible to subscribe to blogs and know when they are updated without having to continually visit the actual site.

There are also commercial tools available to assist in creating RSS feeds. FeedForAll is a standalone application for creating feeds and can be purchased at www.feedforall.com, and DreamFeeder is an extension to Adobe Dreamweaver that enables that program to create RSS feeds from Web pages and can be purchased at http://rnsoft.com.

Embed Multimedia Content in Your RSS

Most traditional RSS feeds are made up of text, and are primarily designed to provide links to content on a Web site. However, an increasing number of designers include multimedia content on their pages with either video or audio files, or both. Recent improvements in the RSS specification have expanded the language to allow for the inclusion of these types of content.

The RSS 2.0 specification added an `enclosure` element for multimedia content. The element may be used within an `item` in the feed. It takes three attributes: `url`, which will contain a path to the content; `length`, the size of the content in bytes; and `type`, the MIME (Multipurpose Internet Mail Extensions) type of the content.

```
<enclosure url="http://www.someurl.com/
media/video.mpg" length="2471632"
type="video/mpg" />
```

Most RSS aggregators that support RSS 2.0 will support media included through `enclosure`. However, the `enclosure` element has several limitations. First, there can only be one `enclosure` element per `item`. Second, it only allows for the inclusion of the size and type of the media, but no other descriptive information. In response to these limitations, Yahoo! created Media RSS, an open module that allows for more control and flexibility on feeds.

You can add the Media RSS module to your feed through the `media` namespace, which you need to declare in the root element of the feed and point to `http://search.yahoo.com/mrss`. The primary element in the namespace is `content`. You must either provide a `url` attribute to the content element, in which you include the path to the media file, or else use a nested `player` element. This element is useful if you plan to use an external media player such as that provided by sites like YouTube. The player element has a required `url` attribute, which will be the path to the player, and optional `width` and `height` attributes.

Embed Multimedia Content in Your RSS

① Open an RSS document in your editor.

② Within the root element's opening tag, add an `xmlns:media` attribute with a value of `http://search.yahoo.com/mrss`.

```
feed - Notepad                                    ①
File  Edit  Format  View  Help
<?xml version="1.0" encoding="UTF-8" ?>
<rss version="2.0" xmlns:media="http://search.yahoo.com/mrss">  ←  ②
        <channel>
                <title>National Park Information</title>
                <description>All the latest information on
                America's National Parks.</description>
                <link>http://www.natlparkinfo.com</link>

                <item>
                        <title>New Site Updates</title>
                        <description>Lots of new content added!</description>
                        <link>http://www.natlparkinfo.com/newcontent.html</link>
                </item>

                <item>
                        <title>NPS News</title>
                        <description>Get the latest news from NPS</description>
                        <link>http://www.natlparkinfo.com/npsnews.html</link>
                </item>
```

③ Within an `item` element, add a `media:content` element's opening tag.

```
<item>
        <title>New Site Updates</title>
        <description>Lots of new content added!</description>
        <link>http://www.natlparkinfo.com/newcontent.html</link>
</item>

<item>
        <title>NPS News</title>
        <description>Get the latest news from NPS</description>
        <link>http://www.natlparkinfo.com/npsnews.html</link>
</item>

<item>
        <title>Yosemite Camping Review</title>
        <description>Our review of camping at Yosemite</description>
        <link>http://www.natlparkinfo.com/review.html</link>
</item>

<item>
        <title>Rafting the Colorado</title>
        <description>Video of a trip down the Colorado River</description>
        <link>http://www.natlparkinfo.com/content/raftingvideo.html</link>
③  →     <media:content |

</item>
```

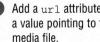
④ Add a `url` attribute with a value pointing to the media file.

```
<item>
        <title>NPS News</title>
        <description>Get the latest news from NPS</description>
        <link>http://www.natlparkinfo.com/npsnews.html</link>
</item>

<item>
        <title>Yosemite Camping Review</title>
        <description>Our review of camping at Yosemite</description>
        <link>http://www.natlparkinfo.com/review.html</link>
</item>

<item>
        <title>Rafting the Colorado</title>
        <description>Video of a trip down the Colorado River</description>
        <link>http://www.natlparkinfo.com/content/raftingvideo.html</link>
        <media:content
            url="http://www.natlparkinfo.com/content/rafting.swf">◄━━④
</item>
```

⑤ Add a closing `media:content` tag.

```
<item>
        <title>NPS News</title>
        <description>Get the latest news from NPS</description>
        <link>http://www.natlparkinfo.com/npsnews.html</link>
</item>

<item>
        <title>Yosemite Camping Review</title>
        <description>Our review of camping at Yosemite</description>
        <link>http://www.natlparkinfo.com/review.html</link>
</item>

<item>
        <title>Rafting the Colorado</title>
        <description>Video of a trip down the Colorado River</description>
        <link>http://www.natlparkinfo.com/content/raftingvideo.html</link>
        <media:content
            url="http://www.natlparkinfo.com/content/rafting.swf">

        </media:content>◄━━⑤
</item>
```

Extra

The `content` element supports thirteen additional attributes, all of which are optional. The `fileSize` attribute allows you to include the size, in bytes, of the media file. Note that the "S" is capitalized. The `type` attribute lets you include the MIME type, while `media` supports values of `image`, `audio`, `video`, `document`, or `executable`. Media RSS supports the concept of grouping content through the `group` element. If this content is part of a group, you can include an `isDefault` attribute to let the player know that this particular content should be displayed or played by default. Again note the capital "D." You can add an `expression` attribute with a value of `full` to indicate that the content is the complete version, `sample` if it is merely a sample or teaser, and `nonstop` if it is being streamed.

Some players will perform better if you provide the `bitrate` attribute for music and the `framerate` for video. You may also specify the `samplingrate` and `channels` to provide that information to the player. The `duration` may allow certain players to inform the user of the length of the media while it is being played. The `width`, `height`, and `lang` attributes allow you to provide additional useful information.

continued ➡

Yahoo! created Media RSS specifically to overcome the limitation as to the type and amount of data that could be provided through the enclosure element. As such, it supports many additional elements in which this information can be provided.

The original specification included an adult element to indicate that the material may be unsuitable for children, but it has been replaced by the more robust rating element. It supports a scheme attribute, which can take a value of simple, declaring the content as adult or non-adult. Alternately, you can use scheme to specify some other rating system, including mpaa, icra, or v-chip.

The title, description, and keywords elements let you more accurately identify the content. The Media RSS specification was developed primarily to allow multimedia content to be submitted via RSS to the Yahoo! search engine, so these elements are important in that respect.

Large images and video can be represented in a smaller, static image through the thumbnail element. It takes a required url attribute to point to the image to be used as a thumbnail.

You can ensure that the people who created the content are recognized and their rights protected by including credit elements with appropriate role attributes and a copyright element, which can take an optional url attribute to provide a link to copyright information.

Text transcripts, closed captioning, or song lyrics can be included via the text element. You can include an optional type attribute, set to plain or html, and start and end attributes to time-code the text to the video or music.

Embed Multimedia Content in Your RSS (continued)

6 Within the media:content element, add a media:rating element's opening tag.

7 Add a scheme attribute set to simple.

8 Set the tag's contents to non-adult or adult as appropriate.

9 Add the closing media:rating tag.

10 Add a media:title element's opening tag.

11 Add an appropriate title and the closing tag.

12 Add a media:description element's opening tag.

13 Add an appropriate description and the closing tag.

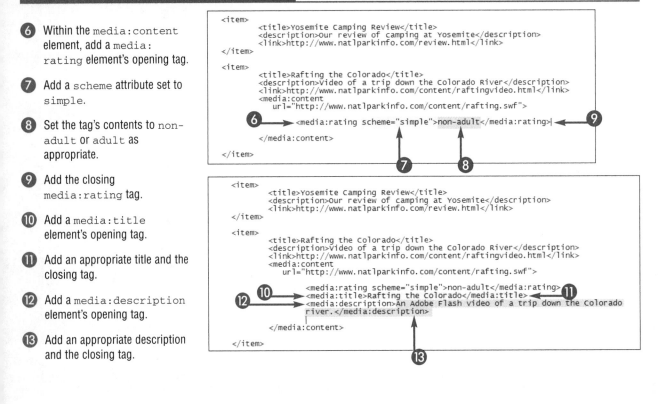

⑭ Add a `media:thumbnail` element's opening tag.

⑮ Add a `url` attribute with a path to a thumbnail that represents the content.

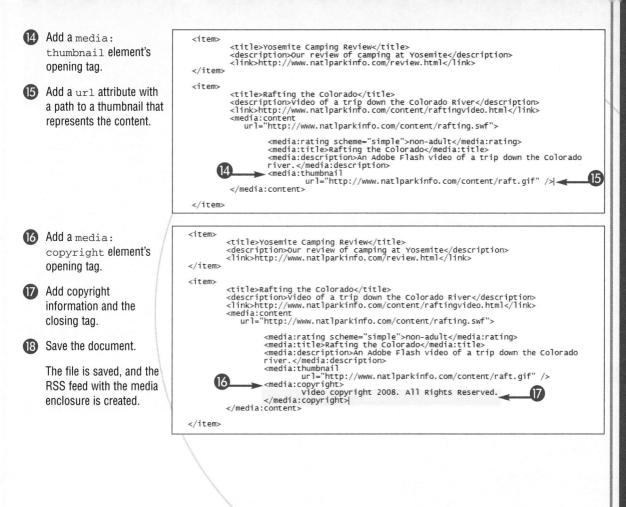

```
<item>
        <title>Yosemite Camping Review</title>
        <description>Our review of camping at Yosemite</description>
        <link>http://www.natlparkinfo.com/review.html</link>
</item>

<item>
        <title>Rafting the Colorado</title>
        <description>Video of a trip down the Colorado River</description>
        <link>http://www.natlparkinfo.com/content/raftingvideo.html</link>
        <media:content
            url="http://www.natlparkinfo.com/content/rafting.swf">

                <media:rating scheme="simple">non-adult</media:rating>
                <media:title>Rafting the Colorado</media:title>
                <media:description>An Adobe Flash video of a trip down the Colorado
                river.</media:description>
                <media:thumbnail
                        url="http://www.natlparkinfo.com/content/raft.gif" />
        </media:content>

</item>
```

⑯ Add a `media:copyright` element's opening tag.

⑰ Add copyright information and the closing tag.

⑱ Save the document.

The file is saved, and the RSS feed with the media enclosure is created.

```
<item>
        <title>Yosemite Camping Review</title>
        <description>Our review of camping at Yosemite</description>
        <link>http://www.natlparkinfo.com/review.html</link>
</item>

<item>
        <title>Rafting the Colorado</title>
        <description>Video of a trip down the Colorado River</description>
        <link>http://www.natlparkinfo.com/content/raftingvideo.html</link>
        <media:content
            url="http://www.natlparkinfo.com/content/rafting.swf">

                <media:rating scheme="simple">non-adult</media:rating>
                <media:title>Rafting the Colorado</media:title>
                <media:description>An Adobe Flash video of a trip down the Colorado
                river.</media:description>
                <media:thumbnail
                        url="http://www.natlparkinfo.com/content/raft.gif" />
                <media:copyright>
                        Video copyright 2008. All Rights Reserved.
                </media:copyright>
        </media:content>

</item>
```

Apply It

Copyright protection applies to any content published in any form, so unless the owner of a video or piece of music specifically grants permission for it to be reused on other sites, it cannot be. Many authors, however, do make their content available while retaining some rights to it under the Creative Commons license. Media that is made available through a Creative Commons license should retain a reference to the license, and the namespace to support this is RSS. You can reference the Creative Commons license in your RSS by adding the appropriate `xmlns` attribute to your root element:

```
<rss version="2.0" xmlns:media="http://search.yahoo.com/mrss"
xmlns:creativeCommons="http://backend.userland.com/creativeCommonsRssModule">
```

Then, within the `content` element for the media, you can add the license element from the namespace:

```
<creativeCommons:license>http://www.creativecommons.org/licenses/by-
nc/1.0</creativeCommons:license>
```

Create a Podcast

Y ou have mostly likely heard of a podcast before, and may already subscribe to several. Most popular radio programs provide podcasts of past shows, and many multimedia Web sites have begun offering them as well.

A podcast is simply an MP3 file with an accompanying RSS file that is published to a Web server. While the name is derived from Apple's iPod player, any MP3 player can be used to listen to the podcast. Many media players today include support for subscribing to podcasts so that as new material becomes available, it is automatically downloaded to the subscriber.

The most complicated portion of creating the podcast is recording the audio file itself. Radio shows are obviously recorded to begin with, already own the equipment to

capture the sound, and presumably already employ professionals who know how to use it; they will have a very easy time with this step. Amateurs, however, may find it intimidating as well as expensive. At a minimum, you will need a good-quality microphone and some software on your computer that can capture the audio and give you the tools to clean it up, edit it, and convert it to MP3 format.

Once you have the audio recorded, you need to create the RSS document that will describe the file and include the content. This will be a standard RSS 2.0 document. Within the item element, you will want to include a title for the podcast, a description, and a publish date, through the appropriate RSS elements. Then, you will include an `enclosure` element with a URL pointing to the MP3 file, a length for the size of the file in bytes, and a type set to `audio/mpeg`.

Create a Podcast

① Create a new RSS document in your editor.

② Add the XML prolog.

③ Add an `rss` element's opening tag with a `version` attribute set to `2.0`.

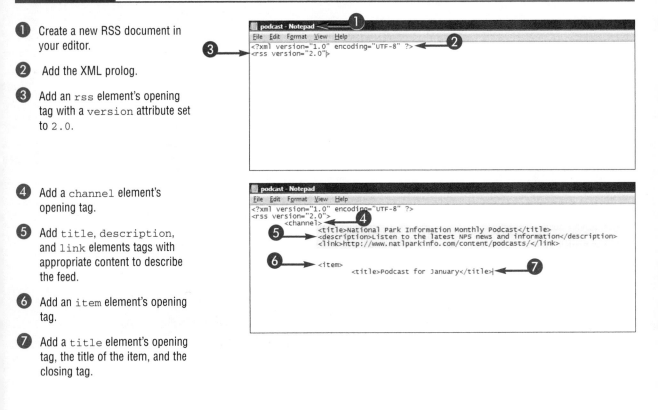

④ Add a `channel` element's opening tag.

⑤ Add `title`, `description`, and `link` elements tags with appropriate content to describe the feed.

⑥ Add an `item` element's opening tag.

⑦ Add a `title` element's opening tag, the title of the item, and the closing tag.

8 Add a `description` element's opening tag, the description of the item, and the closing tag.

9 Add a `pubdate` element's opening tag, the publication date, and the closing tag.

10 Add an `enclosure` element's opening tag.

11 Add a `url` attribute with a value set to the path to the podcast's MP3 file.

12 Add a `length` attribute with a value set to the size, in bytes, of the file.

13 Add a `type` attribute with a value set to `audio/mpeg`, and the closing slash.

14 Add the closing `item` tag, the closing `channel` tag, and the closing `rss` tag.

15 Save the file.

The file is saved, and the podcast is now ready to be published.

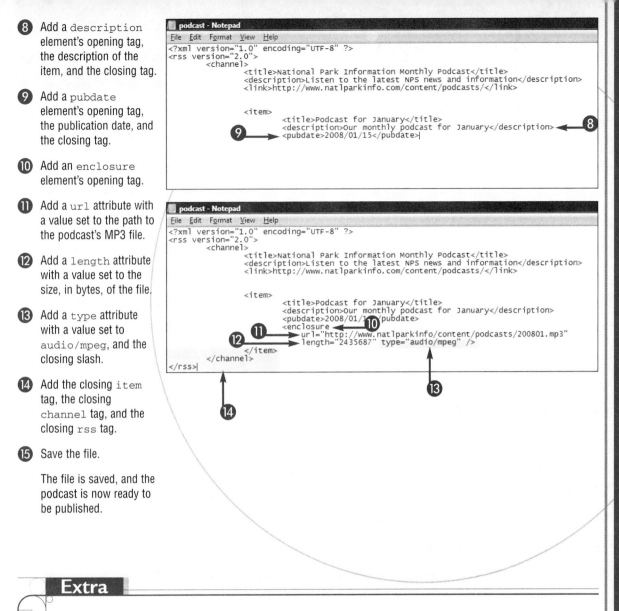

Extra

While professionals will want to use high-end hardware and software to create their audio, many low-cost and free software solutions exist to capture and edit audio. A popular choice is Audacity, which you can download from http://audacity.sourceforge.net. It has a fairly small learning curve, yet includes advanced features if you find you need them.

While low-cost or free software will get the job done, the same unfortunately does not apply to the hardware. The microphones built-in to many laptops, and the cheap ones that ship with many desktop computers, are not going to produce good sound quality. If you want your podcast to sound good, plan on investing in a high-quality microphone. You are also going to need to find a room that is as quiet as possible where you can record without interruption. If you plan to make money off your podcast, you may be able to rent time in a recording studio. If you are instead going to record at home or the office, you need to find a time and place where you can record without interruption from other people as well as phones or other noisy devices.

Publish Your Podcast to iTunes

One of the most popular ways to find and subscribe to podcasts is the Apple iTunes music store. This is accessible to anyone through the free iTunes media player. While many think that iTunes is merely a tool to use to synchronize the music on your computer with your iPod, and see the iTunes store as merely a place to go to legally purchase and download more music, the two actually work together to provide a place for anyone to publish — and even sell — their podcasts.

The actual process of publishing to iTunes is simple, as there is a wizard for doing so in the iTunes product. You click the Publish a Podcast item in the Music Store section of iTunes, provide the path to the RSS document for your podcast, and then log in with your iTunes account. Once submitted, you will need to wait for the podcast to be reviewed by Apple, but once it is, it will appear in the store.

You will need to pay close attention to the title, author, description, and keywords elements in the content section of your RSS document, as these provide the information that iTunes will use to identify the podcast. It does not use the information in the item section.

In addition, there is an `itunes` namespace available that provides several additional features. You can use the `itunes:summary` element to provide a detailed description of the podcast, although you can also use the standard description instead. You should include an `itunes:category` element to allow your work to be properly categorized, which will enable your users to more easily find it.

Publish Your Podcast to iTunes

1. Open an RSS document that contains podcast information in your editor.

2. In the root `rss` element's opening tag, add an `xmlns:itunes` attribute with a value of `http://www. itunes.com/dtds/podcast -1.0.dtd`.

```
podcast - Notepad
File  Edit  Format  View  Help
<?xml version="1.0" encoding="UTF-8" ?>
<rss version="2.0" xmlns:itunes="http://www.itunes.com/dtds/podcast-1.0.dtd">
        <channel>
                <title>National Park Information Monthly Podcast</title>
                <description>Listen to the latest NPS news and information</description>
                <link>http://www.natlparkinfo.com/content/podcasts/</link>

                <item>
                        <title>Podcast for January</title>
                        <description>Our monthly podcast for January</description>
                        <pubdate>2008/01/15</pubdate>
                        <enclosure
                           url="http://www.natlparkinfo/content/podcasts/200801.mp3"
                           length="2435687" type="audio/mpeg" />
                </item>
        </channel>
</rss>
```

3. Make sure you have `title`, `description`, `author`, and `keywords` elements under the channel, and that they contain correct data.

4. Add an `itunes:category` element with a text attribute and an appropriate value.

5. Save the file.

```
podcast - Notepad
File  Edit  Format  View  Help
<?xml version="1.0" encoding="UTF-8" ?>
<rss version="2.0" xmlns:itunes="http://www.itunes.com/dtds/podcast-1.0.dtd">
        <channel>
                <title>National Park Information Monthly Podcast</title>
                <description>Listen to the latest NPS news and information</description>
                <author>Rob Huddleston</author>
                <keywords>National Parks, NPS, National Park System</keywords>
                <link>http://www.natlparkinfo.com/content/podcasts/</link>

                <itunes:category text="Society &amp; Culture" />
                <item>
                        <title>Podcast for January</title>
                        <description>Our monthly podcast for January</description>
                        <pubdate>2008/01/15</pubdate>
                        <enclosure
                           url="http://www.natlparkinfo.com/content/podcasts/200801.mp3"
                           length="2435687" type="audio/mpeg" />
                </item>
        </channel>
</rss>
```

6 Open iTunes.

Note: *In Windows Vista, click Start → All Programs → Apple iTunes → iTunes.*

7 Click the iTunes Music Store button.

8 Click Submit a Podcast.

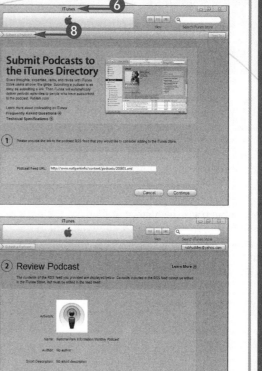

9 In the Podcast Feed URL screen, enter the path to the RSS document and click Continue.

Note: *The RSS feed will need to be uploaded to a Web server first. This is discussed in chapter 19.*

10 Log in to your iTunes account, or create a new account.

11 Review the podcast information and click Submit.

The podcast is submitted and is now available on iTunes.

Note: *Apple reviews each podcast submission to be sure that it is properly categorized. This process may take several days.*

Extra

You can add artwork to your podcast when you publish. This artwork will appear in the iTunes store when users find your podcast. You can do this by including the `itunes:image` element in your RSS document. The element takes a `url` attribute that references the image to be used as the artwork. The image should be a square JPEG or PNG at least 600 pixels on a side. This must be done at the channel level, not the item level.

Currently iTunes supports sixteen top-level categories, and 51 subcategories. The top-level categories are Art, Business, Comedy, Education, Games & Hobbies, Government & Organizations, Health, Kids & Family, Music, News & Politics, Religion & Spirituality, Science & Medicine, Society & Culture, Sports & Recreation, Technology, and TV & Film. Each of the categories except Comedy, Music, News & Politics, and TV & Film have subcategories. The complete list is available at www.apple.com/itunes/store/podcaststechspecs. html#resources. Note that if you reference one of the categories that contains an ampersand in its name, you need to be sure to use the `&amp;` character entity, so, for example, TV & Film would need to be entered in the RSS as `TV &amp; Film`.

Create
a Blog

Web logs, or *blogs*, have quickly become one of the most popular uses of the Web. A blog is really nothing more than a Web site whose content is updated frequently and is generally presented in reverse chronological order. Many blogs are the online diaries of their owners, but increasingly, blogs are being used to provide much or all of the content for sites.

Blogs have been around since the early days of the Web. In fact, some trace the history of blogs to the days of Usenet, before the invention of the Web. The term *weblog* was coined by John Barger in 1997, while Peter Merholz broke the word up, as a joke, into *we blog* in 1999, thus creating the term that has remained in use to today.

The easiest way to create a blog is to use one of the many free online blog services, which handle all of the

backend programming necessary. They provide you with a simple, online control panel into which you can type your entries and manage other aspects of the blog. You can then link to the blog's pages from your main Web site using normal linking techniques.

Blogger is a well-known blog service. The service helped create the current popularity of blogging by providing a simple interface for nontechnically inclined users to create and manage their blogs. In 2003, Google purchased Blogger.

To start blogging, simply go to www.blogger.com and sign up, for free, for the service. They will take you through a series of steps to create an account. You can use an existing Google account if you have one, or create a new one.

Create a Blog

① In a Web browser, go to www.blogger.com.

② Enter a Google username and password.

③ Click Sign In.

● If you do not have a Google account, click Create Your Blog Now and follow the steps outlined on the site.

④ Enter the name you wish to have displayed on the blog.

⑤ Enter the address you wish to use for the blog.

⑥ Click Continue.

7 Choose a template for your blog.

8 Click Continue.

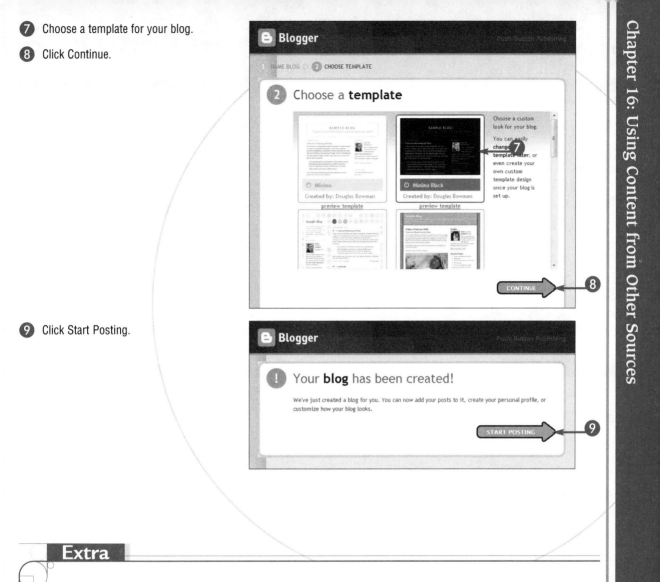

9 Click Start Posting.

Extra

If you want more control over your blog, you can download blog software and run it on your own site. Two popular blogging applications are Moveable Type from Six Apart and BlogCFC from RIAForge. Moveable Type is designed as a professional publishing tool. Six Apart offers a free personal edition, as well as corporate, education, and nonprofit pricing. Moveable Type relies on Perl, which is supported by most Web-hosting companies. Movable Type offers an online control panel from which you can manage your blog's settings and create entries. Its layout is controlled via CSS, and there are many *skins*, or prebuilt layouts, available for download. You can get details about it at www.movabletype.com.

BlogCFC was developed by Raymond Camden. This free, open-source blogging solution is powered by Adobe ColdFusion, so you will need to ensure that your host supports that if you plan to use BlogCFC. The system is at once powerful and easy to use. Like Moveable Type, BlogCFC provides a simple online control panel and a CSS-based layout. You can download BlogCFC from http://blogcfc.riaforge.org.

continued →

O nce you have signed up with the Blogger service, you can begin creating entries from the control panel. At the top of the screen, you will see three basic navigation tabs for the service: Posting, Settings, and Template.

The Posting page allows you to create new posts by filling out a simple HTML form. You can either enter the post in Compose mode, in which you use the toolbar at the top of the form to add formatting controls, or you can use the Edit HTML mode, where you can include any HTML tags you wish. Note that in Compose mode, pressing Enter will add paragraph tags to the entry, while in the Edit HTML mode, you must do that yourself. You can also choose whether or not to allow comments on your posts.

The Settings page lets you modify the title and description of your blog, as well as configure other parameters. Finally, the Template page lets you control the look and feel of the pages. You can choose from one of several dozen prebuilt designs, or the service provides a page in which you can edit the underlying CSS for the blog to create your own layout and design.

As a service provided by Google, Blogger also allows you to include AdSense, which is Google's inline, keyword-based advertising. AdSense ads will appear on your page, keyed to that page's content, and you will receive a commission each time one of your users clicks a link in the ads. You can sign up for an AdSense account and add it to your blog from the AdSense link on the Template page.

Create a Blog (continued)

⑩ From the menu at the top of the Blogger control panel, click Posting.

⑪ Click Create.

⑫ Add a title for the post.

⑬ Add the text for your blog entry.

⑭ Click Post Options.

⑮ Choose to allow or disallow comments.

⑯ Click Publish Post.

The post is published.

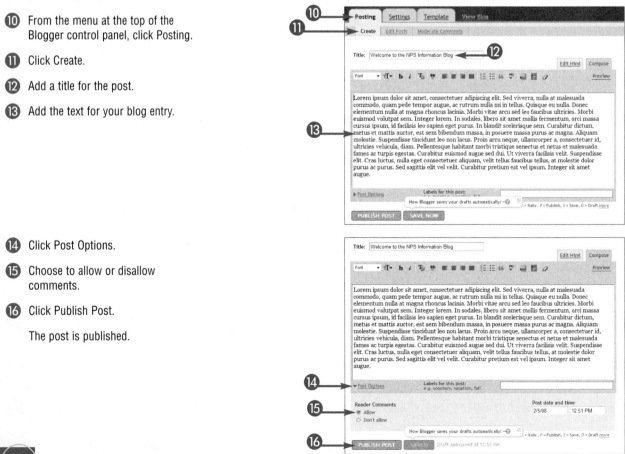

⑰ From the menu at the top of the Blogger control panel, click **Settings**.

⑱ Type a description, and configure the blog using your desired settings.

⑲ Click **View Blog**.

The blog appears in the browser.

Apply It

You can add a link to your blog from your Web site by simply adding it to the site's navigation.

```
<ul>
    <li id="homepagelink"><a href="index.html" title="Home Page">Home</a></li>
    <li id="factspagelink"><a href="facts.html" title="National Park Facts Page">National
Park Facts</a></li>
    <li id="parklistpagelink"><a href="parklist.html" title="List of the National Parks">List
of the Parks</a></li>
    <li id="regionspagelink"><a href="regions.html"><abbr title="National Park
Service">NPS</abbr> Regions</a></li>
    <li id="glossarypagelink"><a href="glossary.html" title="Glossary of Park Service
Terms">Glossary</a></li>
    <li id="contactpagelink"><a href="contact.html" title="Contact Page">Contact</a></li>
    <li id="blogpagelink"><a href="http://yourblog.blogger.com" title="Blog">Blog</a></li>
</ul>
```

Display an RSS Feed on Your Site

The primary means by which blogs share information with one another is through Really Simple Syndication, or RSS. You will want your blog to have an RSS feed, which publishes the headlines to the articles you write, along with links to them, so that others can subscribe and use the feed. At the same time, you may wish to display an RSS feed from another site on your page. This may be a local news site, or a feed from a blog with topics related to your own.

You will need a server-side component to retrieve the RSS feed from the publishing site and convert the XML to HTML to display on your page. It will also need to occasionally return to the site to see if the feed has been updated, and if so, provide that new information to your page. See Chapter 15 for more about RSS feeds.

You could write the necessary script using any of the main server-side technologies, including PHP, ColdFusion, and ASP.NET. However, if you do not know those languages or wish to deal with writing the code, you can also rely on third-party services to provide the translation for you.

One such free service is at www.rss-to-javascipt.com. The site uses JavaScript to call a server-side script, hosted on the RSS-to-JavaScript site, that calls the appropriate RSS feed at regular intervals, translates it to HTML, and then displays the HTML on your page. You can call any valid RSS feed with the service. They provide a form to apply some basic customization of the appearance of the feed's links and text, or you can modify your own CSS to ensure that the feed fits with the rest of your site.

Display an RSS Feed on Your Site

① In your Web browser, go to www.rss-to-javascript.com.

② Click RSS/RDF/ATOM to JavaScript Converter.

The browser navigates to the next page.

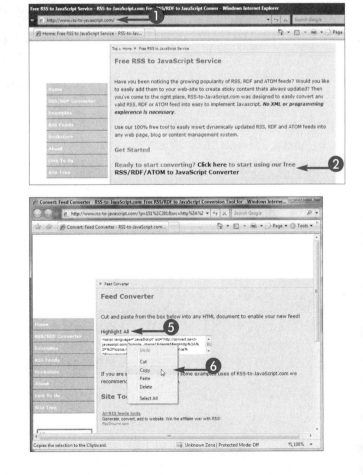

③ Enter the URL of the RSS feed, and select any of the optional configuration choices.

④ Click Generate JavaScript.

The browser opens the next page in a new window.

⑤ Click Highlight All.

⑥ Right-click in the text area and select Copy.

7 Open the Web page on which you wish to display the feed in your editor.

8 In the section of your document in which you wish to display the RSS feed, paste the code you copied in Step 6.

9 Save the page.

10 Open the Web page in your browser.

● The page displays, showing the RSS feed.

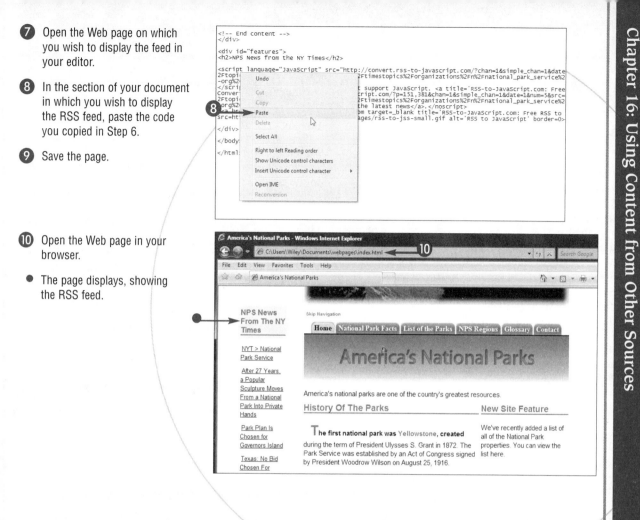

Extra

You should be aware that there are a few disadvantages to using this JavaScript-based approach to displaying an RSS feed. First, should your users have JavaScript disabled, they will be unable to see the feed, and will instead be presented with a plain-text link to the RSS-to-JavaScript site.

Second, search engines will not bother trying to read JavaScript. Placing an RSS feed on your site can improve your overall search engine rankings, as many blogs have a *track-back* feature that displays links back to sites that link to them. Using JavaScript, the search engine will not be able to follow the link from your site to the other, so it will not build the association between the track-back link and your page.

Despite these issues, this and similar services are the simplest way to display RSS feeds.

Show Your Photos with Flickr

As the popularity and ease of use of digital cameras has expanded, so too has the desire to share photos on the Web. Although creating your own photo gallery requires nothing more than XHTML knowledge, many people would rather not have to create their own sites and want something simpler.

Flickr, which Yahoo! now owns, is the most popular of a set of Web sites that exist to allow users to share photos. In addition to simply posting photos, Flickr provides an online community to share pictures, automatic RSS feeds, and many related Web applications.

Flickr offers somewhat limited free accounts, but provides the opportunity to upgrade to a *pro* account with an annual fee. The main difference between the free and paid accounts is the number of photos that can be uploaded per month.

Signing up with Flickr involves using either an existing Yahoo! account or creating a new one. After you are signed up, you can immediately begin uploading and sharing photos. You can make uploaded photos available to the general public, or you can restrict access to certain other users. Flickr automatically makes an RSS feed available for the photo pages as well.

Flickr also provides a *badge*, which enables you to create either an HTML or Flash widget so that you can display your Flickr photos on your own Web site. Setting up the badge involves going through a simple wizard interface on Flickr's site, at the end of which you receive code that you can copy and paste onto your page.

Users have the ability to comment on uploaded photos, creating the community aspect of the site.

Show Your Photos with Flickr

① In your browser, go to www.flickr.com.

② If you do not have a Yahoo! account, click Create Your Account, create an account, and then sign in.

● If you do have a Yahoo! account, click Sign In and then enter your username and password.

After you are signed in, you will be taken to your personal home page within Flickr.

③ Click Upload Photos.

④ Click Choose Photos.

⑤ Navigate to the photo that you want to upload.

⑥ Click Open.

⑦ If necessary, click Add More to select more pictures.

⑧ Set the privacy settings that you want.

Note: *Only public photos can be added to a badge.*

⑨ Click Upload Photos.

The file or files are uploaded.

⑩ Click Describe Your Photos.

⑪ Enter a title and description for each photo.

⑫ Click Save This Batch.

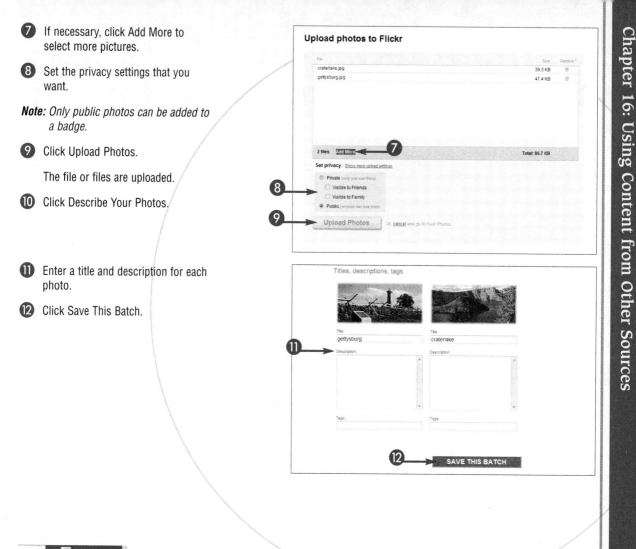

Any time you post content on the Web, you are making it available to a wide audience, so copyright infringement can become a concern. There are many myths out there about copyright, but the most important thing you need to know is that copyright protection is automatic. As soon as you create a unique work, it is protected by copyright.

Flickr is designed as a place to share photos, but that does not mean that copyright protections to do not apply. Using the site's settings, you can restrict who has access to your photos. In addition, if you are going to make photos public, you can choose to apply a Creative Commons license to them, which sets restrictions on acceptable use of your images. Creative Commons offers a variety of restriction levels, from making the photo completely open as long as it is attributed to you, to restricting commercial use, and several others. Flickr provides a description of the Creative Commons choices at www.flickr.com/creativecommons.

continued →

I n addition to using a Flickr badge, there are other tools available that enable you to display Flickr photos on Web sites. Because Flickr has an open application programming interface (API), anyone with programming knowledge can create tools to use Flickr photos.

One such tool is Splashr, available at www.splashr.com. Splashr gives you a set of about 30 templates. Using a Flickr tag or tags, your username, or a photo group, Splashr will generate a presentation of the photos it takes from Flickr, and it provides copy-and-paste code for you to add the presentation to your site. It does not offer much in the way of customization, and the presentations tend to be large files.

Another tool is Badgr, available for download from www.mentalaxis.com/words/badgr. Badgr takes the Flickr Flash-based badge concept one step further in that it

provides considerably more customization options.

Flickr Slidr, from www.flickrslidr.com, is another tool that allows you to insert Flickr slideshows on your site. By filling out a simple form, the page will generate a block of HTML code that you can paste into your editor.

Several other tools, listed at www.flickrbits.com, include Chasr, FSViewr, and PictoBrowser, which simplify the process of adding Flickr photos to your site; Flashr, which provides a programming object that allows you to access Flickr's API in ActionScript for Adobe Flash; and PHPFlickr, which is similar to Flashr for PHP.

The Flickr API is itself well documented and can be viewed at www.flickr.com/services/api, complete with the necessary documentation and code samples, so you can create your own Flickr tools for non-commercial use if you are familiar with another programming language.

Show Your Photos with Flickr *(continued)*

⑬ In your browser, go to www.flickr.com/badge.gne.

⑭ Click An HTML Badge.

⑮ Click Next: Choose Photos.

⑯ Click Yours.

⑰ Click All of Your Public Photos.

⑱ Click Next: Layout.

⑲ Select the options that you want on the layout page.

⑳ Click Next: Colors.

㉑ Select colors to match the color scheme of your Web site.

㉒ Click Next: Preview & Get Code.

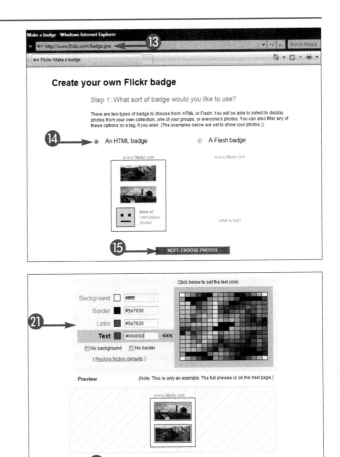

㉓ Select the code in the text area.

㉔ Right-click in the text area and click Copy.

This is the code you need:

All you need to do is copy and paste this chunk of code into your website where you'd like your badge to appear.

㉓

```
<!-- Start of Flickr Badge -->
<style type="text/css">
#flickr_badge_source_txt {padding:0; font: 11px Arial, Helvetica, Sans serif;
color:#6666                    Undo
#flickr_bad                          ortant; margin:0 !important; border: 1px solid rgb
(0, 0, 0) !im      Cut
#flickr_icon                         portant;}
                   Copy
.flickr_badg                         important;}
.flickr_badg        Paste             k solid black !important;}
#flickr_bad                          50px;}
#flickr_www        Delete           center; padding:0 10px 0 10px !important; font:
11px Arial, I      Select All       ortant; color:#3993ff !important;}
#flickr_bad
#flickr_badge_uber_wrapper a:link,
#flickr_badge_uber_wrapper a:active,
#flickr_badge_uber_wrapper a:visited {text-decoration:none !important;
background:inherit !important;color:#3993ff;}
```

㉔

㉕ Open an XHTML document in your editor.

㉖ Paste the code from Flickr.

㉗ Save the page.

The document is saved, and the badge will now display on the page.

```
aboutus - Notepad                      ㉕
File  Edit  Format  View  Help
</div>

<!-- End header -->
</div>

<!-- begin main content -->
<div id="content">

<h1>America's National Parks: Photos</h1>

<p>View our photos online at Flickr.</p>

<!-- Start of Flickr Badge -->
<style type="text/css">
#flickr_         Undo                    11px Arial, Helvetica, Sans serif; color:#000000;}
#flickr_                                 nt; margin:0 !important; border: 1px solid rgb(0, 0,
#flickr_         Cut                     ant;}
.flickr_         Copy                    portant;}
#flickr_                                 black !important;}
#flickr_         Paste                   0 10px !important; font: 11px Arial, Helvetica, Sans
㉖               Delete
#flickr_
#flickr_         Select All
#flickr_                                 -decoration:none !important; background:inherit !impo
#flickr_         Right to left Reading order    ffff;border: solid 1px #5e7630}
#flickr_                                 ; font: 11px Arial, Helvetica, Sans serif !important;
</style>          Show Unicode control characters
<table id                               padding="0" cellspacing="10" border="0"><tr><td><a hr
id="flick        Insert Unicode control character  ▶  3993ff">flick<span style="color:#ff1c92">r</span></st
cellpaddi                               " id="flickr_badge_wrapper">
<script t         Open IME              /www.flickr.com/badge_code_v2.gne?
count=3&c         Reconversion          rce=user&user=45478916%40N00"></script>
</table>
</td></tr
<!-- End of Flickr Badge -->
```

Extra

Inserting a Flash badge is as simple as inserting the HTML badge. You start at the same place, but on the first page of the badge wizard, you select Flash instead of HTML. The Flash badge gives you one less step, as the HTML has the choice of several different layouts but the Flash badge has only one.

The big advantage of the Flash badge is that it contains some simple animation. It randomly selects one of the images in the badge and enlarges it to fill the space of four of the thumbnails. After a few seconds, that image collapses back down and another is randomly selected, repeating the process.

Your users will need to have the Adobe Flash Player installed on their computers in order to view the badge. However, as of September 2007, Flash Player has been installed on over 98.7% of Internet-connected computers worldwide, so very few of your users will have a problem viewing the badge. Most of those users who do not already have the Flash Player will be able to download and install it in a matter of a few seconds.

Display a Google Map on Your Page

Since its release in 2005, Google's take on online maps has revolutionized the online mapping industry, and Google very quickly became regarded as the leading mapping site. Unlike other online maps that existed at the time, Google implemented their maps through Ajax (Asynchronous JavaScript and XML), creating a much richer and more extensible interface. Google maps feature seamless scrolling, the ability to zoom in and out on locations, and the ability to switch to a satellite view to see the location as it actually appears. In some cities, users can even view street-level photos.

Google makes most of their tools available for developers through the Google API, and Google Maps is no exception. Any developer can place a live Google Map on a site, and choose to enable the ability to scroll the map, zoom in and out, and switch between the map and satellite views. The

code for implementing the maps on your page can be found at http://code.google.com/apis/maps. You will need to sign up for an API key, which limits the use of the maps to pages within a single Web site. However, there is no limit to the number of keys one user can request.

After you have requested a key, you can copy and paste the code provided by Google into your XHTML page. The only difficulty is that you need to specify the initial location shown on the map with longitude and latitude rather than a physical address. Developers familiar with JavaScript can implement the Geocoding feature, which enables you to enter a physical address, but the online documentation is not clear about how to integrate the Geocode script with the main maps script, so many beginning developers may find it easier to simply look up the longitude and latitude of their address instead.

Display a Google Map on Your Page

① In your browser, go to http://code.google.com/apis/maps.

② Click Sign Up for a Google Maps API Key.

③ Read the terms of the service.

④ Click the check box stating that you read and agree with the terms.

⑤ Enter your Web site's address.

⑥ Click Generate API Key.

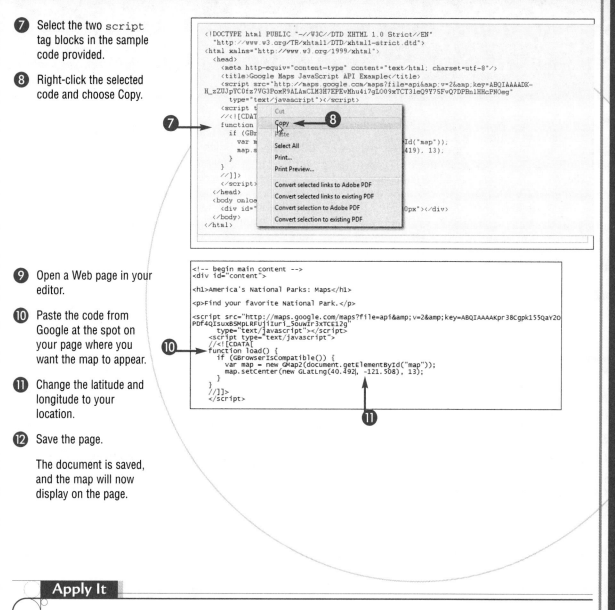

7 Select the two `script` tag blocks in the sample code provided.

8 Right-click the selected code and choose Copy.

9 Open a Web page in your editor.

10 Paste the code from Google at the spot on your page where you want the map to appear.

11 Change the latitude and longitude to your location.

12 Save the page.

The document is saved, and the map will now display on the page.

Apply It

You can add pan and zoom controls to your map by adding a few extra lines of JavaScript:

```
var map = new GMap2(document.getElementById("map"));
map.addControl(new GSmallMapControl());
map.addControl(new GMapTypeControl());
map.setCenter(new GLatLng(37.4419, -122.1419), 13);
```

Display a Google Calendar on Your Site

G oogle Calendar is a free, Web-based calendaring system with features rivaling many costly desktop applications. With Google Calendar, you can add events by simply clicking on the appropriate date, set the length of events, and add additional details. By setting up multiple calendars, you can color-code events to help categorize them.

Calendars can be shared, and the system allows the calendar's owner to determine whether events should be viewable or editable by other users, and can control exactly which users have permissions to view or edit the calendar. Calendars can also be made public so that anyone may view them. Organizations can share a group

calendar by simply setting up an account, creating the calendar, and then adding organization members to the calendar's permissions.

You can either direct users to calendar.google.com to view your events, or you can use the Google API to integrate it directly into your site. Through the API, you can maintain all of the normal functionality of the calendar, but have it appear within the overall look and feel of your site. As with other Google tools, you will first need to obtain a free API key, but once you have the key, adding the calendar to your site is a simple copy-and-paste procedure.

Display a Google Calendar on Your Site

1 In your browser, go to http://calendar.google.com.

2 Enter a valid username and password.

● If you do not have an account, click Create a New Google Account and follow the instructions to create the account.

3 Click Sign In.

4 In your browser, go to http://code.google.com/apis/calendar.

5 Click Embeddable Calendar Helper Tool.

6 Enter a title for the calendar.

7 Adjust other settings as desired.

8 Select the text in the text area.

9 Right-click the selected code and choose Copy.

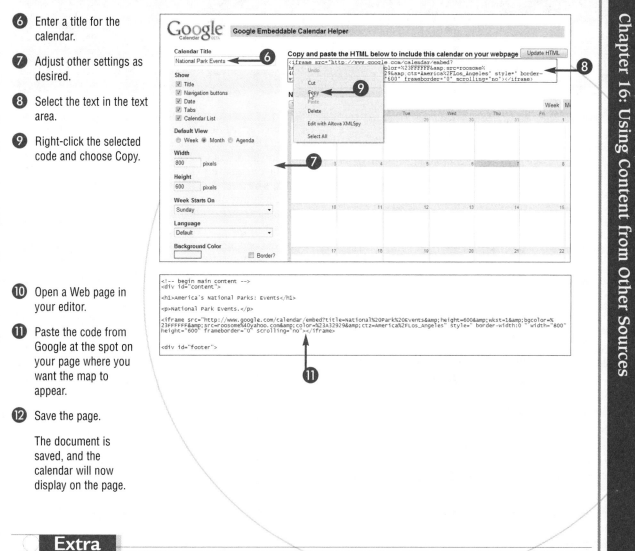

10 Open a Web page in your editor.

11 Paste the code from Google at the spot on your page where you want the map to appear.

12 Save the page.

The document is saved, and the calendar will now display on the page.

You can create multiple calendars within the same Google account if you need to display separate calendars on different pages. Simply return to the Google Calendar APIs page, choose the other calendar you wish to add, and copy and paste the code.

The code Google generates utilizes an iFrame, or inline frame, to display the calendar directly from Google's servers. When you preview the page locally during development, you will only be able to see the calendar if you are actually connected to the Internet.

Google also offer a series of so-called "Calendar Gadgets" that add additional functionality to the page, such as weather reports. Details on the gadgets and instructions on their use are available on the Google Calendar APIs main page.

Display Advertising on Your Page

One of the most effective ways to generate income from your Web site is through advertising. Many of the top Web sites, such as Google, Yahoo!, and MySpace, generate most or all of their income through ads.

While advertising on your site is not likely to generate millions, many smaller site owners are able to cover the costs of Web hosting fees by placing a few ads on their pages. Best of all, the ads themselves will be free to you, so there is no financial risk involved.

Google AdSense is a service that provides free, targeted ads to Web masters. Google will read the contents of your page and generate ads appropriate to that content. Whenever a user clicks an ad, Google receives a payment from the advertiser, and passes a commission back to you.

Ads can be placed anywhere on your page, but they will be most effective near the top or somewhere within the content. They do not need to take up a lot of space on the page. Google offers twelve text-based layouts, eight image layouts, seven video layouts, twelve link-based layouts, seven referral layouts, and several seasonally-themed layouts, allowing designers to apply ads that best fit the appearance of their pages.

As a host of the ads, you have the ability to filter the ads to prevent competitors or those advertising products you feel are inappropriate. Commission paid on ads varies depending on the types of ads displayed.

As with other Google products, displaying AdSense ads on your site is as easy as signing up for a free account and then copying and pasting code on your page.

Display Advertising on Your Page

① In your browser, go to www.google.com/adsense.

② Click Sign Up Now.

③ Fill out the required information to create an account and click Submit Information.

④ Select whether you want to use an existing Google account and provide the login information or sign up for a new Google account.

⑤ When you receive the confirmation e-mail from Google, follow the instructions to complete the registration process.

⑥ From the AdSense main page, click AdSense Setup.

⑦ Click which type of ad you wish to use.

⑧ Click Continue.

⑨ Follow the instructions to customize the ad display.

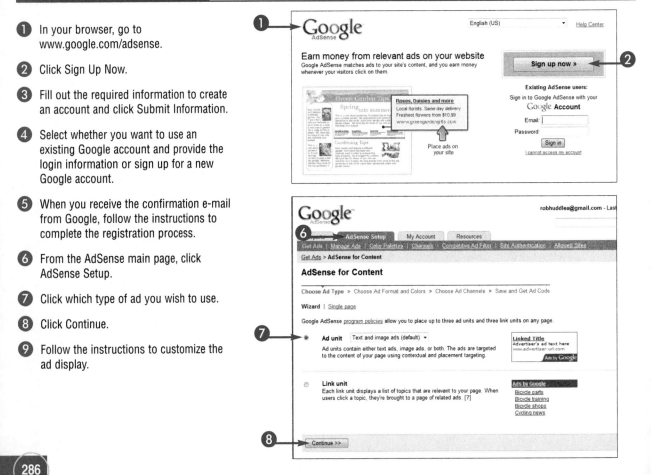

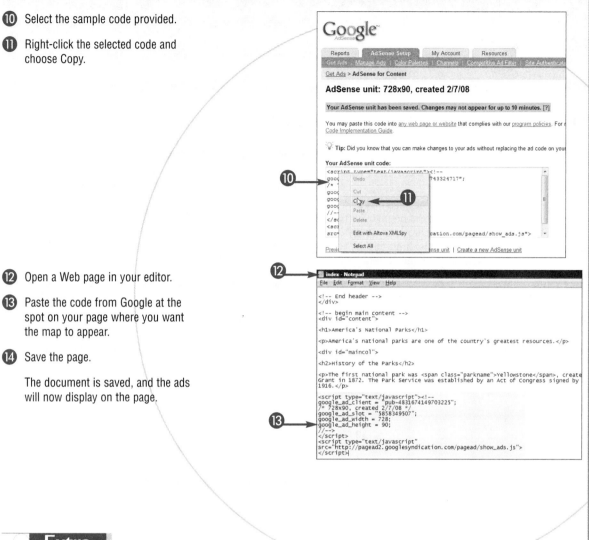

⑩ Select the sample code provided.

⑪ Right-click the selected code and choose Copy.

⑫ Open a Web page in your editor.

⑬ Paste the code from Google at the spot on your page where you want the map to appear.

⑭ Save the page.

The document is saved, and the ads will now display on the page.

Extra

Beyond the potential for income, there is another significant advantage to using Google AdSense. Because the ads are targeted based on the content of your page, Google must scan your page often to be sure that the ads are appropriate, and will therefore be more likely to pick up recent additions to your site. This may not affect your overall page ranking, but may be helpful for blogs and other sites that update content frequently or discuss current topics.

This task is focused on displaying other people's ads on your site, thereby basically making it a sort of online billboard. However, you have the option to do the opposite — be one of the advertisers that other people are displaying. Google implements this side of the business through its AdWords feature. Details are available at adwords.google.com. Microsoft offers an adCenter product to generate ads on its MSN network of sites, which includes msn.com, hotmail.com, and many others. See adcenter.microsoft.com for information.

Add Social Bookmarks

Most Web users have a set of bookmarks of frequently visited sites. However, because these bookmarks are stored by the browser directly on your computer, it is not possible to directly access them from other computers or share them with other users.

The oddly named site del.icio.us describes itself as a "social bookmarking Web site." The basic premise is that instead of bookmarking pages in your browser, where only you can see them, you bookmark pages through the Web site instead. You can then view and use the bookmarks from anywhere and make them available to others.

Like other social sites on the Web, you need to begin by creating a free account. After you have signed up, the site will prompt you to download an extension for whichever browser you are using. The extension will add two del.icio.us buttons to your browser's toolbar. One will allow you to add bookmarks, and the other accesses your saved bookmarks. When you are on a site that you want to bookmark, you can click the button on the toolbar, and the link will be added to your del.icio.us bookmark account instead of to the browser's list of bookmarks. You also have the ability to add tags to the bookmark to make it easier for other users to find them.

The social sharing aspect of del.icio.us is one of its best features. You can go to the del.icio.us Web site and search for bookmarks that others have saved, thereby possibly discovering other sites related to your search topic.

del.icio.us makes the lists of links available via RSS, so any Web site can display the links from the bookmarks by consuming the RSS feed.

Add Social Bookmarks

1 In your browser, go to http://del.icio.us.

2 Click Get Started.

3 Fill out the form to create an account.

---

del.icio.us ← **1**
social bookmarking

» **all your bookmarks in one place**

» bookmark things for yourself and friends

» **check out what other people are bookmarking**

learn more...   » **get started** « ← **2**

---

4 Click Install Buttons Now.

5 Follow the instructions to install the two needed buttons.

---

1 Enter Details   **2** Install Buttons   **3** Button Tutorial

Welcome, natlparkinfoadmin. Your account has been created.

To use del.icio.us, you need to install two buttons into your browser. We recommend that Int users install this simple del.icio.us extension:

del.icio.us/help/ie/success - Microsoft Internet Explorer
File Edit View Favorites Tools Help
Back   del.icio.us TAG
Address http://del.icio.us/

"My del.icio.us" button   "Tag this" button

Install Buttons Now » ← **4**

After starting the installer, please close any open Internet Explorer windows. You'll be automatically when the installer successfully completes.

6 After the buttons are installed, browse to a page that you want to bookmark.

7 Click the Tag button.

8 Click Save.

The new window closes.

9 Click the del.icio.us button.

The del.icio.us page opens.

10 Click the RSS button at the bottom of the page.

11 Right-click the browser's address bar.

12 Click Copy.

13 Open an XHTML document in your editor.

14 Type an anchor element's opening tag.

15 Set the value of the href attribute to the address that you copied in Step 12.

16 Type appropriate link text.

17 Type a closing anchor tag.

18 Save the page.

The document is saved, and your Web site users can now access them through the link on the page.

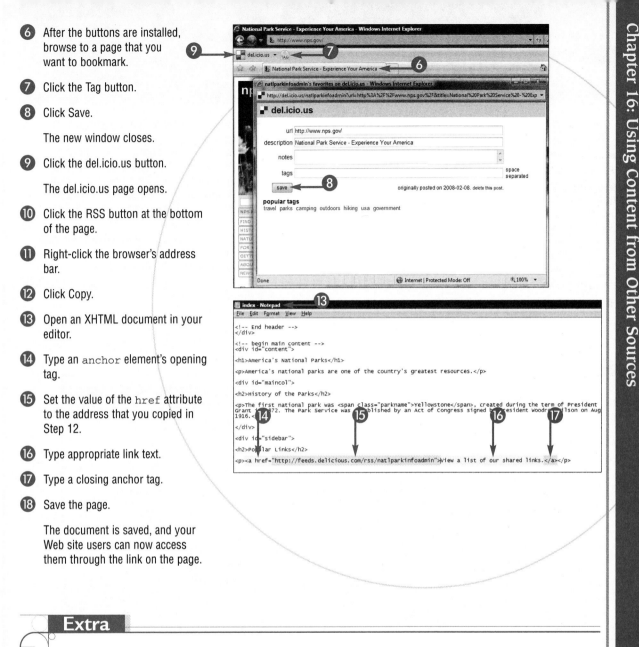

Extra

Many third-party tools have been created to work with del.icio.us. Some of the more useful ones are the browser-integration extensions, available for Firefox and Internet Explorer. These tools enable you to convert your existing browser bookmarks or favorites to del.icio.us bookmarks and to synchronize both, so bookmarks added to the browser will also be added to del.icio.us, and vice versa. There are also several operating system tools that give you desktop or task-tray integration with del.icio.us, so you can go to a bookmark without first having to open your browser.

The del.icio.us site has links to "Save to del.icio.us" buttons and Ajax-enabled tags to add to your site to encourage your users to bookmark your site with del.icio.us.

If you have bookmarked sites with MP3 files, you can add the Play Tagger script, available on the del.icio.us site, to enable users to play the MP3s directly on your page, without your needing to add any additional code.

Add Google Search to Your Site

large sites can be overwhelming and difficult for users to navigate to get the information that they need. Therefore, adding search capabilities to your site will enhance its usability.

Creating your own search on a site would require building a database-driven Web application. Instead, you can use Google's Search API to enable this functionality. By copying some code provided by Google, you can add a Google Search box to any page on your site and give your users the ability to search just within your site or on the Web as a whole. The search is actually performed by Google, so you do not need any technical expertise.

Like many other Google applications, the Search API uses Ajax. Google currently provides six different search tools.

The simple Search box is similar to a search from Google's home page. A blog-restricted search only searches entries on your blog, and a custom search engine enables you to specify which sites should be searched and customize the look and feel of the search box to match your site. Google also provides a news bar to search headlines, a blog bar to search other peoples' blogs, and a blog comment form.

To implement one of the searches, you need to simply sign up for a Google account and then request an API key for a particular site. You will then be given sample code that can generally be copied and pasted directly onto your page. To use the simple search, you will not have to modify the code at all.

Add Google Search to Your Site

① In your browser, go to http://code.google.com/apis/ajaxsearch.

② Click Sign-Up for a Google AJAX API key.

③ Read the terms of the service.

④ Click the check box stating that you read and agree with the terms.

⑤ Enter your Web site's address.

⑥ Click Generate API Key.

7 Select the sample code provided.

8 Right-click the selected code and choose Copy.

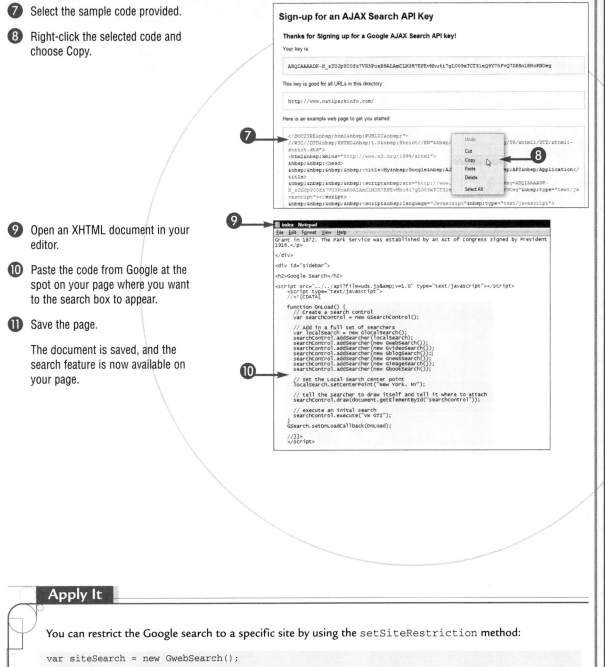

9 Open an XHTML document in your editor.

10 Paste the code from Google at the spot on your page where you want to the search box to appear.

11 Save the page.

The document is saved, and the search feature is now available on your page.

Apply It

You can restrict the Google search to a specific site by using the setSiteRestriction method:

```
var siteSearch = new GwebSearch();
siteSearch.setSiteRestriction("yoursite.com");
searchControl.addSearcher(siteSearch);
```

Understanding Search Engine Optimization

Search engines are a primary way that many users will find your site, so ensuring that your pages will appear as high as possible in the results is a key factor in increasing the number of site visitors.

Early Search Techniques

In the mid-1990s, as the Web began to rise in popularity, the first search engines appeared to help users find information in the exponentially increasing number of pages on the Web. These early search engines relied on Web masters to self-describe their pages by using the `meta` element in HTML to add keywords and descriptions of the page content. Unfortunately, it became too easy to manipulate the system by inserting keywords that contained popular search terms yet had no relation to the page in question.

PageRank and Google

While Larry Page and Sergey Brin were graduate students at Stanford University, they developed a new algorithm that relied primarily on incoming links to a page. Their basic theory is that while a Web master might use misleading keywords on a page, other Web masters would fail to perpetrate the false connections because they would not provide links to it. In other words, while a site might say that it was about a currently popular celebrity in its keywords, other sites are not likely to link the name of that celebrity to a site if it is not about her. This system, dubbed PageRank, became the basis for the company Google, which Page and Brin founded in 1998.

While Google's system was much more difficult to manipulate than older systems, some Web sites developed systems to artificially increase their ranking. Because of this, modern search companies, including Google, Yahoo!, and Microsoft, maintain strict levels of secrecy around the precise details of their search algorithms. An unfortunate reality of being a modern Web designer is that those few unscrupulous Web masters who have found ways to manipulate their search rankings have made it much more difficult for the honest majority to ensure that they get good rankings for their pages.

Content Is King

By far the most important key to getting good search engine rankings is to have good, meaningful content and to be sure to use the proper XHTML elements to code that content. Search engines read the code in your page, and give more weight to text enclosed in heading tags than that in, say, paragraphs, the logic being that the text in headings is what the page is "about."

Another consideration is that pages with good content are more likely to keep their viewers once they have been found. Far too many designers become so focused on getting a good search ranking that they sacrifice the usability of their page. What is the use of getting a good search ranking if your users immediately leave your site because they cannot find the information they want once they get there?

Consider Accessibility for Search Optimization

Because search engines read the code of the page, they approach your page in many of the same ways screen readers for blind users do, so in general, pages that are accessible to disabled users will get higher search engine rankings than those that are not.

Avoid All-Image Pages

Pages that are made up of nothing but images will rank much lower due to their lack of meaningful text for the search engines to read.

A common approach to design is to begin in a program like Adobe Fireworks or Photoshop to create a mock-up of the finished page. Once it is done, this mock-up can be a useful tool in design. However, many newer users want to take the mock-up, which will by definition be an image, and simply place that image on the Web as the finished page. Even through the use of appropriate alternate text, this page will rate very low on search engine results. It will also load very slowly and be difficult to edit later. A better approach is to take the mock-up as a guide for the layout. You can take the portions of the mock-up that should be images from the original and place them in the final product, either through CSS backgrounds or the XHTML `img` element, but the bulk of the page should be text entered directly into the XHTML.

Do Not Rely on Search Engine Optimization Alone

Not every site is necessarily going to benefit from high search engine rankings. Sites that are part of a larger marketing strategy may not rely heavily on search engine results at all. Placing the site's address on billboards or television advertisements may be as, if not more, effective than worrying about one's Google PageRank. Word of mouth can be an effective strategy, as can the use of social networking sites such as MySpace or Facebook, particularly for blogs or small local sites. Search engine optimization should fit within the site's overall marketing strategy.

Manual Page Submission

While most search engines attempt to automatically catalog pages, they also allow Web masters to submit their pages manually. Yahoo!, for example, has a manual submission whereby they will guarantee that your page will appear under certain keywords, although they will not guarantee the exact placement on the results page, and they do charge for this service. Other search engines allow for manual submission but may not guarantee placement, and none make any warrantees as to how long the placement may take, as most manual submissions are verified by hand by staff at the search company.

Follow Search Engine Guidelines

Every one of the major search engines makes a set of guidelines available to assist Web masters in building pages that will get higher rankings. These are not rules that are set in stone, and, in fact, search engines change them frequently, but you should observe them as much as possible.

The techniques used by unscrupulous designers who are attempting to increase their page ranking by fooling the search engines are referred to as *black hat* techniques. These techniques include placing repeated keywords in text with the same color as the background, or in blocks that are hidden through CSS, either through the display or visibility properties or by positioning them off the page. Search engines have both automated and manual processes for attempting to find sites that engage in these practices, and will either lower the site's ranking or possibly remove the site from their databases altogether if they are discovered. As such, the risks of using these techniques outweigh the rewards.

Search Engine Optimizers

Given the importance most sites place on good rankings, an industry of companies that specialize in helping sites develop effective search engine optimization strategies has arisen. In addition, conferences are held around the world throughout the year on the topic. Many of these conferences are attended, and at times sponsored, by the search engine companies.

While most search engine optimization companies look to increase rankings through legitimate, search engine-approved techniques, there are some that specialize in black hat techniques, so care must be taken when selecting a company to be sure that their end result will help, instead of hurt, your page's ranking.

Add Meta Elements

The original method of inserting information into your page to let search engines know what the page was about was by using the HTML `meta` element. The word *meta* is from the Greek meaning "with," and is often used to refer to something that refers to itself. The `meta` element allows designers to add information about the page on which the element appears.

The `meta` element must appear in the head of the document, and can be used any number of times. For search engine optimization, the `meta` element should be given with a `name` attribute, set to either `keywords` or `description`. When using `keywords`, you will add a `content` attribute that contains the list of words. The `content` should be a comma-separated list of the words by which you think users are likely to search for your site. Common misspellings or alternate forms of the

company's name or primary purpose should be included. Search engines have never made specific details available as to how many keywords they will read, but most guesses are that the maximum is around 50.

A `meta` element with a `name` attribute set to `description` will take `content` set to a brief, human-readable paragraph describing the site. Some search engines will display this description under the link to the site on the results page, so a well-written description can result in more users actually visiting your site from the search engine results page.

Be aware that some search engines, Google among them, officially claim to ignore meta keywords and descriptions altogether. While it probably does not hurt your site to add them, it will not help your ranking on the major engines today, so you will need to decide if the effort required to add them is worthwhile.

Add Meta Elements

① Open a Web page in your editor.

② In the `head` of the page, add a `meta` element's opening tag.

③ Add a `name` attribute with a value set to `keywords`.

④ Add a `content` attribute with a value set to a comma-separated list of words.

⑤ Add the trailing slash to close the element's tag.

6 Add a second meta element's opening tag.

7 Add a name attribute with a value set to description.

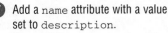

index - Notepad
File Edit Format View Help
```
<!DOCTYPE html PUBLIC "-//W3C//DTD XHTML 1.0 Transitional//EN" "http://www.w3.org/

<!--
Title: America's National Parks
Author: Rob Huddleston, rob@robhuddleston.com
Date: 11/4/07
-->

<html xmlns="http://www.w3.org/1999/xhtml">

<head>

<title>America's National Parks</title>

<meta name="keywords" content="National Parks, America's National Park,
NPS, National Park Information" />

<meta name="description"|

<link rel="shortcut icon" href="images/favicon.png" type="image/png" />

<link rel="stylesheet" href="styles.css" type="text/css" />
<link rel="stylesheet" href="printstyles.css" type="text/css" media="print" />
<link rel="alternate" href="altstyles.css" type="text/css" title="Larger Text" />

</head>
```

8 Add a content attribute with a value set to a brief paragraph describing the site.

9 Add the trailing slash to close the element's tag.

10 Save the page.

The page is saved. The meta tags have been added to the page.

index - Notepad
File Edit Format View Help
```
<!DOCTYPE html PUBLIC "-//W3C//DTD XHTML 1.0 Transitional//EN" "http://www.w3.org/

<!--
Title: America's National Parks
Author: Rob Huddleston, rob@robhuddleston.com
Date: 11/4/07
-->

<html xmlns="http://www.w3.org/1999/xhtml">

<head>

<title>America's National Parks</title>

<meta name="keywords" content="National Parks, America's National Park,
NPS, National Park Information" />

<meta name="description" content="The National Park Information site
provides users with facts, lists of the parks, the regional organization
structure of the National Park system, and a glossary of terms." />

<link rel="shortcut icon" href="images/favicon.png" type="image/png" />

<link rel="stylesheet" href="styles.css" type="text/css" />
<link rel="stylesheet" href="printstyles.css" type="text/css" media="print" />
<link rel="alternate" href="altstyles.css" type="text/css" title="Larger Text" />

</head>
```

Extra

In addition to the keywords and description, the meta element has several other uses. The name attribute can be set to author or revised, in which case content would hold the appropriate value. You can also set name to any value you wish, and accompany it with appropriate content. Search engines and other software do not use these custom names for any purpose, so they are merely for your own use.

Instead of name, you can add the http-equiv attribute. One possible value is content-type, in which you can instruct the browser as to the type of document that is being served through the content — text/html for HTML documents or text/xml for XHTML. Another is expires, in which case you can add a date and time to content after which the browser should request the page from the server instead of using a cached copy. Finally, you can set http-equiv to refresh, and then set content to a number of seconds and path to a page that should be requested after those seconds, thereby redirecting the user to another page or refreshing the current page.

Using Google's Web Master Tools

oogle is far and away the most popular search engine, so any discussion on search engine optimization will by necessity begin with pages being listed on Google. While the company guards their specific search algorithms to attempt to impede the efforts of those who would abuse the service, they do provide a series of tools for Web masters to help them ensure that their pages follow the company's guidelines, as well as tools to track statistics as to which keywords are resulting in the page appearing and how the page ranks.

You can access these tools at www.google.com/webmasters/start. As with other Google services, you will first need to either create a Google account or log in with an existing one. Next, you can add as many sites as you wish to begin tracking. After verifying that you are the owner of the site, you can then begin to view statistics on it.

From a menu on the left edge of the screen, you can view Diagnostics on your site. The Web Crawl tool reports any pages on your site that Google had difficulty cataloging, while the Content Analysis tool lets you know if there is content on your site that Google finds problematic or suspect.

The Statistics section is perhaps the most useful. It allows you to see which keywords are returning your site in Google searches, as well as the keywords from your site that the engine has cataloged, while the Crawl Stats page shows your PageRank in Google.

The Links category displays tables showing the number of sites that link to yours, the number of pages within your site that link to other pages in your site, and the number of automatic Google Sitelinks that have been created.

Using Google's Web Master Tools

① In your browser, go to www. google.com/webmasters/start.

② Click Get Started.

③ Log in with an existing Google account.

● If you do not have an account, click Create a Google Account and follow the instructions to create the account.

④ Type the address of the site you wish to track in the text box.

⑤ Click Add Site.

⑥ Follow the instructions to verify the site.

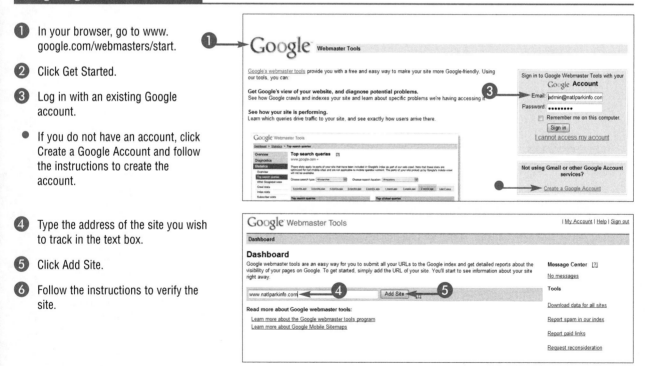

7 Click Diagnostics.

8 Click Web Crawl.

9 View the information provided.

10 Click Statistics.

11 Click What Googlebot Sees.

12 View the information provided.

13 Click Links.

14 Click Pages with External Links.

15 View the information provided, which will show you the number of pages linking to yours.

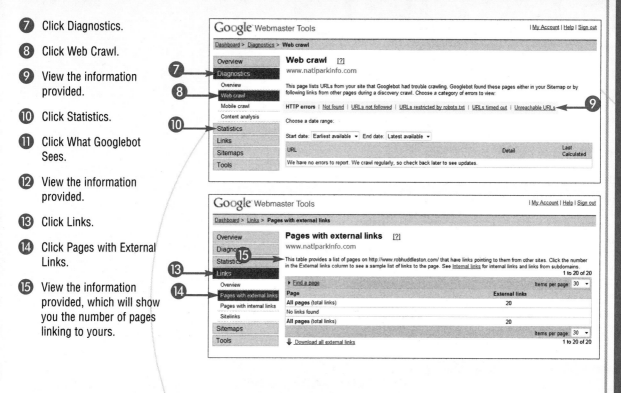

Extra

From the main Dashboard page in the Web master tools, there are four useful links on the far right. The first link allows you to download all of the data from the site on all of the sites you manage. The data will be downloaded as a .csv, or Comma Separated Values, file, which you can open in Microsoft Excel or a similar spreadsheet application. This tool is particularly useful if you manage a series of related sites and want to be sure that your optimization is working.

The second link allows you to report spam, or sites that are using deceptive practices to increase their PageRank. When you search Google for something and come across a page that is showing up in the results but does not relate to the search topic, you are most likely visiting a spam site, and you can use this form to report it. The third link serves a similar purpose, but allows you to report sites that are selling links. Some organizations attempt to capitalize on the fact that the number of sites that link to yours increases your PageRank, a practice that officially violates Google's standards.

The final link allows you to appeal a prior decision by Google to remove your site from their index if they believe you violated their policies.

Create a Sitemap

One of the easiest ways to get Google and other search engines to catalog the pages in your site is to create a sitemap. This special XML file allows you to tell the engine which pages on your site should be added to their index.

Sitemaps for search engines should follow the schema developed at the Sitemap.org Web site. The root element of the sitemap file will be urlset, which will contain an xmlns attribute pointing to the schema at www.sitemaps.org/schemas/sitemap/0.9. Within the root, you will have a series of url elements, which in turn will contain a loc element. The value of the loc element will be the address to the page to be indexed.

You will need to always use absolute paths for your pages, so you always need to begin with the protocol, such as http. If you have pages that can be accessed

through more than one protocol, such as those that can use either http or https, they should only be listed once.

The schema supports three optional elements within the url. The first, lastmod, allows you to specify the date and time at which the page in question was modified, ensuring that search engines will revisit the page to catalog changes. You can also add a changefreq element, which supports values of always, hourly, daily, weekly, monthly, yearly, or never to indicate how frequently the page is likely to change. Search engines will not necessary crawl the page as often as indicated, but it can help. Finally, you can add a priority element, with a value ranging from 0 to 1, indicating the priority of this page within the site and in effect instructing the engine on the order in which pages should be indexed.

Create a Sitemap

① Create a new document in your editor.

② Add the XML prolog.

③ Add a urlset element's opening tag.

④ Add an xmlns attribute with a value of www.sitemap.org/ schemas/sitemap/0.9.

⑤ Add a url element's opening tag.

⑥ Add a loc element's opening tag.

⑦ Add an absolute path to your homepage.

⑧ Add the closing loc tag.

⑨ Add a lastmod element's opening tag.

⑩ Add a value set to the date and time the file was last modified and the closing tag.

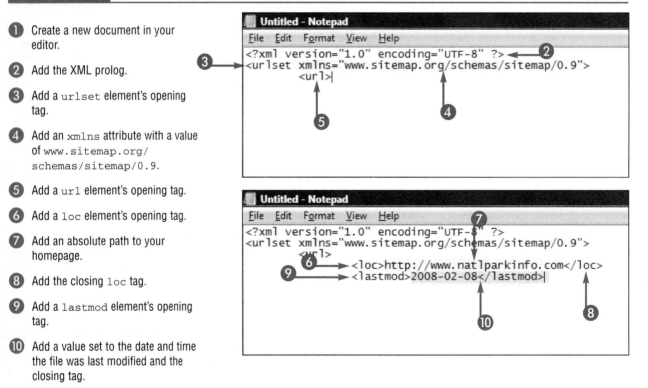

11. Add a `changefreq` element's opening tag.

12. Add an appropriate value and the closing tag.

13. Add a priority element's opening tag.

14. Add a value and the closing tag.

15. Add a closing `url` tag.

16. Repeat Steps 5 to 15 to add additional pages to the sitemap.

17. Add a closing `urlset` tag.

18. Save the file.

19. Open the file in a browser to ensure that it is well-formed.

The file either displays, as shown here, or an error displays.

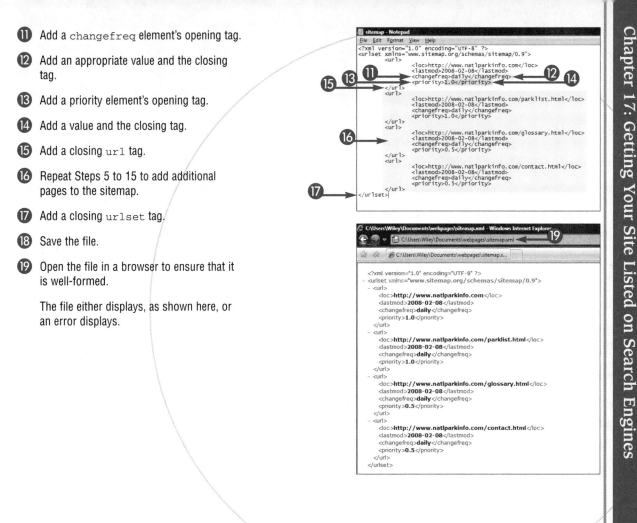

Extra

Many tools exist to create sitemaps automatically. Google includes one as part of its Web master tools called the Sitemap Generator. Unfortunately, it is a Python script that requires execution privileges on the server, which many hosting accounts disallow. However, if you can run it, it will automate the process of creating the script and save you time, especially for very large sites. You can download the Sitemap Generator at https://www.google.com/webmasters/tools/docs/en/sitemap-generator.html.

Sitemaps are most useful on sites with frequent changes, such as blogs. Most blog software includes a tool to generate a sitemap and keep it up-to-date as you add content to the blog. Many blog packages do this automatically, so you never even have to think about it. Check the documentation for your blog to see if it includes sitemap-generation features.

Google also supports subsets of the sitemap protocol for indexing video, mobile content, news, and code search. The Web Master Tools page has details on how to build and use each of these.

Prevent Pages from Being Listed on Search Engines

Occasionally, you may have pages within your site that you do not want to be indexed on search engines. For example, you may have test pages on your site that show developmental stages of upcoming features, or possibly pages you have set up for your own personal use to which you do not want to grant others easy access.

Two methods exist for telling search engines to ignore pages. The first is the creation of a robots.txt file, which you can place on your server in the Web site's root directory. This is a simple text document that will begin with an instruction as to which user agent should be affected by the document. As there is no way to be sure how the search engine's robot will identify itself, you will always use an asterisk to represent all agents. Then, you will have one or more Disallow statements. An asterisk

will disallow indexing of the entire site; a specific folder disallows indexing that folder, and a particular page blocks indexing of the page.

The robots.txt file is a convenient way to block indexing of entire directories, but while it supports individual file blocking, you can also do this using the meta element on the page to be blocked. In this case, you use the name attribute, set to robots, and then set the content to one or more of the following values: noindex, nofollow, index, or follow. If you use more than one value, they should be separated by commas. A noindex value prevents the search engine from indexing the page, while nofollow prevents it from following links on the page. Note that the robots.txt method does not provide for a way to prevent the engine from following links, so you may want to use both the meta element and the robots.txt file.

Prevent Pages from Being Listed on Search Engines

① Create a new plain text document in your editor.

② Type User-agent: *.

③ Type Disallow:.

④ Enter either an asterisk, a path to a directory in the site, or a specific filename.

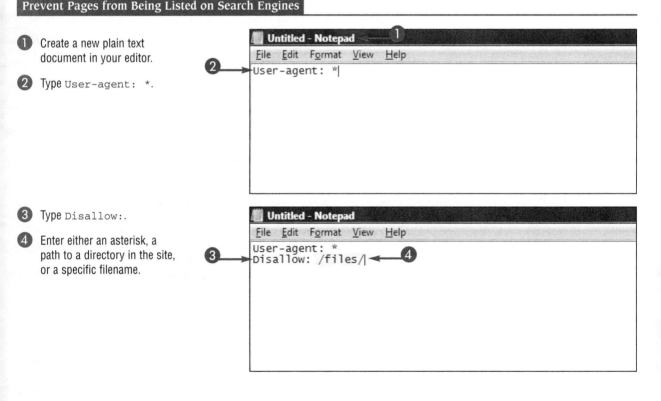

⑤ Repeat Step 4 to add additional `Disallow` statements as needed.

⑥ Save the page.

Note: *Name the file robots.txt, and be sure to save the file in the root of the Web site.*

⑦ Open a Web page in your editor.

⑧ In the head section, add a `meta` element's opening tag.

⑨ Add the `name` attribute, set to `robots`.

⑩ Add the content attribute, set to `noindex, nofollow`.

Note: *Be sure to include the comma.*

⑪ Save the page.

The file is saved. The page should now be ignored by search engines.

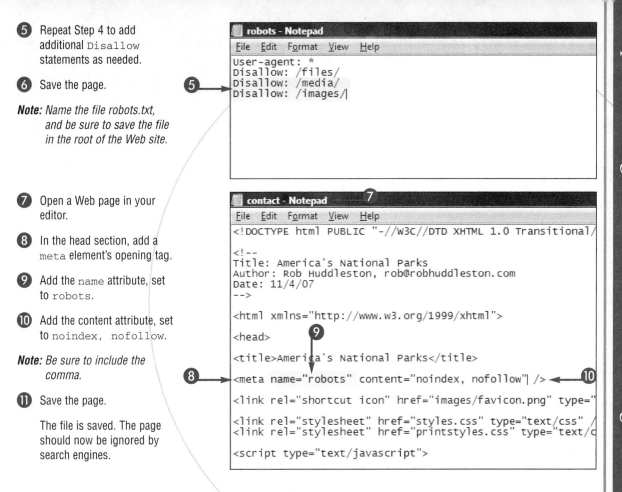

robots - Notepad

File Edit Format View Help

```
User-agent: *
Disallow: /files/
Disallow: /media/
Disallow: /images/|
```

contact - Notepad

File Edit Format View Help

```
<!DOCTYPE html PUBLIC "-//W3C//DTD XHTML 1.0 Transitional/

<!--
Title: America's National Parks
Author: Rob Huddleston, rob@robhuddleston.com
Date: 11/4/07
-->

<html xmlns="http://www.w3.org/1999/xhtml">

<head>

<title>America's National Parks</title>

<meta name="robots" content="noindex, nofollow"| />

<link rel="shortcut icon" href="images/favicon.png" type="

<link rel="stylesheet" href="styles.css" type="text/css" /
<link rel="stylesheet" href="printstyles.css" type="text/c

<script type="text/javascript">
```

Extra

Unfortunately, there is no way to guarantee that search engines will pay attention to instructions in robots.txt files or to the `meta` tag. Some search engines will still display a page that is not indexed in the results, but not provide details such as descriptions, while others may not display it at all.

If you have content that you want to be absolutely certain is not going to appear in search results, you should not place it on the Web. Alternatively, you can place it on the Web but require a password to access it. You will then need to create a log-in form and either set up password security through your Web host or else create your own log in script using a server-side processing language such as Adobe ColdFusion, Microsoft ASP.NET, or PHP.

Avoid Common HTML Mistakes

There are many common mistakes that can make the difference between a successful Web site and one that is a failure. Over time, avoiding these issues will become second nature. Note that everything listed here applies to both HTML and XHTML pages.

Change the Title

HTML editors, both code-based and visual design, will create the basic HTML structure tags for you. These editors will either leave the title blank, or put some generic text in place for you. You need to be sure to change the title of every page to something appropriate for that page.

Adobe Dreamweaver, for example, uses "Untitled Document" as the default title. A Google search on that term brings up close to 40 million pages, almost all of which are documents where the designer forgot to change the title from the default.

Include Character Encoding

You should always include information in the head of your document that identifies the character encoding for that document. This is a somewhat technical way of letting the browser know which set of characters are needed to properly render the page.

Almost every page will properly render if you set the encoding to UTF-8, which has become a de-facto standard for Web pages, e-mail, and most other electronic forms of communication.

The actual code to indicate the encoding uses the `meta` element with the `http-equiv` attribute set to `content-type` and the content set to `text/html; charset=utf-8`.

```
<meta http-equiv="Content-Type"
content="text/html;
charset=utf-8" >
```

Proofread and Spell Check

The Web abounds with examples of extremely poor writing and spelling. Most HTML editors provide a spell check tool, which you should use. Some editors will only check individual pages, while others may have the ability to check all of the pages in your site at once. However, no computerized spell checker is perfect, so it is still necessary to manually proof the documents.

No HTML editors provide a grammar checker, and even if they did, it does not take long using Microsoft Word to discover that the grammar checker is far from accurate. This again is a task that only a human can perform. You also need to double-check your punctuation.

Test Your Links and Do Not Include Links to Future Pages

You must test every link on every page by hand. You need to check not only that the link points to a page and is not "broken," but also that the link points to the *correct* page. Do not rely on automatic link checkers in software, as they can only detect broken links, not incorrect ones.

You should also avoid having links to pages that do not yet exist or that are "under construction." Instead, simply leave the link off until the page it points to is done. A common technique is to go ahead and include the link in the code, but then comment it out so that it does not appear on the page until it is needed.

Include a Document Type Declaration

Even HTML documents need a Document Type Declaration (DTD), or DOCTYPE. Without one, you will not be able to validate your pages. Like XHTML, HTML supports Strict, Transitional, and Frameset DOCTYPE. The DOCTYPE needs to be the first line of code on the page, as some browsers will incorrectly render the page if even a comment precedes it.

Use the Proper DOCTYPE

XHTML documents require a DOCTYPE in order to be valid. You need to decide whether you will create a Strict, Transitional, or Frameset document and begin with the proper DOCTYPE. Be sure that the DOCTYPE includes the complete path to the DTD. This is particularly true if you are using an older HTML editor that may use an improper path.

Avoid Common XHTML Mistakes

hile all of the mistakes mentioned previously with HTML documents apply to XHTML documents, there are several others issues of which you need to be aware when writing XHTML.

Include the Namespace Identifier

The root element of the document, `html`, needs to include an `xmlns` attribute to reference the origin of the namespace. This will always point to www.w3.org /1999/xhtml, so your `html` element's opening tag should be:

```
<html xmlns="http://www.w3.org/1999/xhtml">
```

All Images Must Have Appropriate Alternate Text

Every image on the page, except backgrounds inserted through CSS, must have appropriate alternate text that adequately and accurately describes the image.

Properly Close All Tags

XHTML requires that all tags be closed. Be sure that you do not forget to close container tags, particularly ones that have a lot of content where the opening and closing tags may be hundreds of lines apart. If you use a lot of `div` elements, you should get in the habit of typing the closing `div` tag as soon as you create the opening tag to lessen the chance that you will forget it later. It may also help to put a comment immediately before or after the closing tag to identify it with the opening tag, so if you end up with a series of closing tags at the bottom of your document, you can tell which tag closes which portion of the page.

Escape Characters

You need to be sure to always use the character entities to escape illegal characters in XHTML. The left angle bracket, or less-than symbol, needs to appear as `&lt;`. The right angle bracket, or greater-than symbol, needs to be `&gt;`. The ampersand uses `&amp;` and the quotation mark uses `&quot;`. Documents that do not consistently escape these characters may display properly in the browser, but they will not validate.

Properly Nest Tags

XHTML tags must be properly nested. You need to close tags in the opposite order in which you open them. Therefore, text that is going to be both bold and italic needs to be coded as `<strong><em>Text</ em></strong>`, not `<strong><em>Text</ strong></em>`.

Use Lowercase

XHTML is case-sensitive. All elements and attributes must be lowercase. Attribute values can be mixed-case, but most of the time it will make the most sense to use lowercase for them as well.

Always Include and Quote Attribute Values

Attributes must have values in XHTML. Certain elements in HTML used single-word attributes, such as the multiple and checked attributes in form controls. In XHTML, these must have a value. Every single-word attribute from HTML uses the name of the attribute as its value, so multiple becomes `multiple= "multiple"`.

In addition, every attribute value must be enclosed in quotation marks. You can use either single or double quotes.

IDs Must Be Unique

You cannot reuse an `id` on a page — they must be unique. For example, if you have a series of radio buttons or check boxes and you are using the `for` attribute to associate a label with them, each will need an `id`. However, a lot of designers will write the code for one check box or radio button and then copy and paste it for the others. They will generally remember to change the value, but often forget to change the `id`.

Avoid Common CSS Mistakes

A s with HTML and XHTML, there are certain mistakes beginners frequently make in CSS that you need to watch for and avoid.

Selectors Are Case-Sensitive

CSS selectors are case-sensitive. If you are writing proper XHTML and using lowercase for your elements, then element selectors must be lowercase. Problems more often arise when not matching case on `id` or `class` selectors. If you use mixed case in the XHTML, you must use the same mixed case in the CSS. Therefore, if you have `<div id="mainContent">`, your CSS selector must be `#mainContent`.

Use the Right Font Name

When specifying fonts, be sure to use the proper name, which is the name of the actual font file on the computer. Some applications display a common or friendly name for the font, so they cannot be relied upon. For example, Microsoft Word lists a font called "Comic Sans," but the actual filename in Windows is "MS Comic Sans." Many Web editing tools will be sure to display the correct name, but you may need to look at the files in the Fonts folder to be sure.

Classes Start with a Period, IDs with a Pound Symbol

Class selectors in CSS begin with a period, while `id` selectors begin with a pound sign or hash. You need to be careful to not confuse the two. It is legal although not recommended to have a class selector with the same name as an `id`, so if you use the wrong symbol at the beginning of the selector's name, CSS will not be properly applied.

Shorthands Reset Defaults

When using CSS shorthand properties such as `font`, remember that undeclared values are reset to their default, which may override inheritance. Say, for example, that you have a `div` that includes a paragraph. If your CSS sets the text within the `div` to bold, then normally the paragraph's text would be bold. However, applying the following formatting to the paragraph overrides the inherited bold property as the shorthand does not include it, and thus resets it to the default:

```
font: 90%/1.4em Arial, Helvetica, sans-serif;
```

Property Values Are Rarely Quoted

CSS rarely uses quotation marks around the values of properties. The only time it is legal to use quotes is when the property value is made up of more than one word. In general, this only applies to font names; so, for example, "Times New Roman" must always be quoted. Note, however, that shorthand properties that take more than one value are not quoted.

Always Include Units of Measurement

There is no default unit of measurement in CSS. Unless you are applying a value of zero, you must always include a unit of measurement. If no unit is supplied, some browsers may ignore the property in question, while others will attempt to guess at the unit, yielding unexpected and unpredictable results.

Remember the Differences Between Margins and Padding

Margins exist outside of the box, while padding exists within it. If you are attempting to move an element further from or closer to an adjacent element, you need to adjust the margin. If you are attempting to move the content within the box — for example, push text away from the border — then you need to adjust padding.

Also, margins can accept negative values, while padding cannot; padding can be applied to inline elements, whereas margins cannot.

Adjacent Margins Collapse

Adjacent margins in CSS collapse. For example, the default space between a heading and a paragraph that follows it is simultaneously the bottom margin of the heading and the top margin of the paragraph. Merely reducing one of them will not cause the elements to move closer.

It can often be helpful to remove one of the margins altogether so that you can focus on the other. In the previous example, you might decide to set the bottom margin of the heading to zero, thus allowing you to control the space between the elements by only adjusting the paragraph's top margin.

Remember the Differences Between display:none and visibility:hidden

Setting an element to display:none removes it from the document altogether, while visibility:hidden merely hides it from view. Elements that follow one with display:none will move up into its space, but will maintain the space of a hidden element.

Hiding elements with visibility is useful if you wish to have them appear and disappear through JavaScript, but still maintain their space on the page otherwise. Use display:none to remove elements from the page when designing print style sheets, as you would then want other elements to claim the space.

Only Use CSS Images for Backgrounds

You should only use CSS for images that are backgrounds and do not matter in the content of the page. Ask yourself if the page would still make sense and the user could still get the desired information from it if the image were not there. If the answer is yes, then you can apply a background image through CSS. If no, then you should insert it via the XHTML img element and use appropriate alt text.

Write Proper Hexadecimal

CSS requires that hexadecimal color codes begin with the pound symbol. Most browsers will ignore any color specification that does not include the pound.

Hexadecimal colors are always made up of six digits from 0 to 9 and A to F, although if the color is made of three pairs of values, it can be shortened to three digits, so #00BBFF can be written #0BF.

CSS is not case-sensitive with hexadecimal, so it does not matter if you capitalize the letters or not.

Watch for Inheritance

Many, but not all, CSS properties will inherit to child elements. Applying a font-family of Arial to a div will cause all of the children elements to display in Arial, but applying a top-margin to the same div will not apply the top-margin to its children. Pay attention as you learn CSS to which properties will inherit and which will not so that you can become aware of it as you gain experience using the language.

Watch for Block Properties that Do Not Work on Inline Elements

Every element is defined as being either block or inline. Block elements create their own space on the page, whereas inline elements do not.

Most CSS properties can be applied to either block or inline elements, but a few cannot. For example, margins can only be applied to block elements, while text-align can only apply to inline elements.

You can use the display property to reset an element that is normally inline to block, or vice versa; so, for example, you can apply display:block to the anchor element to set margins.

Avoid Common Design Mistakes

I n addition to technical coding issues, you need to watch for common issues in the actual design and implementation of your pages.

Design Should Serve Content

The Web is without question a visual medium, so you should strive to create visually appealing sites. However, far too many designers fall into the trap of focusing more on the design than the content. You should ask yourself this: Would you be likely to revisit a site that was visually stunning but provided very little useful content? On the other hand, would you revisit a site that was less visually interesting but provided a lot of great content?

Always make sure that your design serves your content, not vice versa. If you have a paragraph of text that will not fit in the design, the design needs to be reconsidered. The same applies to navigation: Do not sacrifice useful links because they do not fit in the design, but rather, redesign the page so that the links will fit.

Focusing on content first and foremost will also, almost by definition, make your pages more accessible to users with disabilities and improve your search engine rankings.

Give Up Control

When building Web pages, you need to accept that there are certain things you cannot control. Among them are the operating system and browser of your users, the size and screen resolution of their monitors, and the presence — or lack — of plug-ins such as Adobe Flash, Adobe Reader, or Apple QuickTime.

Only the last item on that list, the plug-ins, can be reliably tested and controlled. If your page uses Flash or has documentation in PDF, you can display a message on the page informing users that they need to download and install the appropriate player. The other issues are things that you simply need to understand that you cannot control, and need to design around.

You should not worry about the "ideal" or "most popular" screen resolution. Instead, design your page so that the information can be accessed at any resolution. You should not design pages that "work best" on certain browsers or operating systems, but instead create pages that work well in all browsers across all platforms.

You should also give up the notion of creating pixel-perfect designs across browsers and platforms. The unfortunate reality is that browsers render pages differently. They always have, and most likely always will. Do not worry if a particular element on the screen is three pixels further to the left in Internet Explorer on Windows than it is in Safari on a Mac. So long as the page still looks good, and the information is still accessible, you have done the best you can and should move on to other issues that you can control.

Think Like Your Users

The Web is a user-centric environment. You are building a Web site in the hopes that people will visit and come to use the site, but you must keep in mind that there are almost certainly other sites where they can get the same information or products, and that these competing sites are never more than a click or two away. Because your users invest almost nothing to visit the site, they will have a very low threshold for tolerance if they become frustrated on the site.

You need to build your site the way you think your users want it, not the way you want it. Structure your navigation in a way that will make sense to your users. Avoid terminology or jargon that may be confusing to them. Validate your forms to be sure that users submit the correct information, but be sure to inform them up-front as to what you expect for that data, and allow them as much freedom as possible. For example, many people enter dates differently, and your form should be able to accept a date entered in a variety of formats.

The best way to be sure you are reaching this goal is to carefully test your site on real users, and implement as many of their suggestions as you realistically can.

Test Your Pages

Never assume that your page will look the same on your user's computer as it does on yours. You need to check your page in all of the top browsers. This includes the latest two versions of Microsoft Internet Explorer, which are 6 and 7 as of this writing; and the latest versions of Mozilla Firefox and Apple Safari.

You also need to check your page on different operating systems. At a minimum, you need to check your page on both a computer running Windows and on a Macintosh. Most users rely on one or the other, so if you are a Windows user and do not have access to a Mac, either find a friend or coworker who can test your page for you, or find an online forum where you can ask others to test the pages. Yahoo! Groups offers several very popular Web design forums that can serve this purpose.

Use Color Wisely and Pay Attention to Contrast

Color can as easily destroy the design of your page as it can enhance it. Using too many colors can serve as a distraction, as can using colors that do not work well together.

Pay close attention to the contrast between the background and foreground on your page. Too little contrast will make the text difficult or impossible to read. Most users will not have the patience to try to read the text, but will instead simply give up and go to another site.

Be Careful with Fonts

Using too many fonts on a page can be very distracting. Most designs work best with only two or three fonts. You should have one font for your headings and one for your body text, with possibly a third for sidebar or callout text.

Remember that the browser uses device fonts, so the font you choose must be installed on your user's computer in order to be displayed properly. Unless you are working in an intranet, the only fonts that you can be certain will be installed on every machine are Arial, Courier, Times New Roman, and Verdana. You should always provide a list of alternate fonts to use so that the browser has a fallback in case your specified font is unavailable.

Avoid Very Small Text

A disturbing trend in blog design is to use very small text. This can be difficult to read on large monitors with high screen resolutions and for those with poor eyesight. It is better to err on the side of caution and have your text be larger rather than smaller, although text that is too large can be just as hard to read.

Windows users need to also keep in mind that, in general, text on a Macintosh will be rendered roughly 25 percent smaller, so text that is difficult to read in Windows may be impossibly small on a Macintosh.

You should also always use percents or ems to specify your font size to ensure that your user can resize it if necessary, regardless of which browser they use.

Do Not Center Everything

Having all of the text on the page centered is a sure sign of an amateur designer. Centered body text is difficult to read and should always be avoided.

Keep Lines Short

Very long lines of text are hard to read as your eyes get tired as you move across the line. You should make sure that your main body text is enclosed in some sort of container with a width that will prevent the lines of text from becoming too long, particularly as the presence and popularity of wide-screen monitors grows.

Clean Up HTML and XHTML with HTML Tidy

nce you have created your code, you can use HTML Tidy to check and clean up the XHTML or HTML. It was originally developed by Dave Raggett of the World Wide Web Consortium (W3C), but today, it is maintained by a group of volunteer developers.

HTML Tidy does many things to improve the validity of XHTML code. It will find and correct tags that are either lacking a closing tag or have the wrong closing tag; find and correct improperly nested tags; properly nest inline elements inside block elements; fix instances where block elements are invalidly nested within other block elements; add the slash to close empty tags if needed; add missing quotes around attribute values; and report on unknown or browser-specific elements and attributes that are not a part of the official specification. HTML Tidy will reformat your source code, but you can choose

whether it should indent all the code, which results in a slightly bigger but more readable file, or not. HTML Tidy will generate an accessibility report pointing out those areas that may need to be improved to make the document accessible; it will remove any presentational markup, such as the use of font, center, and other purely presentational elements, and replace them with equivalent CSS rules. The program has limited support for pages that contain server-side scripting, and it can parse and clean up XML files as well.

The biggest downside for most users is that although it runs on the Windows operating system, HTML Tidy does not have a graphical user interface. Instead, you need to use the command line to execute HTML Tidy. At its most basic, you can run the program by typing the command `tidy -f errors.txt -m index.html`, which runs the program on the index.html file, editing it in place and generating an errors.txt file with a list of what corrections were made.

Clean Up HTML and XHTML with HTML Tidy

① Navigate to www.paehl.com/open_source/?HTML_Tidy_for_Windows.

② Download the Tidy executable.

③ Extract the file into the directory that contains your XHTML files.

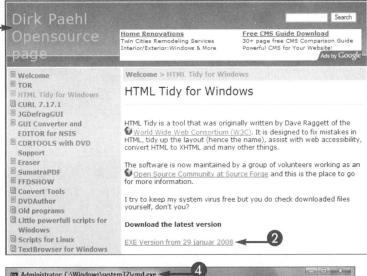

④ Open a Command window.

Note: *In Windows Vista, click Start →*
Run and type `cmd`.

⑤ Type `cd`, followed by a path to the folder into which you extracted Tidy.

⑥ Type `tidy -f errors.txt -m index.html`.

⑦ Press Enter.

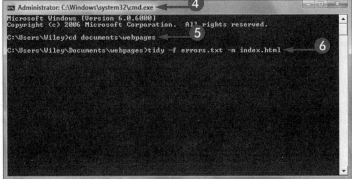

8 Open the index.html file in your editor and observe any changes.

File Edit Format View Help

```
<!DOCTYPE html PUBLIC "-//W3C//DTD XHTML 1.0 Transitional//EN" "http://www.w3.org/

<!--
Title: America's National Parks
Author: Rob Huddleston, rob@robhuddleston.com
Date: 11/4/07
-->

<html xmlns="http://www.w3.org/1999/xhtml">

<head>

<title>America's National Parks</title>

<link rel="shortcut icon" href="images/favicon.png" type="image/png" />

<link rel="stylesheet" href="styles.css" type="text/css" />
<link rel="stylesheet" href="printstyles.css" type="text/css" media="print" />
<link rel="alternate" href="altstyles.css" type="text/css" title="Larger Text" />

</head>

<body id="homepage">

<!-- Begin content -->
<div id="container">

<!-- Begin header -->
<div id="header">

<p><img src="images/yosemitevalley.jpg" alt="Yosemite valley" /></p>
```

9 Open errors.txt in your editor.

If any corrections were made, they appear in the document.

● This text appears if no errors were found.

File Edit Format View Help

```
Info: Document content looks like XHTML 1.0 Strict. ←———●
No warnings or errors found.

To learn more about HTML Tidy see http://tidy.sourceforge.net
Please send bug reports to html-tidy@w3.org
HTML and CSS specifications are available from http://www.w3.org.
Lobby your company to join w3C, see http://www.w3.org/Consortium
```

Apply It

You can create a configuration file to store common settings that you want to have Tidy use. Simply save the file in the folder in which you run Tidy and then let Tidy know that you wish to use it by issuing the `-config` command with the name of the file. A sample configuration file might look like this:

```
indent: auto
indent-spaces: 4
wrap: 80
markup: yes
output-xml: yes
input-xml: yes
show-warnings: yes
numeric-entities: no
uppercase-tags: no
uppercase-attributes: no
char-encoding: latin1
```

Validate XHTML

In order to make the development of Web pages as easy as possible and to easily facilitate backwards compatibility, browsers from the very early days of the Web have been designed to simply ignore bad or questionable code. This means that you can add any markup to your document that you want to, whether or not it is valid, and the browser will not return an error. When it encounters an element, attribute, or attribute value that it does not recognize, it simply ignores it and goes on processing the page as if the offending code did not exist. Although beginners, who often become frustrated at the appearance of constant error messages, may find this lack of errors refreshing, experienced programmers know that troubleshooting errors is far easier than troubleshooting unexpected behavior.

Therefore, you should always ensure that your markup validates as proper XHTML. Although there is currently no browser that natively validates XHTML, there are many free resources available that provide validation, including the Markup Validation Service on the W3C's site. The W3C Validator enables you to validate pages. You can validate pages that are currently online or use a form on the site to upload a page to it for validation.

The W3C Validator is unable to validate pages that lack a correct DOCTYPE, as there is no way for the tool to know which syntax rules it should use without that. It will validate documents that use HTML 4.01 Transitional, HTML 4.01 Strict, HTML 4.01 Frameset, XHTML 1.0 Transitional, XHTML 1.0 Strict, XHTML 1.0 Frameset, or XHTML 1.1.

Validate XHTML

1. In your Web browser, navigate to http://validator.w3.org.

2. Click Validate by File Upload.

3. Click Browse.

4. In the File Upload dialog box, navigate to an XHTML document that contains a valid DOCTYPE.

5. Click Open.

- The file path appears in the upload field.

6 Click Check.

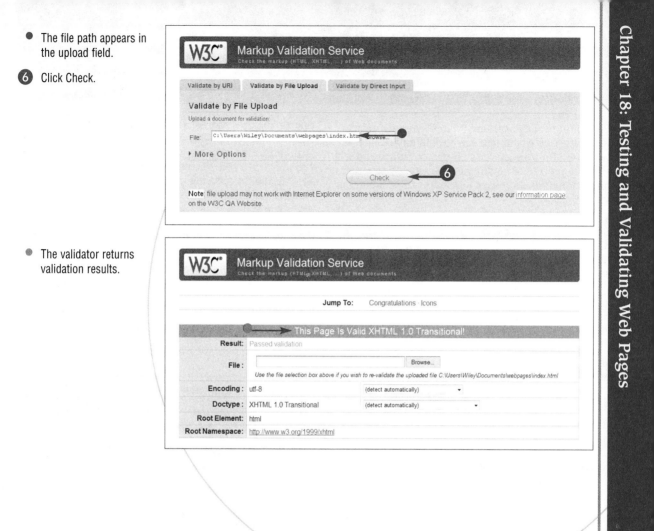

- The validator returns validation results.

Validate CSS

Creating valid Cascading Style Sheets ensures that your page will render correctly in any standards-based browser, such as Firefox or Safari, and will simplify the process of modifying or hacking your CSS to render in non-standards-based browsers such as Internet Explorer 6.

As with invalid XHTML, browsers will unfortunately refuse to return an error message when they encounter bad CSS. Instead, they will either ignore the offending property, value, or rule altogether or they may try to guess at your meaning and give unexpected results.

Before validating your CSS, make sure that you have already validated your XHTML. Browser-rendering problems are much more likely to be caused by invalid XHTML than by invalid CSS.

One simple, free tool for validating CSS is the W3C CSS Validation Service, which you can access at http://jigsaw.w3.org/css-validator. This service allows you to check a CSS file, or the CSS embedded within an XHTML file, by entering a URL to the file, uploading a local file, or directly typing the CSS into a form on the page. The validator analyzes your CSS and either informs you that everything is fine or returns a list of errors on the page, complete with line number references, so that you can fix them.

Although the errors are often highly technical, the W3C also maintains a documentation page for the validator that explains the errors. If your page does validate, the site shows you code that can be copied onto your page to display an icon showing that you have valid CSS.

Validate CSS

BY URL

1. In your browser, go to http://jigsaw.w3.org/css-validator.

2. Enter a URL to a CSS file or a Web page that contains an embedded style sheet.

3. Click Check.

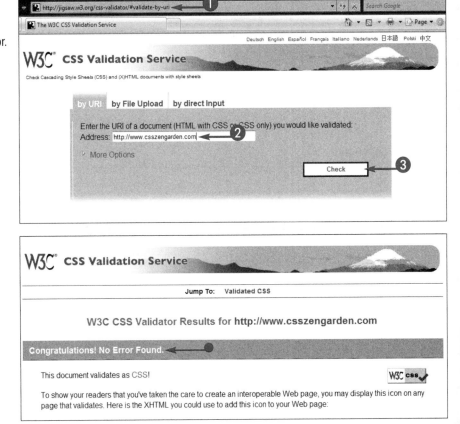

- The results page is displayed, showing either a valid message or error descriptions.

BY FILE UPLOAD

① In your browser, go to http://jigsaw.w3.org/css-validator.

② Click By File Upload.

③ Click Browse.

④ Navigate to and select a CSS file on your local hard disk and click Open.

⑤ Click Check.

● The results page is displayed, showing either a valid message or error descriptions.

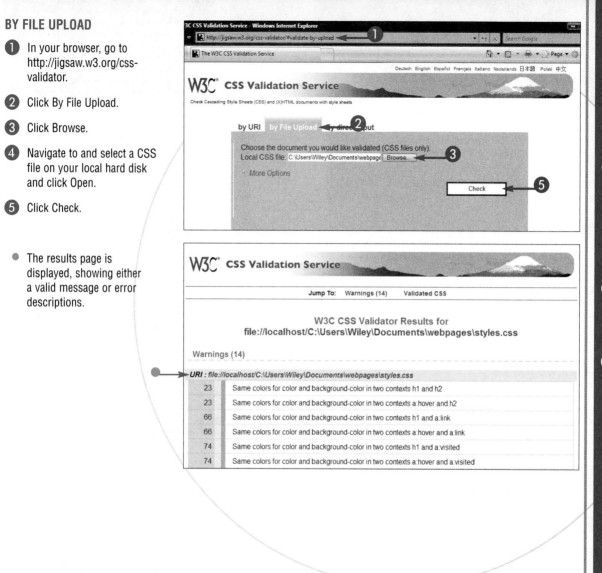

Extra

Adobe Dreamweaver CS3 includes a built-in validator that will not only check the validity of your code, but will also point out potential browser incompatibility issues and provide a link to a Web page where you can read about solutions to browser-specific CSS rendering bugs. To use this feature, open a CSS document in Dreamweaver and then click the Check Browser Compatibility button on the toolbar. This displays the Results panel. If the program detects errors in your CSS, you can double-click the error to go to the relevant line of code. If it detects valid CSS that may nonetheless not render properly in a browser, it displays the error and provides a link to the CSS Advisor Web site, where you can read about solutions to the problem.

Find a Web Host

In order for others to view your Web site, you will need to transfer the files from your local computer to a Web server. If you work for a large company, you may already have access to a server that the company owns, but if you work for a smaller company or are building a personal site, you will probably want to use a Web hosting company.

Web Hosts

Web hosts are companies that rent space on their servers. Using a Web host offers many advantages: You do not need to install, configure, or maintain the server operating system or deal with security on it; you do not need to worry about maintaining the Web server software; and you do not need to deal with hardware issues. With a Web host, you can worry about the design and implementation of your site, and let others worry about the technical details of running a server.

Shared versus Dedicated Hosting

Most Web hosts offer a service called "shared hosting," where your site is on a server with many other sites. If one or more of those sites begins to use too much bandwidth or server resources, the performance of your site might suffer. Most good hosts will monitor this and may move sites that causing problems to less busy servers, but it is a reactionary measure that can only be taken after the problem arises.

Dedicated hosting, offered by many higher-end hosts, allows you to rent an entire server for your site, so yours will be the only one running on the machine. This is, for obvious reasons, a much more expensive alternative, but if the performance of your site is of paramount concern, or if you think your site might become one that needs more resources, you should consider this option.

Shopping for a Host

There are literally millions of Web hosts available — a Google search for "Web hosting" in January 2008 returned 428 million results. Therefore, you will want to spend some time comparison shopping. Hosts have widely varying fees for their services, from free to thousands of dollars per month. They also offer a wide range of services for these fees, so you will need to investigate which ones offer the services you want for the price you can afford.

Domain Hosting

Free Web hosts will generally require that you use their domain name, but most other hosts offer domain hosting, where you can purchase a domain name and use it for your site. Some hosts even offer multiple domain hosting, allowing you to purchase several domains and host them all, either as a single site that has many domains pointing to it, or as separate sites.

Services Offered by Hosts

All hosts should offer a certain amount of disk space, a maximum allowed amount of monthly bandwidth, and some sort of control panel interface to allow you to administer your site. Usually, the hard drive space and bandwidth will be more than sufficient for most sites, although hosts generally offer a la cart options for additional space and bandwidth should you need them.

Hosts will generally offer e-mail services as well, allowing you to use e-mail accounts attached to your domain name. They may also offer server-side scripting features, such as support for PHP, ASP, ASP.NET, and ColdFusion, as well as space on database servers.

All hosts should offer some sort of backup system to protect against data loss on their side, and many will make the Web server logs for your site available, either as a raw data file that you need to analyze yourself or through a graphical interface on the control panel.

As with most things, the more services you opt for, the higher the cost of the package.

Tech Support

All Web hosts should offer technical support, although the level and quality of support you get may vary greatly from one host to the next. In general, only expensive plans will include live phone support. Many hosts now offer a support chat feature that allows you to discuss issues with a technician in real time, and most rely on a support ticket system to handle nonemergency issues. The quality of tech support is the most-often cited reason for people to choose to stay with, or leave, a host.

Hosting Reviews

With the overwhelming number of available Web hosts, it is impossible for a single person to effectively compare all of the options. You should first seek out trusted friends, coworkers, or affiliated businesses to get personal recommendations on hosting.

You can also visit one of several online forums in which users share their views — good and bad — on Web hosts. The forums at www.whrforums.com are a fantastic resource for this information. *Web Host Magazine* offers a categorized search process that allows you to find hosts based on the services they offer on their Web site at www.webhostmagazine.com, and FindMyHost.com offers a search feature, reviews, and a guarantee to assist you in dealing with problems with any host that they recommend.

Signing Up with a Host

Once you have found the host you want to use, you will be able to sign up through their Web site. Most will ask for basic contact and billing information. Many offer monthly or yearly billing, with a discount for longer terms. Once they receive your information, you should receive an e-mail from them with details as to how to log into the control panel and set up other details of your site and with the login information so that you can upload your files to them.

Keep this e-mail, as you may need to refer to it later should you forget your login information or need to contact your host.

Once the registration process is complete, you should be able to upload your files immediately. If you are using domain hosting, there may be delay before the name servers on the Internet recognize the new location of your site, but many hosts provide a temporary address to allow you to access the site in the meantime.

Buy a Domain Name

The easiest way for people to find and remember your site is to have your own domain name. Fortunately, purchasing a domain name is a fairly easy and surprisingly inexpensive task.

To register your own domain, you will first need to find a name that is not taken by someone else and then determine which top-level domain you want to use. Originally, there were three top-level domains open to the public: .com, .org, and .net. Later, the Internet Corporation for Assigned Names and Numbers (ICANN) created others, including .name and .biz. Every country has a two-letter country code as well, and several have made theirs available to anyone, regardless of whether they are a resident or citizen of the country. One of the better known of these is from the island of Tulavu, in the Pacific Ocean, which allows their .tv name to be used around the world.

In 1992, the National Science Foundation asked companies to bid to be granted a contract to develop the domain name system. One company, Network Solutions, entered the winning bid and thus became not only the developer of the system but the first registrar as well. They were later granted the right to charge for registrations, and they maintained a monopoly on the domain name registration system until 1999, when ICANN was created and the system was opened to anyone who wanted to become a registrar. Since then, thousands of domain registrars have come into business, and the prices to register domain names have dropped considerably.

Although registrars will attempt to convince you to use their service by offering packages of domain names, hosting, and other services, the key aspect for finding the one that you want is price. Just as with other services you may use, you will want to spend time comparison shopping to find the least expensive registrar.

Buy a Domain Name

① In your browser, go to www.network solutions.com.

② Type the domain name that you want to use.

③ Click the top-level domain that you want.

④ Click Search.

● The site returns a list of domains that are available.

Note: If no domains are available with that name, Network Solutions offers you close alternatives or the chance to search again.

⑤ If the domain name that you want is available, click Add Domain(s) to Order.

6 On the next page, choose if you want the domain to be private and click Continue.

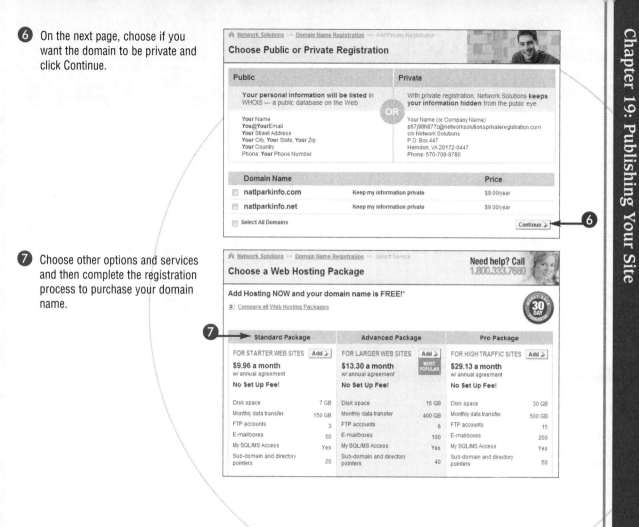

7 Choose other options and services and then complete the registration process to purchase your domain name.

Extra

You need to inform your Web host of your domain name in order for your users to be able to use your domain name to find your site.

After you have registered the name with the registrar, you will need to go back to your hosting provider and get the names of their name servers. This information may also be included in the e-mail you received from the host when you signed up. Then, on the registrar's Web site, you will be able to enter the name server information, which will point the domain name to your site.

Domain names need to propagate through the Web because the servers that convert the names to their corresponding IP addresses cache the information. Usually, this will only take a few hours, but it can take as long as a day or two, so you will need to be patient when you first try to visit your site via its IP address.

Publish Your Web Site Using Windows FTP

I n order for your Web site to be visible to other people, you will need to publish it, or transfer the files from your local machine to your Web host's servers.

Although there are several different technologies available to transfer files, by far the most common is FTP (file transfer protocol). FTP has been used for many years to allow for the transfer of files between often incompatible operating systems and, in fact, predates the World Wide Web.

In order to use FTP, you will need to know the address of the server to which you want to transfer the files and have a username and password set up on the server. This information should be in the e-mail you received when

you signed up with your Web host. You will also need an *FTP client* — software on your computer that you can use to create and maintain the FTP connection. If you are using Microsoft Windows, you can use its built-in FTP client. Windows FTP is automatically installed with Windows, so you do not need to do anything to get it to work.

The big disadvantage to Windows FTP is that it relies on the MS-DOS command window, so it can be very difficult to use if you are unfamiliar with DOS commands. However, it is small and uses few resources, and the fact that it is available at no charge and requires no additional software installation or setup to Windows users may outweigh the need to learn the admittedly arcane DOS commands.

Publish Your Web Site Using Windows FTP

① From the Start menu, select Run.

② Type ftp.

③ Click OK.

The Windows FTP window opens.

④ Type open *address_of_ your_ftp_server.*

⑤ Press Enter.

⑥ Type your username.

⑦ Press Enter.

⑧ Type your password.

⑨ Press Enter.

The FTP server logs you in.

10 Type hash.

11 Press Enter.

12 Type lcd and then the path to the folder on your hard drive that contains your Web page files.

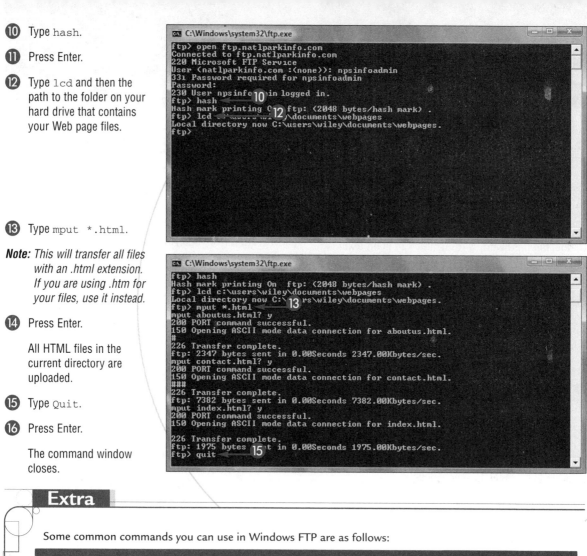

13 Type mput *.html.

Note: *This will transfer all files with an .html extension. If you are using .htm for your files, use it instead.*

14 Press Enter.

All HTML files in the current directory are uploaded.

15 Type Quit.

16 Press Enter.

The command window closes.

Extra

Some common commands you can use in Windows FTP are as follows:

COMMAND	DESCRIPTION
open <server>	Opens a connection to a specified server
user <username>	Specifies a username to log in
dir	Displays a list of the files in the current directory on the server
cd <path>	Changes to a specified directory on the server
lcd <path>	Changes to a specified directory on the client
mkdir <directoryname>	Creates a directory on the server
hash	Displays hash symbols, or pound signs, to show the progress of a file upload or download
get <filename>	Downloads a file from the server
put <filename>	Uploads a file to the server
mget <*.extension>	Downloads all files with the specified extension
mput <*.extension>	Uploads all files with the specified extension
quit	Closes the connection and the command window
?	Displays a list of accepted commands

Publish Your Web Site Using SmartFTP

There are many free and low-cost FTP clients on the market. One very popular one is SmartFTP, produced by software maker SmartSoft. SmartFTP is freeware, so anyone can download and use it free of charge. SmartSoft makes versions of its product for Windows 2000, XP, 2003, and Vista.

SmartFTP supports secure connections. One of the criticisms of FTP, in general, is that everything, including the username and password, is transmitted in plain text and is quite easy to intercept. Secure FTP uses Secure Sockets Layer to encrypt the data transfer. Unfortunately, many servers are not set up to use Secure FTP, so you will need to confirm with your host if they use it. SmartFTP also has a very intuitive graphical user interface to minimize the learning curve when using it. It supports file synchronization, file compression, and file transfer integrity to make sure that files are not corrupted while in transit.

If you or your Web host uses a UNIX-based server, you will need to modify the properties to set the proper permissions on files that you transfer to the server. These properties are called CHMOD for *change mode*. Many FTP applications either do not allow you to modify these properties or else use arcane command-line interfaces that make it difficult. With SmartFTP, you can set these permissions directly within the interface.

The program has an interface that closely resembles most other FTP programs. Once connected to the server, the local files will appear on half of the screen, and the remote files on the other half. You can simply drag files and folders from the local machine to the remote machine, or vice versa. SmartFTP will queue files for transfer, so you can select multiple files and start the transfer and then continue work on other items while the program uploads or downloads your files.

Publish Your Web Site Using SmartFTP

① In your browser, go to www.smartftp.com.

② Click Download.

③ Click the correct version for your computer.

You are directed to the download site.

④ Click Download Now.

● The File Download dialog box appears.

⑤ Click Run.

The file downloads, and the installation program launches.

⑥ Click Next.

⑦ Click I Accept the Terms of the License Agreement and click Next.

⑧ Click Typical.

⑨ Click Install.

The program installs.

⑩ Click Finish.

SmartFTP launches.

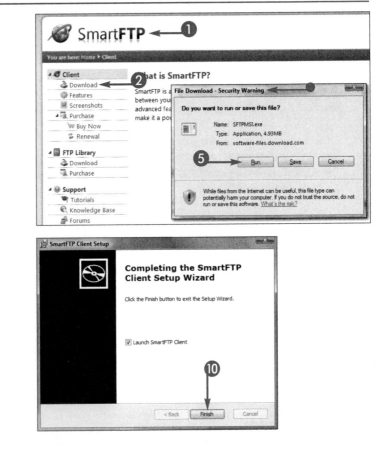

⑪ Click File → New Remote Browser.

The New Remote Browser dialog box appears.

⑫ Type your server address.

⑬ Type your username.

⑭ Type your password.

⑮ Click OK.

The program connects to the server.

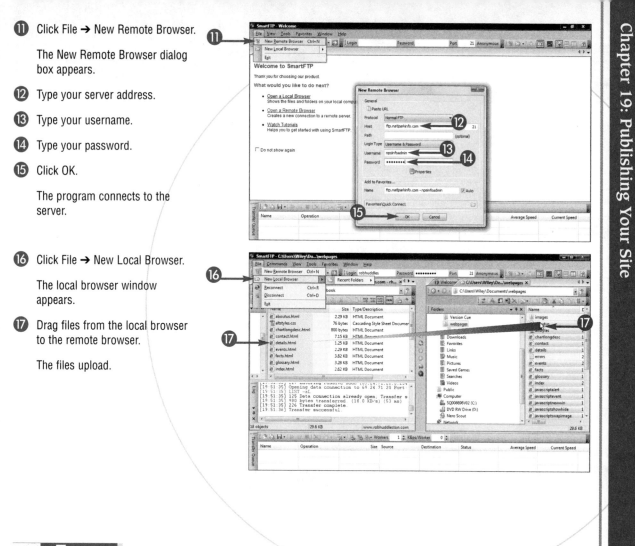

⑯ Click File → New Local Browser.

The local browser window appears.

⑰ Drag files from the local browser to the remote browser.

The files upload.

Most applications for creating, editing, and viewing Web pages files are the same or nearly the same for both Windows and Macintosh. Both platforms have plain-text editors, Adobe Dreamweaver is nearly identical on both, and most Windows-specific software such as SmartFTP will run on MacOS X via Virtual PC, Bootcamp, or Parallels.

In addition, there are many good FTP programs available for use on the Macintosh. One popular one is called Transmit, created by Oregon-based Panic (www.panic.com). It is a lightweight application that is very easy to install and use. Cyberduck (www.cyberduck.ch) is an open-source FTP client for Macintosh that includes many of the same features as other products. Both Cyberduck and Transmit are free.

Interarchy, created by Nolobe in Australia (www.nolobe.com/interarchy), is an extremely powerful FTP client for Macintosh that goes far beyond the capabilities of most other FTP programs. It includes the capability to script downloads to control them dynamically, on-the-fly file conversion and compression, and much more. It is not free, however.

HTML and XHTML
Tag Reference

The following is a complete list of the elements supported in HTML 4.01 and XHTML 1.0, including suggested usage and supported attributes. Unless otherwise noted, the elements and attributes are supported by all "flavors" of both HTML 4.01 and XHTML 1.0.

All XHTML elements accept the following common attributes, except as noted in the text. They are always optional:

COMMON ATTRIBUTE	DESCRIPTION
class	A class selector for the element.
dir	Sets the direction of the element as either left to right or right to left.
id	A unique identifier for the element.
lang	Specifies the language of the element.
style	Applies an inline style to the element.
title	Sets a title for the element.
xml:lang	Specifies the language of the element. If both lang and xml:lang are given with different values, xml:lang takes precedent.

`<a>`

The anchor tag, used for hyperlinks and named anchors. Note that the href and name attributes are mutually exclusive. The common attributes, as well as the following attributes, are supported:

ATTRIBUTE	DESCRIPTION
accesskey	Optional. Sets a keyboard shortcut to access the link.
charset	Optional. Advises the browser as to the encoding of the target link.
coords	Optional. Used for setting client-side image maps along with shape, although it is not supported by any known browser.
href	Required if creating a hyperlink. Defines the path to the target resource.
hreflang	Optional. Tells the browser the language of the target resource.
rel	Optional. Sets the relationship of the target. See the description under link for possible values.
name	Required if creating a named anchor. Defines a name for the anchor, which can serve as the target of another link. Technically only appropriate for HTML and not XHTML, where the id attribute of the target element should be used.
rev	Optional. Sets a reverse relationship. See the description under link.
shape	Optional. Used for setting client-side image maps along with coords, although it is not supported by any known browser.
tabindex	Optional. Controls the order in which the field will gain focus if the user is tabbing through the page. Must be an integer between 1 and 32,767.
target	Optional. Sets the name of the window or frame in which the link should open. Only defined in HTML, as XHTML 1.0 intended to replace it with JavaScript. XHTML 1.1 reintroduced the attribute as valid.
type	Optional. Advises the browser as to the content type of the target.

`<abbr>`

An abbreviation, used to denote a piece of text that should be treated as an abbreviation. Screen readers may read the text as a word rather than sounding out each letter. This element only supports the common attributes. Note that `title` should be used to designate the full text that is abbreviated.

`<acronym>`

Denotes an acronym. Some browsers may use special display properties, such as a dotted underline, when rendering acronyms. Screen readers may read the acronym as a word, rather than sounding out each letter. This element only supports the common attributes. Note that `title`, while technically optional, should always be used to designate the full text that is abbreviated.

`<address>`

This element denotes the address block on a page. By default, most browsers will display text within this tag in italics. This element only supports the common attributes.

`<area>`

This sets coordinates for an image map clickable region. It must appear within a `<map>` tag set. As an empty tag, it must be properly closed. The common attributes, as well as the following attributes, are supported:

ATTRIBUTE	DESCRIPTION
accesskey	Optional. Sets a keyboard shortcut for accessing the region.
alt	Required. Specifies alternative text for the region.
coords	Required. Sets the coordinates of the corners of the shape of the region.
disabled	Optional. Disables the region, making it unclickable. The only legal value is `disabled`.
href	Required. Sets the target resource's location.
name	Optional. Names the region.
nohref	Optional. Specifies that the region has no associated link.
shape	Required. Defines the shape of the region. Possible values are `circle`, `rect`, and `poly`.
tabindex	Optional. Defines the region's order when the user is tabbing through the page. The value must be an integer between 0 and 32,767.
target	Optional. Sets the name of the window or frame in which the link should open. Only defined in HTML, as XHTML 1.0 intended to replace it with JavaScript. XHTML 1.1 reintroduced the attribute as valid.

`<b>`

The `b` element renders the text in bold. While entirely presentational, it has been preserved even in XHTML 1.0 Strict. The `strong` element is preferred as it has semantic meaning. This element only supports the common attributes.

`<base>`

Sets a base hyperlink or target for the page. Must appear within the head. As an empty element, it must be properly closed. Note that the common attributes are not supported for this element.

ATTRIBUTE	DESCRIPTION
href	Required if `target` is not provided. Sets the base path for all hyperlinks.
target	Required if `href` is not provided. Sets the base target for all hyperlinks. Not valid in XHTML.

continued →

\<bdo>

Used for bidirectional override, or to change the direction of text from left to right to right to left, or vice versa. The common attributes, as well as the following attribute, are supported:

ATTRIBUTE	DESCRIPTION
dir	Required. Defines the direction. Legal values are rtl and ltr.

\<big>

This renders text in a larger font size. Only allowed in HTML, and not supported at all by XHTML. Style sheets should be used instead of this element. This element only supports the common attributes.

\<blockquote>

Used to describe a large quotation from another source. By default, text within the blockquote will be indented from both the left and right margins. The common attributes, as well as the following attribute, are supported:

ATTRIBUTE	DESCRIPTION
cite	Optional. Provides a reference to the resource being quoted.

\<body>

This defines the body of the document, which is all the content that will be displayed in the browser window. It must be a direct child of the html element, and is required for all documents. It cannot be repeated. All attributes are optional. All attributes of the element beyond the common set are deprecated in favor of CSS.

\

This is used to create a line break in a block of text. As an empty element, it must be properly closed. This element only supports the common attributes. Older attributes such as clear have been deprecated in favor of CSS.

\<button>

Can be used to create a button, and can only appear within \<form>. The common attributes, as well as the following attributes, are supported:

ATTRIBUTE	DESCRIPTION
accesskey	Optional. Sets a keyboard shortcut for accessing the region.
disabled	Optional. Disables the region, making it unclickable. The only legal value is disabled.
name	Optional. Names the region.
tabindex	Optional. Defines the region's order when the user is tabbing through the page. The value must be an integer between 1 and 32,767.
type	Required. Sets the action for the button. Possible values are submit, reset, and button.
value	Optional. Assigns a value to the button control, which may be interpreted by a server-side script.

\<caption>

This denotes the caption of a table. It must be used within \<table> and must be the first child of that element. This element only supports the common attributes. Older attributes such as align have been deprecated in favor of CSS.

\<cite>

This marks a citation in the text. Browsers will display text in italic by default. This element only supports the common attributes. The title attribute should be used to provide a reference to the original source.

\<code>

This can be used to mark a block as code, usually in onscreen tutorials. Text will be displayed using a monospaced font by default. This element only supports the common attributes.

<col>

This denotes a column of a table. It is used to add styles for the column. It must appear within `<table>`, after `<caption>` but before other code except `<colgroup>`. As an empty element, it must be properly closed. The common attributes, as well as the following attributes, are supported. All attributes are optional.

ATTRIBUTE	DESCRIPTION
align	Determines the alignment of text within the column's cells. Even though this is presentational, it has not been deprecated and is valid even in XHTML 1.0 Strict and XHTML 1.1. Possible values are `left`, `right`, `center`, `justify`, and `char`.
char	Specifies the character to which the text in the column should be aligned if `align` is set to `char`. The default is a decimal point. Not supported by most browsers.
charoff	Sets the offset distance to the first character for alignment. Not generally supported by browsers.
span	Defines the number of columns being defined.
valign	Determines the vertical alignment within the cell. Like align, this is purely presentational but has not been deprecated. Possible values are `top`, `middle`, `bottom`, and `baseline`.
width	Sets the width of cells within the column. Can be measured in pixels, percents, or as a relative value using an asterisk. Another purely presentational attribute that nonetheless remains in the specification.

<colgroup>

Used to group a set of `col` tags together.

Must appear within `table`, after `caption` but before any other code.

Requires one or more `col` elements as children.

This element supports the same set of attributes as `col`. See that listing for details.

<dd>

The definition list description, which marks the definition portion of the list item. It must appear within `dl`. This element only supports the common attributes.

<del>

This marks text as being deleted; browsers will display the text with strikethrough. The common attributes, as well as the following attributes, are supported:

ATTRIBUTE	DESCRIPTION
cite	Optional. Provides a reference, often the identification of the person authorized to delete the text.
datetime	Optional. The timestamp of the deletion. Must be set using the W3C (World Wide Web Consortium) date format, details for which can be found at www.w3.org/TR/1998/NOTE-datetime-19980827.

<dfn>

This marks the definition of a word. Note that this is not used within the definition list, but rather in normal text. This element only supports the common attributes.

<div>

A division, or logical section of your page, usually for style purposes. This element only supports the common attributes. Other attributes such as `align` have been deprecated in favor of CSS.

<dl>

Used to denote a definition list. This element only supports the common attributes.

<dt>

This element sets the term for an item in a definition list. It must appear within `<dl>`. This element only supports the common attributes.

<em>

This marks a word or words for emphasis. Most browsers will render text within `<em>` in italics.

This element only supports the common attributes.

continued ➜

<fieldset>

Used to denote a collection of related form fields. It must be used within `<form>`. Browsers will draw a visual border around the `<fieldset>`. This element only supports the common attributes.

<form>

This is the parent element for a form.. All form controls must appear within the tag set. The common attributes, as well as the following attributes, are supported:

ATTRIBUTE	DESCRIPTION
accept	Optional. Specifies a list of allowed MIME types. Not currently supported by browsers.
accept-charset	Optional. Specifies a list of acceptable character encodings for the values being entered in the form. Not widely supported.
action	Required. The path to the resource that will process the form.
enctype	Optional. The encoding type used to send the data. Possible values are `application/x-www-form-urlencoded`, which is the default; `multipart/form-data`, which must be used if uploading files via the form; and `text/plain`.
method	Required. Instructs the browser as to how the data from the form should be sent. Possible values are `get` and `post`.
name	Optional. A unique name for the form, used by JavaScript. Not supported by XHTML, where an `id` should be used instead.
target	Optional. Sets the name of the window or frame in which the form's result page should open. Only defined in HTML, as XHTML 1.0 intended to replace it with JavaScript. XHTML 1.1 reintroduced the attribute as valid.

<h1>

Used for heading level 1. This element only supports the common attributes. Other attributes such as `align` have been deprecated in favor of CSS for all levels of headings.

<h2>

Used for heading level 2. This element only supports the common attributes.

<h3>

Used for heading level 3. This element only supports the common attributes.

<h4>

Used for heading level 4. This element only supports the common attributes.

<h5>

Used for heading level 5. This element only supports the common attributes.

<h6>

Used for heading level 6. This element only supports the common attributes.

<head>

This element defines the head section of the document. It takes no attributes, and is required for all documents. The `head` must include exactly one `title`, and can include any number of the following elements in any order: `base`, `isindex`, `link`, `meta`, `object`, `script`, and `style`. No other elements may appear in the `head`.

<hr>

This creates a horizontal rule, a visible line across the page. This element only supports the common attributes. Other attributes such as `align` have been deprecated in favor of CSS.

<html>

This is the root element in every document. It is required for all documents. The closing `</html>` tag must be the last tag in the document. Note that the common attributes are not supported for this element, except for `lang` and `xml:lang`, which are recommended.

ATTRIBUTE	DESCRIPTION
xmlns	Required for XHTML, not defined for HTML. Specifies the namespace for XHTML. Its value will always be `http://www.w3.org/1999/xhtml`.

<iframe>

Used to create an inline frame, or "window," in the page into which another XHTML document can be displayed. Note that although this is a frame, it is used within an XHTML Transitional or Strict document, not a Frameset, and appears within the `<body>`. A common belief holds that `iframe` is only supported by Internet Explorer, but it is part of the HTML and XHTML specification and is, in fact, widely supported across modern browsers. The common attributes, as well as the following attributes, are supported:

ATTRIBUTE	DESCRIPTION
longdesc	Optional. Provides a path to a document that describes the frame in detail.
name	Optional. An identifier for the frame.
src	Required. The path to the document to be displayed within the frame.
scrolling	Optional. Determines whether scrollbars will appear if needed in the frame. Possible values are `auto` (the default), `yes`, and `no`.

Several presentational attributes are still supported, although they should be avoided in favor of CSS:

ATTRIBUTE	DESCRIPTION
frameborder	Turns on or off the visible border around the frame. Possible values are 0 and 1, with 0 being off and 1 being on.
height	The height of the frame. Most browsers default this to 150 pixels.
marginheight	The height between the top and bottom interior edges of the frame and its content.
marginwidth	The width between the left and right interior edges of the frame and its content.
name	Assigns a name to the frame for targeting hyperlinks. Not supported by XHTML, where `id` should be used instead.
width	The width of the frame. Most browsers default to 300.

continued →

\<img\>

This is used to add images to the page. As an empty element, it must be properly closed. The common attributes, as well as the following attributes, are supported:

ATTRIBUTE	DESCRIPTION
alt	Required. Text equivalent to the image.
height	Optional. Instructs the browser as to the height of the image, which can speed display and ensure that the layout does not collapse if the image is not displayed.
ismap	Optional. Defines the image as a server-side image map. Rarely used.
longdesc	Optional. Provides a path to a document that describes the image in detail.
name	Assigns a name to the image, which can be used by JavaScript. Not supported by XHTML, where id should be used instead.
src	Required. The path to the source image file.
usemap	Optional. Provides a reference to a map element on the page.
width	Optional. Instructs the browser as to the width of the image, which can speed display and ensure that the layout does not collapse if the image is not displayed.

\<input\>

Used to create text field, check box, radio, hidden, file, and image form controls, as well as buttons, within forms, depending on the specified type. It must appear within the \<form\> tag. As an empty element, it must be properly closed. The common attributes, as well as the following attributes, are supported:

ATTRIBUTE	DESCRIPTION
accept	Optional. List of MIME types to allow. Only used with type="file".
accesskey	Optional. Sets a keyboard shortcut to give the field focus.
alt	Required alternative text if type="image". Not supported by other types.
checked	Optional. Preselects the field. Only used with type="radio" or type="checkbox".
disabled	Optional. Causes the field to be unselectable.
ismap	Rarely used attribute is type="image" and the image is a server-side image map.
maxlength	Optional. Sets a maximum number of characters that may be entered in the field. Only applies to type="text" and type="password".
name	Required. A name for the form field. Not supported by XHTML, where id should be used instead.
readonly	Optional. For type="text", causes the text in the field to be unchangeable by the user. Must be used with a value.
size	Optional. Physical width of the field. May also be set through CSS.
src	Optional. Provides a path to the image. Only used with type="image".
tabindex	Optional. Controls the order in which the field will gain focus if the user is tabbing through the page. Must be an integer between 0 and 32,767.

\<input\> (continued)

ATTRIBUTE	DESCRIPTION
`type`	Required. Sets the type of the form control. Possible values are `button`, `checkbox`, `file`, `hidden`, `image`, `password`, `radio`, `reset`, `submit`, and `text`.
`usemap`	Optional. If `type="image"`, provides a path to the map element if the image is an image map.
`value`	Provides a value for the field. Required if `type="checkbox"`, `type="radio"`, or `type="hidden"`. Optional for `type="text"`, `type="submit"`, and `type="reset"`. Not supported on other types.

\<ins\>

Used to mark text to be inserted into a future draft of a document. The common attributes, as well as the following attributes, are supported:

ATTRIBUTE	DESCRIPTION
`cite`	Optional. Provides a reference, often the identification of the person authorized to insert the text.
`datetime`	Optional. The timestamp of the insertion. See the note above under `del` for proper formatting.

\<kbd\>

This marks text that should be keyboarded in; usually used in tutorials. Browsers will display text in a monospaced font, such as Courier, by default. This element only supports the common attributes.

\<label\>

This denotes text as a label, used on form fields. It must appear with form. The common attributes, as well as the following attributes, are supported:

ATTRIBUTE	DESCRIPTION
`accesskey`	Optional. Sets a keyboard shortcut to give the associated field focus.
`for`	Optional. If the `label` tag is not wrapped around the text and the form control, you can use the `for` attribute to associate the two. The `for`'s value will be equal to the `id` of the control.

\<legend\>

This marks text as a label for a `fieldset`. It must appear as the first child of `fieldset`. The common attributes, as well as the following attribute, are supported:

ATTRIBUTE	DESCRIPTION
`accesskey`	Optional. Sets a keyboard shortcut to give the associated field focus.

\<li\>

This element denotes an individual item in an unordered or ordered list. It must appear within either `ol` or `ul`. This element only supports the common attributes.

\<link\>

This links the document to a related external resource, most commonly CSS. It must be a child of `<head>`. It is always optional, and it can be repeated. As an empty element, it must be properly closed. The common attributes, as well as the following attributes, are supported:

ATTRIBUTE	DESCRIPTION
`charset`	Optional. Defines the character encoding of the external resource.
`href`	Required. The path to the external resource.
`hreflang`	Optional. Identifies the language of the external resource.
`media`	Optional. Identifies the device on which the external resource should be displayed. Possible values are `all` (the default), `aural`, `braille`, `handheld`, `print`, `projection`, `tv`, `tty`, and `screen`.
`rel`	Required. The relationship of the other document. Possible values include `alternate stylesheet`, `appendix`, `bookmark`, `chapter`, `contents`, `copyright`, `glossary`, `help`, `index`, `next`, `prev`, `previous`, `section`, `shortcut icon`, `start`, `stylesheet`, and `subsection`.
`rev`	Optional. The opposite of `rel`, this attribute specifies the reverse relationship of the link.
`type`	Required. The MIME type of the external resource.

continued →

<map>

This is the parent element for an image map, and it requires one or more child `area` elements. Note that `id` is required in XHTML. The common attributes, as well as the following attribute, are supported:

ATTRIBUTE	DESCRIPTION
name	Required in HTML. A name that is used to associate images with this map code. Not supported by XHTML.

<meta>

This element defines additional data about the document. It is always optional and it can be repeated. As an empty element, it must be properly closed. Note that the common attributes are not supported for this element, except `lang` and `xml:lang`. Either `http-equiv` or `name` must always be used.

ATTRIBUTE	DESCRIPTION
content	Required. Defines the content of the information.
http-equiv	Sets a value for an HTTP header. Possible values are `content-type`, `expires`, `refresh`, and `set-cookie`.
name	Names the content. Possible values are `author`, `description`, `keywords`, `generated`, `revised`, or a user-defined value.
scheme	Provides more context for the browser to use in interpreting the data.

<object>

This is used to embed external files, usually multimedia such as Flash or QuickTime. The common attributes, as well as the following attributes, are supported. All attributes are optional.

ATTRIBUTE	DESCRIPTION
accesskey	Defines a keyboard shortcut to access this object.
archive	URLs to relevant resources.
classid	Sets a Windows Registry key for the plug-in needed for the object. Not supported on Gecko-based browsers such as Mozilla Firefox.
codebase	Used to resolve URLs within the object. Usually set to the base URL of the current page.
codetype	The MIME type of the code.
data	The path to the object's data.
declare	Defines an object that should be declared rather than instantiated.
height	The height of the object.
name	Names the object. XHTML 1.1 removed this in favor of `id`.
noexternaldata	Denotes that the object requires no data.
standby	Text to display while the object loads.

<object> (continued)

ATTRIBUTE	DESCRIPTION
tabindex	Controls the order in which the object will gain focus if the user is tabbing through the page. Must be an integer between 0 and 32,767.
type	The MIME type of the object's data.
usemap	Specifies an image map to use with the object.
width	The width of the object.

<ol>

This element marks an ordered, or numbered, list. It must contain one or more <li> tags for the items. This element only supports the common attributes.

<optgroup>

This groups a set of option tags within a form's select list. Most browsers display optgroup as a bold unselectable item. It must appear within select and must contain one or more option tags. Optgroups may not be nested. The common attributes, as well as the following attributes, are supported:

ATTRIBUTE	DESCRIPTION
disabled	Optional. Disables the group of options, making them unselectable.
label	Required. The text to display in bold (for Windows) or as the top-level menu (for Macintosh).

<option>

This will set individual items within a select list. It must appear within either select or optgroup. The common attributes, as well as the following attributes, are supported. All attributes are optional.

ATTRIBUTE	DESCRIPTION
disabled	Disables the options, making it unselectable.
label	The text to display to the user. If not provided, value will be used.
selected	Preselects the option, causing it to appear by default in the drop-down list.
value	The value of the selected item.

<p>

A paragraph of text. This element only supports the common attributes. Other attributes such as align have been deprecated in favor of style sheets.

continued →

\<param>

Parameters for controls of an object can be set with this element. It must appear within `object`. As an empty element, it must be properly closed. The common attributes, as well as the following attributes, are supported:

ATTRIBUTE	DESCRIPTION
name	Required. A unique name for the parameter.
type	Optional. The MIME type of the parameter.
value	Optional. The parameter's value.
valuetype	Optional. The type of the parameter's value. Allowed values are `data`, `ref`, and `object`.

\<pre>

This denotes preformatted text. Text within these tags will respect whitespace. It is very rarely used. This element only supports the common attributes in HTML. In addition to the common attributes, XHTML supports one additional attribute:

ATTRIBUTE	DESCRIPTION
xml:space	Denotes that the parser should preserve the whitespace. The only legal value is `preserve`.

\<q>

This element designates a short quotation used within text. Some browsers will automatically place double quotation marks around the text. The common attributes, as well as the following attribute, are supported. All attributes are optional.

ATTRIBUTE	DESCRIPTION
cite	A reference to the source of the quotation.

\<samp>

This can be used to show code samples. Browsers will display text using a monospaced font. This element only supports the common attributes.

\<script>

This element designates a block of code containing some kind of client-side script, usually JavaScript. It is legal in either the `head` or the `body`. The common attributes, as well as the following attributes, are supported:

ATTRIBUTE	DESCRIPTION
charset	Optional. The character encoding of the script if referencing an external script.
defer	Optional. Instructs the browser that the script will not generate output, so it can continue rendering the page even if the script has not yet executed. The only legal value is `defer`.
src	Optional. A path to an external script block. Note that if used, the `script` tag will be empty. However, it is not legal to close it with a trailing slash. Instead, you must provide an explicit closing `script` tag.
type	Required. The MIME type of the script. Usually `"text/javascript"`.
xml:space	Optional, only supported in XHTML. Instructs the parser to preserve whitespace. The only legal value is `preserve`.

\<select>

This creates a drop-down menu form control. It must be used within `form` and must contain one or more `option` or `optgroup` tags. The common attributes, as well as the following attributes, are supported:

ATTRIBUTE	DESCRIPTION
accesskey	Optional. Sets a keyboard shortcut to give the field focus.
disabled	Optional. Causes the field to be unselectable.
multiple	Optional. Allows for multiple selections. HTML documents may present this attribute without a value; in XHTML, it must have a value of `multiple`.
name	Required. The name of the control.

<select> (continued)

ATTRIBUTE	DESCRIPTION
size	Optional. The number of options to display onscreen. If `multiple` is not used, the default is 1, whereas if `multiple` is used, the default will vary from browser to browser.
tabindex	Optional. Controls the order in which the field will gain focus if the user is tabbing through the page. Must be an integer between 1 and 32,767.

<small>

This renders the text in a smaller typeface. Another of the purely presentational elements that has remained in the language, although it should ideally be avoided in favor of style sheets. This element only supports the common attributes.

<span>

This can be used to apply a style definition where no other inline element exists or makes logical sense. This element only supports the common attributes. Most frequently, you will apply either an `id` or `class` (or possibly both) to reference a selector in your CSS.

<strong>

This creates strongly emphasized text. Browsers display text within `strong` using a bold typeface. This element only supports the common attributes.

<sup>

This is used for superscript, which displays text above the normal line of text. This element only supports the common attributes.

<style>

This element defines an embedded style sheet. It is optional. Because XHTML documents are technically XML, a properly formed document would require the contents of the `style` element to be enclosed in a CDATA section. However, browsers may not properly support this, and some will not correctly render the CSS if it is included, so it is often ignored. Note that the common attributes are not supported for this element.

ATTRIBUTE	DESCRIPTION
media	Optional. Identifies the media type to which the styles should be applied. See the attribute's listing under `link`, previously in this section, for allowed values.
title	Optional. Identifies an embedded style sheet.
type	Required. The MIME type of the contents. Will be set to `text/css`.
xml:space	Optional. Only valid for XHTML, it instructs the parser to preserve whitespace in the style sheet. The only valid value is `preserve`.

<sub>

This is used for subscript, which displays text below the baseline. This element only supports the common attributes.

<table>

This designates a table. It must include one or more `tr` elements, which must in turn include one or more `th` or `td` elements. It can optionally include a single `caption` element, a single `thead` element, a single `tfoot` element, and a single `tbody` element, none of which need to appear together, and may include one or more `colspan` and `col` elements. The common attributes, as well as the following attributes, are supported. All attributes are optional.

ATTRIBUTE	DESCRIPTION
border	The width of the border of the table. A value of 0 will cause the border to not render at all. Technically, the values are given in pixels, although most browsers will display a 3-D effect on the border, causing it to be thicker than actually specified. It is one of several purely presentational attributes that are still supported but should be avoided in favor of style sheets.
cellpadding	The padding within the cell of a table. As not all browsers support the CSS `padding` property for table cells, this is still commonly used.

continued

continued →

\<table\> (continued)

ATTRIBUTE	DESCRIPTION
cellspacing	The space between cells of a table. While presentational, until browser support for margins on table cells or table-collapse improves, this will continue to be commonly used and it is in fact supported by XHTML Strict.
frame	Determines on which sides of the table the border should be drawn. Allowed values are above, below, border, box, hsides, lhs, rhs, vsides, and void. The same effect can be achieved with greater control through style sheets.
rules	Determines where to draw rules — the lines between the cells — in the table. While part of the specification, it is not widely supported. Possible values are all, cols, groups, none, and rows. The same effect can be achieved with greater control and better support through style sheets.
summary	A text description of the table. Used to improve accessibility.
width	The width of the table, specified in either pixels or percentages. Another presentational attribute that is still supported but should be replaced by style sheets.

\<tbody\>

This defines a set of rows as the body of the table. It is useful for applying styles to a section of the table. In some browsers, tables with tbody will scroll, and others provide better printed output. It must appear within table and must contain at least one tr. The common attributes, as well as the following attributes, are supported. All are optional.

ATTRIBUTE	DESCRIPTION
align	The alignment of text in the cells within the section. A purely presentational attribute that is nonetheless still in the specification. Allowed values are left, center, right, justify, and char.
char	Sets a character by which the text in the cells should be aligned, if align is set to char. Not supported by browsers.
charoff	Sets the offset of the alignment character. Not supported by any browser.
valign	The vertical alignment of text within the cells of the section. A purely presentational attribute that is nonetheless still in the specification. Allowed values are top, middle, bottom, and baseline.

\<td\>

This represents table data, used to designate a cell of a table. It must be used within tr. Any elements allowed within body are allowed within td. The common attributes, as well as the following attributes, are supported. All attributes are optional.

ATTRIBUTE	DESCRIPTION
abbr	Sets an abbreviated version of the cell's contents, to be read by a screen reader.
align	See the description under thead.
axis	Conceptualizes the contents of the cell for possibly organizing and rendering the table differently.
char	See the description under thead.
charoff	See the description under thead.
colspan	Sets the number of columns across which this cell should span.
headers	Defines the headers for this cell. The value is a space-separated list of the ids of the appropriate header cells.
rowspan	Sets the number of rows which this cell should span.
scope	Specifies if this cell provides header information. Possible values are row, col, rowgroup, and colgroup.
valign	See the description under thead.

\<textarea\>

This defines a multiline text field. It must appear within `form`. The common attributes, as well as the following attributes, are supported:

ATTRIBUTE	DESCRIPTION
cols	Required. The physical width of the text area, in characters.
disabled	Optional. Disables the field, causing it and its contents to be unselectable.
name	Required. The name of the field.
readonly	Optional. Causes the user to be unable to modify the contents.
rows	Required. The physical height of the field, in rows of text.

\<tfoot\>

This defines a row or rows as the footer of the table. Some browsers will allow for greater control of the table if using this along with `thead` and `tbody`. For example, most tables will repeat the contents of `tfoot` at the bottom of each page if a very long table is printed. It is also useful for applying styles to the table. It must appear within `table`, and oddly, after the `thead` but before the `tbody`, although the browser will render it below the `tbody` rows. It must contain at least one `tr`. This element supports the same attributes as `tbody`. See that listing for details.

\<th\>

This is used in place of `td` for header cells in a table. The default display of `th` content is bold and centered. It must be used within `tr` and usually within a `thead` section. This element supports the same attributes as `td`. See that listing for details.

\<thead\>

This is used in conjunction with `tbody` and `tfoot` to define logical sections of a table. It must appear within `table` and must contain at least one `tr`. This element supports the same attributes as `tbody`. See that listing for details.

\<title\>

This sets the title of the document. It must be a child of `<head>`. It takes no attributes and is required for all documents.

\<tr\>

This defines a table row. It must be placed within `table`, `thead`, `tbody`, or `tfoot` and must contain one or more `th` or `td` tags. Text or other content cannot be placed directly within a `tr`. The common attributes, as well as the following attributes, are supported. All attributes are optional.

ATTRIBUTE	DESCRIPTION
align	Determines the alignment of text within the column's cells. Even though this is presentational, it has not been deprecated and is valid even in XHTML 1.0 Strict and XHTML 1.1. Possible values are `left`, `right`, `center`, `justify`, and `char`.
char	Specifies the character to which the text in the column should be aligned if `align` is set to `char`. The default is a decimal point. Not supported by most browsers.
charoff	Sets the offset distance to the first character for alignment. Not generally supported by browsers.
valign	Determines the vertical alignment within the cell. Like align, this is purely presentational but has not been deprecated. Possible values are `top`, `middle`, `bottom`, and `baseline`.

\<tt\>

This denotes teletype text, usually rendered in a monospaced font such as Courier. This element only supports the common attributes.

\<ul\>

This sets an unordered, or bulleted, list. It must contain one or more `li` tags for each item of the list. This element only supports the common attributes.

\<var\>

This designates text as being a variable, such as in a program. Browsers will display its contents as italic by default. This element only supports the common attributes.

XHTML Frameset

hile frames are being used with decreased frequency, they are still supported under the XHTML Frameset specification. In order for a frames document to validate, it must use the Frameset document type declaration. Frames pages support the following elements and attributes.

<frame>

This element defines an individual frame in a frameset. It is only valid in documents using the XHTML 1 Frameset document type definition. One `frame` element is required for each row or column defined in the parent frameset. As an empty element, it must be properly closed. The common attributes, as well as the following attributes, are supported:

ATTRIBUTE	DESCRIPTION
frameborder	Determines whether a border will appear between frames. Valid values are 0 for no border and 1 for a border.
longdesc	Sets a path to a document to provide a detailed description of the frame and its contents, similar to the attribute's use with img. No browser supports it.
marginheight	The height, in pixels, of the inner margin between the top and bottom edges of the frame and its contents.
marginwidth	The width, in pixels, of the inner margin between the left and right edges of the frame and its contents.
name	Optional but recommended. Uniquely names each frame. Not supported in XHTML, which uses id instead.
noresize	Optional. Instructs the browser to allow or disallow user resizing of the frame. The only legal value is noresize, although HTML documents may present the attribute with no value.
scrolling	Optional. Instructs the browser to allow or disallow scrolling on the frame. Possible values are auto (the default), yes, and no.
src	Required. Defines the path to the document that will fill the frame.

<frameset>

This defines a group of frames. It is only valid in documents using the XHTML 1.0 Frameset document type definition. It will appear in lieu of the body, and it can take itself as a child. The common attributes, as well as the following attributes, are supported. All attributes are optional.

ATTRIBUTE	DESCRIPTION
cols	Defines the size of the columns into which the browser window will be divided. Can be specified in either pixels, percentages, or a wildcard.
rows	Defines the size of the rows into which the browser window will be divided. Can be specified in either pixels, percentages, or a wildcard.

<noframe>

This defines a section of the page to be displayed if the browser does not support frames. Browsers that support frames will completely ignore the contents of `noframe`. As only very old browsers do not support frames, its usefulness is questionable, although providing content in `noframe` can improve search engine results. Its first child must be `body`. All elements and attributes supported by XHTML Transitional are allowed within the body of the noframe. It takes no attributes.

Event Handlers

JavaScript events can be called from the XHTML or HTML document through an *event handler*, an attribute in the element designed to call the event.

Any element that supports the other common attributes supports the following event handlers:

ATTRIBUTE	DESCRIPTION
onclick	Triggered by the user clicking the mouse button once on the element's content.
ondblclick	Triggered by the user clicking the mouse button twice on the element's content.
onkeydown	Triggered by the user pressing and holding down a key on the keyboard.
onkeypress	Triggered by the user pressing down a key on the keyboard. In practice, most browsers treat onkeydown and onkeypress the same.
onkeyup	Triggered by the user releasing a previously-held key on the keyboard.
onmousedown	Triggered by the user pressing and holding the mouse button while over the element's content.
onmousemove	Triggered by the user moving the mouse.
onmouseout	Triggered by the user moving the mouse away from the element's content.
onmouseover	Triggered by the user moving the mouse over the element's content.
onmouseup	Triggered by the user releasing the mouse buttons while over the element's content.

All form controls and the anchor element support all of the previous event handlers, as well as

ATTRIBUTE	DESCRIPTION
onblur	Triggered when the form field or anchor loses focus, usually by the user either tabbing or clicking into another field or anchor.
onfocus	Triggered when the form field or anchor gains focus, usually by the user either tabbing or clicking into the field or onto the anchor.

The input, select, and textarea elements also support all the previous event handlers, as well as

ATTRIBUTE	DESCRIPTION
onchange	Triggered when the contents of the field change, such as the user selecting another option in a select list or overwriting default text in a text box or text area.

The input and textarea elements, but not select, further support

ATTRIBUTE	DESCRIPTION
onselect	Triggered when the text box or text area's contents are selected, usually by the user clicking and dragging over the contents.

The form element supports all of the events mentioned in the first section, as well as

ATTRIBUTE	DESCRIPTION
onreset	Triggered when the user clicks a button with a type of reset.
onsubmit	Triggered when the user clicks a button with a type of submit.

The body element supports

ATTRIBUTE	DESCRIPTION
onload	Triggered when the page initially loads in the browser. This is the default event, and any JavaScript not contained within a function will be automatically executed.
onunload	Triggered when the page unloads from the browser. Unloading occurs when the user goes to another page either by clicking a link, typing an address manually, or clicking a favorite or bookmark, or when closing the browser. In general, users will find most onunload scripts extremely annoying, so they should be used with caution.

Deprecated Tags

X HTML 1.0 deprecated many tags from older versions of HTML, meaning that they are no longer considered part of the specification and should not be used. Primarily, these tags represent presentational code — tags that exist solely to describe how something should be displayed, rather than its logical place in the structure of the document.

While many of these elements are supported by browsers and will still work, they should be avoided.

<applet> This was used to embed a Java applet; the `object` element can be used instead.	**<embed>** This was used to embed external media files. Officially, the `object` element has replaced it, but Internet Explorer still requires its use.
<b> This designated text to be displayed as bold; either `<strong>` or CSS can be used instead.	**<font>** This set the size, color, and/or typeface of text; CSS can be used instead.
<basefont> This set a default font for the document; CSS can be used instead.	**<i>** This set text as italic; the `em` element or CSS can be used instead.
<bgsound> This added a background sound to the document. It was never an official part of the HTML specification, and it only worked in Internet Explorer. There is no real equivalent to this element in any modern specification.	**<isindex>** This was an early method of identifying that a document should be indexed by search engines. It has no known modern browser or search engine support, and proper, valid markup and other search engine techniques should be used instead.
<big> This made text one size bigger; CSS can be used instead.	**<keygen>** This was an early, Netscape-only attempt at securing form submissions. It has never been supported by any other browser, and even modern versions of Netscape do not support it. Secure Sockets Layer is the modern replacement.
<blink> A Netscape-only tag that caused text to blink, it was never officially recognized by the specification. A combination of CSS and JavaScript could be used to achieve the same result.	
	<layer> An early Netscape-only block element for styles and positioning, this was replaced by the `div` element.
<center> This centered a block of code on the page; CSS can be used instead.	**<marquee>** This was Microsoft's answer to `blink` although it created scrolling text. Although many non-Microsoft browsers (including Firefox) support this element, it has never been part of any specification. Cross-browser, standards-based scrolling text can be achieved through JavaScript and CSS.
<dir> This created a directory list; the `ul` element is most often used in its place.	

\<menu\>

This was another early list type. Most designers rely on unordered lists for menus.

\<multicol\>

A Netscape-only tag for generating multi-column text. It was never supported outside of the Netscape browser. Modern multi-column layouts are achieved through CSS.

\<nobr\>

This designates a block of text that will not wrap, even if it results in horizontal scrolling. There is a CSS property that achieves the same affect, but few designers use it as horizontal scrolling is widely regarded as an effect to be avoided.

\<noembed\>

This set content, usually text, that would appear if embedding an object via the embed element failed. As embed is no longer supported, it logically follows that this is not either.

\<nolayer\>

This set content to display if the page used the layer element so that non-Netscape browsers could have content to display. The universal support for div makes this meaningless.

\<noscript\>

This designated alternative content for browsers before the script element was widely supported. Modern universal support for script renders this moot.

\<s\>

This element created the same effect as strike, so it was removed to avoid redundancy.

\<small\>

This rendered text one size smaller, and has been replaced by CSS.

\<spacer\>

This created a specified amount of space in early Netscape browsers, and was primarily used to hold together complex table layouts. It has been replaced by CSS positioning.

\<strike\>

This created strikethrough text and has been replaced by CSS.

\<u\>

This underlined text. It was not recommended as it confused users who may have thought that the text was a hyperlink, although the effect can still be achieved through CSS.

\<wbr\>

This indicated a potential word breakpoint, and was used within the nobr element. As nobr is no longer valid, it made no sense to keep this element.

Named Colors

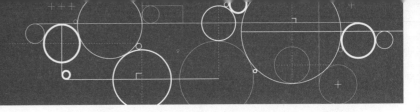

Specifying colors by name, rather than hexadecimal or RGB (red, green, blue), is considered by many as the most user-friendly method. The following reference provides the names supported in the XHTML specification, and their hexadecimal equivalent.

Supported Colors

According to the XHTML Specification, only sixteen colors are supported by name:

COLOR	HEXADECIMAL
aqua	#00FFFF
black	#000000
blue	#0000FF
fuchsia	#FF00FF
green	#00FF00
gray	#808080
lime	#00FF00
maroon	#800000
navy	#000080
olive	#808000
purple	#800080
red	#FF0000
silver	#C0C0C0
teal	#008080
white	#FFFFFF
yellow	#FFFF00

Character Entities

The following reference lists every character entity supported by XHTML, its character equivalent, and the ASCII character code that can be used in its place.

ASCII Characters

Note that the ' entity is only valid in XHTML, not HTML.

CHARACTER	DESCRIPTION
&amp;	ampersand, &
&apos;	apostrophe, '
&gt;	greater than symbol, >
&lt;	less than symbol, <
&quot;	double quotation mark, "

Latin-1 Characters

CHARACTER	DESCRIPTION	CHARACTER	DESCRIPTION
	non-breaking space	&iexcl;	inverted exclamation mark, ¡
&cent;	cent sign, ¢	&pound;	pound sign, £
&curren;	currency sign, ¤	&yen;	yen sign, ¥
&brvbar;	broken vertical bar, ¦	&sect;	section sign, §
&uml;	spacing diaeresis, ¨	&copy;	copyright sign, ©
&ordf;	feminine ordinal indicator, ª	&laquo;	left-pointing double angle quotation mark, «
&not;	not sign, ¬	&shy;	soft hyphen, -
&reg;	registered trademark sign, ®	&macr;	spacing macron, ¯
&deg;	degree sign, °	&plusmn;	plus-or-minus sign, ±
&sup2;	superscript two, ²	&sup3;	superscript three, ³
&acute;	acute accent, ´	&micro;	micro sign, µ
&para;	paragraph sign, ¶	&middot;	middle dot, ·
&cedil;	cedilla, ¸	&sup1;	superscript one, ¹
&ordm;	masculine ordinal indicator, º	&raquo;	right-pointing double angle quotation mark, »
&frac14;	fraction one quarter, ¼	&frac12;	fraction one half, ½
&frac34;	fraction three quarters, ¾	&iquest;	inverted question mark, ¿
&Agrave;	Latin capital letter A with grave, À	&Aacute;	Latin capital letter A with acute, Á

continued

Character
Entities (continued)

Latin-1 Characters (continued)

CHARACTER	DESCRIPTION	CHARACTER	DESCRIPTION
&Acirc;	Latin capital letter A with circumflex, Â	&Atilde;	Latin capital letter A with tilde, Ã
Auml;	Latin capital letter A with diaeresis, Ä	&Aring;	Latin capital letter A with ring above, Å
&AElig;	Latin capital ligature AE, Æ	&Ccedil;	Latin capital letter C with cedilla, Ç
&Egrave;	Latin capital letter E with grave, È	&Eacute;	Latin capital letter E with acute, É
&Ecirc;	Latin capital letter E with circumflex, Ê	&Euml;	Latin capital letter E with diaeresis, Ë
&Igrave;	Latin capital letter I with grave, Ì	&Iacute;	Latin capital letter I with acute, Í
&Icirc;	Latin capital letter I with circumflex, Î	&Iuml;	Latin capital letter I with diaeresis, Ï
&ETH;	Latin capital letter ETH, Ð	&Ntilde;	Latin capital letter N with tilde, Ñ
&Ograve;	Latin capital letter O with grave, Ò	&Oacute;	Latin capital letter O with acute, Ó
&Ocirc;	Latin capital letter O with circumflex, Ô	&Otilde;	Latin capital letter O with tilde, Õ
&Ouml;	Latin capital letter O with diaeresis, Ö	&Oslash;	Latin capital letter O with stroke, Ø
&Ugrave;	Latin capital letter U with grave, Ù	&Uacute;	Latin capital letter U with acute, Ú
&Ucirc;	Latin capital letter U with circumflex, Û	&Uuml;	Latin capital letter U with diaeresis, Ü
&Yacute;	Latin capital letter Y with acute, Ý	&THORN;	Latin capital letter THORN, Þ
&szlig;	German sz ligature, β	&agrave;	Latin small letter a with grave, à
&aacute;	Latin small letter a with acute, á	&acirc;	Latin small letter a with circumflex, â
&atilde;	Latin small letter a with tilde, ã	&auml;	Latin small letter a with diaeresis, ä
&aring;	Latin small letter a with ring above, å	&aelig;	Latin small ligature ae, æ
&ccedil;	Latin small letter c with cedilla, ç	&egrave;	Latin small letter e with grave, è
&eacute;	Latin small letter e with acute, é	&ecirc;	Latin small letter e with circumflex, ê
&euml;	Latin small letter e with diaeresis, ë	&igrave;	Latin small letter i with grave, ì
&iacute;	Latin small letter i with acute, í	&icirc;	Latin small letter i with circumflex, î
&iuml;	Latin small letter i with diaeresis, ï	&eth;	Latin small letter eth, ð
&ntilde;	Latin small letter n with tilde, ñ	&ograve;	Latin small letter o with grave, ò
&oacute;	Latin small letter o with acute, ó	&ocirc;	Latinsmall letter o with circumflex, ô
&otilde;	Latin small letter o with tilde, õ	&ouml;	Latin small letter o with diaeresis, ö
&oslash;	Latin small letter o with stroke, ø	&ugrave;	Latin small letter u with grave, ù
&uacute;	Latin small letter u with acute, ú	&ucirc;	Latin small letter u with circumflex, û
&uuml;	Latin small letter u with diaeresis, ü	&yacute;	Latin small letter y with acute, ý
&thorn;	Latin small letter thorn, þ	&yuml;	Latin small letter y with diaeresis, ÿ

Latin Extended-A

CHARACTER	DESCRIPTION
&OElig;	capital ligature OE, Œ
&oelig;	lowercase ligature oe, œ
&Scaron;	capital S with caron, Š
&scaron;	lowercase s with caron, š
&Yuml,	capital Y with umlaut, Ÿ

Latin Extended-B

CHARACTER	DESCRIPTION
&fnof;	small f with hook, ƒ

Spacing Modifiers

CHARACTER	DESCRIPTION
&circ,	circumflex accent, ^
&tilde,	tilde, ~

Greek

CHARACTER	DESCRIPTION
&Alpha;	Greek capital letter alpha, A
&Beta;	Greek capital letter beta, B
&Gamma;	Greek capital letter gamma, Γ
&Delta;	Greek capital letter delta, Δ
&Epsilon;	Greek capital letter epsilon, E
&Zeta;	Greek capital letter zeta, Z
&Eta;	Greek capital letter eta, H
&Theta;	Greek capital letter theta, Θ
&Iota;	Greek capital letter iota, I
&Kappa;	Greek capital letter kappa, K
&Lambda;	Greek capital letter lambda, λ
&Mu;	Greek capital letter mu, M
&Nu;	Greek capital letter nu, N
&Xi;	Greek capital letter xi, Ξ
&Omicron;	Greek capital letter omicron, O
&Pi;	Greek capital letter pi, Π

CHARACTER	DESCRIPTION
&Rho;	Greek capital letter rho, P
&Sigma;	Greek capital letter sigma, Σ
&Tau;	Greek capital letter tau, T
&Upsilon;	Greek capital letter upsilon, Y
&Phi;	Greek capital letter phi, Φ
&Chi;	Greek capital letter chi, X
&Psi;	Greek capital letter psi, Ψ
&Omega;	Greek capital letter omega, Ω
&alpha;	Greek small letter alpha, α
&beta;	Greek small letter beta, β
&gamma;	Greek small letter gamma, γ
&delta;	Greek small letter delta, δ
&epsilon;	Greek small letter epsilon, ε
&zeta;	Greek small letter zeta, ζ
&eta;	Greek small letter eta, η
&theta;	Greek small letter theta, θ
&iota;	Greek small letter iota, ι
&kappa;	Greek small letter kappa, κ
&lambda;	Greek small letter lambda, λ
&mu;	Greek small letter mu, μ
&nu;	Greek small letter nu, ν
&xi;	Greek small letter xi, ξ
&omicron;	Greek small letter omicron, o
&pi;	Greek small letter pi, π
&rho;	Greek small letter rho, ρ
&sigmaf;	Greek small letter final sigma, ς
&sigma;	Greek small letter sigma, σ
&tau;	Greek small letter tau, τ
&upsilon;	Greek small letter upsilon, υ
&phi;	Greek small letter phi, φ
&chi;	Greek small letter chi, χ
&psi;	Greek small letter psi, ψ
&omega;	Greek small letter omega, ω
&thetasym;	Greek small letter theta symbol, υ
&upsih;	Greek upsilon with hook symbol, λ
&piv;	Greek pi symbol, ϖ

continued →

Character
Entities (continued)

General Punctuation

CHARACTER	DESCRIPTION
&bull;	bullet, ·
&hellip;	horizontal ellipsis, ...
&prime;	prime, '
&Prime;	double prime, "
&oline;	overline, ¯
&frasl;	fraction slash, /

Letter-like Symbols

CHARACTER	DESCRIPTION
&weierp;	script capital P, ℘
&image;	blackletter capital I, ℑ
&real;	blackletter capital R, ℜ
&trade;	trade mark sign, ™
&alefsym;	alef symbol, ℵ

Arrows

CHARACTER	DESCRIPTION
&larr;	leftward arrow, ←
&uarr;	upward arrow, ↑
&rarr;	rightward arrow, →
&darr;	downward arrow, ↓
&harr;	left-right arrow, ↔
&crarr;	downward arrow with corner leftward, ↵
&lArr;	leftward double arrow, ⇐
&uArr;	upward double arrow, ⇑
&rArr;	rightward double arrow, ⇒
&dArr;	downward double arrow, ⇓
&hArr;	left-right double arrow, ⇔

Mathematical Operators

CHARACTER	DESCRIPTION
&forall;	for all, $\forall$
&part;	partial differential, ∂
&exist;	there exists, $\exists$
&empty;	empty set, $\varnothing$
&nabla;	nabla, ∇
&isin;	element of, $\in$
&notin;	not an element of, $\notin$
&ni;	contains as member, $\ni$
&prod;	n-ary product, Π
&sum;	n-ary sumation, Σ
&minus;	minus sign, $-$
&times;	multiplication sign, $\times$
&divide;	division sign, $\div$
&lowast;	asterisk operator, $*$
&radic;	square root, $\surd$
&prop;	proportional to, $\propto$
&infin;	infinity, $\cdot$
&ang;	angle, $\angle$
&and;	logical and, $\wedge$
&or;	logical or, $\vee$
&cap;	intersection, $\cap$
&cup;	union, $\cup$
&int;	integral, $\int$
&there4;	therefore, $\therefore$
&sim;	tilde operator, $\sim$
&cong;	approximately equal to, $\cong$
&asymp;	almost equal to, $\approx$
&ne;	not equal to, $\neq$
&equiv;	identical to, $\equiv$
&le;	less than or equal to, $\leq$

Mathematical Operators (continued)

CHARACTER	DESCRIPTION
&ge;	greater than or equal to, $\geq$
&sub;	subset of, $\subset$
&sup;	superset of, $\supset$
&nsub;	not a subset of, $\not\subset$
&sube;	subset of or equal to, $\subseteq$
&supe;	superset of or equal to, $\supseteq$
&oplus;	circled plus, $\oplus$
&otimes;	circled times, $\otimes$
&perp;	up tack, $\perp$
&sdot;	dot operator, .

Miscellaneous Technical

CHARACTER	DESCRIPTION
&lceil;	left ceiling, $\lceil$
&rceil;	right ceiling, $\rceil$
&lfloor;	left floor, $\lfloor$
&rfloor;	right floor, $\rfloor$
&lang;	left-pointing angle bracket, $\langle$
&rang;	right-pointing angle bracket, $\rangle$

Geometric Shapes

CHARACTER	DESCRIPTION
&loz;	lozenge, $\lozenge$

Miscellaneous Symbols

CHARACTER	DESCRIPTION
&spades;	black spade suit, ♠
&clubs;	black club suit, ♣
&hearts;	black heart suit, ♥
&diams;	black diamond suit, ♦

XHTML 1.1

The newest version of XHTML is version 1.1. The primary goal was to modularize the language. Gone are the so-called "flavors" using the different document type declarations. Instead, the hope was that developers would apply only those "modules" of the language necessary for the goals of their page.

While this would potentially expand the language and allow for more extensibility, its overly complex approach has acted as more of a deterrent to its adoption. XHTML 1.1 is currently in the Working Draft stage at the W3C, meaning that it is not yet a recognized standard, although some browser support exists for some of its features.

The Future

The W3C and other standards organizations continue to press ahead with new revisions to the languages. Below is a brief synopsis of the state of the next versions of XHTML, HTML, and CSS as of this writing. Please note that everything mentioned next is subject to change in the final specifications.

XHTML 2.0

The W3C plans to continue the push towards modularization with the next version of XHTML.

XHTML 2.0 is also in Working Draft stage, and it is a more controversial version as it breaks backward compatibility with XHTML 1.0, 1.1, and HTML. It will introduce such advancements as XForms and XFrames, both of which serve as XML-based replacements for their HTML predecessors. No current browser supports XHTML 2.0.

HTML 5.0

Due to the unpopularity of XHTML 1.1 and 2.0's complex modularization schemes, a group within the W3C began work on a new version of HTML instead. They plan to keep the three "flavor" system of the current specification, while adding many new elements to assist in design.

LOGICAL LAYOUT CONTAINERS

Today, CSS-based layouts rely on the `div` element with logical `id`s, such as "header" or "content." While this system certainly works, many argue that `div` has no real semantic meaning, and the natural inconsistency that will arise from different designers choosing different `id`s can cause problems when trying to port Web pages to other sites. Therefore, HTML 5.0 will contain semantically logical container elements such as `header`, `content`, `sidebar`, and `footer`. The current plan is that these elements will be block elements and will be treated by future browsers in the same way they currently handle the `div` element, but the fact that they will be separate elements will make creating style sheets easier, and should improve accessibility as well.

NAVIGATION LISTS

Most designers who attempt to code to the standards use the unordered list element — `ul` — to code the navigation on their pages. While the argument that navigation is nothing more than a list of links certainly holds, HTML 5.0 plans to render the argument moot with the introduction of the `nl` element, thereby creating a semantically logical navigation container. As with the new layout elements, the `nl` would also mean simpler style sheets and more accessibility.

HTML 5.0 TIMEFRAME

The Working Draft of HTML 5.0 was released on January 22, 2008. The stated goal of the project's team is to have the specification completed by 2010.

CSS 3.0

The next generation of CSS has already been released in pieces, and there is currently some scattered browser support for its features. The primary focus after CSS 3.0 appears to be the addition of new, more powerful selectors and addressing of some often cited shortcomings of the CSS 1.0 and 2.0.

CSS 3.0 TIMEFRAME

As has been mentioned, some aspects of CSS 3.0 have been released. The full specification is due, it is hoped, within the next few years after this writing. However, as there are aspects of CSS 2.0 that are still not supported by browsers a full ten years after its release, there is little hope that CSS 3.0 will enjoy full browser support in the foreseeable future.

CSS
Reference

The following is a reference to the commonly used properties and values in CSS 1.0 and 2.0. Note that styles used exclusively for alternate media types such as aural and Braille are excluded.

Font and Text Properties

Font and text properties provide for control over the appearance of text on the page.

PROPERTY	DESCRIPTION
font-family	Specifies the typeface to be used. Any font can be named. If the font name contains more than one word, it must be enclosed in quotation marks. It is generally recommended that a comma-separated list of fonts be provided.
font-size	Allows for setting the size of text. Units of measurement supported include pixels, points, picas, percentages, ems, exes, inches, centimeters, and millimeters, although pixels and percentages are recommended. The unit of measurement must always be given.
font-style	Sets the text in italic. Possible values are normal, italic, and oblique, although the last is rarely supported.
font-variant	Allows for setting text in small caps. Possible values are normal and small-caps.
font-weight	Makes the text bold or not bold. Possible values that are nearly universally supported are normal and bold. The specification also states values of bolder, lighter, and 100, 200, 300, 400, 500, 600, 700, 800, and 900, theoretically allowing the designer to give various degrees of boldness, but no browser currently supports any of these values.
font	Shortcut property that allows the designer to give values for font-style, font-variant, font-weight, font-size, line-height, and font-family in a single property.
text-align	Sets the horizontal alignment of text on the page. Possible values are left, right, center, and justify.
text-decoration	Sets or removes underlining and other decorative text effects. Possible values are none, underline, overline, line-through, and blink.
text-indent	Indents the first line of a block of text by the specified value.
text-transform	Changes the case of text. Possible values are none, capitalize, lowercase, and uppercase. capitalize makes the first letter of each word uppercase; uppercase sets every letter in uppercase.
line-height	The space between lines in an element.
word-spacing	The space between words within an element.
letter-spacing	The space between characters within an element.
vertical-align	The vertical alignment of an element. Note that not all browsers support vertical-align fully, and in particular many do not support it within table cells.

Color and Background Color Properties

Use the `color` property to set the foreground or text color and `background-color` to set the background color. Any XHTML element within the `<body>` tag, including `<body>` itself, can take either of these properties.

Colors can be specified as RGB (red, green, blue) values, named colors, or hexadecimal, with the latter being the preferred method. If using hexadecimal, the value must always be preceded by a pound sign (#).

Box Model Properties

The CSS Box Model defines the area in which elements exist and is made up of three basic sections: padding, borders, and margins.

Padding

Padding defines the space within an element. Any element, either block or inline, can take padding.

PROPERTY	DESCRIPTION
`padding-top`	The amount of space above the element, before the border.
`padding-bottom`	The amount of space below the element, before the border.
`padding-right`	The amount of space to the right of the element, before the border.
`padding-left`	The amount of space to the left of the element, before the border.
`padding`	The shortcut property that allows you to specify all four padding values at once. If a single value is given, it will be used for all four sides. Two values specify padding for the top/bottom and left/right, and four values set padding for top, right, bottom, and left, in that order.

Borders

Borders are visual boxes around elements. Any element can take borders.

Borders consist of three properties: the visual style, the color, and the width. Borders can be set for each side individually, or using shortcuts, for all sides at once.

BORDER STYLES

Modern browsers support the following values for `border-style`. Older browsers may not support all of these, but should degrade nicely to a solid border:

STYLE	DESCRIPTION
`none`	No border will be drawn.
`hidden`	Except in tables, this is the same as `none`. In tables, the property will suppress borders when used along with `border-collapse`.
`solid`	A single line.
`double`	A double line. The browser determines the space between lines.
`dotted`	A series of dots make up the border. The exact shape and position of the dots is up to the browser.
`dashed`	A series of dashes, with the exact position determined by the browser.
`groove`	A line with shading to create a slight indented 3-D effect. The shading is determined by the browser.
`ridge`	The opposite of `groove`, `ridge` uses shading to create a raised appearance.
`inset`	The browser shades two sides of the border to create the effect of the box being lowered below the page. As with other properties here, the exact shading is left to the browser.
`outset`	The opposite of `inset`, with the box apparently raised above the page.

continued ➡

BORDER PROPERTIES

The syntax for specifying the borders of a box depends on whether you want to set the width, style, or color, and on which sides of the box will need a border.

PROPERTY	DESCRIPTION
border-top-style	Sets the style for the top border.
border-bottom-style	Sets the style for the bottom border.
border-right-style	Sets the style for the right border.
border-left-style	Sets the style for the left border.
border-top-width	Sets the width for the top border.
border-bottom-width	Sets the width for the bottom border.
border-right-width	Sets the width for the right border.
border-left-width	Sets the width for the left border.
border-top-color	Sets the color for the top border.
border-bottom-color	Sets the color for the bottom border.
border-right-color	Sets the color for the right border.
border-left-color	Sets the color for the left border.
border-style	A shortcut property that enables you to set the style of the border for all four sides at once. If one value is given, it will be used for all four borders; two values set the top/bottom and left/right borders, and four values set each individually, in the order top, right, bottom, left.
border-color	A shortcut property that enables you to set the color of the border for all four sides at once. If one value is given, it will be used for all four borders; two values set the top/bottom and left/right borders, and four values set each individually, in the order top, right, bottom, left.
border-width	A shortcut property that enables you to set the width of the border for all four sides at once. If one value is given, it will be used for all four borders; two values set the top/bottom and left/right borders, and four values set each individually, in the order top, right, bottom, left.
border-top	A shortcut property that enables you to set the properties for the top border in a single line. The properties are specified as width, style, and color in a space-separated list.
border-bottom	A shortcut property that enables you to set the properties for the bottom border in a single line. The properties are specified as width, style, and color in a space-separated list.
border-right	A shortcut property that enables you to set the properties for the right border in a single line. The properties are specified as width, style, and color in a space-separated list.
border-left	A shortcut property that enables you to set the properties for the left border in a single line. The properties are specified as width, style, and color in a space-separated list.
border	A shortcut property for specifying all the properties for all four sides of the border at once. Properties are given as a space-separated list in the order width, style, color.

Margins

Margins define the space around an element. Only block elements can take margins.

PROPERTY	DESCRIPTION
margin-top	The amount of space above the element.
margin-bottom	The amount of space below the element.
margin-right	The amount of space to the right of the element.
margin-left	The amount of space to the left of the element.
margin	The shortcut property that allows you to specify all four margin values at once. If a single value is given, it will be used for all four sides. Two values specify the margins for the top/bottom and left/right, and four values set the margins for top, right, bottom, and left, in that order.

Other Box Properties

The following properties can also be applied to boxes.

PROPERTY	DESCRIPTION
width	Sets the width of an element. The default is 100%, but any valid unit will work. Inline elements cannot use width.
height	Sets the height of an element. The default is equal to the height of the content, but any valid unit will work. Inline elements cannot use height.
display	Controls how the element is displayed on-screen. Values are none, which essentially removes the element from the page; block, which causes the element to be displayed in its own space and can take widths and margins; and inline, which causes the element to appear within a line with elements before and after it.

List Properties

The following properties control the appearance and layout of lists.

PROPERTY	DESCRIPTION
list-style-type	Sets the style for the bullet or number. Common values are none, disc, circle, square, decimal, lower-roman, upper-roman, lower-alpha, and upper-alpha.
list-style-image	Replaces the bullet with an image, using a URL to the graphic file.
list-style-position	Sets the indentation of the list. outside, the default, creates a list with hanging indents, and inside wraps subsequent lines of the list item all the way to the margin.

continued ➡

CSS Reference
(continued)

In CSS, any element can take a background image. Note that images that are important for the content of the page should be inserted using the XHTML `<img>` tag.

PROPERTY	DESCRIPTION
background-image	The URL to the image being used as a background.
background-repeat	Sets the tiling of the image. Possible values are `repeat` (the default), `repeat-x` (only tiles vertically), `repeat-y` (only tiles horizontally), and `no-repeat`.
background-position	The position of the image, relative to the top-left corner of the element.
background-attachment	A value of `fixed` causes the image to remain in place, even if the browser window is scrolled, whereas a value of `scroll` (the default) causes the image to scroll up and down with the browser window.
background	A shortcut property for specifying other background properties. A single value can be given for image or color, or more than one property can be given in a space-separated list.

The following properties are used by designers to control the layout of elements on the page.

PROPERTY	DESCRIPTION
float	Causes an element to allow other elements to float next to it. Accepted values are left, right, and none (the default). Standards-based browsers require that position:relative be provided when using float.
clear	Causes an element to not float, if the prior element allowed it to. Values are left, right, both, and none (the default).
position	Allows you to define how the element should be positioned on the page. The default value for position is static.
relative	Allows you to move the element in relation to its original position on the page. An element using relative position remains in the flow of the document, so other elements will not move into its original space. Using position:relative requires that you also specify either top, left, right, or bottom. As noted earlier, most browsers require this property if also using float.
absolute	Allows you to place an element anywhere on the screen. Absolutely positioned elements will be removed from the flow of the page, and other elements will not stay out of their way, often causing overlapping content. Using position:absolute requires that you also give values for its position from a corner of the parent element, using either top and left, top and right, bottom and left, or bottom and right.
fixed	Places an element on the screen that will not move, even if the browser window is scrolled. Some browsers, including Internet Explorer 6, do not support position:fixed and will simply ignore it. (Internet Explorer as of version 7 supports position:fixed.)
visibility	Controls whether or not elements can be seen onscreen. Values are visible and hidden. Unlike display:none, an element set to visibility:hidden will still be "seen" by other elements on the screen, so their space will be respected.
z-index	Sets the stacking order of elements that overlap. The value can be any integer from 0 to 32,767, with elements with higher numbers appearing on top of elements with lower numbers.
overflow	Controls how content should be displayed if a height is given that is smaller than the content. The default is visible, which means that all content will be shown, although some browsers will still respect the height in regard to drawing the bottom border and placement of other elements. Other values include scroll, which causes a scrollbar to appear whether or not it is needed; auto, which creates a scrollbar only when needed; and hidden, which crops the content at the given height.

Web Accessibility Guideline Reference

Two primary sets of guidelines exist for checking that a site is accessible to persons with disabilities.

The World Wide Web Consortium's (W3C) Web Accessibility Initiative released a set of checkpoints for accessibility, organized into three priority groups. Priority one represents a set of guidelines the designer must follow for the document to be considered accessible, as they cover key concepts that, if not achieved, will make it impossible for the disabled to effectively use a site; priority two contains checkpoints that should be followed as they cover significant barriers to accessibility; and priority three is a set of checkpoints that may be followed, representing items that make it somewhat difficult, but not impossible, for disabled users to interact with the site.

Priority One Checkpoints

For general usage:

- Every non-text element, such as images, graphic representations of text, image maps, animation and video, sounds, and so on, must have a text equivalent, provided through either alternate text, a long description, or the element's content.
- Do not rely on color alone to convey information. For example, if you have required fields on a form, do not state that those fields are indicated through red text. Instead, be sure to provide some alternative means of identifying the element that does not rely on color.
- In situations where the natural language of the text may change, clearly identify the change.
- Organize documents so that they are still readable in the absence of style sheets. In other words, be sure that the page is readable and still makes sense with style sheets missing or disabled.
- If you have dynamic content such as video or Flash animation, be sure that text equivalent is updated whenever the actual content changes.
- Avoid anything that causes the screen to flicker.
- Use clear, simple language on the site.

For image maps:

- Provide redundant, text-based links for any region of a server-side image map.
- Use client-side, rather than server-side, image maps whenever possible.

For tables:

- Clearly identify row and column headers.
- Clearly associate headers with data cells for tables that have more than one logical level of headers.

For frames:

- Give each frame a logical, descriptive title.

For applets and scripts:

- Ensure that the page is usable in the absence of scripts or applets. For example, do not use menus that are generated solely through JavaScript unless alternative, non-script-based navigation is also available.

For multimedia:

- Provide auditory descriptions of important information from the visual track of multimedia content.
- Ensure that alternate content, such as Closed Captions, are synchronized with the multimedia content.
- If it is impossible to create accessible multimedia content, provide a link to an alternate page that disseminates the same content and that is updated as often as the multimedia content.

Priority Two Checkpoints

For general usage:

- Ensure that you maintain sufficient contrast between foreground and background colors. This falls under priority two checkpoints for images, and priority three checkpoints for text.

- Use markup languages such as XHTML or HTML instead of images to convey information.

- Be sure to use proper grammar on your pages.

- Use style sheets for layout and presentation.

- Use relative, rather than absolute, units for values in XHTML, HTML, and CSS.

- Use header elements to convey the document's structure.

- Use the proper markup for lists and list items.

- Properly mark up quotations, and do not use elements such as `blockquote` purely for indentation.

- Ensure that dynamic content is accessible or that alternate content is provided.

- Avoid content that blinks.

- Do not create pages that automatically refresh.

- Do not redirect the user to another page using markup, but rather ensure that the server controls redirects.

- Do not have new windows opening without informing the user.

- Use the proper and most up-to-date markup.

- Do not use deprecated features or markup.

- Break up large blocks of content into smaller, but still logically appropriate, sections.

- Clearly identify the target of a link. Avoid ambiguous link text such as "click here."

- Provide metadata about the layout of a site, through a site map, table of contents, or similar method.

- Be consistent in your navigation.

For tables:

- Do not use tables for layout, unless you ensure that tables can be linearized and still make sense.

- When using tables for layout, do not use structural markup for the visual formatting. For example, do not use headings just to achieve bold text.

For frames:

- Describe the purpose of each frame and their relationships.

For forms:

- Always explicitly associate labels with form fields, and properly place the label relative to the field.

For applets and scripts:

- Ensure that event handlers are not dependent on a particular input device, such as a mouse.

- Avoid movement on pages.

- Ensure that programmatic elements are directly accessible. This is a priority one checkpoint if the content is not presented elsewhere in some other form.

- Make sure that elements with custom interfaces can be operated by any input device.

- Use logical, rather than device-dependent, event handlers.

continued

Priority Three Checkpoints

For general usage:

- Specify the expanded form for abbreviations and acronyms.
- Identify the natural language of the document.
- Create logical tab orders for links and form controls.
- Provide keyboard shortcuts for important links and form controls.
- Provide non-link, printable characters as separators for adjacent links.
- Allow users to receive documents according to their preferences.
- Use navigation bars to provide access to the site's navigation, thereby ensuring that it is not hidden within the content.
- Group related links and provide methods to bypass the group.
- If providing search functionality, be sure that it can be used by those with different skill levels and preferences.

- Distinguish headings, paragraphs, and lists.
- Clearly describe document collections.
- If using multiline ASCII art, provide a way to skip it.
- Use graphics or auditory presentations to supplement text if doing so facilitates comprehension.
- Be consistent in the styling across pages.

For image maps:

- Provide redundant text links for client-side image maps.

For tables:

- Provide summaries for tables.
- Provide abbreviations for header cells.
- Provide a linear alternative to tables that lay out text in parallel columns.

For forms:

- Include default, place-holding characters in editable text fields and text areas.

Section 508 Guidelines

In the United States, federal and other governmental bodies must create sites to adhere to the standards set forth in Section 508. These are comprised of sixteen rules for accessibility.

(a) A text equivalent for every non-text element shall be provided (for example, via `alt`, `longdesc`, or in element content).

(b) Equivalent alternatives for any multimedia presentation shall be synchronized with the presentation.

(c) Web pages shall be designed so that all information conveyed with color is also available without color; for example, from context or markup.

(d) Documents shall be organized so they are readable without requiring an associated style sheet.

(e) Redundant text links shall be provided for each active region of a server-side image map.

(f) Client-side image maps shall be provided instead of server-side image maps except where the regions cannot be defined with an available geometric shape.

(g) Row and column headers shall be identified for data tables.

(h) Markup shall be used to associate data cells and header cells for data tables that have two or more logical levels of row or column headers.

(i) Frames shall be titled with text that facilitates frame identification and navigation.

(j) Pages shall be designed to avoid causing the screen to flicker with a frequency greater than 2 Hz and lower than 55 Hz.

(k) A text-only page, with equivalent information or functionality, shall be provided to make a Web site comply with the provisions of this part, when compliance cannot be accomplished in any other way. The content of the text-only page shall be updated whenever the primary page changes.

(l) When pages utilize scripting languages to display content, or to create interface elements, the information provided by the script shall be identified with functional text that can be read by assistive technology.

(m) When a Web page requires that an applet, plug-in, or other application be present on the client system to interpret page content, the page must provide a link to a plug-in or applet that complies with §1194.21(a) through (l).

(n) When electronic forms are designed to be completed on-line, the form shall allow people using assistive technology to access the information, field elements, and functionality required for completion and submission of the form, including all directions and cues.

(o) A method shall be provided that permits users to skip repetitive navigation links.

(p) When a timed response is required, the user shall be alerted and given sufficient time to indicate more time is required.

INDEX

A

`<a>` and `</a>` tags, 38, 46–47
abbr element, 65, 254
abbreviations, Web page uses, 65, 254
absolute paths, 37, 40–41, 53
absolute positioning, 160–161
Access Board, guidelines, 232
acronyms, Web page uses, 254
`action` attribute, 184–185
`active` pseudo-class selector, 124–125
ADA. *See* Americans with Disabilities Act
adCenter, Microsoft, 287
address element, 33, 250–251
Adobe ColdFusion, 214
Adobe Contribute, templates, 179
Adobe Dreamweaver CS3
    AP Elements tools, 161
    cross-platform visual editor, 11
    DreamFeeder extension, 263
    JavaScript support, 8
    scripting language support, 215
    templates, 179
    Web accessibility shortcomings, 239
Adobe Flash Player, 280
Adobe GoLive, visual editor, 11
Adobe Macromedia HomeSite, 10
Adobe Reader, JavaScript support, 8
AdSense ads, 274, 286–287
advertising, Web pages, 286–287
AdWords, Google, 287
`after` pseudo-element, CSS, 148–149
aggregators, RSS feeds, 260
Ajax. *See* Asynchronous JavaScript and XML
`alert` function, JavaScript, 216–217
`align` attribute, `caption` element, 235
alignments, text, 100–101
`alt` attribute, 54–55
alternative text, 54–55, 207, 240–241, 303
Americans with Disabilities Act (ADA), Web accessibility law, 233
ampersand (&) character, 248–249
anchors, `<a>` and `</a>` tags, 38
angle bracket-exclamation point-dash dash (<!--) opening comment, 30
angle brackets < and > characters, 3
animations, GIF, 50
AOL (America Online), 12
Apache Software Foundation, 15
Apache Web Server, 15
Apple iTunes, 270–271
Apple Safari, browser history, 13
Arabic numerals, ordered lists, 79
arguments, `open` function, 224–225
Arial font, 90
arrow characters, XHTML, 344
artwork, podcast addition, 271
ASCII characters, XHTML, 341
assets, Web site file structure, 36
assistive technologies, 19, 23, 32–33, 54–55, 109
Asynchronous JavaScript and XML (Ajax), 9
Atom, RSS development, 260–261
attribute values, XHTML mistakes, 303
attributes, 3–4, 337. *See also individual attributes*
Audacity, podcasts, 269
audio content, 232, 268–271

B

background colors, CSS, 349
background images, 305, 352
`background` shorthand property, CSS, 112–113
`background-attachment` property, 110–111
`background-color` property, 106–107
`background-image` property, 108–109, 172–173
`background-position` property, 110–111, 172–173
`background-repeat` property, 108–109, 172–173
backgrounds, 106–111
badges, Flickr photo sharing, 278–279
Badgr, Flickr tool, 280
bandwidth, Web host service, 315
BBEdit, Macintosh code editor, 10
`before` pseudo-element, CSS, 148–149
block properties, CSS, 305
block-level elements, 22–23, 25, 82–83, 114–117
`blockquote` element, 252–253
BlogCFC, blog builder, 273
Blogger, blog service, 272–275
blogs, 252–253, 250–267, 272–275, 299
`<body>` and `</body>` tags, 18–19
body section, paragraph, 24–25
boldface text, 22–23, 32–33, 98–99
bookmarks, social, 288–289
`border` attribute, 58, 68
`border` shorthand property, CSS, 123
border styles, CSS property, 349
`border-collapse` property, CSS, 127
`border-color` property, CSS, 116–117
borders, 58, 68, 116–117, 177, 349–350
`border-style` property, CSS, 116–117
`border-width` property, CSS, 116–117
bottom, CSS background keyword, 110
box models, 121, 183, 349–351
`<br>` and `<br />` tags, 26–27
British pound, £, 248
browsers. *See also* Web browsers
    case-insensitive HTML elements, 3
    copying/pasting external links, 40–41
    CSS (Cascading Style Sheets), 6
    custom cursors, 133
    design mistakes, 306
    favorites icon display, 60–61
    `fieldset` element background, 211
    font matching process, 103
    font types, 90
    JavaScript code error, 230–231
    JavaScript support, 8
    `legend` element background, 211
    link testing, 48–49
    link tooltip display, 46–47
    list indentation controls, 130–131
    opening a new window, 224–225
    PNG (Portable Network Graphics) format support, 51
    pop-up blockers, 224–225
    source code comment, 30–31
    source code viewing, 31
    whitespace-insensitive HTML, 3
    XHTML, 5
bulleted lists, 76–77, 128–129
bullets, 77, 128–129
`button` element, HTML, 208–209
buttons, 51, 204–207

INDEX

INDEX

INDEX

INDEX

INDEX

Read Less–Learn More®

Visual®

There's a Visual book for every learning level...

Simplified®

The place to start if you're new to computers. Full color.

- Computers
- Creating Web Pages
- Mac OS
- Office
- Windows

Teach Yourself VISUALLY™

Get beginning to intermediate-level training in a variety of topics. Full color.

- Access
- Bridge
- Chess
- Computers
- Crocheting
- Digital Photography
- Dog training
- Dreamweaver
- Excel
- Flash
- Golf
- Guitar
- Handspinning
- HTML
- Jewelry Making & Beading
- Knitting
- Mac OS
- Office
- Photoshop
- Photoshop Elements
- Piano
- Poker
- PowerPoint
- Quilting
- Scrapbooking
- Sewing
- Windows
- Wireless Networking
- Word

Top 100 Simplified® Tips & Tricks

Tips and techniques to take your skills beyond the basics. Full color.

- Digital Photography
- eBay
- Excel
- Google
- Internet
- Mac OS
- Office
- Photoshop
- Photoshop Elements
- PowerPoint
- Windows

...all designed for visual learners—just like you!